LIFE AFTER DARK

A History of British Nightclubs
and Music Venues

DAVE HASLAM

SIMON &
SCHUSTER

London · New York · Sydney · Toronto · New Delhi

A CBS COMPANY

First published in Great Britain by Simon & Schuster UK Ltd, 2015
This paperback edition published by Simon & Schuster UK Ltd, 2016
A CBS COMPANY

1 3 5 7 9 10 8 6 4 2

Simon & Schuster UK Ltd
1st Floor
222 Gray's Inn Road
London WC1X 8HB

www.simonandschuster.co.uk

Simon & Schuster Australia Sydney
Simon & Schuster India New Delhi

The author and publishers have made all reasonable efforts
to contact copyright-holders for permission, and apologise
for any omissions or errors in the form of credits given.
Corrections may be made to future printings.

A CIP catalogue record for this book
is available from the British Library.

Paperback ISBN: 978-0-85720-699-2
Ebook ISBN: 978-0-85720-700-5

Prin...ed and bound by CPI Group...

CONTENTS

Intro   Wonderwalls, gold dust,
discos become Tescos   vii

Chapter One   Bare-necked ladies, shaggy-looking
Germans, everyone is drunk   1

Chapter Two   Dream palaces, degenerate boys,
jazz-mad dancing girls   34

Chapter Three   A bare room with lightbulbs, raves,
what happened next   65

Chapter Four   Merseybeat, flashing eyes, a leg-over   98

Chapter Five   Pills, thrills, not keeping music live   128

Chapter Six   Cosmonauts, light shows,
Clapton takes acid   160

Chapter Seven   Soul power, Big Julie, 'You Make
Me Feel (Mighty Real)'   193

Chapter Eight   Secret gigs, home-butchered hair,
love action at the Roxy   227

Chapter Nine   Posers, the Krays, a tribe called 'goth'   258

Chapter Ten   Tape machines, modern drugs,
unknown pleasures   278

Chapter Eleven   The Wild Bunch, headless pigeons,
a track with no name   310

Chapter Twelve   Police raids, the Prodigy in a bingo
hall, an MC in a cupboard   344

Chapter Thirteen   Celebrities, more ecstasy, music is life   370

Outro   Michael Stipe's shoe, the cocktail from
Hull, worlds emerge   393

Acknowledgements   422

Sources   423

Notes   425

Index   442

INTRO

Wonderwalls, gold dust, discos become Tescos

In most cities there's a club or venue, maybe two or three; places that cast a spell on a particular community, and spaces where a generation or two enjoyed unforgettable gigs, regulars experienced life-shaping moments, or found a lover, or danced until dawn. For so many people, nightclubs and music venues are the source of a lifetime's music taste, best friends and vivid memories. Someone in their late teens in Portsmouth in 1966 might suggest the Birdcage as an example, and then pour out a hundred mod memories. Someone fourteen or fifteen years older might suggest Cy Laurie's jazz club in Ham Yard in Soho in the early 1950s, where basement raves went through until dawn. We can trace many examples of the way venues have nurtured communities away from the mainstream, most potently in the history of gay clubbing. For music lovers in South Yorkshire in the 1980s, the Limit and the Leadmill in Sheffield hosted memorable live gigs and club nights but – in common with other significant clubs and venues – in doing so they were providing somewhere that like-minded people gathered, socialised, collaborated even, good times unfolding, ideas sparking into life.

As well as being sites of personal and communal importance, clubs and venues have had a significant role to play in shaping music history; the likes of Eric's in Liverpool, the Dug Out in Bristol, the Twisted Wheel and the Haçienda in Manchester, the 'Soul II Soul' sessions at the Africa Centre, the Maritime Hotel in Belfast. Witness too clubs like 'UFO' in London, and venues including Mothers in Birmingham and the Magic Village in Manchester, which nurtured the psychedelic scene; and almost all major acts and DJs fashioned the foundations for their careers performing at grassroots venues. Britain's small venues have always been crucial in the development of the country's international reputation for innovative music and fashions.

Poignantly and disconcertingly, there's no trace left of many of the significant music venues we'll visit in this book. The Dug Out has become a restaurant, the Magic Village has been demolished, clubs have become car parks, discos have become Tescos. The new Ham Yard Hotel in London, close to Piccadilly Circus, buried a building with an amazing history, including a basement where Cy Laurie held his jazz raves, the same basement which, just a few years later, was the site of a club called the Scene, a pioneering, amphetamine-filled mod hangout which will feature at length in our story. We'll also hear of other great clubs that have been located in Ham Yard, including the Hambone, founded in 1922 as a bohemian cabaret club and one of the most notorious nightspots of its time. When one regular, Trevor Allen, wrote the Hambone into his novel *We Loved In Bohemia*, a reviewer described the club as a 'shrine of anti-convention and the home of talented rebels'.

Big clubs, corporate superstar DJs, the commercial mainstream and dance halls all feature in the chapters that follow but, to be honest, most of the time I'm prejudiced in favour of the dives. Or if not the dives as such, then the pioneers; the clubs and venues that have innovated not imitated, who have shaken things up. That's when cultural activity is at its most exciting and effervescent, creating new scenes and future possibilities, with inspired and maverick pioneers ignoring or pushing against the mainstream – even if, as with the New Romantics, for example, they become the new mainstream. But that's fascinating, too; how misfit kids and talented rebels gathered under a mirrorball between four walls of a venue can knock culture into a new phase. These venues are at the heart of our story.

Clubs and venues like Bolton Palais, Nottingham's Rock City and the Barrowland Ballroom in Glasgow have played a central role in towns and cities for years and become embedded in the cultural and social life of a community in the same way that, traditionally, a university, cathedral or a factory might have done. Liam Gallagher recently explained the attraction of the Haçienda: 'For people who went there it was their church.' The depth of these connections explains why news of the closure of venues can be greeted like a dagger in the heart of the city, with shock and mourning.

It's hard to imagine what Liverpool would be like if the Cavern or 'Cream' had never existed, or a career for the Animals without the plethora of jazz and r&b clubs in Newcastle. And what would the 1930s have been like without Mecca dance halls? Through the following chapters, we'll celebrate some of the more remarkable, unforgettable, distinctive and pioneering clubs and venues around the country. We'll also discover the identity of the man dubbed 'King of the Ravers', find out the club Muhammad Ali visited, the venue where blow jobs were all the rage and the music hall where a performer killed a heckler.

Over the following pages we'll go nationwide, from Newcastle upon Tyne to Newport in South Wales. Arguably the most significant Newport venue of recent decades is TJ's, a live music venue run by the late John Sicolo, which created and nurtured an alternative scene in the 1980s, a compelling example of the value of venues that kick against musical and cultural homogeneity. When John Sicolo died in 2010, one contributor to a BBC radio show in his honour said TJ's was invaluable to teenagers in the Welsh valleys who weren't at home in either the 'strait-jacket masculinity' of rugby clubs or the high street discotheques. It's also said that TJ's was where Kurt Cobain proposed to Courtney Love.

We'll travel the country, but travel back in time too. It's not only the different experiences of each generation that are intriguing but the similarities too. When you're eighteen you hit the town and tend to think you and your friends are the first to discover cool venues, staying up late, losing your friends, losing your way, but this is Friedrich Engels writing about Manchester in the early 1840s: 'On Saturday evenings, especially, when wages are paid and work stops somewhat earlier than usual, when the whole working class pours from its own poor quarters into the main thoroughfares, intemperance may be seen in all its brutality.'

Despite the reputation of the British for being reserved, there are long traditions of hedonism in this country, citizens living for the weekend. When Engels was writing, for the urban poor after a week of being ground down by factory bosses and mill owners, intoxication and music wasn't just escapism; it was like sticking two fingers up at the bosses. It was as much an exercise in reclaiming life as enjoying it.

Life after dark can be chaotic and perilous, something of a secret time, a lost time, when in our actions what's normal doesn't apply, a chance for some casual flirting or sexual encounters, to seek pleasures, to look different, to be different, to be lost in music, to indulge in some daft craziness that in the morning we may regret but the following week may repeat. Some months ago a friend of mine went to a Bank Holiday event at a club in Leeds. It was crowded and underlit. There was a group of lads in there he described as 'shady'. They were dealing, intimidating, occupying the dark corners. Occasionally they took off, barging across the room and, when a girl stood up to them, she fell to the floor and they started kicking her. The doormen seemed somehow in league with or in awe of the gang and it wasn't until much later that they were cleared off the premises. Some venues might feel like home to you, but there are also always nightclubs and venues you may not want to revisit the next week, let alone three decades later.

As we'll see over the coming chapters, life after dark is under-documented and often hidden, and occasionally it's on the edge of the law or in defiance of it: a tale of dark corners, gangland protection rackets, errant doormen, moral panics, ecstasy deaths. Actresses doing cocaine, cross-dressers, bare-necked girls getting off with sailors in Liverpool music saloons, we'll meet them all.

The approach in this history isn't encyclopedic, in the sense of attempting to include every nightclub or venue that's made a contribution to life in British towns and cities, and to the progress of every band or genre; there are thousands of places that could make such claims. What follows includes a broad outline, from Victorian music halls, through the jazz age to the present day, via beat clubs, mods, psychedelic happenings, funk, soul and rave. But also, at points through the story, a number of key clubs are documented at length, and there's some detailed focus on specific and significant bands, DJs, scenes and promoters. My own time promoting live shows and DJing at clubs like Haçienda has fed my passion for nightclubs and music venues. But the larger picture inspires me too; the sense that people for centuries have made or found their special nightlife spaces, in the same cities as us, maybe the same streets. I love having that sense of kinship with life after dark in the past. I love the idea propounded by the writer Aldo Rossi that there's a collective memory attached to buildings. Maybe we can also tease out some of these memories?

Just a short walk from Ham Yard, deeper into Soho, another building with a rich nightlife history still stands: it's 69 Dean Street, on the corner of Meard Street. In the autumn of 1978 a club night called 'Billy's' opened in the basement; the venue, at the time, was called Gossips. Billy's was hosted and promoted by Steve Harrington, who, emboldened by punk (and having seen the Sex Pistols in Caerphilly), moved from South Wales and took to calling himself Steve Strange. At Billy's, Strange worked alongside his flatmate Rusty Egan (from the band the Rich Kids), who became the club's DJ.

The 'promoter' in the world of clubs and venues is the person who originates an event. Some venues have an in-house promoter; many promoters work independently though, as Steve Strange did at Gossips. The independent promoter has to find the talent, secure a venue – perhaps by hiring a hall or club, perhaps taking a midweek night because it's cheaper – sort out the ticketing and publicity and accept the financial risk. Done right, and built on good foundations, promoting can be a lucrative activity. During one recent financial year, live music promoter Simon Moran, founder of SJM Concerts, was said to be the highest-paid director of any business in the northwest of England, receiving a salary of £6.9m.

A first visit to the Haçienda might have inspired you to change your music collection or your wardrobe, or you might have met people you'd fallen in love with. But in addition, important clubs and venues were and are also a catalyst for activity outside of their wonderwalls: bands, DJs, a legacy, a mythology. The story doesn't end when the last customer leaves.

The people who organised and frequented Billy's (along with graduates of similar clubs of the era – including the Rum Runner in Birmingham, and Blitz, Strange and Egan's next venture) went on to define and disseminate a sound and a flamboyant look that became known as 'New Romantic'. The scene had its genesis in two or three small, left-field clubs. This is where it starts: clubs and venues. And it was the same with the mods, with the Beatles, with the Sex Pistols, with acid house. It's within the four walls of the club that the first stirrings of a new wave are to be found.

The Dean Street Townhouse hotel and restaurant now inhabits the building at 69 Dean Street. It's in an area that was semi-derelict and ill-lit in the crumbling Soho of the 1970s, but now has a monied, satisfied atmosphere. In the restaurant the wallpaper features muted shades of green in a design reminiscent of the early 1950s, the Festival of Britain era. When I visited recently I met some of the staff, young and helpful, and willing to show me around. Cecilia, Jacob, Josh and I wandered upstairs and down, but found no sign of the building's contribution to the story of London's nightlife – a contribution that's much more than housing Billy's. I told them some of the people who'd danced and partied at 69 Dean Street – Henri Matisse, Tallulah Bankhead, Fred Astaire and Noël Coward – but I'm not sure which names they recognised from the depths of the past, nor those from more recent history like Boy George, Steve Strange, and Robert Smith of the Cure. Robert Smith visited when a club called the 'Batcave' opened on the top floor of the building in July 1982. Marc Almond, too; they knew Marc's name, and told me he sometimes visits the Townhouse's restaurant and has a bite to eat. I dropped more names, and then explained the story.

Nos. 69 and 70 Dean Street were two separate homes, built in the 1730s by John Meard for aristocratic families at a time when Soho was a self-contained district, with a reputation for housing a cosmopolitan community of traders, architects and artists. In 1834, composer Vincent Novello and his son Joseph took over No. 69, from where they ran a music publishing business; as it developed, they erected two upper floors to accommodate a printing press before purchasing No. 70 in 1875, creating the first link between the two buildings. In 1901, both Nos. 69 and 70 were turned into industrial premises and then in the mid-1920s the Gargoyle Club was opened on the upper floors by aristocrat David Tennant, which was reached via a lift. The grandest spaces for dining and dancing in London in the 1920s included the Café de Paris. But the Gargoyle was different, more intimate, less staid, and open all hours. And because you had to find the entrance door and then take a lift to the top floors, it had an air of secrecy. The subscription was four guineas per annum.

By day the Gargoyle tended to be the haunt of artists and

writers looking for a drink and a chance to escape work. At night-time it became a favourite with the so-called Bright Young Things, a group of aristocratic types with a conspicuously dissolute lifestyle given over to spectacular parties. Many of the leading Bright Young Things were regulars at the Gargoyle, including Brenda and Napper Dean Paul, and Stephen Tennant. Stephen was owner David's homosexual brother and a man, by all accounts, of much style and theatricality, with a 'prancing' gait and an ultra-flamboyant dress sense. At the end of the 1920s he represented fashion at its most extreme, and had taken to wearing lipstick and gilding his fair hair with gold dust. If he'd time-travelled forward fifty years, there's no doubt Stephen Tennant would have been ushered straight in by the door staff at Billy's.

The 1920s witnessed a boom in public dancing; new dance halls were opening and other venues were installing new, improved dancefloors. The ballroom on one floor of the Gargoyle, with a jazz orchestra in attendance, was a major feature but there was also a coffee room and drawing room, and a rooftop terrace and bar. Among the regular visitors to the Gargoyle, one name stands out: Henri Matisse. Matisse was a personal friend of David Tennant and regularly visited the Gargoyle in the early years of the club; Tennant ended up with two Matisse paintings gifted to him by the artist. He displayed one of these (*The Red Studio*) in the bar at the Gargoyle and the other (*The Studio, Quai St Michel*) on the club's stairs.

In the post-war period, the Gargoyle became a little passé, and never regained its pre-war status as the original in-crowd moved on. Its membership list remained impressive in the 1950s, though – it included Lee Miller (the gorgeous, talented photographer and muse of Man Ray) and the spy Guy Burgess. In the 1950s, while the Gargoyle remained open on the upper floors, another private club, the Mandrake, opened in the basement. Although its official address was 4 Meard Street, owing to various linked basements, it shared the same building. The proprietor of the Mandrake was Boris Watson, who acquired the leases of adjoining basements and knocked through walls until he was able to put a music room in the cellar, the same cellar space that would be used by Billy's in the 1970s, directly underneath where the restaurant now is.

As well as his passion for demolishing partition walls, Boris Watson loved chess – he invested in a dozen chess boards and made them available to all patrons – but it was mainly a private drinking club, one of many in Soho. The strategy was to create a constitution, a committee and a membership list. English licensing laws in the 50s stipulated that pubs stopped serving at two-thirty in the afternoon, shut at three and did not reopen until seven at night, but the law could be swerved by means of private-club licences, which allowed for drinking in the afternoon and after-hours.

I explained to the staff at the Dean Street Townhouse that if they'd been here one evening in the late 1950s, the chances are there would be two jazz bands playing on the premises; up the lift in the Gargoyle there would be Alec Alexander's band, and down the twisting stairs in the Mandrake an in-house combo, including pianist Joe Burns, Percy Borthwick on bass and Robin Jones on drums, which welcomed impromptu jazz sessions with visiting musicians.

After looking around the basement of the Townhouse, where many of the rooms are now store cupboards, Jacob took me to the top floors, where there are beautiful bedrooms and the same rich, hushed ambience as the restaurant. I didn't tell him that after Gargoyle's had shut, the top floor had become a strip club; if I had, I'd have felt the need to whisper it.

On an assignment for *The Face* late in 1982, Derek Ridgers took some photographs of people involved with Gossips, and looking at these, I realised with Cecilia that the club entrance was down the side of the building; not on Dean Street but round the corner, on Meard Street. There are two fire exits there now. It seems to be the case that the door on the left was where the lift would have been to take Stephen Tennant and friends up to his brother's Gargoyle club, and Marc Almond up to the Batcave. And the door on the right would take you to the ground floor and down into the basement, where artists like Edward Burra might spend an afternoon dining at the Mandrake, and late in 1978 Steve Strange, peering at the outfits in the queue, would grant entry to the lucky few, down an unmarked stairwell, to a couple of dark rooms and a mirrorball.

On Meard Street we recreate the scene as best we can. Cecilia stands outside the fire exit, strikes a pose and we laugh. Jacob joins us and takes a look at the photographs. He says he'd heard from his dad it was a bit rum around these parts in the old days.

CHAPTER ONE

Bare-necked ladies, shaggy-looking Germans, everyone is drunk

Music halls 150 years ago were key buildings and major commercial businesses, frequented by thousands of regulars; the raucous, communal, mass night-time entertainment of the day, part pub and part nightclub, part circus and part talent show. They'd present onstage a mix of comic and sentimental songs, magic tricks and satirical sketches. In some of them more sensationalist entertainments were available: human freaks, tightrope walkers, troupes of Red Indians and cross-dressing singers. The story of the British music halls also includes ersatz nudity, evidence of break-dancing in Liverpool a century and a half ago, an early attempt to create a mirrorball, and the sad story of the failed escapologist.

The standard audience tended to be young workers and families, but some of the halls were said to be the centres of vice and violence, frequented by prostitutes, drunken sailors and ne'er-do-wells. There are music venues in our current era that carry a heavy vibe but I've never seen the likes of this sign posted outside a tavern in 1872: 'All persons are requested, before entering the dancing saloon, to leave at the bar their pistols and knives, or any other weapon they may have about them'.

Moral guardians, local churchmen, temperance campaigners and disapproving newspaper editors kept a close watch on music halls. Their fear was that Victorian values of sobriety and respectability could be undermined by the halls; that the working class, unfortunate women, and youths might be corrupted by risqué comic songs and the occasional glimpse of female skin in an environment of heavy drinking and enlivened passions, when instead they could be working, learning or praying. One of the first music halls was the Star in Bolton, owned and run by Thomas Sharples. In the mid-1840s, on some nights, 1,500 people would attend his venue, but his business suffered a setback after a fire in 1851. Having started work on the repair and rebuild, Sharples set a reopening date but his application for a new licence was opposed by some local religious groups, who petitioned the magistrates to deny a licence not just to the Star but to all other singing saloons in the town, claiming that they were 'flood-gates of vice and licentiousness'.

In most parts of Britain there are still buildings that reveal a little of their past as a music hall, especially ones built in the late Victorian or Edwardian eras. Of those built earlier, there are several where elements of the facade of the building remains, for example the Gaiety Music Hall on Nelson Street in Newcastle upon Tyne where, visible from the street, above the door is a tablet inscribed 'MUSIC HALL 1838'. In the case of the Alexandra Music Hall in Canterbury, built in 1850, with a variety of uses since – including some time as a shop and a current life as a student-friendly pub called the Penny Theatre – the basic layout and structure of the music hall is still apparent.

Some mid-nineteenth-century music halls didn't last longer than a decade or two. As well as at the Star in Bolton in 1851, there were dozens of fires, including at the Surrey Music Hall in Sheffield (1865) and St James's Hall in Liverpool (1875). Sometimes the halls were rebuilt, but some couldn't fight off increased competition or closed in the early twentieth century when other forms of entertainment arrived (the cinema and the wireless). In the last hundred years, of course, venues of all kinds have been destroyed by German bombs, and property developers.

Of those venues that are more extensively intact, Hoxton Hall in London and the Britannia Panopticon Music Hall in Glasgow are two surviving mid-nineteenth-century music halls, but both are in a parlous state and engaged in fundraising for much-needed restoration work; both offer visitor tours and occasionally hold events. Two more have received Heritage Lottery Fund payouts, which have enabled them to carry out repairs and refurbishment: Wilton's in London and the City Varieties in Leeds (the City Varieties also received over £5m from Leeds City Council). Both of these also offer guided tours and visits.

The City Varieties, like many of the first music halls, evolved out of existing ad hoc musical activity in a pub, in this case the White Swan, which had been established in 1760 and served drink and food. The pub had a function room above the bar which hosted informal 'free-and-easies', a traditional feature in all sorts of pubs when customers and enthusiastic amateurs would gather and entertain each other with songs. These were often accompanied by a piano and presided over by a 'chairman', a master of ceremonies who, in most cases, had a little wooden mallet with which he rapped for order before announcing the next singer. Other informal outbreaks of carousing and sing-songs would occur in pubs, of course. Travelling players might show up, carrying perhaps fiddles or tambourines, or musicians touring with a fair, or street performers on a night out would visit.

Sometime around 1857 Charles Thornton became the licensee of the White Swan, and after just a few years he was encouraged to construct a music hall as an attachment to the pub. He did this in an ambitious fashion, creating a 2,000-capacity room with a high stage at one end and a gallery at the other, rows of benches along the walls and a few tables and chairs at ground level.

The City Varieties is on Swan Street, which runs between

Lands Lane and Briggate, a narrow street and perhaps not easy to find. If you approach from Lands Lane you'll see Swan Street running down the side of Betfred. From Briggate, look out for the Ann Summers shop and you'll see Swan Street. Grace is the member of staff from the City Varieties who leads the tours; she knows the place well, having first visited the hall fifteen years ago when she signed up in the youth theatre there. The tour I attended on a brisk Wednesday morning was sold out. There were twenty-six of us, and it was busier than Ann Summers (even though they had a sale on). One couple told Grace they bought tickets for the pantomime every year, but the rest of us were first-timers.

People have been going out and getting drunk and tracking down pleasure and entertainment for hundreds of years. In London, by the 1840s, the range of venues where music was part of the entertainment included outdoor pleasure gardens like the Cremorne, or supper clubs like the one run by W.C. Evans on King Street, on the edge of Covent Garden. Pubs had long been a traditional feature of life in hamlets, villages, towns and ports of Britain, as were street entertainments, theatres, taverns and broth-els. Some venues blurred definitions between, for example, taverns and brothels. St George's Tavern in Belgrave Road, Pimlico, would regularly feature men-only free-and-easies in the pub's function room: women who were invited to attend were most likely 'daughters of joy', as prostitutes were sometimes called.

What was new in Britain in the mid-nineteenth century was the rapid growth of new industrial towns like Leeds, Manchester, Birmingham and elsewhere. Families from rural villages, Ireland and, to a lesser extent, Europe, looked to find work in the new manufacturing industries, the factories, the mills. Manchester, for example, grew from a small market town of 48,000 people to a bursting metropolis of 455,000 in the space of fifty years (1801 to 1851).

The 1851 census revealed that for the first time in British

history more people were living in towns and cities than in the countryside. Owing to this mass migration, the poor living conditions and the unregulated factories, most areas of many cities were chaotic and unhinged. The urban poor were rootless, strangers, worked to the bone; for these reasons, there was a widespread and almost desperate demand for night-time entertainment in the 1830s and 1840s. In addition, in 1851 around half the entire population was under twenty years old. Like each and every single, active, young person of every generation, the wish of the young Victorians was not to be kept inside the house, but to seek pleasure, and partners. This urban working class, these new communities, were looking for hedonism, sensation and escape.

To help meet this demand, the Theatres Act of 1843 relaxed the rules governing places of entertainment, especially entertainment on licensed premises. Some informal campaigning had been going on. In 1840 Sam Lane was running the Union Saloon in Shoreditch, east London, which despite not being licensed as a theatre was offering onstage entertainments, including sketches and songs. When the authorities prosecuted and fined him, he led a demonstration march, challenging the authorities with the slogan 'Freedom for the people's amusements'.

The Theatres Act triggered a sharp rise in the number of pubs building stages and offering not just free-and-easies but more formally organised live performances, or setting up designated 'music saloons' in adjacent rooms of buildings. The owner of the St George's Tavern, Charles Morton, took over the Canterbury Arms off Westminster Bridge Road and, after operating it for a number of years as one of the first music halls in the country, in 1856 refurbished it to the tune of £25,000. Audiences flocked there to hear patriotic or comic songs, and marvel at acrobats, magicians and the likes of Dan Rice the Clown ('And His Wonderful Performing Dogs').

Not all music halls were on the scale of the ones built by Charles Morton or Charles Thornton; many weren't much more than an add-on or a function room. Writer R.J. Broadbent documented the Liverpool music halls of the nineteenth century in his book *Annals of the Liverpool Stage*, and while a number of music halls were respectably conducted in Liverpool, from his writing it's clear there were others of a more or less disreputable kind. Broadbent describes an un-named music hall on Williamson Square which appears to have been some kind of pick-up joint, with a less than sophisticated musical offering: 'After ascending a flight of very rickety stairs we reach the concert-room – a long, narrow apartment in a filthy state. Congregated round the bar inside are a number of bare-necked, lightly dressed girls, women and foreign sailors, all in various stages of intoxication.'

The author also visits the more respectable Parthenon Music Saloon run by J.G. Stoll on Great Charlotte Street, also in Liverpool. The doors of the Parthenon opened at 6.30 p.m. and the programme of entertainments commenced at 7 p.m. As with other big halls, acts had a certain slot they were contracted to fill for a designated amount of time, which was advertised in a printed programme. In this era in most singing saloons and early music halls there was no admission charge as such, but customers gained admittance by buying a refreshment ticket for perhaps 3d (about 1p) which they would then exchange at the bar for drinks. At some venues, waiters would take orders for drinks and young lads would walk the floor with cigars and programmes for sale.

Along with Thomas Sharples and J.G. Stoll, by the end of the 1840s there were numerous venue owners in the provinces who already had thriving music-hall-style businesses, including John Balmbra in Newcastle. Balmbra's was opened on the first floor of the Wheatsheaf public house and became a landmark in the town. It was there that George 'Geordie' Ridley performed the song 'Blaydon Races' in 1862. It's still sung on Tyneside today. The opening verse includes the lines, 'I took the bus from Balmbra's and she was heavy-laden / Away we went along Collingwood Street, that's on the road to Blaydon.'

The music hall and theatre world at the time was lively enough to sustain a magazine, *The Era*, concerned with matters theatrical and associated interests (including the licensed trade). A notice in *The Era* on 12 March 1865 carried an advertisement for Thornton's Music Hall promising an 'Astounding Array of Novelties'. Top of the bill on the opening night was Herr Schalkenbach, who had invented what he called 'the extraordinary Piano Orchestra Electro Moteur'. It ended up being a lifetime's work for Herr Schalkenbach, building and perfecting his early version of an electric organ, a very large construction (about the height of two pianos) which had the means to create whooshing sounds and percussion with drums, cymbals and gongs. He toured the invention, later appearing at the Metropolitan Music Hall in Paddington, Crystal Palace and elsewhere. Even more ahead of his time, this one-man Kraftwerk created a soundtrack to an imaginary shipwreck and devised a light show to complement the music he made. His act was deemed to be 'vastly impressive' by one reviewer.

The structure of the Leeds City Varieties is pretty much as it was when it was built by Charles Thornton. The sightlines even from the upper gallery are good, although when the venue was packed you'd expect to be jostling for position. According to *The Era*, there was also a spacious retiring room for the performers and a suite of dressing rooms immediately behind the stage. Grace takes us backstage, where the walls are covered with health and safety advice.

Although the structure and layout remain the same, much of what we see on the City Varieties tour are later additions, including the furnishings, the carpet, the gold leaf on the balcony fascia and the sturdy wooden chairs in the stalls at a comfortable angle. It was more basic when it first opened and Herr Schalkenbach played his electro piano; the venue was upgraded with the addition of balconies down the side and theatre-style seating later in

the nineteenth century. Most of the changes were made after
Charles Thornton leased the hall to John Stansfield (and
ploughed his money into a retail arcade just down the road
instead, an arcade that's still in operation), and then when Thomas
Dunford took over (it was during his tenure that, in 1894, the
name was changed to the City Varieties). It enjoyed another
upgrade in 1898 when it was bought by Fred Wood. Billiards and
supper rooms were attached. The following year the 'Clog
Dancing Championship of the World' took place at the City
Varieties.

Upgrades of this sort were common among music halls in the
last two decades of the nineteenth century, partly because, after
fires and other disasters, the authorities were demanding improve-
ments. But also proprietors hoped that by smartening up the
venues and making them more comfortable they might attract a
more bourgeois, wealthier audience. The recent work at the City
Varieties has concentrated on returning the venue to an approximation of how it might have been in 1900 rather than back to its
earliest days. You can see the wisdom in the decision; it's now a
very comfortable, working theatre, having featured in the recent
past magicians and tribute bands, as well as the annual pantomime.

Grace asks us to imagine what this fine and gilded auditorium
would have looked like in the hall's first phase, in the 1860s,
before the Heritage Lottery Fund, before the various Victorian
refurbishments, and without the gold-leaf balcony adornments,
the theatre seating and the swirly carpet. She explained that in the
late 1860s, despite the spectacular entertainment, by today's standards the venue was at the very roughest end of rough and ready,
with a wooden floor covered with sawdust to absorb dirt, spilled
alcohol and, it seems, much worse. There would be a few tables
scattered around, chairs, some stools. 'It would be different, very
different,' Grace tells us. 'There'd be drink sloshing around and
people standing, chatting, calling out to each other, it would be
packed, noisy.' And then she points up to the lower of the two

balconies: 'Young men who were up there would occasionally relieve themselves over the balcony onto the people below.'

Grace repeats the phrase 'rough and ready' a few times, referring to the hall, but life in general for the working class in Leeds and elsewhere was rough and ready. In those boom towns with their rapidly growing populations, housing was a mess, with gross overcrowding, insanitary conditions and exploitation by landlords. The working poor were inhabiting a cross between the Wild West and a shanty town.

Law makers were playing catch-up – the provisions of the Theatre Act reflected that, as did initiatives in the workplace that belatedly attempted to regulate working conditions and hours of work. The Factory Act of 1847 limited a working day for women and children to ten hours and the Factory Act of 1850 closed some loopholes and, among other things, formalised standard practice in the textile districts like Manchester that all work would end on Saturday at 2 p.m.

Some workers in the textile, mining and other industries would absent themselves on some or all Mondays. This wasn't covered by law or regulations, it was simply custom in certain districts. This day off was dubbed 'St Monday' and would follow a Saturday payday and a night on the town. In some cases workers who'd grown up in rural or other traditions were resistant to regimented regular work imposed by mechanised manufacturing industries and given the choice between earning a few extra pennies or a day off, took the time off, especially if they were being paid piece-work and could earn the money back by increasing their productivity another day. Some just wanted to enjoy drinking time. A royal commission on employment in 1842 found that Mondays in mining communities were 'chiefly spent by the adults in intemperance or recovering from the effects of it, or sometimes mere physical repose'.

Sunday evening offered an extra chance for some carousing. Angus Bethune Reach toured Manchester and the surrounding districts, documenting the lives of the working poor, working hard, playing hard. There's both fear and exhilaration in his account of being out on the Oldham Road one Sunday evening in 1849: 'The public houses and gin shops were roaring full. The whole street rung with shouting, screaming and swearing, mingled with the jarring music of half a dozen bands.'

On corners or near markets, passers-by would be entertained by street performers, including singers with a surprisingly wide repertoire. One of the public houses Angus Bethune Reach may have visited that evening was the George & Dragon on Swan Street, where the entertainment included songs known as 'broadsides', often songs with a local connection, like 'Manchester's Improving Daily', and 'The Manchester Town Hall Waltz'.

The liveliness of music-filled nights out in public houses and the fast-growing variety of local, comic and romantic songs were easily transferable into more formal music hall programmes. In addition, performers and proprietors incorporated such pieces as Rossini's overture to the opera *William Tell* and selections from the operatic works of Vincenzo Bellini in their programmes. In fact, some pieces from the classical canon became well known to almost everyone, even the street urchins, thanks to choirs, bands, organ grinders and street performers.

While the working class visited music halls and pub function rooms and experienced music and dancing on the street, the well-to-do had private clubs, charity balls and events in private houses. Thomas De Quincey came from a comparatively well-off family, who were wealthy enough to live among green fields two miles outside Manchester. He was an enthusiastic opium user and published *Confessions of an English Opium-Eater* in 1821. He would go to the opera or to music recitals at least once a week, carrying with him small tinctures of laudanum (a solution of crude opium in alcohol). He called these 'portable ecstasies' and said they enhanced his experience of listening to music.

De Quincey recalled having stones thrown at him by street

urchins on his way to school, but apart from that there was very little interaction between the social classes. All had their own entertainments, traditions, venues. There was talk that the Alexandra in Manchester attracted sons of factory owners and wealthy merchants but it was assumed they were there for the prostitutes rather than the music performances.

The landowning aristocracy had been the unchallenged power in Britain but the factory owners and the wealthy merchants were new money, the bosses in the new world of large-scale industrial manufacturing. The new wealth in Leeds was in the hands of the mine-owners, the merchants and the textile barons. Taking as a model those London haunts of the ruling class, like Boodle's and the Carlton Club, two houses on Albion Square were procured and, in 1852, opened as a prestigious gentlemen's club; it was a meeting place for the town's leading business and professional men, with a lavish classical interior including coffee, smoking and dining rooms, and a ballroom. It was all very different to Thornton's Music Hall, 200 yards away.

In London, much of the social scene of the rich and aristocratic revolved around 'coming out', the formalised structure by which unmarried young female debutantes would be launched into the world in order to attract prospective husbands. The process took place during a 'season' of dinner parties, court occasions and gala balls. During the Regency and early Victorian era, the season ran from just after Easter to the end of June, but later in the nineteenth century it shifted a little and reached through to 12 August, the Glorious Twelfth as it is known, the start of the shooting season. At this point it was expected that the aristocracy and the gentry would have left London and taken themselves off to their country homes; the single men would put the search for a wife on hold and go hunting for red grouse instead.

The young ladies were expected to deport themselves in very particular and controlled ways, not just at the dances but at all times. They'd be accompanied by a chaperone (usually an older female relative) and were expected to be elegant and to have what Lord Byron called 'a floating balance of accomplishment', including the ability to ride a horse, and perhaps to be able to play the piano or to sing. There were rituals and rules for every situation, including those when, in the company of her chaperone, a young lady might chance upon a male. A well-brought-up young lady (and by implication a potential wife) was expected never to look back after anyone in the street, or catch the eye of a man at a social event, or at church, or the theatre.

It was a relentless few months for the young ladies during the season, when they would be attending three or four parties every night and arriving home at dawn. As with all grand balls and private dances, there were strict conventions covering who could dance with whom, how often, and in what way men and women could observe each other or converse. The liberties of the young ladies, on the face of it, were few, but a little bit of assertive behaviour was acceptable within clearly defined boundaries. For example, a young lady could engage in flirtation at a dance, by use of her fan. If she was to fan herself slowly, it was a sign she was engaged or otherwise unavailable. A fast fan indicated she was independent and not spoken for. A fan shut indicated there was no chance of an encounter, but on the other hand, a deliberate, repetitive opening and shutting of her fan was a very positive come-on. As in any era, you wouldn't want to send or read the signals wrongly.

The aristocracy liked to feel virtuous but usually preferred to combine philanthropy with some pleasure, some conspicuous consumption and a chance to see and be seen. Not just during the season, but year-round and in all towns, there would be glitzy charity events. In April 1845 a grand fancy-dress ball, in aid of the funds for the formation of public baths and washhouses in Manchester, was held in the Free Trade Hall. According to one account: 'The display was very picturesque and made a great impression.' It continued to be the case that most nights out dancing for the well-to-do would be mainly dinner dances in grand halls, or special or charity ticketed balls.

In stark contrast to those nightlife venues where there was a value to being noticed, parading and being part of a glittering high-society occasion, there were other nightlife venues that preferred to be out of sight, including those where gambling or prostitution were a feature. The most extreme example of hidden venues were those where homosexual and cross-dressing men would meet in secret; taverns with function rooms, or select and secret coffee houses, or private homes known as molly houses. The molly houses made every attempt to stay away from the public gaze as they were genuinely outside the law and fraught with danger, given that sodomy was not only illegal but carried the death penalty (it remained a capital offence until 1861).

Rictor Norton in his book *Mother Clap's Molly House* tells the story of one famous molly house on Field Lane in Holborn, one of the estimated 200 or so operating in the first decades of the eighteenth century. Margaret Clap (aka 'Mother Clap') rented out rooms to tenants and provided food, drink and entertainment. The social and cultural aspect of Mother Clap's seems to have been important to her and her visitors (other venues were probably not much more than male brothels).

One Sunday evening in February 1726 forty customers were arrested in a raid on Mother Clap's premises. Police investigations had included a number of undercover constables infiltrating the network. At the subsequent trial, the evidence of one, a Constable Samuel Stevens, was key. He reported that 'Sometimes they would sit in one another's laps, kissing in a lewd manner and using their hands indecently. Then they would get up, dance and make curtsies, and mimic the voices of women.' Of those arrested, three men were found guilty of sodomy and were hanged (Gabriel Lawrence, William Griffin and Thomas Wright). The history of molly houses is littered with similar moments, raids and executions, including a raid in 1810 on a pub in Vere Street, to the west of Lincoln's Inn Fields in London. In addition to activities and parties similar to those at Mother Clap's, it was said that there a homosexual priest, the Reverend John Church, presided over 'gay marriages' at the venue. As a result of the Vere Street raid, two men were hanged for sodomy.

To avoid the gaze of the public and police, there were strategies gay men and women developed as the nineteenth century progressed: secret networks, drag balls in private houses or function rooms hired often under false pretences. On Friday 24 September 1880 the Temperance Hall at Hulme Place on York Street in Hulme, just to the south of Manchester city centre, was hired under the name of the Pawnbrokers' Assistants' Association. Unbeknown to the steward managing the hall, in reality the event was an assembly of men attending a party. Some of the forty-seven men there were dressed in 'fantastical fashion', according to later press reports, and almost half 'in the garb of women'. The party was raided at two o'clock in the morning and all the men present were arrested.

The following day in court it was revealed that Detective Sergeant Jerome Caminada and the men in his charge in Manchester had instigated undercover surveillance of various assembly rooms since the previous Christmas. The drag ball organisers at the Temperance Hall had done all they could to ensure their privacy; most of the windows had been covered over with calico or paper. Caminada and his men used a ladder to look through a high window at the back of the building to espy the assembly for several hours, until the nature of the proceedings were confirmed to the police.

The police also gained knowledge of the secret code to access the drag ball – seven knocks, followed by the password 'sister'. They rushed in, along with a group of local men enlisted by the police for the evening, and after a few brief struggles the arrests were made. Most of the attendees were from Manchester and Salford, including a waiter from Weaste and a stonemason from

Lower Broughton. Nine men had travelled across the Pennines from Sheffield. One of the witnesses told Mr Cobbett (prosecuting on behalf of the police) and the magistrates, that the dancing he witnessed at the party was too indecent and disgusting to describe. Mr Cobbett said that everything pointed to the event being 'one of the foulest orgies that ever disgraced any town'.

On the surface the police action seems heavy-handed, the language grim, but curiously, as the court proceeded, the magistrates and Mr Cobbett appeared to engineer the least draconian outcome, pressing for leniency. Despite acting on behalf of the police Mr Cobbett suggested a 'mild outcome' and, taking his advice, the magistrates decided merely to have the partygoers bound over for twelve months. None of the most extreme charges were laid, and the private lives of the accused remained unexplored. It could be that some of the accused were known in the wider community and were being protected from a long drawn-out trial or that the authorities had decided Manchester needed to hide the scandal as best it could. Whether Caminada felt he'd got an appropriate result after nine months of surveillance and a major use of manpower is another matter.

Such was the division and ignorance between classes, even though music halls weren't hidden away out of necessity as molly houses were, they were in effect unseen by the upper echelons of society; or at least, if acknowledged, considered part of an underworld they'd not venture to. News of how the working poor would be entertained would reach the wider world through newspaper reports of fires or disasters, when coverage would be marked by a shock that such places were doing a roaring trade in the middle of the city, frequented (as the papers would have it) by women, young men, and 'street Arabs'.

The activities and audiences at the music halls were often caught up in ongoing debates regarding drunkenness, although it was really only working-class intemperance that was considered problematic and targeted by a number of mainly failed initiatives.

These included the Beerhouse Act, passed during the reign of William IV in 1830, which aimed to wean the populace off their ever-increasing desire for gin by encouraging beer drinking instead. So the act maintained controls on the sale of spirits but, for a payment of two guineas, allowed anyone to set up as a beerhouse with little or no regulation. Dozens of premises opened. An eyewitness at the time noted the carnage that ensued: 'The new Beer Act has begun its operations. Everyone is drunk. Those who are not singing are sprawling.'

In music hall venues, where shouting and drunkenness were the norm, performers could struggle to get the attention of the audience and there was always room, as Grace at the City Varieties says, for 'an act that was eye-catching'. For the working poor – with a routine pretty much consisting of, wake up, work in a factory or mill or workshop all day, go home, eat a sugar sandwich, go to bed, wake up, go to work, go home, eat a sugar sandwich – when a Saturday night came round they were ready for something totally bizarre, out of the ordinary. Many music halls were designed so that trapeze and high-wire acts could perform, and music hall proprietors often booked so-called 'freak show' performers like Siamese twins and Anna Swan, the Nova Scotia giantess. At the Surrey Music Hall in Sheffield, Thomas Youdan had a penchant for presenting performing dogs.

Music hall songs would cover subjects including life in the local town, the world of work, and love and marriage (depictions oscillating wildly between sentimental portrayals of true love and cynical songs about hen-pecked husbands, and between bawdy tales of extramarital affairs and censorious denunciations of adultery). During the nineteenth century there was much public sympathy for the plight of old and wounded soldiers. According to one historian, when singer Charlie Godfrey began performing a sketch about a neglected old soldier forced to beg, 'The War Office took steps to have the sketch "barred" as it threatened to be "prejudicial to recruiting".'

Generally (and for good reasons), commercial operators, required to apply annually to renew their licence, avoided antagonising the authorities. These realities partly explain the conservative nature of music hall songs. It was as if there were tacitly agreed parameters: songs about poverty were popular, but songs proposing radical solutions to poverty or inequality weren't. Concern at the plight of old soldiers notwithstanding, most songs about Britain at war were unfalteringly patriotic. Audiences had paid their hard-earned cash and left their woes at home; they wanted to be entertained.

Later in the nineteenth century, among the performers who toured nationally, many of the most popular were those who incorporated stock characters into their act. The halls generally dealt in caricatures, like the shy maiden and the gruesome mother-in-law. Actor/comedian George Leybourne became nationally known for his portrayal of 'Champagne Charlie', a parody of an idle, hedonistic posh boy. One of the biggest stars of the late Victorian and Edwardian periods was Vesta Tilley, who began her full-time career at Day's Concert Hall on Smallbrook Street in Birmingham. She was a gifted and celebrated male impersonator who performed various comic character roles, including Monty from Monte Carlo, and Burlington Bertie.

Journalists visiting music halls to report on the entertainment rarely found much that they considered of any artistic value. J. Ewing Ritchie paid a visit to a venue close to Brick Lane, where, on payment of a shilling, he was ushered into a very handsome hall to witness some 'uninteresting bicycling by riders in curious dress'. Comic singing, relieved by risqué dancing, seemed to be the staple amusement of the place; when one of the female performers indecently elevated a leg, immense was the applause from the 'rough element' at the back of the hall.

One of the other forms of entertainment witnessed by Ewing Ritchie was minstrelsy, a tradition born in America but popular in Britain from the 1840s onwards. White performers blacked their faces with burnt cork or greasepaint or shoe polish, and with a range of props, including woolly wigs, created caricatures of black people and performed songs, sketches and dances. After Ewing Ritchie had watched someone dressed as a black man singing 'a lot of low doggerel about his "gal"', he didn't criticise it for being offensive or demeaning, but for being shallow: 'It is a curious thing that directly a man lampblacks his face and wears a woollen wig, and talks broken English, he at once becomes a popular favourite.'

In the 1860s, under the stewardship of Sam Hague, St James's Hall in Liverpool was one of Britain's most celebrated music and dance venues, with a strong line-up of 'blackface' performers. Received industry wisdom was that, curiously, many audiences were more entertained by songs and dances from white blackface minstrels than genuine black Americans, but St James's Hall also featured a ten-member black minstrel troupe recruited by Sam Hague in the 1860s on a visit to the American state of Georgia. The troupe, dubbed 'the American Slave Serenaders', became successful, billing themselves as 'the only combination of genuine darkies in the world'.

Clog dancing had a long tradition in both America and Britain, going back to the mid-nineteenth century, and accomplished clog dancers were a common attraction at music halls. On 18 July 1866, on the opening night of the Cambridge Music Hall in Toxteth, the Leno family appeared, including young brothers Henry and George (the latter would later take the stage name Dan Leno on the way to becoming a celebrated music hall performer). They were billed as 'Mr. and Mrs. Leno, the Great, Sensational, Dramatic and Comic Duettists and The Brothers Leno, Lancashire Clog, Boot and Pump Dancers'.

Other engagements in Liverpool for the Leno family followed. In April 1867, George, Henry and their parents appeared at St James's Hall performing various dances onstage, including clog dancing. But on this occasion part of their act was described as

'American breakdown dancers'. It appears that break-dancing, all the rage in the late 1970s and early 1980s, might have had some roots in much older traditions. And, in common with the hip hop era, the breakdown dances seem to have been taken up by agile kids of a young age, who grew proficient in them and performed them as party pieces and in public. In 1866 Dan and Henry Leno were then aged six and eight years respectively.

The breakdown was one of a number of dances first performed by slave children (also known as 'contraband children'), sometimes accompanied by an older slave playing an African 'banja', the forerunner of the American banjo. In areas of New York, Irish immigrants with their tradition of jigs and reels were mixing with the children of slaves and former slaves and a cross-fertilisation of dance styles occurred. In the early 1840s the American impresario P.T. Barnum had a young dancer called Johnny Diamond on his books. He'd been spotted dancing for cash at the old Fly Market in New York City. Barnum toured Diamond around America, taking on all-comers in dancing competitions. Another celebrated dancer of the breakdown and a dozen or more other dances was Master Juba (William Henry Lane). Juba (named after the Giouba, a hand-clapping and foot-stomping dance created by slaves) came to Britain with a minstrel company and his fame was such he danced before Queen Victoria in Buckingham Palace.

Dance competitions and other contests were a regular feature in music halls, sometimes with a bizarre twist. Henry Pullan in Bradford regularly presented singing contests open to members of the audience. To differentiate his hall from others, he took to requiring the guest singers to carry a live, squirming piglet in their arms while they sang. Ramping up the hilarity further, he then got the singers (still holding the piglet) to get on a donkey, which was then paraded around the stage while the song was sung. In addition to ludicrous live pig and donkey combinations, music hall proprietors could resort to real bottom-of-the-bill fare like these entertainments described in *The Era*: 'Guessing the number of pins or peas in a glass bottle; getting coins out of a bowl of treacle with the mouth.'

There were, of course, also particularly stringent guidelines set out to outlaw the chances of halls presenting scantily clad women onstage, although most music hall proprietors found a happy alternative with what were called *tableaux vivants*. These were living statues, performers in appropriate dress creating a still scene, usually from history or a myth or legend. Subjects for *tableaux vivants* in the music hall included sensational moments of Greek or Roman history (for example, 'Brutus Ordering the Execution of his Son'), but most often performers created scenes which required an underdressed young lady. The trick was the use of flesh-coloured body stockings, which avoided contravening laws on nudity. Among the most popular were scenes featuring Lady Godiva, Adam and Eve, the Goddess Diana, Helen of Troy or one or more of the Sultan's harem (one often-performed tableau was entitled 'The Sultan's Favourite Returning from the Bath'). In retrospect a key ingredient in so many of these *tableaux vivants* appears to be titillation, but Victorians were to a degree in denial about this, as if the choice of presenting a mythical or historical or biblical figure or Roman goddess requiring young women to assume a state of undress was somehow a coincidence.

Audiences appreciated dramatic scenes. The Millstone Concert Hall in Bolton presented a re-enactment of the Siege of Sebastopol featuring backdrops painted by George Martin and directed by T.H. Merridy. Merridy specialised in producing large-scale battle re-enactments, often involving pyrotechnics and spread over several acres, including at Pomona Gardens in Manchester. Originally known as the Cornbrook Strawberry Gardens, the Pomona Gardens were developed as public pleasure gardens by James Reilly in 1868 and included many attractions such as a ballroom (the Pomona Palace) and multiple leisure attractions in the gardens, from dog shows to archery classes.

*

The proprietors of the halls were generally colourful characters, chancers, pioneers and idealists who stamped their personalities on their venues and rarely delegated any of the big decisions, and often acted as chairman. They invariably enjoyed the status ownership of a successful hall gave them in the town. In many ways, those music hall proprietors shared the mentality of many of today's club promoters and not a dissimilar business model. They would take the risk and pay the fees for the night's entertainment and commission advertisements, handbills and posters. The successful ones knew how to find and nurture a regular audience.

Among those with the highest profile in their home town was Thomas Youdan in Sheffield, the centre of the steel trade, a town of grinders, razorsmiths, edge-tool fitters and scissor filers. Thomas Youdan moved there from Doncaster and became a silver stamper, then began to run a pub on West Bar, the Spink's Nest, building around it, adding rooms and creating a new venue that became known as the Royal Casino. He incorporated a spacious ballroom, a concert hall and a museum. When the chaotic affairs of the aristocratic Hunloke family of Wingerworth Hall caused them to find a buyer for the wild animals that had been collected there, Youdan snapped them up and opened a menagerie. The Royal Casino was, in fact, everything but a casino. It later became known as the Surrey Music Hall.

Youdan became a powerful member of the community, not least because in the 1860s his Surrey Music Hall was the biggest building in Sheffield (the locals hadn't got round to building a town hall), and he was responsible for some of the most striking cultural activity in the area, indulging in various crazy schemes. In early 1856, to celebrate the end of the Crimean War, Youdan commissioned a four-ton cake from local confectioner George Bassett. Bassett used over 10,000 eggs in the recipe but when slices were distributed to the old and needy Bassett and Youdan were deluged with complaints that it was undercooked and therefore inedible.

In 1858 Youdan became involved in local politics, being appointed as a workhouse guardian and then taking a seat on the local council, but a suspicion lingers that not all was quite as it seemed with Thomas Youdan. He was attracting a couple of thousand people to his premises two or three times a week, and, like show-business characters in later eras, was embedded in the political establishment and involved in charity work. He was for-ever engaged in feuds with local venue owners, was several times in court for operating illegal raffle and lottery competitions, and had a shady private life. There was controversy concerning the paternity of a child born to one of his barmaids, who had been only fifteen when the child was conceived (there were allegations, which never went to court, that he'd raped the barmaid). He denied being the baby's father but the courts found against him and he paid 2/6 (12½p) per week support for the following thir-teen years. In March 1865 the Surrey Music Hall was destroyed by fire but within weeks Youdan had bought the old Adelphi Theatre in Furnival Road, which he reopened as the Alexandra Music Hall later the same year.

Sam Hague's St James's Hall was another venue that ended up destroyed by fire, in 1875. According to one account, 'The whole of the roof, the scenery, dresses, and interior of the hall soon became a charred mass of ruins. Poor Hague when he saw the destruction of his popular hall cried like a child.' Unfortunately Herr Schalkenbach's famous electric organ, which had travelled safely all around Western Europe, including Paris where Herr Schalkenbach demonstrated it to Napoleon III, was in temporary storage at St James's and was wrecked in the fire.

Despite the frequent campaigns by anti-alcohol temperance groups including the formation in 1853 of the United Kingdom Alliance for the Suppression of the Traffic in All Intoxicating Liquors, who would picket outside halls or licensing sessions and raise petitions, the prevailing wisdom among magistrates and police was that alcoholic excess was more likely to be found in pubs, beerhouses and gin palaces than in music halls. In addition, many music hall proprietors developed close and often financial relationships with the local police, giving themselves some leeway in the event of any incident or complaint. Furthermore, in all the government-led committees and enquiries (like the 1852 Select Committee on Public Houses), along with a need to be mindful of public morality there was also a desire to protect and enhance the tax revenues accruing from alcohol sales.

Music halls were occasionally the site of violence. Genuine troublemakers could cause disruption to an evening's entertainment, but it was rare. In Manchester, the Victorian streets were home to 'scuttler' gangs, hooligans with a level of infamy which matched any gang in modern times, and on a par with the 'peaky blinders' of Birmingham. John-Joseph Hillier was one scuttler with a well-earned reputation for violence (he was jailed a number of times for attacking people with a butcher's knife). Originally from Ireland, he grew up in Salford and was a gang member by his early teens. A scuttler had a certain look – hair well plastered down, a peaked cap worn at an angle, a white scarf, a union shirt, a heavy belt with a big buckle, iron-shod clogs and coarse cotton trousers cut like a sailor's, with 'bell-bottoms'.

Hillier became the leader of the 'Deansgate Mob', based in Manchester city centre and recruiting from the densely packed housing around where the high glass restaurants and corporate office blocks in Spinningfields are now situated. His mob frequently hunted down and attacked a rival gang who were based at a music hall, the Casino on Peter Street, and would do battle inside the hall. He revelled in his notoriety: when newspapers dubbed him the 'King of the Scuttlers', he had the phrase sewn onto the front of his jersey.

In reality, it's unlikely halls were any more dangerous than the street outside (and possibly less so); Deansgate, for example, was described by a local policeman as 'a plague spot' of violent crime. The halls were frequented by a mix of the working poor and the lower-middle class, courting couples, husbands and wives, work-mates and children. They would draw an audience from the locality and in those close communities everyone tended to know each other and some of the older men would intervene if ruffians were ruining the night.

As well as debates about the role of the music hall in encour-aging intemperate drinking, and concerns about the content of the entertainment being less than uplifting, a further issue was prostitution, a widespread, blatant trade in Victorian Britain, par-ticularly in London. That London was rife with vice was partly because there was a bigger reserve of well-off men who would pay for sex, and an ongoing supply of hot-blooded soldiers and sailors passing through the city. But prostitution is always present where there's poverty, and women had a slightly different social standing in London as a result of the different opportunities for female workers. Factories and mills further north employed thousands of people, male and female, and a young woman could make a rela-tively good living as a factory operative. In London there were almost no large-scale manufacturing industries, and the most common jobs for working-class women were very poorly paid: domestic servants, for example, including nursemaids. The researcher/journalist Henry Mayhew suggested in the late 1850s that soldiers were notorious for 'hunting' nursemaids walking with prams in the park. He claims that a nursemaid or a shop-girl would prostitute herself, not full-time, but occasionally allowing herself to be accosted on the street: 'She prostitutes herself for her own pleasure, a few trifling presents or a little money now and then.'

Mayhew visits a music hall above a pub on Ratcliff Highway in the East End of London where benches have been pushed back against the walls to create a central dancefloor. He doesn't hesitate to label the women present as prostitutes, here, he thinks, to pick up sailors. He watches them, calling them 'brazen-faced' and describ-ing them as 'dressed in gaudy colours, dancing and pirouetting in a fantastic manner'. The orchestra of four musicians (a fiddle, a cornet and two fifes or flutes) he describes variously as 'bearded' and 'shaggy-looking' ('probably Germans', he concludes). The music and the waltzing he finds to be 'exhilarating in the highest degree'. By the end of the evening he is less judgemental of the women in the venue, noting that they're the most enthusiastic dancers. But he remains unimpressed by the male patrons: 'The faces of the sailors were vacant, stupid and beery.'

In general, by the 1870s, even the most judgemental could see that the music hall reflected the ubiquity of prostitution rather than created it. Nevertheless there were one or two halls which seemed to encourage vice, and they were to be found in the West End of London rather than in the poorer districts. The Argyll on Great Windmill Street, for example, owned by wine merchant Robert Bignell, attracted some of the wealthiest and most dissolute men and achieved notoriety for its masquerade balls and unceasing rumours that prostitutes operated on the premises. All over London there were lodging houses where prostitutes and clients who'd met on the streets or in pubs or music halls could find privacy, at the cost of a shilling or two per hour. Rooms near the Argyll were the most lucrative in London.

An American, Daniel Kirwan, documented an evening out at the Argyll Rooms in his book about social inequality, *Palace and Hovel: Or, Phases of London Life*. He suggests the vast majority of men are there without their wives. The women, meanwhile, dazzle Kirwan with their silks and satins and velvets, rich jewels and gold ornaments. The men, many of them in full evening dress, he describes as 'in respectable society'. The women not so: 'No virtuous woman ever enters this place,' he declares. Downstairs with 'the vulgar herd' he reckons it's chiefly clerks and tradesmen dancing the waltzes and quadrilles with various partners. Upstairs in the gallery things move up a level, there are various titillating paintings, groups of wealthy aristocratic gentlemen and numbers of 'fast women'. He's introduced to Kate

Hamilton, a former art student and once a great beauty, who controlled the trade in women at the Argyll and other venues.

The Argyll Rooms temporarily lost its licence in 1857 on the grounds that it promoted 'great social evils'. After arguing that its closure increased local street prostitution a licence was granted again by the Middlesex magistrates, although the venue remained controversial and Bignell lost his licence for music and dancing again in November 1878 and the Argyll Rooms closed. As with anxieties about intemperance, the police, magistrates and most newspapers of the day – in all but the most extreme cases – favoured pragmatism. This attitude was neatly summed up by a policeman Henry Mayhew met in 1862: 'The British Queen, a concert-room in the Commercial Road, is a respectable, well-conducted house, frequented by low prostitutes, as may be expected, but orderly in the extreme, and what more can be wished for? The sergeant remarked to me, if these places of harmless amusement were not licensed and kept open, much evil would be sown and disseminated throughout the neighbourhood.'

There were tidied-up, morally irreproachable 'people's concerts' in the 1840s and 1850s hosted by organisations like the Glasgow Total Abstinence Society and the Leeds Rational Recreational Society. Pressure groups like these and other bodies campaigned for local authorities to build and run civic buildings that could host such events in more morally uplifting surroundings. St George's Hall in Liverpool and Colston Hall in Bristol were both built with this in mind. Colston Hall opened in 1867 with three auditoriums: the main theatre was mostly used for live concerts, and the smaller halls for such music hall staples as minstrel shows and *tableaux vivants*.

In the last decades of the nineteenth century, the unhinged, unregulated chaos of urban life became a little tamer, and challenges to the social order from the Chartists and trade unionists had largely been brought under control. The relative prosperity of the era encouraged conformity among the populace and wide-spread investment in civic buildings and in leisure. In 1867 Queen Victoria laid the foundation for the Royal Albert Hall of Arts and Sciences, an ambitious building that took four years to build and aimed to rival the Cirque d'Hiver in Paris. On open-ing, however, and for nearly a century afterwards, the acoustics were derided (then partially fixed – in 1969, 135 large fibreglass acoustic diffusing discs were attached to the ceiling to cut down the echo).

During the 1890s, as new building regulations were intro-duced, proprietors refurbished their halls with Romanesque arcading, palatial staircases, oak carving and French Empire pilasters, and programming began to reflect more aspirant tastes. In many venues the original music hall audiences – the working poor (casual labourers, apprentices, soldiers, factory workers of both sexes, dockers, servant girls and families) – found them-selves joined by middle-class audiences (including the likes of tradesmen, office managers and civil servants). In some establish-ments in the early days of the music hall members of the audience could arrive late, and come and go as they pleased, but a night out at a music hall was now a more formal occasion, closer to practices at the so-called legitimate theatre.

Another sign of the taming of the music hall industry was the rise of the chains – operators controlling and operating multiple venues. With only a few exceptions, the waywardness and local idiosyncrasies of the halls were replaced with standardised enter-tainment at venues owned by the chains. J.G. Stoll at the Parthenon in Liverpool was succeeded by his son, J.G. Stoll (Jnr), who married a widowed actress with children from her previous marriage, Roderick and Oswald. Subsequently, on the death of their stepfather, the two brothers assisted their mother in the management of the Parthenon. Oswald Stoll then began building a chain of music halls and became one of the major players in the industry. Edward Moss was another operator with several halls and

variety theatres. Moss Empires was created when the two com-
petitors combined (Stoll became the managing director of the
company), and became the largest of the music hall chains.

These developments in the music hall industry, though, including concessions to middle-class tastes, were no defence when
competition came from the cinema. Audiences in search of
escapism and entertainment flocked to see so-called 'moving pictures' in the first two decades of the twentieth century, and many
music halls closed, or were themselves converted into cinemas.
The City Varieties took to showing films on some nights of the
week, but they continued to find there was a demand for talent
shows, and also instigated regular wrestling contests.

As we shall see in the next chapter, after the First World War
the jazz wave crashed over Britain and a generation was swept up
by it, and by the end of the 1920s the younger crowd were more
likely to be found in dance halls on Fridays and Saturdays than old
music halls. The remaining music halls were more widely known
as variety theatres; comedy was now the staple diet. Harry Joseph
took over the lease on the City Varieties in 1941 and, in the
quest for financial survival, found a number of inspired ways to
entice locals to his venue. According to Grace, on one occasion he
presented a young woman attempting to hypnotise an alligator live
onstage. I asked her how the alligator got on and off stage, as there
didn't seem room backstage to manoeuvre him (or her). She said
she didn't know if it was a him or a her and wasn't sure where the
alligator was kept. However, we both agreed we'd have paid sixpence to see such a thing.

In the 1950s, it wasn't so much other kinds of live entertainment as the rise in home entertainment which threatened to keep
crowds away from venues like the City Varieties, notably the
increasing availability and popularity of television. Harry Joseph
began to programme attractions that television didn't include. In
a typical bill from 1962 he would present a selection of strippers –
Francesca, Maria and Renee – with other performers providing

comedy capers and a risqué revue like *Who Goes Bare?* But he also forged a lucrative alliance with the new medium, scoring a coup in 1953 when the City Varieties became the home of the weekly BBC show *The Good Old Days*.

The Good Old Days, a more than slightly sanitised and nostalgic TV series, was a feature of the TV schedules for thirty years. The audience dressed in period costume and the chairman was Leonard Sachs. His role was one of the elements that had survived through the music hall era, inherited from the tradition of free-and-easies, and evolved into a performance in its own right. Sachs would introduce the entertainers with extravagant phrases delivered in a very elaborate approximation of aristocratic speech.

Almost 2,000 performers were filmed during *The Good Old Days* at the City Varieties, many of them household names then and since, including Ken Dodd, Bernard Cribbins, Roy Castle, Morecambe and Wise, and the great Les Dawson. Les Dawson was a bridge between the music hall of a hundred years before and the light entertainment of the day, a master of *double entendres*, more than proficient at the piano forte, with a range of memorable onstage characters, and he always raised a titter with jokes about the wife's mother.

Other TV shows have had one foot in the heyday of the music hall, among them *The Black and White Minstrel Show*, which was on prime-time TV from 1958 to 1978, complete with blacked-up characters and stereotypes galore. The show was much mocked and parodied and the subject of a petition calling for its end as early as 1967. Since its cancellation, *The Black and White Minstrel Show* has come to be seen more widely as an embarrassment, despite its huge popularity at the time. Less controversially, in our present era we've educated ourselves to expect Saturday night TV to include a number of the elements of a night out as it might have been presented by Thomas Youdan or Harry Joseph: talent shows, dance competitions and even performing dogs.

Leeds City Varieties closed in 2009 and reopened, refurbished, in 2011. Wilton's Music Hall – the other hall to receive major funding for refurbishment – evolved from a pub on Grace's Alley in Stepney, east London, called the Prince of Denmark (also known as the Mahogany Bar). The Prince of Denmark was the haunt of sailors, thieves and prostitutes. It appears John Wilton hoped that by building a music hall behind the pub he could bring a bit of calm to the otherwise disorderly premises. Wilton's Music Hall opened on 28 March 1859, packed with 1,200 people and with John Wilton in the chair. The entertainers in its earliest days included a resident choir and resident comics, including Sam Collins, a London-born former chimney sweep who presented himself as an 'Irish' singer; Mr and Mrs Randall, the character duologuists; and Mr Charles Sloman, well known for his improvisatorial talents, who was also Wilton's first designated music director.

In the building of the hall, John Wilton prioritised the acoustics but didn't underspend on the decor or the structure. One feature, a 'sunburner', created by Messrs Defries and Sons of Houndsditch, was a huge piece of lighting equipment; although there was no means of rotating it, it was not unlike a giant mirror-ball. It hung from the ceiling covered by a combination of more than 20,000 prisms, shards and spangles, all illuminated by the flickering flames of hundreds of tiny gas burners, throwing light into the corners and across the room. The sunburner had a system of ventilation that produced a continual current of fresh air. *The Era* was impressed: 'However crowded the room may be, as it was on the opening night, not the least inconvenience is felt from the heat.'

Despite John Wilton gaining a reputation as an authoritative chairman and the presence of two doormen at the entrance to the venue, Wilton's was never going to find a wholly respectable audience, given the character of the neighbourhood and the realities of life in the East End at the time. These realities included a thriving sex trade. In 1862 a brothel 'of the very lowest and most infamous kind' just a few doors away from Wilton's was closed down after the arrest and conviction of the owners. Prostitutes also operated in Wilton's itself. On arrival at the hall men with their wives would make for the ground floor of the auditorium, whereas men looking for a less respectable encounter knew to go upstairs to the gallery. Given the clandestine nature and the passing of time, our knowledge of the activities of the prostitutes doesn't extend much beyond a sense of dubious goings-on and dark dealings. For example, one of the rooms off the main auditorium was registered for use as a 'Finishing school for young ladies'.

The refurbishment of Wilton's has taken the venue back to its condition in 1878, some nineteen years after it first opened and a few years after John Wilton had moved on to manage the refreshment department at the Lyceum Theatre in the West End, but most significantly, just after it reopened following a fire in August 1877. It feels very much like a first-generation, unregenerated music hall, especially in contrast to the 1900-style City Varieties. It's bare, dark, atmospheric.

Wilton's didn't have much of a life after 1878, closing as a licensed music hall in 1881. There's evidence, however, that it remained open in some guise, perhaps operating illegally (there are reports of female prize-fighting and women singing shocking songs 'of blasphemous indecency'). The next owners, though, came from a different part of the moral scale: Wesleyan Methodists, who took over the building and used it as a mission until 1957 when it was sold to Coppermill Rag Warehouse.

In the modern era, after being semi-derelict for several decades, Wilton's has had various periods of fundraising and refurbishment, enough to provide a space for a number of events, including actress Fiona Shaw in an adaptation of *The Waste Land* in 1997, *Mojo* magazine presenting the Black Keys in 2008, a stage version of *The Great Gatsby* in 2013 and a showing of Fritz Lang's silent film *Metropolis* with a live musical accompaniment in

2015. Like the City Varieties, guided tours are available. Mine started with a piece of cake in the Mahogany Bar and ended with a drink in the gallery bar. It was only early evening, about seven o'clock, but also in the bar were a couple in their twenties in a tight embrace, kissing (with tongues and everything). I fancy they'd been roused by a combination of wine and the aura of licentious history.

Undoubtedly, though, the most shocking episode in Wilton's history occurred on 25 November 1863. Peter Melloy was a regular and popular performer at the venue. One evening he was singing at a charity event and the hall was packed with an estimated thousand people. But a large man in the audience – one Thomas Bunn – started to heckle Melloy, telling him to get off the stage. Then he got up from his bench and stood at the front of the stage shouting, 'Shut up, we have had enough of that.' Melloy was wearing a felt hat (it was part of his act) and he threw it at Bunn, and the two then got into an altercation during which Bunn continued to shout 'insolently and impertinently' (according to one account). Those who were seated rose to see what was happening and Melloy jumped off the stage and punched Bunn twice on the head. Bunn fell, and was taken to the supper room and then the bar-parlour, where he was still unable to stand. He was then carried home to St Mark's Street where he died less than an hour later. According to James Sequira, a surgeon who discovered internal bleeding in Thomas Bunn's brain, the blows received were most certainly the cause of death.

Melloy went on trial at the Old Bailey on an indictment charging him with the manslaughter of Thomas Bunn. Extraordinarily, even the wife of the dead man was among those in the court who called for leniency on account of the provocation Melloy had suffered when her husband interrupted his songs. At the trial much was made of Thomas Bunn's drunken state (he'd tried to start a fight that afternoon in the Three Tuns). The court was told that the singer was a 'well-conducted and on all occasions a well-disciplined man'. It took the jury just five minutes of deliberation to find Peter Melloy guilty of feloniously killing and slaying Thomas Bunn, but the jury strongly recommended mercy 'on the grounds of gross provocation'. For killing the heckler, the singer was sentenced to just fourteen days' imprisonment.

CHAPTER TWO

Dream palaces, degenerate boys, jazz-mad dancing girls

In the 1920s and into the 1930s there was a huge rise in the number of public dance halls. Some were relatively small and local but by the mid-1930s every town or city centre had a major dance hall, holding a couple of thousand people or more. Grand and palatial, these were the 'palais de danse' that within a generation had replaced music halls and variety theatres as favourite sites for Saturday nights out.

Most people were living in substandard housing, without access to anything remotely glitzy, but the likes of Bolton Palais, Streatham Locarno and Barrowland in Glasgow offered colour and thrill and sophistication. And not just in the interwar period, but beyond. In the early 1950s trombone player Eddie Harvey would tour with various dance orchestras: 'The dance halls we played in were dream palaces. They really were. They were just lovely places to go and great places to cop off. That always happened on the last number. That's when everyone made their move.'

There were also some borderline-illegal venues where flouting convention was the convention; for example, many of the less salubrious London clubs in Soho and the West End attracted drug-dealers, prostitutes, thieves, gangsters, police bribes and police raids. The Hambone was the kind of all-night venue that attracted a mix of bohemian artists, actors and actresses, and underworld characters. I can imagine a night out there being an exciting, powerful experience. You'd leave the glittering lights of Piccadilly Circus and move into the relative darkness of Windmill Street and then take a left into Ham Yard. Once through the door you'd follow an iron balustrade up a flight of steep stone steps, and with each step the banging drums and blasts of a saxophone grew louder. You might have to push your way past a girl in scarlet at the top of the stairs, but then you'd be in.

Ethel Mannin's 1925 novel *Sounding Brass* includes a depiction of the Hambone and its clientele. She suggests that many of the patrons are men present with women who aren't their wives (including one of the central characters, a shady married man who falls for a long-legged dancer). At the club, Mannin describes the musicians: four men playing saxophone, concertina, flute and drums, and a fifth member 'at a baby grand piano, a pianist who might have been a masculine woman or a feminine man'.

In contrast to some of the goings-on in Soho, and certainly by today's standards, the average glitzy palais de danse – where singles made their move, couples courted, and everyone danced their troubles away – were chaste places indeed. The most likely time for some action would be at the end of the night during the walk home, but not in the dance hall, where venue operators kept an eye open for intimate shenanigans.

When the Mecca organisation built up an empire of dance halls from the late 1920s onwards, they introduced strict rules about acceptable behaviour drawn up by head office and com-municated to every staff member. Respectability was a reputation most dance hall managers craved, and most audiences expected. Some people were always on the lookout for instances of exces-sive fun, however. A leading Methodist, Lord Rochester, warned,

'Dancing has been known to lead to impurity of thought, desire and practice.'

Bolton Palais was one of a number of palais de danse built with a 'sprung' dancefloor (another example is the Ritz in Manchester); its oak and walnut dancefloor was mounted on over 500 spiral springs. At most of the halls, surrounding the designated dancefloor would be small circular tables, with chairs. There would be balconies, a jazz band would perform from the stage, and cloakroom and toilet facilities would often be in the basement. The staff – bar staff, usherettes and cloakroom attendants – would wear uniforms of some kind.

Nottingham Palais opened on 24 April 1925 with a billiard saloon attached. Dancing would take place most evenings at 8 p.m., with daily *thé dansants* (tea dances) at 3 p.m. The venue had a large illuminated globe in its entrance hall, and inside was a fountain sending water twenty feet into the air, illuminated by rainbow lighting. Nottingham Palais has survived, though at some cost to its dignity and having undergone several large-scale refurbishments in recent years, it's now the Oceana, featuring, every Thursday, a night called 'OMG'.

Many of these palais-style public dance halls from the first half of the twentieth century, however, were turned into bingo halls or have disappeared beneath shopping centres, ring roads or apartment blocks. In Glasgow, the Dennistoun Palais was closed in 1962, converted into a Fine Fare supermarket and finally demolished to make way for flats. Galliard Homes have built a housing block, Vision 20, on the site of the Ilford Palais, a former cinema opened as a palais de danse on Boxing Day 1925.

So many of these dance halls remain deep within the communal memory of the towns and cities in which they were situated. On websites with strong local history content, the message boards about nightlife are often full of remembrances of old music venues and nightclubs. We associate going out dancing to favourite venues with our younger, more carefree days, but sometimes the strongest memory is a missed moment, an unrequited passion, a love that never blossomed. Many local papers carry a weekly column where readers try to reconnect with people they met at the palais and have never seen since, someone they shared a glance or a dance with still held in their memory, soundtracked by a certain tune perhaps. Not all letters or posts reflect memories full of poignancy or great fondness. On one website dedicated to celebrating life in Ilford, a former habitué of the Ilford Palais posted: 'Outside the Palais my girlfriend's brother had his jaw broken.'

The Hammersmith Palais de Danse opened in west London in October 1919, and in the 1970s and beyond hosted live performances by the likes of Slade, U2, PiL, the Ramones, Siouxsie and the Banshees, New Order and the Notorious B.I.G. We'll make mention of the Hammersmith Palais throughout the next chapters and will discover the identity of the last man to invade the stage at the venue. But even if the Hammersmith Palais had closed after just a few decades, it would still have been considered a significant venue; it was the first of its kind, the blueprint for all the plush public dance halls that followed, and the venue that kicked off the Roaring Twenties in spectacular style.

Hammersmith Palais was opened by two American entrepreneurs, Messrs Booker & Mitchell, who bought up an old skating rink and gave the building an amazing makeover. It was so vast, done up so sumptuously, and – featuring the big new thing, ragtime – it made an immediate impression. The *Daily Express* gave the Palais an outstanding review: 'This new super-palace of jazz and other dances of the day is declared to be without its equal as a dancing hall anywhere in Europe.'

Crowds flocked there; some reports claim over 6,000 attempted to attend the opening night. For the first nine months, the resident ragtime band were the Original Dixieland Jazz Band, who began their run of engagements sharing the stage with a dancer, Johnny Dale, employed to help excite the crowd and to display the latest dance steps. This wasn't universally well received: one reviewer likened his moves to a 'filleted eel about to enter the stewing pot'; another claimed the Dixieland Jazz Band 'is doing its best to murder music'.

The Original Dixieland Jazz Band had been approached to star at the Hammersmith Palais after having already appeared at Rector's on Tottenham Court Road, where their popularity grew so quickly a move to a bigger hall was required. Nevertheless, one commentator declared that Londoners 'are bewildered by the weird discords'. Hammersmith Palais generated its own newsletter, the *Palais Dancing News*. In its first issue, in April 1920, the newsletter published an interview with the band's founder Nick La Rocca, who appeared happy to stoke the controversies. He described his band's music as 'outbursts', saying, 'I even go so far as to confess we are musical anarchists.'

Ragtime made an impact across the range of venues; it was the first jazz craze, an import from America which was first heard in Europe around 1900. Its non-European and syncopated beat marked it out as very different from the waltz, which had dominated dancefloors through the Victorian era, and from other traditional dances. In his 1970 book *The Edwardians*, J.B. Priestley recalled being at a theatre and experiencing 'the syncopated frenzy' of ragtime for the first time in 1913. He'd seen a performance by the Hedges Brothers and Jesse Jacobson – a singing trio (the youngest Hedges brother, Elven, also played piano, saxophone and banjo) – who'd journeyed from America to accept a major music hall contract in England and were sent on tour. White musicians, with their roots in vaudeville, they were far from being what might be considered authentic, but to Priestley their irresistible ragtime rhythms were potent: 'It was as if we had been still living in the nineteenth century and then suddenly found the twentieth century glaring and screaming at us. We were yanked into our own age, fascinating, jungle-haunted, monstrous.'

Priestley was recalling all this over half a century later, so his observations may well be coloured by hindsight, but he captures something of the various and ambiguous responses to early jazz. The music seemed primal and alive – which was thrilling to some listeners, but dangerous to others. Those twenty minutes in an old Yorkshire music hall, he wrote, signalled 'the end of confidence and any feeling of security, the nervous excitement, the frenzy, the underlying despair of our century'.

This, of course, was before sound recording was widely available – radio emerged in the early 1920s, and only a lucky few had access to phonographs and gramophones – so in 1919 jazz was almost exclusively a live experience, mostly first reaching working-class listeners, as it did Priestley, through song and dance revues at the theatre. A monied few, though, had enjoyed access to jazz from just before the First World War at luxury private clubs hosting dinner dances. Murray's in London, for example, had a restaurant on the ground floor and a large wood-panelled ballroom below, where the house band, led by the black American banjoist/vocalist Gus Haston, was often still in full swing at 5 a.m.

Thus, in the years prior to the opening of the Hammersmith Palais, the working class hadn't had the pleasure of taking to a big public dancefloor and dancing to the weird discords of ragtime, though interest was very strong. The Palais experience turned a rumour into a phenomenon, opening just a year after the end of the First World War, when the country had suffered the grievous loss of hundreds of thousands of young men on the battlefield; this led to two contradictory responses. One was a headstrong rush to hedonism, seizing the opportunity to enjoy life and feel free, but the second was a perception that so soon after the war the frivolity was disrespectful to the dead (Vera Brittain described the young as 'light-hearted and forgetful').

All sorts of venues in the jazz age were pressed into service to meet the demand for dancing. Dance fans in villages and small towns would make do with sports halls and church halls, and in

some city districts the main dance venue was the local swimming
baths. Swimming baths had been built during the late Victorian
and Edwardian leisure boom, in part for a very practical reason –
to provide the washing facilities that many working-class homes in
this era lacked – but also to provide leisure opportunities. Many
baths became dance venues in the winter months, including the
Alhambra in Nelson (Lancashire), Thornton Heath Baths
(Croydon) and Thimblemill Baths (Smethwick). At Thimblemill
Baths the main pool was drained every October and the area
boarded over with a sprung maple floor. It took two days to drain
the pool and two weeks to construct the floor. As well as dancing,
through the winter months the baths became the venue for fetes,
boxing and hairdressing.

With their water features, balcony bars and uniformed staff, the
big public dance halls put a little bit of luxury within reach of the
whole nation. In addition, an increasing number of exclusive,
ostentatious private clubs were operating in London through the
1920s and 1930s. One was Ciro's, which opened in 1915 on
Orange Street in the heart of the West End of London, with
high-spec decor, ornate pillars and mirrors, and a sliding roof
that could be opened in the summer. It was a high-society haunt
appealing to the upper classes, offering evening dinner dances
and stage shows usually featuring a small jazz orchestra and a
troupe of dancing girls. As well as Murray's and Ciro's, other
exclusive venues in London included the Kit Cat Club, and Café
de Paris, both members only, levying a charge of 10/- (50p) or
more for dinner dances. London was the only city in the country
at the time that could sustain expensive private clubs of this sort;
if you'd gone up to Lancashire with ten shillings you'd have had
several great nights out paying 7d (3p) for a pint of beer.

The manager at Murray's was from Chicago and went under
the pseudonym of Jack May. He was one of a number of colourful characters embedded in the Soho nightlife scene, alongside
the likes of Freddie Ford and Kate Meyrick. Kate Meyrick ran

several venues, the main one being at 43 Gerrard Street in Soho. Throughout the 1920s the activities that went on there were said to include drug-taking, prostitution and after-hours drinking. She evaded sanctions other than occasional fines, which might lead us to suppose she was paying off the police and the authorities. Nevertheless, she had many a day in court when prosecutors waded in with colourful descriptions. 'It is called a dancing club,' said one in 1919, of 43 Gerrard Street, 'but it would be no exaggeration to call it a dancing hell – an absolute sink of iniquity.'

Jack May, meanwhile, was often alleged to be involved in dealing cocaine and opium, although the most notorious opium dealer in the Soho clubs of the 1920s was Chinese restaurant owner the Brilliant Chang, who was implicated in more than one high-profile drug-related death and the subject of sensational media stories. As well as opium and cocaine dealing and addiction, all-night drinking, flighty females and men dressed as women also triggered moral panics between the wars.

Youngsters (by which I mean people in their late teens) habitually face – or even court – parental disapproval of their lifestyle choices and music tastes. The perception of the 'generation gap' became widespread in the 1960s but, as I've documented in my book *Manchester, England* and elsewhere, there was a good deal of incomprehension and hostility among parents when youngsters began frequenting dance halls and other jazz venues in the 1920s. Jazz had arrived and, within a generation, all the Saturday night rituals had changed: the routines, the clothes, the venues, the music. Older generations tended to disapprove especially of the less well-appointed, more down-market venues. When discussing a visit to a dance hall in Manchester, one woman recalls, 'My father would have killed me if he'd known. It was a right dive.'

Such is the magnitude of the shift in what's deemed respectable, it's hard to imagine the formalities and strictures that governed behaviour in public dance halls seventy or eighty years ago. Even with the Mecca codes of conduct in place, the morally uptight could still be taken aback by activities we'd consider the height of innocence. In the 1930s, the Mass Observation initiative encouraged 'ordinary' people to record diaries and thoughts. One middle-class contributor to Mass Observation reported on a visit to Streatham Locarno: 'I was surprised at the amount of open intimacy, the numbers of arms round shoulders and the number of people holding hands quite openly.'

People were accustomed to doing all their living, working and leisure close to home – school, work, cinema, pubs and dance hall all within a few streets of their front door – but the palais de danse often drew their audience from a number of districts, bringing people together. This cultural opening-up of life was in part possible thanks to the improving transport infrastructure in the early 1920s, especially the freedom to explore the city by omnibus. Dance halls like Hammersmith Palais were considered social levellers; compared to the strict demarcations of music halls, the mix was conspicuous. Ciro's prided itself on its exclusivity – the likes of Hammersmith Palais, on the other hand, gloried in their openness.

With neither the popular touch of mainstream venue operators, nor the criminal connections most Soho club owners enjoyed, one club owner was something of an anomaly: Frida Strindberg, the divorced second wife of August Strindberg, the Swedish playwright. Frida founded the Cave of the Golden Calf in the low-ceilinged basement of a warehouse on Heddon Street (off Regent Street) motivated by high ideals; she hoped to create an avant-garde hangout in the middle of London offering artistic and challenging cabaret entertainments of the kind that could be found at her inspiration, the Kabarett Fledermaus in Vienna. In the run-up to the opening of her club, Mrs Strindberg told the press that the venue was to be 'a place given up to gaiety', and that its interior decorations would be 'brazenly expressive of the libertarian pleasure principle'.

She employed the painter Spencer Gore to create and commission artworks and decorative items from talented young British artists, including Jacob Epstein, Eric Gill and Wyndham Lewis. But the weeks prior to a nightclub launch are always fraught, and this was no exception. Gore struggled with Mrs Strindberg over the decorative scheme, telling his friend J.D. Turner, 'Days and days I have spent arguing about the colour of the walls and ceiling. Most irritating thing I ever had to do with.'

The Cave of the Golden Calf opened in June 1912. Eric Gill made a statue of a golden calf for the foyer, Gore contributed a Gauguin-esque triptych, but the contribution towards the stage decoration from Wyndham Lewis was possibly not what Mrs Strindberg had in mind; he painted a drop curtain depicting raw meat. Syncopated musical entertainment was provided on a small stage by a fierce-looking pianist and his wife, a singer. There would be cabaret and poetry recitals through until dawn. Frida struggled to keep on top of the paperwork. The audiences seemed happy listening and dancing to ragtime and drinking all night, but found the entertainments a little too much of a challenge. Many young aristocrats ventured in, however, and a fair proportion of them were homosexual, or so it's said (the Cave is mentioned in Philip Hoare's 1997 book *Wilde's Last Stand*). The pink pound wasn't as strong as it would be a hundred years later, and the Cave went bankrupt and closed in 1914.

From 1914 onwards, the opportunities for American musicians to work in London clubs increased. That occasion when Henry Mayhew visited a pub on Ratcliff Highway and described the shaggy-haired German musicians rocking an East End music hall wasn't a one-off; for decades, clubs and venues had called upon the services of German musicians. From the outbreak of the First World War, for obvious reasons, this was no longer possible. In addition, many young British musicians were joining the armed forces. It fell to American musicians to fill the jobs gap.

African-American musicians schooled in the jazz clubs of New

York were soon in Britain, many of them thanks to the organisational skills of Will Cook, who formed the Clef Club in 1912, a booking agency for black musicians that became a point of contact for European promoters. Murray's had led the way by hiring Gus Haston, and the next musician to make the transatlantic crossing was Dan Kildare, drafted in from New York to provide the music at Ciro's. In March 1915 he assembled some fellow Clef Club musicians, sailed for England and began rehearsals for the Ciro's opening in May. There were seven people in the band: three banjos, string bass, drums, piano and vocals.

The band were invited to play at several private parties and charity events, attended by the likes of the Prince of Wales, Winston Churchill and various dukes and earls. At an open-air concert for convalescing soldiers in the summer of 1915, a columnist at the high-society magazine *Tatler*, signing herself 'Eve', reported the band were raucously received: 'The men simply loved it, of course, shrieked the ragtime choruses and revelled in the fearful din and encored everything, and altogether were a much more appreciative audience than the usual Ciro's ones, who are generally busy eating, of course.'

Despite those good works, the decision to open Ciro's in May 1915 while the country was at war was its undoing, as popular opinion began to build against upper-class hedonists who were dining, dancing and philandering the night away while thousands of ordinary young British men were being killed on the battlefields of northern France. In the 1914 Defence of the Realm Act the government introduced new regulations cutting liquor licence hours. As a result, in Soho in particular, late-night drinking and dancing went underground, and clandestine establishments opened. Beyond the law in respect of late-night drinking, other illegal activities tended to swirl around these establishments, including gambling and prostitution. The heat stayed on Ciro's; when MPs began to lodge complaints about the activities of the club and its clientele, the police were forced to act. In April 1917, the club was shut down.

Ironically, aside from its patrons' hunger for all-night dancing, Ciro's was probably one of the least criminally minded of the private clubs in London at the time. Vice and drug-dealing in Soho and the West End before and during the war wasn't confined to clubs or music venues. For a time, a sandwich shop at 89 Shaftesbury Avenue – said by police to be patronised by 'prostitutes and Continental undesirables' – was the centre of a drug-dealing operation. It was masterminded by a Swiss man, Georges Wagnière, who was arrested at a raid on the shop and deported.

As well as mounting surveillance operations, the police would also receive letters and anonymous tip-offs, but were also involved in taking bribes. Jack May was often mentioned in correspondence, including in a letter sent by Eton-educated Captain Ernest Schiff. In December 1915 he wrote directly to the Attorney General, Sir John Simon: 'A very bad fellow, Jack May, is the proprietor of Murray's Club in Beak Street – a quite amusing place. But for vice or money or both he induces girls to smoke opium in some foul place. He is an American and does a good deal of harm.'

Despite allegations aplenty, May, whose real name was Gerald Walter, evaded prison, possibly because he really was an innocent abroad or perhaps because he had friends in high places (politicians and top military personnel frequented his club, and it's said that plans for the first British tanks were signed off there late one night in 1915), or because he had the money to pay off the right policemen and to engage effective but expensive lawyers. On the other hand, his accuser, Captain Schiff, was a shady character, an inveterate gambler, a pimp and a blackmailer. His days were numbered. In March 1919 he was killed by the father of a young woman he was attempting to entice to work for him as a prostitute on the streets of the West End.

When politicians, newspaper editorials and the likes of Lord Rochester fulminated against jazz and dance halls, it was clear they were out of step with the general public. When Leyton's urban district council in east London made attempts to ban jazz dances at local venues, including the baths, describing such dancing as 'morally bad', the local populace defended the dances and the prohibition didn't work. Nevertheless, controversies continued to be stirred up. There were fundamental objections to live jazz (other than distaste at a dancer wiggling round like a filleted eel); musical experts, for example, denounced jazz as 'rhythm without melody'. Various moral guardians objected to the 'negro' origins of the music. Priestley's use of 'jungle haunted' was one of the less derogatory examples of the word 'jungle' attached to jazz.

Popular culture, however, embraced American influence generally: the excitement of jazz, the enchantments of Hollywood, the dirty realism of James Cagney films. It also absorbed culture from further afield; soon, dancers would be attempting the Argentine tango and the Brazilian samba. Popular culture in the first half of the twentieth century was at odds with that strand of British culture that's always been wary of foreign ways and imported ideas.

There are many examples of how the developments and excitement surrounding taking to the dancefloor for a couple of hours on a Saturday night reflected or created deeper cultural trends. When traditionalists listed regrettable changes in British society, jazz was always mentioned. In 1926 the *Manchester Guardian* declared, 'Short skirts, lipsticks, vulgar films, sex novels, jazz. There is almost no end to the list of abominations.' *The Times* said that jazz was 'one of the many American peculiarities that threaten to make life a nightmare'.

Not only was there resistance in some quarters to anything un-British, which by definition and implication was a bad thing, but the very act of listening and dancing to jazz – unbuttoned, raucous ragtime – was a clear break from tradition, from 'old-time' dances like the Lancers and the waltz. There was now a desire for dances that were less formal than they had been in the Victorian era. To social commentators of the time, this seemed symbolic of a loosening of pre-war conventions, a development which some regretted, but others enjoyed.

Perhaps this rebellion on the dancefloor was leading to a more modern world, less despotic and hierarchical? Or, in the words of another newspaper, 'In the ballroom the up-to-date dances are the antithesis of the mechanical rule-bound movements insisted upon by the dancing masters of the late Victorian period.' It's appropriate that the journalist uses the word 'masters'. Finding some freedom from male control was one of the attractions for women of dance halls. The chance of a dalliance with some lad was also possible, particularly at certain venues, like the Palais (later named the Princess) on Barlow Moor Road in Chorlton, Manchester, as one woman remembers: 'My sister met her future husband at the dance hall in Chorlton. Oh! It was the picking-up place, yes.'

The new opportunities and excitements afforded by the public dance halls were bound up with other signs of female emancipation during and after the First World War, including steps towards granting women the vote and, in 1921, Marie Stopes opening Britain's first family planning clinic. Powering this changing status was the role women had played during the war; it's reckoned a million women were added to the British workforce between 1914 and 1918, taking up multiple trades in industry, transport and munitions.

It's noticeable how enthusiastic women were about dancing in the 1920s, enrolling in dance schools, tuning into radio, being first in the queue at dance events hosted by workplaces or churches, embracing more than just the music, more than the dance steps, and much more than close encounters with men. Indeed many women were happy to go out dancing without any expectation of dancing with men; given that a generation of men had been decimated by the war, women were used to being surrounded by other women, and at the dance hall it was perfectly acceptable for women to be seen dancing together.

The rising popularity of dance music venues and dancing as a pastime fuelled activity in the fashion industry. The majority of men owned a good enough suit, but for young women in their search for a perfect outfit, the choice was better than it had been pre-war, with the wider use of glamorous material like rayon and mass-produced clothing. The excitement of planning and shopping and getting ready would remain part of the ritual of going out. In 1939, one of Mass Observation's contributors, a 23-year-old typist, described the joys of her going-out rituals like this: 'Preparing for a dance is half the fun to my mind. Getting one's frock ready. Wondering whether you shall have your hair done.'

A passion for dancing reflected or reinforced the change in the status of women after the First World War; it was as if going dancing was the defining feature of the liberated, independent woman. Newspaper columns and letters pages were filled with analysis on the 'modern woman', who was reckoned to be a 'dancing girl', a 'jazz-mad dancing girl' or a 'flapper'. The self-confidence of the flappers, with their fashionable short haircuts and higher hemlines, was striking. The lighter fabrics and loose fit of the flapper dresses were specifically designed with dancing in mind.

Flappers were conspicuous only in cosmopolitan pockets in major cities, but the sense that jazz and dance halls were fuelling female liberation was nationwide. It was a modern development that seemed to cause consternation among older men who feared the shifts in gender relations. One article in the *Manchester Evening News* in February 1920 described flappers as 'social butterflies', and condemned the 'frivolous, scantily-clad, jazzing flapper, irresponsible and undisciplined'.

Some newspaper correspondents yearned for a return to old-fashioned values and an end to women taking up masculine habits like smoking in public, and expressed disillusionment with the frivolous, flirty females of the 1920s. One male letter writer to the *Daily Express* was moved to share this theory: 'The majority of men much prefer a girl of modest disposition – that is, one who does not smoke, flirt, or jazz.'

In her 1932 novel *Women of the Aftermath*, writer Helen Zenna Smith expresses her vexation that the men who a few years earlier had 'called on women when the man-power supply gave out unexpectedly' were now advising women after the war to 'get back to your dust-pans and your kitchens'. In the novel, Hettie, the wife of a former soldier, is terrorised by him and escapes into a decadent, bohemian life, taking a job as a professional dancer.

Many of the larger dance halls employed professional dancers. These were the so-called 'sixpenny dancers' who would congregate in designated areas and who customers could hire by the dance during the evening. These professionals were not only potential dance partners, but they also engaged in exhibition dancing at intervals throughout the evening. Female customers were likely to be as assertive as the men. If they were keen to dance with a man and a professional was available, women wouldn't be expected to hold back: 'If partners are slow in coming forward, we go to the "pen" and pick our own professional dancing men at so much a dance.'

Hettie, in *Women of the Aftermath*, finds the job sleazy and exploitative. It certainly wasn't always so, but there were definitely issues surrounding the sixpenny dancers. In 1933 three managers at the Kosmo Club on Swinton Row in Edinburgh were found guilty of living wholly or in part on the earnings of prostitution of dance partners or instructresses. Witnesses came forward to allege that men who were 'desirous of having immoral relations' could pay thirty shillings for a dance partner for the evening with the understanding the dancer would also leave the Kosmo with the customer (twenty of the thirty shillings were retained by the club's management, the rest went to the young woman). Several of the women involved, including a 'dance instructress' from

Manchester, admitted that they went on to indulge in sexual activity.

However, the dance music business provided many other employment opportunities for women, from cigarette girls and waitresses to venue managers. Betty Lyons ran the Hammersmith Palais in the 1930s. She had a reputation in the industry for being forward-thinking and proactive. In August 1937 she visited dance halls in America and Canada to find ideas and inspiration and make new contacts.

Women were employed as instructors, some at the dance schools set up by venues, Streatham Locarno among them. Lessons were crucial. Women and men who were skilful dancers were well regarded (according to one chap interviewed by historian Judith R. Walkowitz: 'A woman's dancing skills trumped her looks at the dance hall'). Freestyling and improvisation weren't considered appropriate and there were numerous reports of untrained dancers causing havoc, much to the annoyance of professionals like Phyllis Haylor and Alec Miller, who described a scene at a dance hall minutes after exhibition dancers had performed a Charleston: 'Hundreds of wild youths endeavoured to copy their kicking and stamping steps and to adapt them to the ballroom, with disastrous results. It was positively unsafe to go within two yards of any couple performing these ridiculous antics.'

Of all the jobs in music venues and dance halls in the 1920s and 1930s, the most prestigious was that of band leaders. Venues would vie for the services of popular band leaders, but the most powerful of them would resist being tied down if more lucrative work was offered to them elsewhere. Hammersmith Palais was regarded as the top of the tree for dance band leaders. Lou Preager became a household name when he took the job at the Palais, from where the BBC regularly broadcast his orchestra's performances.

Another favourite BBC band leader was the violinist Bert Ambrose, who was born in the East End of London but served his apprenticeship in New York, working alongside Emil Coleman at Reisenweber's restaurant. Back in London in the early 1920s he featured at the Embassy Club on Bond Street, but his ambitions were hampered by the Embassy's policy banning radio broadcasts from the venue. Ambrose knew the profile garnered from radio was key to gaining a recording contract and moved on to the May Fair Hotel on Stratton Street, from where he made multiple broadcasts for six years. In 1937, in partnership with the American band leader Jack Harris, he took over ownership of Ciro's. For a short while they employed the gifted pianist Art Tatum at the venue, but the Ambrose and Harris partnership didn't last.

As we'll see, a downturn in the economy in the second half of the 1970s had a deleterious effect on some venues, but didn't bring a halt to nightlife. If anything it boosted activity, as evidenced by the rise of disco and punk in the last years of that decade. The years of economic depression in the 1930s were similarly buoyant. Even in areas badly hit by job losses, nightlife thrived. In Glasgow, the Barrowland Ballroom was founded by Margaret McIver, a widow bringing up nine children. She'd built up the Barrowland Market (known locally as the Barras), and the ballroom was an extension of that business, opening on Christmas Eve 1934 with a dance for all the stallholders. Stylish throughout, the front of the building was graced with a sign in the shape of a man pushing a barrow suspended above the front door. Mrs McIver approached drummer Billy McGregor and he formed a resident dance band, Billy McGregor and the Gaybirds.

The 1930s also witnessed the emergence of Britain's most powerful dance hall brand – Mecca. Mecca was headed by C.L. Heimann, a native of Denmark who came to Britain as a teenager and worked for a catering company called Ye Mecca Cafes. Heimann persuaded his bosses to buy their first dance hall, Sherry's in Brighton, and to appoint him manager. This was 1927.

He made a roaring success of the venture and Mecca took ownership of other dance halls all around the country, including the Ritz in Manchester and the Tottenham Palais (renamed the Tottenham Royal by Mecca), and within a few years Heimann had control of Mecca's dance hall operation. Working alongside the Scottish entrepreneur Alan Fairley – who owned the Locarno Ballroom on Sauchiehall Street in Glasgow – Heimann continued to build the empire, rolling out more Locarnos nationwide, including the one in Streatham. Ruth Ellis worked there in 1948; she was the last woman in the UK to be hanged, after killing her lover David Blakely in 1955.

From the outset, Heimann concentrated on incorporating set standards of customer service, and homogenised the entertainment offered at every Mecca venue. Among other activities, Mecca established the magazine *Dance News,* which promoted the activities in their halls and discussed dances and reported on special events. In a later chapter we'll meet a generation of club promoters in the 1990s – the likes of Darren Hughes and James Barton at Cream – who built brands and were credited with not just reflecting but moulding public tastes. C.L. Heimann was probably an even more powerful figure in nightlife history. In 1938 he was described as one of 'the cultural directors of the nation'.

The boom in leisure enjoyed by the working class and lower-middle class included a passion for the cinema, with many of the bigger picture houses benefitting from investment from individual entrepreneurs and national chains. There was plenty of jazz and dancing in films of the era. Academic Catherine Feely has made a study of a diary kept by Frank Forster. Frank visited a cinema almost every night throughout 1934 and 1935 ('first and foremost in order to leave the house' says Feely).

In 1935 Frank Forster was in his mid-twenties, living in Chester with his parents and working on a building site. He espoused various left-wing causes and ideas, had no girlfriend and not much contact with women at all. And it's likely his unhappiness was compounded by being a young man of the left adrift in Chester, a small city that insisted on electing Tory MPs all through the 1930s. While sitting on his own in darkened cinemas watching the likes of Fred Astaire, he hatched a plan which he confided in his diary in September 1935: 'It has now become imperative that I should take up dancing if I am to feel at home in the company of women.' And not just the company but the proximity: 'I must get some experience of sexual association, in the form of dances.'

A few weeks later he invited a woman whom he had met at a Workers' Educational Association class to accompany him to a few dances. Aware that being a good dancer was a much-prized accomplishment, he'd imagined himself an Astaire-esque expert, but after these visits his diary records he had proved 'not much of a success'. There was also no improvement to his love life. Frank resorted to desperate measures, including signing up to a Communist summer school in the hope of meeting young women there.

Hesitant and a little too unworldly even for the Chester singles scene, we can only imagine what Frank would have made of some of the shenanigans away from the tightly controlled and respectable venues. In all cities there were opportunities for sharp or illegal practices. Down south, in Soho, moral codes were malleable. At the Falstaff on Oxford Street, one of the bar staff, Mark Benney (real name Henry Degras), wrote a memoir of his days there (*Low Company*, 1936): 'All the thieves and prostitutes of London came there to spend their money, and they demanded licence. Women for ten shillings a bet walked naked through the rooms. Men walked openly from group to group vending stolen articles. And on the dancefloor men lifted the skirts of girls as they passed and smacked their bare buttocks.'

Through the 1920s and 1930s, Ham Yard and its immediate environs featured bohemian hangouts, sometimes attracting a mix of the upper-class party set and hard-core villains, including the Blue Lantern (next door to the Hambone, and identified by journalist and writer D.J. Taylor and others as a key venue for the Bright Young Things) and the New Avenue. The New Avenue, owned by Freddy Ford, was the site of numerous gang battles. In 1927 Ford was jailed for receiving stolen goods, by which time he'd changed the name of the New Avenue to the Havinoo, apparently to mimic the way cockneys affecting a posh accent liked to pronounce the word. At his trial, a police officer claimed Ford's Havinoo was nothing more than a room full of thieves, male and female.

The determination of the authorities to clamp down waxed and waned, but during the watch of Home Secretary William Joynson-Hicks in the second half of the 1920s there was something approaching a 'war on clubs', and the likes of Kate Meyrick found her venues under police pressure. Even before he initiated a more authoritarian approach, Meyrick's venue at 43 Gerrard Street was raided at least twice in 1924 and at the end of that year she was sentenced to six months for selling liquor without a licence. In 1928 she was arrested again, this time as part of an investigation into 'C' Division's Sergeant George Goddard, a corrupt policeman who'd been operating a protection racket for nearly a decade. The various court fines and the payments to bent coppers barely dented Kate Meyrick's profits, though; she claimed she'd made half a million pounds running clubs, lived a carefree life, and sent her children to expensive public schools. One of them, her second daughter Dorothy Evelyn, married Edward Russell, 26th Baron de Clifford, a friend and follower of the British fascist leader Oswald Mosley.

The press rarely failed to report on salacious goings-on in clubs. Although homosexuality was illegal at the time, colourful characters like Stephen Tennant were usually indulged by the press. But at other times, the press and the public were openly hostile to gay men. Court cases were routinely brought against men hosting cross-dressing parties or importuning on the street. In 1926, after two men were charged in connection with activities at a dance hall in Marylebone, the *Daily Mail* reported on some of the evidence against them: 'Acts of the grossest nature were witnessed.'

The Running Horse on East Chapel Street, Mayfair, was a venue frequented by gay men and lesbians and was placed under police surveillance in 1936. Officers later reported that 'two youths in the bar had their hair waved and their faces and lips made up', and there were present 'three women of masculine appearance. Their hair was cut short in manly fashion, and they wore costumes of collars and ties and no hats.'

Gay men found imaginative ways to socialise, including regularly infiltrating a ball at the Albert Hall. Lady Jeanne Malcolm was a socialite and the hostess of the annual Servants' Ball at the Albert Hall from 1930 onwards. Her aim was to provide the opportunity for servants to enjoy the kind of lavish nights out the upper classes were accustomed to. The ticket prices were low and, to avoid embarrassment of any servants unable to afford formal evening wear, the balls were fancy dress. Within a few years, the cross-dressing community had begun to frequent the Servants' Ball. They weren't servants; they just liked dressing up as women, in coloured silk blouses and tight-hipped trousers, with rouged lips and painted faces.

There was disquiet among some social commentators and writers of anonymous letters to MPs and the police. Some of the attendees were described as 'degenerate boys', 'male prostitutes' and 'sexual perverts'. For a few years the drag outfits were allowed to add to the gaiety of the occasion, but then the Servants' Ball organisers banned cross-dressing men. 'No Man Impersonating a Woman Will be Admitted' the tickets read.

Cost was often a deciding factor when it came to picking a hall to visit on a Saturday night, and location too, of course. In the 1930s different styles of music had developed. There would be dance bands who would play in a sweet style, perhaps characterised by the lilting sound of a violin section, but others would play in a more raucous, 'hot', stomping fashion in which the saxophone or the muted trumpet were signature instruments. A correspondent in *Melody Maker* regretted the hot style, describing it as 'loud and quick, unharmonious and cacophonous'. Of a similar mindset, Jack Hylton was one of a number of high-profile band leaders who considered it worth eliminating 'crudeness' to ensure jazz was more commercially palatable and he openly talked of the need to neutralise its 'jungle' origins.

There's plenty of evidence, though, that by 1937 music lovers and thrill seekers in London looking beyond the lilting rhythms of dance orchestras had several clubs to choose from, among them Jig's on St Anne's Court (an alley between Wardour Street and Dean Street), the Nest on Kingly Street, and Jack Isow's Shim Sham Club at 37 Wardour Street (later the Rainbow Roof and, later still, part of the venue that would go on to house the Flamingo). These clubs were noisy, tough and interracial. Ideally they would have featured African-American musicians but there were legal restrictions on work visas for American musicians imposed by the Musicians' Union. The black British (mostly West Indian) musicians who took the stage did their best to channel the rhythms and attitudes of Harlem in their playing. The band at the Shim Sham was directed by George 'Happy' Blake, from Trinidad. He and his brother Cyril had a profound influence on British jazz, helping to introduce calypso and Latin American influences.

If some halls were known for 'hot jazz' no doubt there were others noted for 'hot girls'. Almost all of the halls were dominated by the young but in most towns there was a hall or two where older customers congregated. Tony's Ballroom next door to the Birmingham Hippodrome on Hurst Street was always said to be multi-generational.

Some clubs catered for a specific clientele. According to researcher Allison Abra, the Royal dance hall in north London was known for being a 'Jewish hall'. Young men and women with an Irish Catholic background were often committed members of the Gaelic League, who would hold regular ceilidh dances, often on a Sunday. In Manchester in the 1930s there were two very active branches: the Craobh na Laimbe Deirge and the Craobh Oisin. The city had a number of thriving venues in the 1930s, including the Ritz on Whitworth Street, with its sprung dancefloor. In 1937 the George & Dragon on Swan Street in Manchester began a new phase in its development when the stage was moved from one end of the hall to jutting out halfway up a wall. It was a question of economics; by putting the stage up there the then owner Ernie Tyson freed more floor space to pack in drinkers. The bands accessed the stage up a ladder. That's how the venue got a new name: Band on the Wall.

Whatever the music and the type of club, all venues faced disruption in September 1939 with the outbreak of the Second World War. Towns and cities were blitzed by German bombers. Between September 1940 and May 1941 there were nearly 150 full-scale raids on the UK. During the Blitz some dance venues were used as air-raid shelters (including Thimblemill Baths in Smethwick) but some took direct hits and a number were destroyed (including Tony's Ballroom in Birmingham).

Most dance halls stayed open during the Blitz. Partly this was because warnings would be sounded but then no incendiaries would drop, and this happened often enough to create a degree of complacency. But there was also a determination in the general population not to allow German bombing raids to put an end to the good life. In the case of the Café de Paris, patrons – who included celebrities, debutantes and members and associates of the royal family – were also reassured by its basement location. Staff and customers felt safe twenty feet underground; but unfortunately they were proved wrong. On the night of 8 March 1941 two bombs hit the building and it appears that one fell through a ventilation shaft and landed right in front of the stage. Band leader Ken 'Snakehips' Johnson was decapitated, and over thirty more staff, diners and dancers were killed in the raid; nearly a hundred others were injured. Looters took advantage of the tragedy and were seen stealing handbags and removing jewellery from the dead and dying.

In north London, a busy neighbourhood dance hall on Green Lanes, Palmers Green, was destroyed and another was hit in southwest London in November 1943 when a German bomb landed on 35 Putney High Street, devastating several shops, starting fires and killing eighty-one people in the top-floor Cinderella Dance Club, the ground-floor Black & White Milk Bar and outside. Most of the casualties were under twenty-three years old.

The Second World War brought another bout of soul-searching and media controversy about flighty females, largely triggered by the presence of the American armed forces in Britain from January 1942. A phrase became common parlance: 'yank hunting', to express the phenomenon of British women actively seeking out the GIs. Generally, however, it appears that condemnation was reserved for women who hung around outside military camps or approached Americans in pubs. Dance halls seemed to be considered a safe place for some harmless flirting. One woman is quoted by Philomena Goodman in *Women, Sexuality & War* (2001): 'The Yanks were all over,' she says. 'You danced with them but you knew what kind of reputation you would get if you went out with Americans.'

During the war business stayed strong at the Barrowland Ballroom in Glasgow partly thanks to the presence of American servicemen. Glasgow was a busy transit city where troops disembarked after their Atlantic crossing to await transportation to camps around Britain. On their arrival in Britain, the servicemen would watch a film preparing them for what they would find out on the town on shore leave, including the fact there was no 'colour bar' in bars and dance halls. As we will see in a later chapter, this wasn't quite the case, but it was still very different from what the white American servicemen or the African-Americans had experienced at home.

African-American servicemen in particular caused a stir in the Glasgow dance halls as many of them were great dancers, experts in the lindy hop and various versions of the jitterbug, notably one called 'the collegiate shag'. The GIs hit the town and hit on the girls. Sometimes such goings-on and conflicts over girls caused trouble in the city but it's said that most of the trouble was between white and African-American servicemen rather than between Americans and locals. Policing the dance halls during the Second World War was made a little more complicated by the presence of US military police outside Glasgow dance halls, complete with their white gloves and night sticks.

Once again, as they had in the First World War, women had jobs in munitions factories and took up trades that had previously been monopolised by men. With so many male musicians conscripted into the armed forces, there were also jobs and opportunities for female musicians. The female contribution to most dance bands had been restricted to providing vocals, although there were some notable female players famous for their proficiency as musicians – including the much-lauded American drummers Mary McClanahan and Viola Smith. During the war band leader Ivy Benson became a star in Britain, and her Ivy Benson All Girl Orchestra toured extensively and were, for a while, in-house band on BBC Radio. Her lead trumpet player Gracie Cole went on to form her own all-girl orchestra.

For many of the bigger dance halls, the late 1940s witnessed a return to pre-war music and programming. But it's always a mistake in culture to assume all is settled. Times will change, and you can be sure that out of sight somewhere people are going off on a tangent, inventing or reinventing new, maverick, challenging ways of doing things. So it was after the war. Even while the mainstream – the big halls and BBC radio – dominated, two new strands of jazz were emerging, both of them in opposition to the prevailing idea of what was standard.

As a result of restrictions on foreign musicians, the respectability of the music sought by band leaders like Jack Hylton and by closely directed and controlled dance halls, nightlife and the music that powered it had become too predictable. Radio had nurtured an even bigger audience for jazz but in general what you'd hear on the radio erred on the bland side, and were most often broadcasts from the sedate environs of hotel ballrooms. The millions tuning in to the likes of Jack Payne from the Hotel Cecil or the band led by Jack Hylton were experiencing a 'domesticated' version of jazz, according to one commentator.

Jazz had always had a disruptive ingredient, but its power was being neutralised. Some musicians and music fans more adventurous in their tastes made a point of looking for music outside the mainstream, including a number who began to be attracted to the work of Charlie Parker and Dizzy Gillespie, and the free-form stylings of bebop. Saxophonists Johnny Dankworth and Ronnie Scott were both members of the *Queen Mary*'s orchestra when the ship journeyed over to New York in 1947, her first trip after the war. They took themselves off to 52nd Street to find Charlie Parker and returned to London, enthused and eager. They were among the very first of a small but influential group of musicians and their fans who took to 'modern jazz', as it was called. Writing at the end of the 1950s, David Boulton defined modern jazz thus: 'More often than not "Modern Jazz" is a descriptive title given to the new music which originated as "bop", "re-bop" or "be-bop".'

Maverick musicians and music fans, fired by a spirit of self-organisation, created a new generation of jazz clubs, non-mainstream alternatives to the dance halls and restaurant venues with their dinner dances. One of these is the venue now known as the 100 Club, founded in 1942 in the basement of 100

Oxford Street; as we'll see, it has had a part to play in British music history for more than seventy years. Another was the Fullado on New Compton Street, previously the Bouillabaisse, a drinking club with a clientele drawn mainly from the West Indian community and a regular hangout favoured by black US servicemen. Bebop became the dominant style at the Fullado. Laurie Morgan was a drummer in dance bands who would make his way to the club after work: 'Bebop was like a clarion call. This new world was going to come.'

Those musicians who ventured into bebop and other modern jazz styles were reacting against the blandness of the mainstream but others who were also looking for an alternative went in a different direction; back to a time before commercial imperatives had taken over, to an era when compromise and radio-friendly formulas weren't on the agenda. That led them back to New Orleans to the works of the likes of Jelly Roll Morton and King Oliver, and inspired an interest in what was called 'revivalist' jazz. Gramophone records were key to this interest. In 1936 the Brunswick record label issued an album devoted to King Oliver's Creole Jazz Band, then came the first British release for a Bessie Smith album. Via these gramophone recordings people had a chance to hear authentic, older, purer forms of jazz for the first time.

Musicians like George Webb began to plot ways to promote revivalist jazz. He formed the Dixielanders, using the Red Barn in Barnehurst, near Bexleyheath in Kent, as a base. Humphrey Lyttelton joined the Dixielanders in 1946 and later recalled the chin-stroking seriousness of the Red Barn: 'Jazz was a serious music ... to be studied and you could not give it full attention when you were being buffeted and trampled underfoot by dancers. At the Red Barn people who jogged about in their chairs too vigorously were discouraged by petulant frowns from their neighbours.' Through the 1950s both Webb and Lytteltton would be involved in venues in Soho and the West End that would be catalysts for new sounds and styles.

In the mid-1950s jazz began to lose its place at the centre of nightlife. Some venues from the first half of the century survived, others didn't. Thimblemill Baths hosted the Beatles in November 1962, as well as the Rolling Stones (March 1964), the Kinks (February 1965) and the Who (January 1966). Most of the artworks commissioned by Mrs Strindberg's Cave of the Golden Calf disappeared, but a study for some of the mural decoration by Spencer Gore is now owned by the Tate. The site on which the Kosmo in Edinburgh stood and the surrounding few streets were levelled in 1966 to make way for what is now the St James shopping centre. After a spell of being owned by a dental hospital, the old Ciro's now houses archive and administration departments of the National Portrait Gallery. The Café de Paris is still open and trading, over ninety years after its launch, with dining available in the Titanic Ballroom and cabaret every Friday. Murray's, in various incarnations, thrived on Beak Street for several decades (Christine Keeler worked there as a hostess in the early 1960s), but closed in 1975 and is now a Byron restaurant.

The Palais in Chorlton became the Princess, and in the early 1960s hosted Thursday 'Stag Nights' featuring up to seven strippers an evening. The first Locarno in Glasgow was reinvented as a discotheque, Tiffany's, in the 1960s and then a live music venue, hosting bands like the Dead Kennedys (September 1981) and U2 (December 1982). Barrowlands was destroyed by fire in 1958, then rebuilt and reopened on Christmas Eve 1960. It remains a high point of any touring band's schedule, with a reputation for passionate crowds. Hammersmith Palais was finally demolished in 2012 by Parkway Properties.

Booker & Mitchell, who built and opened the Hammersmith Palais de Danse, also took over a pickle and jam warehouse owned by Crosse & Blackwell at the top of Charing Cross Road, and in 1927 turned it into the Astoria, a cinema and ballroom. The Astoria was, significantly, the first major dance hall in the West End of London. It later became the venue for the gay club Bang, and for numerous live gigs, including the Manic Street Preachers, Radiohead and Nirvana. It closed for good at the beginning of 2009 to be demolished to make way for Crossrail.

The Bolton Palais was a flagship Mecca hall, where the popular weekly TV show *Come Dancing* would occasionally be filmed. *Come Dancing* was devised by Mecca's boss Eric Morley in 1949, originally featuring dance instructors giving advice about the likes of the samba, the tango, the foxtrot and the quickstep. Then a competitive element was introduced, with teams formed from different areas of the country, and filmed in various halls. One evening in March 1960, ten million people tuned in to watch the East Midlands in competition with a team from the West Midlands at Nottingham Palais. This proved to be the peak of its popularity – then came the Beatles and their generation that led to a mass exodus from the established rituals and venues of ballroom dancing (and indeed bebop and trad jazz), but nevertheless *Come Dancing* stayed in the TV schedules until 1998 and in 2004 was remixed and relaunched as the hugely popular *Strictly Come Dancing*.

The Locarno Dance Hall in Streatham, which opened in 1929, became in turn the Cat's Whiskers (1969), the Studio (1984), the Ritzy (1990) and Caesars Night Club (1995). Paul Simonon, who would go on to be in the Clash, went dancing to ska in the early 1970s when it was the Cat's Whiskers, and later that decade and into the 1980s weekends featured the likes of DJ Steve Walsh whipping up the crowd with records by the Fatback Band, Odyssey and McFadden & Whitehead. Kingsley Amis namechecks the Streatham Locarno in his novel *The Riverside Villas Murder*, making mention of its gold chairs.

From 1994 the Streatham club was owned by Fred Batt, who gave it the name Caesars the following year. He presented professional female boxing contests there and also introduced cage fighting. The venue featured in films, such as Guy Ritchie's movie *Snatch* and the ITV show *Stiletto Ghetto*. Batt is a renowned demonologist and was troubled by dark shapes inhabiting the place.

During its empty hours he claimed to hear the sound of scream-ing, footsteps and creaking doors opening on their own. He believed that the ghost of a woman was present in the club. At first it was thought the ghost could be that of Ruth Ellis, but an attempt by Yvette Fielding and others to make contact with her spirit during the second series of the TV show *Most Haunted* in 2003 was unsuccessful.

CHAPTER THREE

A bare room with lightbulbs, raves, what happened next

I'm on a stage where Muddy Waters, the Who, Oasis and the Sex Pistols have performed; where the Kinks played the week they topped the charts with 'You Really Got Me'; where Siouxsie of the Banshees made her live debut and the Damned ducked when Sid Vicious threw a pint glass; where the White Stripes played their first ever gig in Europe; where DJs Gilles Peterson and Paul Murphy packed out jazz nights in the 1980s. I'm excited, even though it's a Tuesday afternoon and the only people watching me standing on the stage are a sound engineer testing the speakers and Jeff Horton, the man who owns the venue: the 100 Club, on Oxford Street. Jeff is used to indulging visitors who walk in off the street and stand in the venue a while, reminiscing or imagining. 'It's no problem,' he says.

Live music began at the 100 Club on 24 October 1942, when it was known as the Feldman Swing Club, and continues to this day. It's set back off the street through an entrance to a multi-occupancy office block between two shops that looks like it might take you to a meeting with a recruitment consultant or financial adviser, but you go to the right and through a door and down the stairs, with the pay-desk on the landing, before bending to the left and into the hall. Jeff's been working here for thirty years, and has been in sole charge of the club since 2001, when he succeeded his father Roger, who took over the club in 1964 when Jeff reckons there were probably over 200 live venues in the West End and Soho.

The first thing you notice are the pillars down the middle of the venue, at least three of which look like they'd cut off sightlines to the stage. The size and the layout mean you can't ever be more than about forty feet from the stage. You're right there, a flick of sweat away from the performers. Its history is acknowledged via dozens of photographs lining the walls, including those of Ken Colyer, Mick Jagger, Alice Cooper and Humphrey Lyttelton. For a few years in the mid-1950s the club was named after the latter and became the Humphrey Lyttelton Club.

A survey published in 1951 estimated that three million people went out dancing to palais-style dance halls every week, and that the vast majority were between the ages of sixteen and twenty-four. At that point in the 1950s, restrictions that had been put into operation during the war were still in place, including limits on the sale of tea, confectionery, sugar and meat (the formal end to food rationing didn't come until 1954). Despite the war still casting a shadow over life, and despite the twin social pressures of respectability and conformity suffocating some aspects of personal expression, the enthusiasm shared by those three million dance music fans who filled venues from the Barrowland Ballroom in Glasgow to the Hammersmith Palais is evidence that, although the 1950s has often been characterised as the grey and dull decade before the Swinging Sixties, there were good times to be had.

Furthermore, the years after the war also witnessed the beginnings of a shift in nightlife habits, away from the mainstream, nearer the boundaries of conformity, and seemingly out of sight of the researchers. There was a boom in jazz clubs run by musicians taking it upon themselves to find spaces to play. The majority of musicians made a living playing with the big bands at public dance halls and private functions but craved intimate places like Feldman's, often in basements, where, away from their commercial engagements, they could showcase their talents and indulge their passion for left-field music of various kinds. Two styles in particular appealed: modern jazz inspired by the likes of Dizzy Gillespie, and trad jazz recapturing the sound of jazz pioneers like Jelly Roll Morton or King Oliver. According to Humphrey Lyttelton, 'Young people – not necessarily jazz fans – began to desert the big dance halls for the more informal jazz club atmosphere.'

These informal jazz clubs in basements and, later in the decade, other small venues like coffee bars, skiffle clubs, cellars with juke boxes, and pub function rooms featuring folk nights, were populated by musicians and other creative types, clued-up entrepreneurs and crusaders for new music. As we'll see, throughout the 1950s these informal spaces, animated by the spirit of self-organisation, played a part in laying the foundations of what came later, the so-called Swinging Sixties.

When Roger Horton took over Humphrey Lyttelton's old club in 1964, he'd been working for a jazz promotions company called Jazzshows alongside George Webb from the Dixielanders. Jazzshows became more heavily involved in the 100 Club and Roger became the venue manager, then a director, and finally the proprietor. At this point it was being advertised as the Jazzshows Jazz Club. He was aware that other kinds of music were also in demand, and in February 1964 he changed the name to the 100 Club. Roger instinctively knew he was going to have to be flexible in his booking policy. 'My dad changed the name to the 100 Club because of the address, and because it didn't have the word "jazz" in the title,' says Jeff.

Jeff was in his teens in the mid-1970s, and began to take an interest in the affairs of the club. He recalls the problems of that era, with industrial strife resulting in the country being on a three-day week and electricity often shutting off between 6 p.m. and 9 p.m. 'There were a lot of times we were shut in the seventies because you couldn't open without electricity and by the time you put it back on nobody was about or bothering to venture out. I remember the early seventies being a pretty difficult time.'

Ron Watts used to promote gigs in the Home Counties in the late 1960s, including at the Nag's Head in High Wycombe. He maintained his High Wycombe connections but also began promoting at the 100 Club, where he mostly booked blues acts. At one of Ron's shows at High Wycombe Technical College in 1976, the Sex Pistols played on a night when Screaming Lord Sutch was headlining. Roger was impressed and offered to promote a Sex Pistols show at the 100 Club in March 1976, on a Tuesday night. The gig was a mess. Johnny Rotten got drunk, tried to start a fight with the rest of the band and stalked out of the club, but Ron offered them a residency starting a few weeks later.

The association between the Sex Pistols and the 100 Club culminated in September 1976 when Ron Watts promoted a two-day punk festival featuring the Pistols, the Clash, Buzzcocks and the Damned. 'When punk came along in 1976 the club got a whole new lease of life,' says Jeff. 'I think the punk festival in '76 was probably the moment where the club changed forever because it's still the single most important occasion, the thing the club's most associated with, above all the other brilliant things that we've done.'

On the second night of the festival, when the Damned were playing, Sid Vicious lobbed a beer glass at the stage and it broke against one of the pillars and inflicted a severe injury on a young woman in the audience. The police were called and Vicious ended up in Ashford Remand Centre, though he was released after some spurious alibis were offered in his defence. Despite this sorry incident, punk's champions in the press – although few in number at this point – judged the festival a huge success. Caroline Coon wrote a two-page spread for *Melody Maker* declaring: 'The 600-strong line that stretched across two blocks was indisputable evidence that a new decade in rock is about to begin.'

It wasn't all about punk. In the late 1970s reggae also became a feature of the programming at the 100 Club. There was a Saturday soul night hosted by Capital Radio's Greg Edwards. DJ Ady Croasdell's 6T's Northern Soul night made its 100 Club debut in May 1980, and through the 1980s African musicians Fela Kuti, Miriam Makeba and Hugh Masekela, and Youssou N'Dour all appeared at the club. Looking back to the 1980s Jeff Horton also picks out the jazz DJs who used to fill the club on a Friday night, people like Gilles Peterson and Paul Murphy. 'You'd have people coming in every single Friday night, even if they didn't know the band because they knew it was going to be completely packed. It was the DJs who were really, really important. The band would bring in so many people but the DJ would make sure it was completely sold out.'

Another DJ-led night, 'Popcorn' featuring DJs Paul Hallam and Dave Edwards, filled the venue every week in the late 1990s, by which time another wave of emerging bands had found a home at the 100 Club. This was kick-started when Chris York from SJM phoned Jeff and they came to an agreement over new band showcase nights. The first of these, in September 1992, featured a relatively unknown Suede, who were followed in the next few years by up-and-coming bands like Oasis, Cornershop, Catatonia and Travis. In July 2001, the White Stripes played their first-ever European show at the club.

Despite staging as many successful events as it ever had, the rising costs of running the venue, including a rates bill of £4,000 a month and year-on-year leaps in rent, had created a situation where it looked unlikely that the 100 Club could survive. In September 2010 the *Evening Standard* splashed the story of its imminent demise on its pages, as did the *NME*, and a hundred other magazines and websites. Jeff was inundated with support, including from Paul McCartney who offered to perform a lunchtime show. Just over 300 people attended, a sell-out as you'd expect, with all the £60 tickets sold. McCartney played for almost two hours. 'People had flown in from Chicago, all over North America,' remembers Jeff. 'It was the most extraordinary show, just the best; and fantastic to get that kind of seal of approval from someone like that.'

The 100 Club is one of the longest-running live music venues in the world. There's been no break since 1942, though there have been difficult times. The venue is still independently owned, just as it was in its first days when the Feldmans opened the venue. Their background was in the garment trade; in 1942 Joe Feldman was working as the manager of a clothing factory on Gerrard Street, and his sons Robert and Monty worked there too, as pattern cutters and designers. The boys were into jazz: Robert on clarinet and Monty on accordion played at parties, bar mitzvahs and youth club dances as the Feldman Trio with their young brother Victor as drummer. Victor was particularly talented and even when he was just eight years old he was already attracting attention as a rising star.

On a walk along Oxford Street after leaving work one evening in 1942, Robert passed 100 Oxford Street and wandered down into the basement, where he found Mac's Restaurant and immediately planned setting up a jazz club on the premises. The pillars weren't ideal, but he thought maybe a feature could be made of them, or he could hide them with some potted palm trees. He came to an arrangement to host a live jazz club on Sunday nights. At first Joe was sceptical about the project but, perhaps seeing it as a chance to showcase the talents of child prodigy Victor, he stepped in and added some financial backing. Robert and Monty began to make enough money to give up their work as pattern cutters, while Joe got more involved and headed the operation.

George Webb, who'd launched his Dixielanders at the Red Barn, had connections to the 100 Club, which predated his work with Roger Horton at Jazzshows by a decade. In 1943 the Dixielanders also became the first revivalist jazz group to play at Feldman's when the editor of *Melody Maker*, Ray Sonin, persuaded Robert Feldman to book them. The gig worked – the sound suited the intimate basement – and other revivalist and traditional jazz acts followed, including the Crane River Jazz Band formed by former merchant navy seaman Ken Colyer.

Colyer was of the opinion that mainstream jazz by the late 1940s was overly commercialised, controlled by an industry of compliant venue owners, record companies, and the BBC. He saw something political in the anti-commercial philosophy behind the sound, and he wasn't the only one. A leftist political edge to revivalist jazz was clear at the time. George Webb, for example, was booked by the Young Communist League for various events in central London in the early 1950s. And when in 1958 the Campaign for Nuclear Disarmament set off from Trafalgar Square on a protest march to Aldermaston – the designated centre of Britain's nuclear weapons industry – the marchers were led by Ken Colyer's band playing 'When the Saints Go Marching In'.

Modern bebop fans and those in the other camp – the revivalists and traditionalists seeking to reproduce the authentic pre-commercial jazz – each had favoured venues. When the 100 Club was being run by Humphrey Lyttelton and his manager Lyn Dutton the music policy continued to be mostly traditional jazz, whereas modern jazz fans would gather at venues like Club Eleven. Club Eleven started in 1948, founded by musicians connected with bands Johnny Dankworth and Ronnie Scott had formed following their visit to hear Dizzy Gillespie in America. It was situated in Ham Yard, in the basement of the building that had housed the Hambone. In the late 1940s there was also a boxing gym on the first floor and, it was said, a strip club on the premises too (perhaps in the rooms where the Hambone had been).

Ham Yard already had a reputation for unregulated good times, and for venues operating a little distance from the letter or spirit of the law. Club Eleven fitted into this tradition. There were ten musicians involved including Ronnie Scott, Hank Shaw, Leon Calvert, Laurie Morgan and Tony Crombie. An eleventh member, Harry Morris, a non-musician, took care of the financial side. Fullado mainstay Denis Rose organised many of the jam sessions there. Occasionally he'd ask Don Rendell to fill a vacancy in the Eleven. 'It was a rough place – a kind of old ramshackle sort of bare room with lightbulbs,' Rendell later recalled. 'There was no effort to beautify the place, none. The interest in jazz was growing, but the point was, it was the in place. It was the hip place.'

The trad jazz and modern jazz split was tribal in a way that became very familiar in later decades; young people were making choices about where they went out, and who they hung out with, the music they favoured and the clothes they wore. That you could define yourself in the world with your dress was nothing new; it was something urban gangs like the scuttlers and peaky blinders had understood. As did the flappers, causing a stir with their haircuts and hemlines.

Enamoured of Charlie Parker, Dizzy Gillespie and the early Miles Davis, the bebop crowd studied the looks and style on album sleeves and developed a determination to live out a notion of cool. Music and fashion were at the heart of the lifestyle, and the club you frequented was where you demonstrated your attitudes and allegiances; the mythologies were strong, and would get stronger. You only had to read Jack Kerouac to get that, or take a look at the cover of one edition of his 1958 novel *The Subterraneans* which, in the words of the blurb, was an unabashed portrayal of 'weird lives and wild loves in a jazz-haunted, desire-tormented world'.

There were cells of bebop fans – subterranean, underground (literally and culturally) – who'd escaped to venues where the music, look, language and behaviour wouldn't be countenanced anywhere else. On occasions, Club Eleven would be enveloped in a haze of marijuana, and some of the musicians on the scene used heroin. If you visited Club Eleven you'd soon become aware the drug use had an effect on the performances. Bill Le Sage, who played with the Johnny Dankworth Seven, remembered: 'The bands would play one number for forty minutes. Then take a ten-minute break while they tried to think of the next tune to play.'

After a year in Ham Yard, Club Eleven moved to a venue on Carnaby Street. At the new premises, Club Eleven suffered a major drugs bust on 15 April 1950, when around forty police officers raided the place. They searched the 200 attendees, made ten arrests, and discovered an empty morphine ampoule, a small packet of cocaine, some prepared opium and a large number of cigarettes containing Indian hemp. The newspapers pounced on the goings-on, and ran stories of 'drug-crazed beboppers'.

Denis Rose was one of the musicians questioned after the raid and he was turned over to the military police when it was discovered he had absconded from the army. Ronnie Scott was another of the arrested men and was charged at Marlborough Magistrates Court under the Raw Opium Regulations and Dangerous Drugs Act. At the court, the chief inspector was asked to present his evidence: 'The Club is a bebop club run by musicians who recently moved from other premises,' he began. The presiding magistrate interrupted: 'What is bebop?' The chief inspector didn't go in for a particularly sophisticated explanation: 'It's a queer form of modern dancing; a Negro jive.'

It's understandable perhaps that a magistrate wasn't keeping abreast of music trends, but it was also the case that, with the exception of small pockets of interest, the general public was unaware or unimpressed by developments in jazz, the works of Miles Davis, or the use of recreational drugs by the 'jazz-haunted'. The establishment was keen to keep a lid on everything, wary of weird thinking; a hangover from the wartime desire not to rock the boat. All kinds of activity were suspect: for example, in 1952 authorities in Newcastle, believing that jazz audiences brought trouble to venues, banned a concert featuring Nat King Cole and Johnny Dankworth.

The early 50s tendency to expect conformity would lessen in the following decades, but throughout the decade and beyond, whether out of naivety or ignorance, plenty of ordinary folk weren't quite sure what to make of beatnik-type activity. As late as 1960 a journalist on a Sheffield paper was acknowledging that 'the sight of a teenage figure walking the streets in an oversize sweater and faded blue jeans horrifies the average Sheffield citizen'.

Despite hostility from the authorities and wariness or incomprehension from the general populace, venue owners, musicians and mavericks continued pushing the boundaries of music and nightlife. In 1952 and 1953, for the lucky few, there were opportunities to attend all-night music venues. The lucky ones were those who knew where to look or who to follow: certain characters like Cy Laurie, George Melly and Mick Mulligan.

Visiting a modern jazz club was a cerebral or spiritual experience; the use of reefers and heroin was hardly conducive to banging out high-energy music. At the Red Barn, revivalist jazz audiences were discouraged even from foot-tapping and audiences at Feldman's would nod their heads but remain seated. Cy Laurie's was different to all these; at his venue you'd leap around to party music, dance music – they called it a 'rave'.

Cy Laurie hosted his trad jazz raves in the basement space on Ham Yard vacated by Club Eleven when they moved to Carnaby Street. Cy was a clarinet player rumoured to have a proper job – as a gravedigger – and had previously run a weekly club at the Seven Stars on Bromley High Street. He did little to spruce up the space – it remained a dark, grubby basement – but even with a low-quality sound system and dilapidated sofas, the music had a much more direct dance appeal than strung-out modern jazz.

We were never told about our antecedents during the rave years at the end of the 1980s, at 'Shoom', 'The Trip' or the Haçienda, or raves near Blackburn or the M25. At the Haçienda we knew we hadn't invented staying up all night – we knew about the Northern Soul all-nighters, Wigan Casino, and the speed and scooter scenes – but we didn't know the word 'rave' was being used to describe an all-night dance party back in the early 1950s and that subsequently the word would be used again, when the Who played Brighton's Florida Rooms during the height of mod, for example.

Unlike the DJ-led raves of the late 1980s, back in 1952 and 1953 it would be a live band whipping up a frenzy. On occasions George Melly and his bandmate Mick Mulligan would throw all-night basement parties at their rehearsal room on Gerrard Street, Soho. Mick Mulligan was described in *Melody Maker* as 'King of the Ravers'. His story is told in George Melly's memoir *Owning Up*, a wonderfully evocative story of his early jazz years, including days and nights spent touring in Britain, suffering the nation's B&Bs, confrontations with promoters and venue owners, and enjoying knee-tremblers with playful females. Melly was always gifted with the ability to extract fun out of the most unglamorous situations.

Despite George Melly's story-telling prowess, you'd be hard-pressed to develop a mythology that playing live up and down the country in the 1950s was anything on a par with the intense subterranean life portrayed in a Kerouac novel. Singer Elaine Delmar was on the northern club circuit playing two or three gigs a night and then getting the milk train home. Her sets would come second in priority to the night's bingo session and onstage she'd be faced with a restless audience, likely at any time to get up and wander off to go and buy a pie to have with their pint. She recalls: 'There'd be lots of booze, lots of smoke and rowdiness – the chairman of the club would come onstage saying, "Come on, give a bit of support, give the poor cow a chance!" Dreadful.'

Cy Laurie's weekly trad jazz raves were lively, full of dancing and popular with St Martin's School of Art students. There was a certain look sported by the regulars. The lads tended towards corduroy trousers, short chunky sweaters, duffel coats and short, thoughtful-looking beards. The girls liked dirndl-style circular dresses, curtain-hoop earrings and black stockings. Black was the default colour for most outfits. There'd be some dancers in sandals, some barefooted. The goings-on at Cy's appealed beyond the schisms; lured by bohemian, unrationed enjoyment, even young people who didn't consider themselves 'trad' fans made their way to the venue.

As the decade progressed, the smaller scenes and activity away from the major dance halls were developing in cities all over Britain. In Newcastle, for example, despite the local council's ban on Nat King Cole, the city was building a strong jazz scene. Back in the 1930s, the Newcastle Rhythm Club had hired or taken possession of a succession of venues and function rooms, including, in 1954, the Mahogany Hall in the Royal Arcade. The following year, George Pearson took the Central Labour Club on Melbourne Street and opened the New Orleans Club.

Many of the important and influential musicians who'd emerge in the late 1960s and early 1970s were enjoying their formative years in clubs and venues in the 1950s. Bryan Ferry is just one example. A teenager, his visits to the New Orleans Jazz Club made an impression, and it wasn't just the music, it was the whole experience. Later he recalled being inspired by the otherworldly atmosphere: 'To me it was just like being in a movie set; people smoking and drinking and then this band were playing who were really good.'

The in-house band at the New Orleans Club was the Mighty Joe Young Jazzmen, who featured a trumpet player called John Walters, a former art student. Another young musician who was a regular performer at the club was Nigel Stanger, who became more than proficient on the alto and tenor saxophones, piano and Hammond organ, and went on to play with the likes of Herbie Goins at the Flamingo, John Mayall and, in 1993, on Bryan Ferry's album *Taxi*.

Eric Burdon was a local lad who also spent some of his formative years in the New Orleans Jazz Club, which is wonderfully apt given that a song about a house in New Orleans later made the reputation of his band, the Animals. In one interview Burdon later recalled his crowd hanging out in the cooler clubs in Newcastle, describing his bunch of friends as 'like a motorcycle gang without the motorcycles. They were tough, hard-drinking and listened to American music.'

Burdon had met John Steel at Newcastle College of Art and Industrial Design. In early 1957 they were in a band together, the Pagan Jazzmen, with Burdon on vocals (and trombone) and Steel on trumpet. Among the other musicians was a banjo player; they were that kind of band. But they were also switched-on young men with their ears and minds open. Within a year they had a rhythm & blues band; they were no longer jazzmen. The banjo player bought an electric guitar, Steel swapped to playing drums and they became the Pagans. The Pagans added piano player Alan Price. The stuttering evolution of these various line-ups was replicated nationwide in 1956 and 1957 in other groups as the arrival of rhythm & blues and rock & roll made an impact.

The impact of rock & roll was first delivered not at clubs or live venues, but cinemas. The cinema in the 1920s and 1930s was

influential in spreading the sounds of jazz and now in the 1950s
would do the same for a new sound. Two films in particular featured rock & roll numbers and caused controversy and
consternation, on a few occasions triggering riotous disturbances
by what were identified as teddy boys. The 1955 film *Blackboard
Jungle* was the first: it included the song 'Rock Around the Clock'
performed by Bill Haley and the Comets. Subsequently there
was a spin-off film, *Rock Around the Clock,* shown early the next
year.

Cinema had this role because rock & roll wasn't easily available on radio and tours by the stars were few and far between.
The only time Elvis set foot in Britain was in 1960 when he
broke his journey in Prestwick airport in Scotland on his way
back home to America from his military service in West
Germany (although the theatre impresario and Everton FC
chairman Bill Kenwright has made claims Elvis had been to
London in 1958, secretly sightseeing with Tommy Steele).
Exposure to rock & roll at the cinema had a visceral impact,
partly and thrillingly because cinemas had a far better PA than
you'd get at Cy Laurie's or the New Orleans Club. Exposed to
the volume, the kick of the bass drum, the power of the guitars,
Roger Eagle was one of many young Britons who left a cinema
in 1955 with a lifetime devotion to music ahead of him. He later
recalled seeing the likes of *Rock Around the Clock* and *The Girl
Can't Help It*: 'For the very first time you could see and hear this
incredibly powerful music. If you can imagine what it's like in a
cinema with rock & roll being played through a cinema sound
system, it was extremely exciting, because there's a huge bass res-
onance there.'

Fuelled by sensationalised press coverage and panic, a number
of local authorities banned screenings of *Rock Around the Clock*,
including those in Bristol, Liverpool, Warrington and Carlisle. At
some cinemas there was a police presence outside – or on occasions, inside – but little trouble. The music was the draw, and –

apart from a bit of dancing in the aisles, which to some cinema operators was scandalous enough – most outbreaks of hooliganism occurred during the boring bits when the songs ended and the storyline recommenced.

Despite the high profile of films like *Rock Around the Clock*, the 1950s witnessed a steady downturn in cinema attendance from amazing highs in the 1930s, mostly as a result of the increasing ownership of televisions. The response of some cinema owners was to refurbish and transform their premises into bona fide music venues fit for touring bands and local talent contests. In 1957 Bill Haley played at the Gaumont in Coventry and elsewhere including the Manchester Odeon (where backstage he met some cousins from Cumbria; his mother was born in Ulverston). When Jerry Lee Lewis embarked on his first British tour, venues included the Gaumont State cinema in Kilburn, although the tour was cut short when the press revealed that his new bride, who was travelling with him, was only thirteen years old.

Skiffle was Britain's home-grown hybrid of rock & roll, blues and folk. It took off at the end of the 1950s among the young, not just as music to listen or dance to, but also to perform. Very few people could afford electric guitars and amplifiers, but a skiffle line-up – acoustic guitar, tea-chest bass that you could make yourself, and a washboard – was do-it-yourself entertainment, a form of cheap thrills. Lonnie Donegan's commercial success in 1955 triggered further interest in skiffle.

Donegan's early work dates back to 1953. When Ken Colyer and Chris Barber were booked for their jazz sets they began to break up the shows with skiffle, with various line-ups. Colyer and Alexis Korner were at the core of most, often with Lonnie Donegan on vocals. Soon these skiffle performances began to attract attention and audiences. By July 1953 *Jazz Journal* was describing the 'electric atmosphere' of these skiffle sessions and praising Donegan's version of 'John Henry' and Colyer's rendition of 'How Long Blues'. Out of this ad hoc, unhyped activity,

Donegan emerged with his version of 'Rock Island Line', credited to the Lonnie Donegan Skiffle Group, but an arrangement originally conceived by Lead Belly. It became a massive hit.

During the second half of the 1950s, there were signs of new energies on the outskirts of culture, perhaps as a result of the 1944 Education Act, which had opened up secondary education to young people with working-class origins. According to novelist Keith Waterhouse, author of *Billy Liar*, it was: 'An upstart generation who instead of becoming factory fodder had come up through the grammar schools and red-brick universities and was now ready to take the world on.'

A new generation wanted to make its own world, find its own place, and space. In 1953, the sense that alternative ways of thinking needed developing lay behind the founding of the Theatre Workshop by Joan Littlewood in a crumbling Victorian theatre in Stratford in the east London borough of Newham. Geographically, and in most other ways, it was some distance from the established West End theatres. There was a sense of self-organisation and a political impulse in their anti-establishment philosophy, similar to that of the likes of left-leaning jazzers such as George Webb. The English Stage Company at the Royal Court provided another antidote to mainstream theatres.

In many towns and cities, there were tea shops and coffee houses, many of them branded by Lyons or Kardomah, frequented by all kinds of people; popular meeting places, they were useful assignation sites for courting couples. A variation on the coffee house theme arrived in the 1950s, however, with the introduction of Gaggia machines, capable of producing espresso and cappuccino coffees, and the juke box. Often these emergent coffee bars were independently owned, and attracted teenagers. Many of them provided live skiffle. They were cool in the way established social spaces such as public houses weren't. According to Adrian Horn, 'In the late 1940s and 1950s teenagers perceived pubs as old-fashioned, lacklustre and dreary, and frequented by old men playing outdated pub games.'

Among the most significant coffee bars in the late 1950s was the 2i's on Old Compton Street in London where all kinds of interesting people gathered, and even the doormen went on to greater things (Peter Grant, for example, became manager of Led Zeppelin). Singer (and, later, broadcaster) Wally Whyton observed: 'The coffee bars were the first places where you could hang about for an evening, spend a shilling on a coffee, go in at nine and come out at eleven, and nobody bothered you, nobody said you had to have a second cup of coffee.' He became a member of the Vipers Skiffle Group, who would advertise themselves as playing 'Blues and Folk Music' at venues like the Bread Basket Espresso Coffee Bar on Cleveland Street (near Goodge Street station). The Vipers featured Tommy Hicks in their line-up, and were the first resident band at the 2i's.

On the far end of the ground floor was a narrow staircase leading down to a smaller cellar room in which there was a makeshift stage of milk crates with planks on top and, on the wall, a couple of speakers; this was where the live music was performed. While he was with the Vipers, Tommy Hicks was spotted by music impresario Larry Parnes, became Tommy Steele and covering American hits (with a band, the Steelmen), began to have UK chart success. A number of other stars were discovered or performed at the 2i's, including Joe Brown, Eden Kane, Hank Marvin, Adam Faith and Paul Gadd (later better and infamously known as Gary Glitter). Cliff Richard also had a residency with the Drifters, who renamed themselves the Shadows after the American soul group the Drifters threatened legal action.

Coffee bars were popular in their own right, but it's also noticeable how many evolved into informal music venues. They had no alcohol licence so were subject to few restrictions on use and hours; a few, in Soho and other busy nightlife areas, were 24-hour establishments. If there was no inclination or space for live music, there was always room for the most important piece of furniture: a loud, well-stocked juke box. It's reckoned there were fewer than a hundred juke boxes in Britain at the end of the Second World War, but over 15,000 by 1958. It was considered a symbol of Americanisation and a controversial cultural transformation. Richard Hoggart in his 1957 book *The Uses of Literacy* was clearly concerned about what he called the 'spiritual rot' evident in the sight of coffee and milk bars. He claimed those who hung out at such places – 'the juke box boys', he called them – exhibited 'no aim, no ambition, no belief'.

Despite Hoggart's disdain, the coffee bar experience proved irresistible to the young, more attractive than dance halls or pub function rooms or working men's clubs. Colin MacInnes describes all this in his novel *Absolute Beginners* in 1958: 'You could see everywhere the signs of un-silent teenage revolution,' he writes. 'Everywhere you go the narrow coffee bars and darkened cellars with the kids packed tight.'

Not for the first or last time in our story, entrepreneurs were making a space, attracting a crowd, creating a scene. In Newcastle upon Tyne, a young man called Mike Jeffery had dropped out of his degree course at the University of Newcastle to run the Marimba Coffee House on High Bridge Street. His venue was unlicensed, which meant that teenagers were welcome. The Marimba offered jazz sessions every Saturday from midnight until three in the morning, but the venue also became a daytime hangout. It offered lunch for four shillings (20p) and an 'atmosphere with a difference'.

One of the foremost jazz musicians in the area was Mike Carr. He was a travelling salesman by day, specialising in bulk sales of Mars bars, but by night he played keyboards in various jazz combos alongside Malcolm Cecil. He got to know Mike Jeffery and later became partners with him running the Downbeat Club from 1960, another hangout for Eric Burdon.

In the history of significant venues it makes sense to celebrate the most conspicuous in every era, but at the same time we should be aware of the smaller, marginal enterprises that innovate and nurture ideas and music; ideas and music that may disappear without trace but may reach and change public consciousness months or even years later. We've already seen this at Billy's, Club Eleven and elsewhere. It's worth pointing out too how many popular musicians who were young kids in 1957 and then went on to careers in rock music, at some point featured in a skiffle group: for example John Lennon and Paul McCartney, Van Morrison and Jimmy Page.

'What happened next' is always part of the story. Later, we'll discuss the Sex Pistols playing at the Lesser Free Trade Hall in Manchester, a celebrated occasion when the legacy of the event had a huge significance. We'll also visit clubs in the 1980s, some unnoticed at the time, but which were key to creating the scene in the 1990s. Victor Feldman, the youngest of the Feldmans who launched the venue that became the 100 Club, enjoyed a career as a drummer and vibraphone player but then had even more success as a hardbop pianist, especially after he'd emigrated to the USA in 1957. He worked with the likes of Woody Herman, featured on Miles Davis' 1963 album *Seven Steps to Heaven* and went on to work outside of jazz, with Frank Zappa, Joni Mitchell and Tom Waits.

Many venues carried a sense of potential within their walls, as well as a coffee machine, pillars in the wrong place, a juke box and perhaps a stage. In Liverpool, the Jacaranda was founded in 1957 by Allan Williams, who converted an old watch-repair shop on Slater Street into a coffee bar, which became a coffee bar club when Williams opened the small, spartan, brick-floored basement. Through the late 1950s, the Jac became a favourite of local musicians, including members of the skiffle group the Quarry Men, and the band they became – the Beatles. The Jacaranda was also a hangout for the local Afro-Caribbean community, including the calypso star Harold Philips, who had journeyed to England in 1948 on the MV *Empire Windrush*. Philips had a variety of jobs in the 1950s, including as a builder and barman. Taking the stage name Lord Woodbine, he joined Gerry Gobin's All Caribbean Steel Band, playing a tenor pan; they played regularly at the Jacaranda Club.

So many coffee bar enterprises would also turn out to be the starting point for music business careers. Danny Betesh was one of those involved at the El-Rio in Macclesfield in 1956; fast-forward ten years to the mid-60s and he was being described as 'the most important agent and promoter based in Northern England'. Mike Jeffery moved from the Marimba to the Downbeat and then Club A Go Go; from there he would go on to be Jimi Hendrix's manager. In Leeds, the family that owned the Del Rio coffee bar on Basinghall Street later ran the In-Time Disco in the Merrion Centre, which had a timepiece theme, with the DJ housed inside a large open pocket watch.

In the 1958 film *Expresso Bongo*, talent agent Johnny Jackson discovers teenager Bert Rudge (played by Cliff Richard) singing in a coffee bar and gives him the name Bongo Herbert as a first step to being groomed for stardom. The success of the film spawned yet more coffee bars, including one unashamedly calling itself Expresso Bongo in Morley, near Leeds (it's now the Ho Ho Chinese takeaway).

When Joan Littlewood went out on a limb to stage Shelagh Delaney's ground-breaking play *A Taste of Honey,* the Theatre Workshop was one of a number of cells of maverick artistic activity in the 1950s that would serve as a catalyst for major cultural change. Another enlightened and influential young woman, Mary Quant – in a different field of expertise and not sharing Littlewood's political and social views – had nevertheless also grasped that the emerging generation were on the lookout for alternatives to the obvious. Mary Quant's Bazaar was one of the pioneering boutiques, located out in Chelsea, west London, and established in 1955 when Mary Quant was just twenty-one years old. According to one cultural historian, 'She single-handedly reinvigorated the idea of modern British fashion.' Boutiques like Bazaar were as different from your average department store as the Royal Court was to theatres around Leicester Square, and as a modern jazz club was different to a dance hall.

It's what happened in these small venues during the 1950s that laid the foundations for what happened in the 1960s. It was where the new ideas were born, ideas that were a bit 'out there'. In the mid-1960s Dennis Hopper would enjoy Swinging London: 'It was just amazing,' he'd say. 'The dance clubs and the jazz and these packed places, it was just incredible.' That was the time when the seeds bloomed, the new culture emerged, Mary Quant's work reached public consciousness, and clubs like the Flamingo created and connected with the zeitgeist.

The Flamingo was founded when Jeff Kruger hosted an evening of jazz in the basement of the Mapleton Restaurant in Coventry Street in 1952 and then christened the venue with the new name. He managed to generate such a buzz about the opening night, it was said that it required forty policemen to control the crowds. Live jazz included appearances by amazing female singers like Sarah Vaughan, Ella Fitzgerald and Billie Holiday.

In 1957 the Flamingo moved to Wardour Street, by which time another name later associated with the success of the venue, Rik Gunnell (who would run the legendary all-nighter sessions there), had also been active for several years, having named his first venture into jazz promotion the 2-Way Club, held on Thursdays at 100 Oxford Street from 1952. On the upper floor of the building that housed the Flamingo was the Whiskey A-Go-Go, one of the few clubs in the area licensed to sell alcohol.

A booming nightlife feeds into a lively retail sector. In the late 1950s, snappy dressers among the young men in London headed to Vince in Piccadilly. Vince sold young men's clothes that had colour in them and weren't restricted to the traditional common-sense materials like tweed, wool or gabardine. At one time John Stephen worked there, before setting himself up as a designer and establishing a number of boutiques on Carnaby Street, including His Clothes and Male West One; these became a destination of choice for daring young men who appreciated colour. Ian McLagan of the Small Faces recalled: 'Before that all you had was the same clothes your dad wore. Life suddenly was colourful.'

At the sharp end of fashion were the mods, who'd developed (and indeed taken their name) from their taste for modern jazz, its methodology and mythologies. Their mod styles were continuing to evolve, a few steps ahead of the straights, taking inspiration from the irresistible attractions of Miles Davis and Chet Baker, who came to prominence after joining the Gerry Mulligan Quartet from 1952, and the emergence of tenor players like Wardell Gray and Dexter Gordon.

Among those who stalked the streets paying attention to the details of mod living was Pete Meaden. In 1960 Andrew Loog Oldham – who later managed the Rolling Stones – would hook up with Meaden and comb the West End and Soho; always checking Austin's on Shaftesbury Avenue first and always swerving the shops selling the ubiquitous post-war grey or black suits, lusting instead after the likes of a bottle-green mohair suit with a paisley lining.

In May 2013 I met Andrew in Liverpool and, with some encouragement, he reminisced about his younger days. He's always made and taken great opportunities. Six months after leaving school he was working at Bazaar with Mary Quant. In October 1959 Ronnie Scott opened a venue in a basement at 39 Gerrard Street; Andrew Loog Oldham wanted in, so he called

Ronnie Scott's partner at the club, Pete King. Andrew asked for work and got it.

Ronnie Scott's held just a hundred people in a very cramped room – so cramped it was easier to serve drinks at the tables than to ask people to walk to the bar. Andrew Loog Oldham became the club's first waiter, working at Ronnie Scott's from seven till midnight throughout the week and till 1 a.m on Saturdays. Licensing regulations insisted they had to provide food, which was one of Andrew's duties. 'There was a Pakistani restaurant and we didn't have a food licence so we'd take orders and I'd get the food and bring it back and I also hung the coats.'

A working compromise was found to the Musicians' Union ban on visiting jazz musicians initiated in the mid-1930s, in the form of an exchange arrangement with the American Federation of Musicians, so Ronnie Scott was able to host bebop artists from America, many visiting the UK for the first time. British jazz musicians and fans were hungry to hear the black American musicians. 'It was a public service, putting on those American acts, it was incredible,' says Andrew, recalling particularly performances by Zoot Sims. Another act that made an impression on him was Harold McNair, the super-cool flute player. He'd imagined a life sound-tracked by Miles Davis, and there he was, at midnight, in a jazz club. It was really happening: 'Before that, everything was second-hand. Zoot Sims, man, it was like getting on a plane, it allowed you to be in America.'

Half a mile away, the Marquee began life in the basement of the Academy Picture House at 195 Oxford Street. The original plan of the owner, George Hoellering, was to run a ballroom with a circus-themed decor, complete with green, red and white marquee-style awnings. Despite the fancy furnishing, a Steinway piano and an espresso coffee lounge, Hoellering couldn't attract an audience, so pianist Dill Jones and his manager Peter Burman took over the programming at weekends. They presented their first 'Jazz at the Marquee' event in January 1958. Despite their boast that at the Marquee you could 'meet the stars at the most modern jazz rendezvous in the world', Jones and Burman also struggled to fill the venue.

Soon, Harold Pendleton was called in and offered the space. Pendleton, who ran the National Jazz Federation, saw the location of the Marquee as a positive: it was halfway between Humphrey Lyttelton's club at 100 Oxford Street, and the Flamingo on Wardour Street. At 100 Oxford Street you'd expect to hear trad, at the Flamingo modern jazz – so, as befitting the location, Pendleton decided to programme both.

With a number of small scenes and music evolving, some venues stuck to purist and niche audiences, while others opened up their programme. Even at the 2i's, for example, skiffle and jazz co-existed for a year or two. It was the same at the Cavern in Liverpool: jazz and skiffle were the club's mainstays in the first years. Two acts on the opening night of the Cavern on 16 January 1957 were local, proven jazz outfits (including the Merseysippi Jazz Band). The other act was the Coney Island Skiffle Group who, needless to say, were not young New Yorkers from Coney Island.

One of the most famous music venues in our history, the Cavern, was opened by Alan Sytner, partly inspired by clubs in Paris. Sytner was in his early twenties, but he'd already been to Paris and tasted the nightlife of the Quartier Latin, and set his heart on opening a jazz club in his home town along the lines of Le Caveau on Rue de la Huchette. His father, a local GP, put up some cash and a local estate agent showed them potential premises including an old cellar that had been used as an air-raid shelter in the basement of a warehouse on Mathew Street. Even the narrow streets suggested something of the ambience of Paris to young Alan and, echoing Le Caveau in its name, the Cavern was born.

The Cavern continued to offer nights playing both traditional and modern jazz and skiffle, but Sytner banned rock & roll from the venue. Elvis Presley and Jerry Lee Lewis had both had Number One singles by mid-1958 but in general rock & roll was associated with scruffs and teddy boys, and few club owners wanted a clientele of that kind.

On 7 August 1957 the Quarry Men were booked to play a short skiffle set between two jazz bands at the Cavern. It was a quiet Wednesday; there was no huge fanfare. The Quarry Men at the time included Pete Shotton, Len Garry and Colin Hanton, and one young man who would go on to star in the Beatles – John Lennon. In defiance of Sytner's ban on rock & roll, midway through their set Lennon persuaded the rest of the band to play Elvis Presley's 'Don't Be Cruel'. Although this irked the club owner, the band was booked again, and on this occasion Paul McCartney was part of the Quarry Men. In the middle of 1958 they stopped performing with a banjo and a tea-chest bass and put some proper distance between themselves and the skiffle scene, although it would be 1960 before they had a regular drummer, Pete Best, by which time the Quarry Men had become the Beatles.

Over in Newcastle, Eric Burdon, John Steel and Alan Price, now in thrall to the Joe Turner album *The Boss of the Blues*, were leaving pure jazz behind and getting deeper into rhythm & blues. As the Kansas City Five they took some gigs at the New Orleans Club and the Downbeat, but in May 1962 Alan Price went missing and threw in his lot with the Kontors alongside Chas Chandler. Eventually, out of all the chopping, changing, joining and leaving, the Animals would emerge.

Skiffle triggered deeper interest in rhythm & blues (which isn't surprising given that 'Rock Island Line' had been a reworking of a Lead Belly song) but also in American folk music (a number of songs Woody Guthrie wrote or played, including 'Grand Coulee Dam', were skiffle standards). Interest in down-home, non-glitzy folk and work-songs with American roots was marked by an increase in folk clubs, often held in pub and function rooms.

Myra Abbott initiated the Hoy at Anchor folk club in Southend: 'Its main ethos was uncommercial music – we wanted to provide an alternative,' she said.

In this era Ewan MacColl began hosting 'Blues & Ballads' events. Some skiffle groups transformed into folk groups, including the Ian Campbell Folk Group (originally the Clarion Skiffle Group), who opened their 'Jug o'Punch' folk club at Digbeth Civic Hall in Birmingham and played regularly at the Crown pub on Station Street (where they recorded their debut album). Dave Swarbrick was a member of the group in its early days (he later featured in Fairport Convention). Both guitarist Spencer Davis and pianist Christine Perfect also appeared with Ian Campbell's group before going on to enjoy illustrious careers. In Edinburgh, among the plethora of folk events was a Thursday folk club at the Crown Bar run by various hands, including Bert Jansch, Robin Williamson and Clive Palmer, which helped develop their later careers in Pentangle (Jansch) and the Incredible String Band (Williamson and Palmer).

The Troubadour was a coffee house with a cellar on Old Brompton Road in Earls Court that became one of the most significant venues during the British folk revival of the late 1950s. When Bob Dylan first visited England in late December 1962 he went out in London looking for the kind of scene analogous to that in Greenwich Village. Pete Seeger suggested he track down Anthea Joseph, who ran events at the Troubadour, which he did. One evening he played there with Richard Farina and Martin Carthy, a simple set-up; no microphones, no lights, no stage. He also hung out at the King & Queen, behind Goodge Street station, where he sang three songs at the invitation of Carthy. On his return to the States he wasn't particularly effusive about his time in London, complaining it was cold, but he did find at least one thing to report: 'The English can do the twist by moving only one leg,' he told an interviewer.

Some of the demand for alternatives to the established music venues in the 1950s came from the West Indian community. The dominant force were the Jamaicans, who'd brought with them various customs, including the music they'd enjoyed in the Caribbean and the notion of sound systems to deliver that music. Sound systems had emerged in Jamaica in the late 1940s; each would invariably include a record selector, an MC and technicians to transport and set up big box speakers. They were a team – tight-knit, community or family-run enterprises that took the music to the people, playing outdoors or at venues, often in competition with other sounds.

Setting up a sound system outdoors wasn't such an attractive idea in cold, rainy Britain, but they established a presence at house parties (variously known as 'blues' or 'shebeens'), church halls and community centres. These first sounds in Britain would be playing Fats Domino, Jimmy Reed and calypso, as they did back home, helping keep connections and Jamaican identity strong. Two aspects of this activity need underlining: the spirit of self-organisation inherent in sound-system culture, and that sound systems were among the first examples of DJs playing vinyl to provide the entertainment on a night out. Sound-system operator Duke Vin (real name Vincent Forbes) later explained his motivation: 'I couldn't find nowhere for a dance. The country was dead. So I started my own system. People started using basements in houses that were packed till morning.'

That sound systems existed outside mainstream music venues was out of necessity as much as desire. Black people faced discrimination in housing and jobs, and in clubs. There were plenty of city-centre venues that would deny black people entry to a club based solely on their colour. Back in 1929, the Locarno in Streatham was involved in controversy when the proprietor, H.S. Kingdon, imposed a colour bar. 'Our attitude is this. We do not believe in mixing water with wine or black with white. The Locarno Dance Hall is for white people only.'

There's an uncomfortable history here, but it's worth noting that Mr Kingdon faced a backlash from customers appalled at his decision. The local newspaper was inundated with letters critical of him and the Locarno dropped the door policy. Discrimination of this sort was not illegal, and it wouldn't be until the 1965 Race Relations Act outlawed operating a colour bar in a pub or club. Until then, it's hard to know exactly how many clubs operated an implicit or explicit colour bar, but a number of cases became high profile, including that of the Scala in Wolverhampton in 1958, where the proprietor Michael Wade refused admission to black men. Despite protests to the licensing authorities the premises had its licence renewed. It wasn't until a change of ownership that the colour bar at the Scala was lifted.

By this time sound systems had moved into certain specific clubs (there were said to be several dozen basement clubs run by West Indians in south London alone). They were also conspicuous at public sound clashes, when the sound systems would often play in competition with each other, as happened in Jamaica. 'The Big Five Night' was a promotion at Lambeth Town Hall in November 1957, advertised as featuring 'the Five Greatest Sounding Systems battling for the 1957 Club Championship of Sound and Record'. Vincent 'Duke Vin' Forbes triumphed: his sound system had an unrivalled reputation, as a selector he knew how to wow a crowd.

Self-organisation in the Afro-Caribbean community extended to other activities at the end of the 1950s, with a Caribbean Carnival held at St Pancras Town Hall in January 1959. For the next few years it alternated between the Seymour Hall (at Marble Arch) and the Lyceum, and from 1965 onwards Carnival was situated in Notting Hill.

In the late 1950s sound systems weren't the only vinyl-led nights out in Britain. Some of the programme at rhythm clubs like the one in Newcastle would involve the jazz aficionados gathering to listen to albums. Various entrepreneurs were also beginning to look into importing the idea of record hops from America, where DJs (particularly Alan Freed, and others with a following on the radio) could attract hundreds of kids to live roadshows, playing records in venues and sports halls. A version of these record hops was already happening in Yorkshire, under the auspices of Jimmy Savile.

In 1944 Savile was declared unfit to be called up into the armed forces, and instead was drafted to work in the mines; during a shift at Waterloo Colliery, he was injured in an accident and it took three years for him to recover. He began hiring venues close to where he lived in Yorkshire, playing dance records on customised gramophones and charging admission whenever and wherever he could get a function room. For decades, when people got dressed up and went out they had danced to a live band and there were plenty of people sceptical that the idea of people dancing to records would catch on. But hard work, commercial nous and a box of mid-tempo 78s by the likes of Joe Loss, Lee Dorsey and Jack Teagarden established Savile as a successful operator of these prototype mobile discos.

The old-style variety theatres that had evolved out of the music hall were continuing to lose customers, some of them becoming bingo halls. TV was a cheaper source of live entertainment and the younger generation had more exciting nightlife options. Some variety theatre managers, like Harry Joseph at the City Varieties in Leeds, found a small but loyal audience for strippers and revues like *Who Goes Bare?* but, with only a few exceptions, variety theatres were in a bad way by the end of the 1950s. Moss Empires and other businesses did their best to chase the market. In August 1956, the Rockets – a group formed by the former Club Eleven bebopper Tony Crombie – was signed for a tour of variety venues, and described as 'the first full-time rock & roll outfit in the country'.

A reviewer who attended a gig by the Rockets at the

Sunderland Empire reported in the *Sunderland Echo*: 'I enjoy good jazz, and I can tap my feet to a pulsating rhythm as well as most, but I found the renderings of Mr Crombie's Rockets to be nothing more than clangourous, ear-splitting uproar.' Rock & roll, of course, was on its way to becoming louder still. We can only hope that when Black Sabbath played at the Bay Hotel in Sunderland in 1969 the newspaper sent a less fragile reporter.

Over in Newcastle, important names were on the move. John Walters, the trumpet player for the in-house band at the New Orleans Jazz Club, later became a producer on John Peel's radio show. Bryan Ferry moved on from hanging out at the New Orleans Jazz Club to frequenting the Club A Go Go. He'd also attend art school, where exposure to art and ideas, together with his formative experiences at the clubs, fed into his dream of finding a role on the music scene. Malcolm Cecil went on to play with some music greats, including sessions on the Stevie Wonder albums *Talking Book* and *Innervisions*. He'd left Newcastle in the early 1960s and joined Alexis Korner's Blues Inc., which also featured harmonica player Cyril Davies. Davies and Korner had both moved from skiffle into blues, and together ran the London Blues and Barrelhouse Club, a venue that after sparsely attended first months went on to attract the likes of Muddy Waters and Memphis Slim.

Between 1956 and 1962 – those years between the first UK hit for Elvis Presley and the first hit for the Beatles – groups were getting together at the grass roots, emerging, hungry, playing their first gigs; also, older musicians and fans of various genres self-organising, offered plenty of alternative choices in live music venues, certainly in Britain's larger conurbations. Alternative ways of performing live, consuming music and going out dancing to music had been established, a drift away from big bands playing sweet swing or Dixielanders playing to serious, seated audiences. Coffee bar dance clubs reinforced and normalised the change that Cy Laurie's allies helped pioneer. It was those jazz clubs that had begun to flourish in the early 1950s that became a model for going out: basement clubs, the music cranked up really high, a sense of nonconformist rebellion. When jazz had long lost its allure, later generations had new excitements but would continue to appropriate and appreciate raucous, underlit cellars.

What's striking about the late 1950s is the range of venues. Groups had plenty of places to play: function rooms, dance halls, youth clubs, swimming baths and coffee bars. In Sheffield, bands like Ricky & the Rebels would play all these sorts of venues, as well as wedding receptions and private functions. In addition, on Sunday nights they'd often play at one of a number of cinemas around Attercliffe: the Regal, the Plaza, the Adelphi or the Globe.

Elsewhere in Sheffield, Club 60 was formed by Terry Thornton, a musician who, among other things, tried to promote rock & roll at City Hall, only for the council to deny him use of the venue. He'd been working on a plan to create a space for young, adventurous music lovers, which would be part nightclub and part jazz club, but where you might also expect arty-type poetry. In the spirit of the times, he opted to try to make something happen out of nothing, opening Club 60 in an old pub cellar, which he refurbished with the help of local art students and music fans. It was billed as 'The local jazz club with the continental atmosphere'. Sheffield's citizens grew more accustomed to the sight of teenagers in blue jeans.

Nationwide, more coffee bars turned into coffee dance clubs. In Manchester the Left Wing on Brazennose Street described itself in advertising material as a 'beatnik-type' coffee bar promising reduced-rate admission for 'feminine-type cats'. It would later house the Twisted Wheel club, with Roger Eagle installed as the club's DJ. That was in 1963, by which time disc-only nights and DJs were becoming an accepted part of British nightlife – although the trend was causing some consternation in the established nightlife industry. The Association of Ballrooms, for example, was panicking. *Melody Maker* on 6 June 1959 announced the news that 'Bosses of Britain's ballrooms plan to probe the wave of disc hops which are springing up all over the country,' explaining that, 'These record sessions, often run in village halls, teenage clubs and civic centres, have already put some dance proprietors out of business.'

In the early 1960s both Ronnie Scott's and the Marquee would move to new premises. Terry Thornton would go on to establish one of Sheffield's most celebrated clubs, the Esquire. Cyril Davies and Alexis Korner promoted a weekly blues night at the Ealing Jazz Club, which played a part in the early days of the Rolling Stones. Lord Woodbine opened a number of semi-legal clubs, including the New Cabaret Artists Club on Upper Parliament Street, Liverpool, where an early line-up of the Beatles (John, Paul, George and Stu) played, backing Janice, a Mancunian stripper. And the 100 Club survived.

On 10 June 2007 the 100 Club staged George Melly's last ever gig. The eighty-year-old singer was dying of lung cancer and suffering badly with emphysema. His wife called up Jeff Horton and said George knew he was close to dying and he wanted one last hurrah at the 100 Club. 'How long's he got?' asked Jeff. 'He could be dead any day now,' was the reply, which was a problem, as Jeff didn't have any spare dates in the diary for at least three weeks. Still, a gig was agreed and George kept going and kept going. A few days before the show his wife called Jeff again, not with bad news but just to let him know what George was saying: that his wish was that he would drop dead on stage on the night. Jeff was perturbed: 'I said, "Well, that might be great for George but I really hope it doesn't happen".'

That evening, when George Melly arrived at the club in his wheelchair, he was accompanied by several medical staff and Jeff's office resembled a field hospital, complete with drips and other supplies. 'He was amazing,' says Jeff. 'The smoking ban was on but we still let him have a smoke on stage. Even though he was so ill, he pulled this thing off absolutely brilliantly. I think that show and the anticipation of it prolonged his life a little, as I don't think he died until about three or four weeks after.'

The BBC was there, filming the event, and the footage includes George being lifted on and off the stage in his wheelchair. The stage Louis Armstrong, the Who, the Sex Pistols, the White Stripes and Siouxsie and the Banshees have performed on. The stage George Melly didn't die on.

CHAPTER FOUR

Merseybeat, flashing eyes, a leg-over

Noddy Holder is sitting with me discussing the venues he played when he was in Slade, and before; when he was playing local gigs around the West Midlands. He'd just seen a photo of Slade at their height – all four of them: Dave Hill, Jim Lea, Don Powell, and Noddy – taken by Harry Goodwin in the aftermath of a show at Belle Vue in Manchester in April 1975; they're pictured surrounded by trashed seats.

In the first three years of the 1970s most Slade singles would end up at Number One and most Slade tours would involve noise and chaos, mass singalongs from thousands of lads ('headcases, a lot of them' says Noddy, fondly) and screaming girls, and those broken seats. They were banned from some venues, but loved it, encouraging the audience, feeding the frenzy. Noddy remembers audiences foot-stamping during 'Get Down and Get With It' on the verge of bringing down balconies. 'It was like mayhem when the gig finished and the hall emptied, the seats were wrecked. We paid fortunes in insurance for venue repair. Our insurance bill was phenomenal.'

Slade were rowdy but showbiz too. They wanted their live shows to be exciting and unforgettable. In performance, including on TV of course, they'd look for outlandish outfits and headgear to wear. Dave Hill was always eccentrically dressed. Before Slade he wore a cloak around town. Noddy shakes his head. 'I mean, wearing a cloak round Wolverhampton in 1966? Everyone was, "Look at that fella!" Whereas Jim, Jim hated all the dressing up, hated it with a vengeance.'

Noddy's *pièce de résistance* was a hat made of mirrors. His mirror hat is considered such a sight of significant historical interest that the British Music Experience at the O2 requested to exhibit it, but Noddy said no, it's too precious. 'The effect live was stunning,' he explains. 'We had to black out the whole arena and then we had a pencil beam but the mirrors were big, a good few inches across, so it was like a mirrorball but a massive mirrorball and the beams would come off and they'd be proper beams, like spotlights, and I could light the audience up, and when the spotlight hit them they'd go mad.'

When I take him back to his roots, to the days when music became his life, we spend most of the time talking about Mary Regan (known as Ma Regan), who ran a circuit of venues in the West Midlands. Originally from Ireland, Mary and her husband Joe had arrived in the area before the war and opened tea shops in the Birmingham area. They then began acquiring dance halls, including a former snooker hall in King's Heath (which they named the Ritz) and two venues both called the Plaza – one in Handsworth (in the old Rookery Picture House cinema) and one in a cinema on Halesowen Road in the centre of Old Hill. Old Hill is to the west of Birmingham and to the south of Wolverhampton, deep in that area of the West Midlands known as the Black Country. The Regans opened the Old Hill Plaza as a live music venue in 1962.

I'd heard some of the story behind the Cavern and the rise of the Beatles, and the importance of the 'Crawdaddy' in the case of the Rolling Stones, but I hadn't heard Ma Regan's name. The more Noddy told me, the more I appreciated her role in the first half of the 1960s, a very fertile period for British music, and an era when teenage consumers were becoming a major cultural and economic force; that rising demand for record players, personal radios, fashions, nights out.

In this chapter we'll trace the electrifying effect of the rise of the Beatles, the role of venues like Ma Regan's and the Club A Go Go in Newcastle, the proliferation of beat groups, and also those inspired by a deeper interest in rhythm & blues like the Rolling Stones and the Animals. And we'll examine the effect of all this activity beyond Britain, and beyond music.

Noddy talks about some of the other people for whom Ma Regan's venues were a launchpad for later success, people who went on to be in the Move, the Electric Light Orchestra, the Moody Blues, Black Sabbath, Emerson, Lake and Palmer, and Led Zeppelin. It turns out Robert Plant even had a spell DJing at one of Ma Regan's venues – the Plaza in Old Hill. And the Plaza in Old Hill was where he met John Bonham.

The Black Country in the early 1960s was an area of high employment; local factories were busy and always recruiting apprentices. One such place was Birmingham Sound Reproducers, whose headquarters were at the Monarch Works in Powke Lane, Old Hill, half a mile from the Plaza. BSR had 2,500 employees making budget amplification equipment, turntables and component parts for other companies to use in their products, including the famous mega-selling Dansette record player.

As evident from the flappers and the trad-jazzers, for example, it's something of a misrepresentation to suggest that before the 1960s the young weren't identifiable or economically active, with their own music, venues and fashions. Conflict between the generations is age-old. However, what can be generally agreed is that the period between the early 1950s and the middle of the 1960s witnessed a shift in power in that conflict, partly through weight of numbers, and partly because the booming Western economies created full employment and put money in the pockets of teenagers.

The youth of the early 1960s were hungry for entertainment, and for something other than the music their parents liked. Around the country teenagers, mostly lads, hundreds in every city, dozens in every town, were forming bands. They'd been energised by rock & roll and some, though not all, had been through a skiffle phase, but that had lost its novelty factor. Former skiffle bands like the Quarry Men had dropped the washboard and banjo and recruited a drummer. Many of the groups were competent, almost all were derivative, but such was the demand even those who were never going to breach the charts could fill their diaries with live appearances.

In our current era there's been something of a resurgence in live music, but nothing compares to the first half of the 1960s. Britain's first and most successful rock generation performed relentlessly, on the road and at their key residencies; the Beatles at the Cavern, the Rolling Stones at the Crawdaddy and the Animals at the Club A Go Go. At their residency, or on tour, it wasn't unusual for bands to play two or more engagements per evening, with a matinee thrown in for good measure. Bands would start by playing clubs, pub and hotel function rooms, cricket clubs and so on, and then perhaps move up to gigs in ballrooms and theatres. Travelling into the city centre wasn't always possible or desirable; people tended to be happy to work and play close to home, family members lived in your locality, you worked close to home – perhaps in the local factory – and you frequented one of the local pubs. Down the road was a cinema and a dance hall.

In among this sense of tight-knit communities, tiny scenes developed based in town or neighbourhood venues, anywhere a mile from a factory or a workshop or warehouse, anywhere with a few streets. Imagine being sixteen or seventeen and after work grabbing something to eat and then walking half a mile to the Old Hill Plaza and queuing with 400 other lucky ticket holders and seeing 'Little' Stevie Wonder, the Who, the Beatles, the Rolling

Stones. Going somewhere local that could bring life to your world and your world to life.

In addition, for the young would-be musicians, the foundations for dozens of successful careers in music were laid in these neighbourhood venues. It's imperative for a band to have somewhere they can perform, somewhere their friends can get a bus to. It gives them a chance to develop a sound and build an audience. If you were a young lad living in Stourbridge, Dudley or Walsall, and you had the talent and worked your backside off, then you might get a break – the Plaza Old Hill might be a launchpad.

Of all the musicians Noddy worked with or bumped into on the Ma Regan circuit, only a small minority made a career from music, but the apprenticeship was invaluable; those that made it went far, and in all directions. Noddy was telling me about all the bands he was in before Slade, in and around Walsall and the Black Country. The young Neville Holder had enjoyed a musical upbringing – his mother played the violin and his father, a window-cleaner, liked to sing in local pubs – and as a teenager played in bands including the Phantoms, the Memphis Cutouts and Steve Brett & the Mavericks. He'd been in several bands before he took lead vocals; initially he was a guitarist. The bass player in an early line-up of Steve Brett & the Mavericks was Dave Holland, who ended up with a hugely successful jazz career, playing alongside Stan Getz and Chick Corea and appearing on Miles Davis's *Bitches Brew* album.

Before Dave Hill and Don Powell joined Noddy in Slade, they were part of the Vendors, who were booked regularly by Ma Regan, and then they formed the 'N Betweens and got themselves a residency playing every Monday evening at the Old Hill Plaza. Even when Slade got together, their first gigs were many, various and tiny, but from the start always showbiz and always value for money. They had a regular gig in a community centre in Walsall on Sunday nights that they dubbed 'The Sunday Service', and Noddy would go onstage dressed as a vicar. He tries to remember the name of the venue (he thinks it was Aldridge Community Centre), but even many of the ones he can remember have long since disappeared. It was a long time ago and Old Hill seems a long way away. We're ordering off a menu at the Grill on New York Street in Manchester and Noddy decides he might have ostrich. The young waiter asks how he'd like it. 'Medium,' says Noddy. He looks at me and says, 'I guess that's how you have ostrich, isn't it?'

It's worth reminding ourselves that wherever British rock music ends up – multimillionaires with multiple homes (Paul McCartney with $800m stashed away and Mick Jagger $305m), gigs for royal jubilees, award ceremonies, champagne, sponsors' logos, a table at the Brits, or the singer from Slade ordering ostrich in a relatively fancy Manchester restaurant – it was founded on a network of mildewed venues, beat clubs, roughly furnished function rooms, grim basements and grotty cellars.

Few were grottier than the Cavern, Mathew Street, Liverpool. Paul McCartney's father offered a ton of encouragement to his son, but he was never a fan of the Cavern. 'You should be paid danger money to go down there,' he told Paul.

The Beatles played the Cavern 292 times; the first occasion was in February 1961, well over three years after the Quarry Men's debut. By the time of their last show at the venue, in August 1963, they were pop stars. The Cavern is where they honed their talent and built a fan base. Gerry Marsden, of Gerry and the Pacemakers, said the place 'stank of disinfectant and stale onions and was hot, sweaty and oppressive'. One of the reasons Alan Sytner sold the place was that he baulked at the cost of maintaining it, knowing that the most pressing refurbishment was to improve the 'ventilation system'. Also, he'd run out of money. 'I had terrible advice,' he later said. 'There wasn't anyone telling me not to buy another sports car or go to Paris.'

When Sytner sold the club in 1959 there was no sense that the history of the Beatles and the Cavern would be so entwined. Up to the end of 1961, in fact, the band was most closely associated with the Casbah – a coffee bar and music venue run along similar lines to the Jacaranda but out of the city centre, spread through several basement rooms in a large Victorian house in West Derby. The Quarry Men featured on the Casbah's opening-night bill on 29 August 1959, and Paul McCartney and John Lennon got involved setting up the venue for its opening, painting walls and ceilings to brighten up the basement. The group also had a brief Saturday residency, playing for £3 a night. Four decades later, looking back, McCartney wanted credit to go the Casbah. 'People know about the Cavern, but the Casbah was the place where all that started. We looked upon it as our personal club.'

The Casbah was founded and run by Mona Best as a venue for local music-loving teenagers (her son, Pete, was the drummer in a group called the Blackjacks). She knocked down dividing walls, rigged up a Dansette and showcased live music. There were soft drinks and coffee available. In addition to the Quarry Men, the Blackjacks also performed there regularly, as did Cass & the Cassanovas (who later became the Big Three).

As with so many important venues, the Casbah developed as somewhere to hang out. It wasn't just about the music or the live events, it was a space that all kinds of budding artists and interesting young folk gravitated towards, felt at home and met up in, plotted and planned. It was there that John Lennon and Paul McCartney persuaded Stuart Sutcliffe to play bass in the group one evening. Sutcliffe couldn't play bass but the logic was irresistible: he'd won £65 in an art competition so he could afford to buy one, he looked cool, and he was John's best friend. 'We were sitting with a cup of cappuccino trying to persuade Stuart to get this bass,' McCartney later recalled. 'He said it was a painting prize and he was supposed to buy canvases with the money and anyway he couldn't play. We said we'd teach him and it was at the Casbah that we actually talked him into it.'

During the first months of the Casbah, the Quarry Men

metamorphosed into the Silver Beatles, and Allan Williams from the Jacaranda set them up with gigs in Hamburg. Pete Best, perfectly placed, became the band's new drummer. The fledgling Beatles had their first extended stay in Hamburg in the second half of 1960 with residencies at the Indra and the Kaiserkeller. While there, they worked hard and played hard on a diet of youthful enthusiasm and Preludin, a legal amphetamine they were able to buy at the chemist.

One of the non-chemical factors that gave them energy and motivation, as with other groups who loved rock & roll and started out playing skiffle, was their disdain for the light entertainment passing for youth culture in Britain at the time. On returning from their first visit to Hamburg, they celebrated with a pre-Christmas gig at the Casbah, and a hand-drawn poster was produced advertising the 'fabulous' Beatles, helpfully describing them as a 'rock combo'. Another phrase which was just coming in vogue and might have been used by Mona Best was 'Big Beat', then being applied to post-skiffle bands like the Beatles, who had lost their banjos and gained a drummer – home-grown bands, usually four lads with a grounding in rock & roll who wanted to avoid the smoothed-out crooner stylings of Marty Wilde, Adam Faith and friends. It was this strong beat their music carried which inspired the origin of the description 'Big Beat' – later shortened to 'beat' – rather than any connection with beatniks or beat poetry. It might be Johnny Burnette-style rockabilly, Chuck Berry covers, or versions of pop hits, but what was always of paramount importance was that the 'beat groups' played music you could dance to.

If there's one man responsible for the close connection between the Beatles and the Cavern it's not Alan Sytner, it's Bob Wooler, who'd been working alongside Allan Williams in various ventures. Williams opened the Top Ten Club on Soho Street, promising lots of work to Wooler, but the venue was burned down after just six days so he went back to hanging around the Jacaranda, and that's where he met the Beatles. He'd not heard them play but promised to do what he could to get them some gigs, the first with promoter Brian Kelly at Litherland Town Hall. Wooler later recalled doing the deal with Kelly. 'I rang him up from the Jacaranda. I asked for eight pounds for them. Kelly offered four; we settled on six.'

Wooler attended the Litherland show, and instantly appreciated the Beatles weren't as flimsy as the other bands on the local circuit. It was their first major gig outside the in-crowd coffee bars of Liverpool and the band made a real impact, dressed differently from all the other groups, head-to-toe in black, including leather jackets. The local girls thought they might be German, having heard the group had just arrived from Hamburg. It's this Litherland Town Hall gig that John Lennon later identified as a breakthrough moment. 'We stood there being cheered for the first time. This was when we began to think that we were good,' he later said. 'It was only back in Liverpool that we realised the difference and saw what had happened to us while everyone else was playing Cliff Richard shit. Mind you, seventy per cent of the audience thought we were German, but we didn't care about that. Even in Liverpool, people didn't know we were from Liverpool. They thought we were from Hamburg. They said, "Christ, they speak good English!" which we did, of course, being English.'

The Cavern's new owner, Ray McFall, was building a new audience. Not jazz, not skiffle, not rock & roll – beat groups. At the Cavern on 25 May 1960 the first evening advertised as a 'Beat Night' was held, and the bill that evening included Rory Storm & the Hurricanes (their line-up included drummer Ringo Starr). By the end of that year Beat Nights and lunchtime sessions were a fixture at the club, and McFall had recruited Bob Wooler to organise the shows and act as the club's disc jockey and compere. It wasn't long before the Beatles were installed as a resident band.

Another ingredient in the rise of the Beatles was their manager,

Brian Epstein. Alerted to their rising reputation by Bill Harry, the man behind the magazine *Merseybeat*, Epstein first set foot in the Cavern on 9 November 1961 to see the Beatles perform. He considered them a bit scruffy. Being dressed in black could be an obstacle to commercial success, he decided, so he facilitated a change that saw them ditch the leather jackets and become lovable mop-tops.

Brian Epstein was ambitious, astute and happy for his band to sacrifice a bit of credibility in order to reach the public eye. If you had a wholesome image then you pleased crowds, promoters and venues and you earned cash. That's just how things were. Noddy recalls 1964 and his time in the Memphis Cutouts, all clean-cut, with a big repertoire of snappy cover versions and a wardrobe of matching suits. The Memphis Cutouts got gigs, including plenty of well-paid wedding engagements, and being attired in matching royal-blue coats with black velvet trimmings was a definite plus point. When one of the other Cutouts, 'Bern' Burnell, had some of his gear stolen backstage at Wolverhampton Civic Hall, losing the coat was traumatic. Bern was bereft, telling the local paper, 'I don't mind somebody hiding it as a joke, but now it's past that. I need it for the engagements we've got lined up and I can't get another in time.'

With Epstein installed as the Beatles' manager, in addition to adjustments to the band's wardrobe renewed attempts were made to find them gigs. The right kind of gigs, too; not just to earn some sort of wage, but to boost their public profile and, when the time came, to help sell records. Some of their shows, going back to when they were the Silver Beatles, were far from profile-building. In May 1960 they'd gone up to Scotland on a short tour, making their Scottish debut at the town hall in Alloa, but only as the backing band for Johnny Gentle. The gigs had been organised by impresario Larry Parnes, and also featured Alex Harvey and His Big Beat Band.

At a residency like the one the Beatles had at the Cavern, you could hope to count on the support of friends, friends of friends, regulars and locals, and then you'd look to take the next step: to ballrooms and theatres and to move beyond the locality. This wasn't always possible, if there was no demand and no national record release. But Brian Epstein promised the Beatles a record deal and more national gigs. He sent them to play all over the country, often to small or unimpressed crowds. An historic building dating back to the 1830s, the Subscription Rooms were run by Stroud Urban District Council, who booked the Beatles to play there on 31 March 1962. It was so bad it was memorable. 'Hardly anyone showed up for a start, which was not wonderful,' Paul McCartney later said of the event. 'A group of teddy boys started throwing coins and we ended up picking them up.'

A few months later the Beatles recruited a new drummer, Ringo Starr, from Rory Storm & the Hurricanes. The classic John, Paul, George and Ringo line-up played their first show together on 18 August 1962 at the Hulme Hall in Port Sunlight. Audiences were growing; 500 people attended. Port Sunlight on the Wirral peninsula is a small town built by Lever Brothers to accommodate workers in its soap factory, and is relatively easily accessible from Liverpool. However, the band's fanbase was still localised, and when their single 'Love Me Do' was released in early October 1962 it crawled up the charts to Number 17 in the hit parade.

On 11 January 1963 the Beatles journeyed to the Black Country, after a lunchtime set at the Cavern, having been booked for two gigs in one evening; both shows were presented by Mary Regan. Once Ma Regan had established a small circuit of venues, she'd book bands to play two, sometimes three, of them on the same night. Local bands or touring bands, she worked them all hard. When the Beatles were booked at the Old Hill Plaza, they'd been scheduled to also appear at the Ritz in King's Heath, but January 1963 was in the middle of the coldest winter for decades and the band were unable to make the eleven-mile journey across

Birmingham to the venue so the gig was rescheduled for 15 February. (That same week saw them at the Azena Ballroom, Sheffield, at a gig organised by a young Sheffield lad, Peter Stringfellow. Stringfellow had just served a short prison sentence for selling stolen carpets and was at the beginning of his career as a successful nightclub promoter and owner.)

The Old Hill Plaza's role in music history is well hidden. It's safe to say that, in comparison to Liverpool, Old Hill's tourist infrastructure is somewhat underdeveloped. The glitterati generally give this part of the Black Country a swerve. In 1963 Old Hill was a world away from the centre of any kind of media interest, aside maybe from the local evening paper, the *Express & Star*.

The Black Country was hard at work helping to create foundations for the country's wealth, just as it had been for a hundred years or more. The area's engineering traditions, all banging noise and hard graft, consisted of dozens of small factories, forges and workshops making chains, hooks, bolts, pressings and specialist items of metalwork. Factory owners could make a few bob making sheet metal, iron chains and nails, and many of the local musicians worked in the industry, including a young man called Tony Iommi, the guitarist with the Rockin' Chevrolets, a band you'd see dressed in matching red lamé suits and playing regularly on the Ma Regan circuit.

At first glance, the Black Country probably looked very much like a man's world, but Ma Regan reigned in an area where female entrepreneurs were not unknown among all this metal-bashing. In the mid-nineteenth century, Eliza Tinsley founded one of the most lucrative factories in Britain in the area, employing around 4,000 people making nails, rivets, chains and anchors. It's also worth pointing out that in this part of the world – as in other working-class areas of the country – in most households the wives controlled the purse strings. They'd be given any pay packets earned in the family and distribute pocket money to the men. Hard-working and trusted, Ma Regan took an active part in the club, picking the bands and doing the deals. Husband Joe was a more than competent compere and would dress in an evening suit with a black bow tie and make sure the bands got on and off the stage at the set times and introduce them from the stage in his lilting Irish accent.

For bands operating locally they considered it a big step if they could impress Ma Regan. She'd hold auditions and pick only the best bands. It wasn't just a chance to play with a band like the Beatles, or to be part of a big Saturday night event; even a spot on a Monday night was coveted, if you could oust the 'N Betweens. Every year there was a Big Beat Contest at the Wolverhampton Gaumont and the grand prize for winning was an audition with Ma Regan.

Ma Regan didn't forget the inability of the Beatles to complete January's engagements exactly as agreed upon, though, and she reminded Brian Epstein a few times that the band now owed her a favour. In the first six months of 1963 the Beatles had released two more top-selling singles and a debut album, and Epstein – probably quite rightly – thought his band had outgrown the likes of Ma Regan. Nevertheless, she called in the favour and on 5 July 1963 the Beatles travelled down from Liverpool to play the Old Hill Plaza again. Also on the bill that evening were two local beat groups, Dane Tempest & the Atoms (winners of a Big Beat contest) and Denny Laine & the Diplomats.

All these groups, most live groups in fact, were there to move the crowd. If you visited the Old Hill Plaza to see the Beatles you expected to dance. You wouldn't be there to stand in ranks or politely clap; groups performed, audiences danced. The Beatles zinged through their set, playing numbers like 'Twist and Shout' and 'Long Tall Sally' with both prowess and passion. But they also played their own compositions, including 'Please Please Me', 'Love Me Do' and 'I Saw Her Standing There'.

Regulars at the Plaza Old Hill continued to enjoy the fruits of Ma Regan's work. A month after the Beatles had played there, the headliners were the Rolling Stones. The gig on 10 August was not only the first visit by the Stones to the Midlands, it was their first headline show outside the Home Counties. As we saw with the Beatles, local venues and a local following were a launchpad. And the very early days of the Stones were focused in the southeast of England.

For a small contingent of music lovers in the Southeast, although Merseybeat was an improvement on Marty Wilde and Adam Faith, it was still a bit clean-cut, and they had started digging deeper, into the roots of rock & roll, into black rhythm & blues, tuning in to the American Forces Network and finding in the likes of John Lee Hooker music that was raw and radical. One of their favourite venues was a hotel ballroom on Eel Pie Island where Arthur Chisnall ran nights, originally featuring the likes of George Melly and Ken Colyer, then moving into r&b, with Long John Baldry, John Mayall and others.

This crew of young blues aficionados began to frequent the Ealing Jazz Club, situated below a tea shop across the road from Ealing Broadway station, with an entrance down narrow steps into an alley running between the tea shop and a jeweller's. The Jazz Club had been in existence since January 1959 but began to embrace blues in 1962 when Cyril Davies and Alexis Korner of Blues Incorporated moved on from the London Blues and Barrelhouse Club and set up a regular 'Rhythm and Blues Night'.

It's always said there was something a little bit middle class and nerdy about this crew. But they were absolute enthusiasts, more than a little obsessed with the work of Muddy Waters, Buddy Guy, John Lee Hooker and others. Eric Clapton was among them. For John Mayall, who later recruited Clapton to the Bluesbreakers, those nights at Ealing Jazz Club were inspiring. 'Ealing is obviously the foundation and starting point of everything.'

Chris Dreja, a founder member of the Yardbirds, later recalled:

'At this stage, it was a very elite clique, a bunch of like-minded, quasi-art-school types. There were only a handful of people – us, the Rolling Stones, a few others. We'd meet up in the cloakroom of the art school, or some damp flat in Ealing, with an import record that someone had found.'

It was at the Ealing Jazz Club on 7 April 1962 that Mick Jagger and Keith Richards met Brian Jones when Jones was performing with Cyril Davies and Alexis Korner's Blues Incorporated. They soon had a group up and running – Jagger, Richards and Jones, plus Ian Stewart and Dick Taylor – calling themselves the Rollin' Stones (lifting their name from a Muddy Waters song).

By September 1962 the Rollin' Stones had a weekly residency at Ealing Jazz Club, although, like every young act, their line-up was subject to change. In December that year bassist Bill Wyman joined, followed in January 1963 by drummer Charlie Watts. The Stones at this time were ambitious, but less for commercial success than to be able to demonstrate their purist credentials. Bill observed: 'We weren't a pop band, we just got together and played the blues music we liked to play. And if we could play in front of a few people who liked it, well, that was the ultimate at that time.'

The Stones were building a reasonable following via the Marquee, Ealing Jazz Club, Eel Pie Island Hotel and their numerous other London and Surrey club gigs. Interest in rhythm & blues spread beyond a handful of aficionados and a number of industry insiders were championing the Stones, including Giorgio Gomelsky from the Piccadilly Jazz Club. He'd be key to getting them a gig that established them at the forefront of the new wave: at a function room in a pub next to the River Thames, the Station Hotel, Richmond. Gomelsky had started to put live music on at the Station Hotel, which, for his sessions there, he'd renamed the Crawdaddy, taking the name from a Bo Diddley song. One group that had been playing at the Crawdaddy regularly was the Dave Hunt R&B Band, which briefly featured Ray Davies, who later formed the Kinks.

Gomelsky gave the Rollin' Stones a first engagement at the Crawdaddy one snowy night, 24 February 1963, on the strength of which they secured a residency. It's said that the second or third time they played the audience was a hundred, which the band considered amazing (Bill Wyman says that only six people turned up to one of their 1963 shows at Ealing Jazz Club).

At the Crawdaddy the Stones connected not just with a hip crowd, but a hip crowd mad with excitement. Their response to the Stones was to dance, shout and leap about; within two months they were swinging off the rafters. Brian Jones was the band's organiser and prime mover in the early days although, once the Crawdaddy took off, Gomelsky became the band's de facto manager. He loved the band's attitude: 'They were playing with guts and conviction. They were playing blues, but they weren't an academic blues band. The Rolling Stones were more like a rebellion. At the Crawdaddy people just went beserk.'

Some of the excitement at the venue was generated by its out-of-the-way location and the sense of a secret scene that engendered. Most Sundays through the summer the Stones played a late-afternoon session at Ken Colyer's club at Studio 51, and then went on to the Station Hotel for their Crawdaddy engagement. Making a success of both led to fees of £25 at Colyer's and £50 at the Crawdaddy.

The impact of the Beatles and the Stones wasn't instant, but then you'd go out one week and you'd see a few boys wearing winklepickers instead of brothel-creepers, ditching turn-ups and favouring drainpipes, and the white girls dressing like they were the Shirelles. And all the while Matt Monro thought he was going to be riding high in the hit parade for the foreseeable future. The week the Stones started at the Crawdaddy, top of the charts was Frank Ifield with Norrie Paramor & His Orchestra with 'The Wayward Wind', but eight weeks later the Beatles had their first Number One, 'From Me to You'.

It was at the Crawdaddy that the Beatles, invited by Gomelsky,

saw the Rolling Stones perform for the first time one Sunday in
April 1963. The Fab Four arrived looking every inch the pop
stars, dressed in long suede coats and matching hats which they'd
picked up on their latest Hamburg trip. The visit triggered a
reciprocal invitation. A few days later the Beatles were at the
Royal Albert Hall, their first appearance there, performing for the
BBC Light Programme 'Swingin' Sound '63', and they invited
the Stones to see the show.

As we shall see, for Paul McCartney the 'Swingin' Sound'
event was notable for non-music reasons. For the Stones, on the
other hand, the Beatles made many and various impressions upon
them. Keith liked the Beatles because he was interested in their
chord sequences. For Mick and Brian, sat on the front row, witnessing the show and with memories of those suede coats still
vivid, their desire to become pop stars on a par with the Beatles
was cemented.

Back at their residency at the Crawdaddy, a long way from the
showbiz shenanigans onstage and backstage at the Albert Hall, the
audience the Stones had built up was growing. Word reached
Andrew Loog Oldham who, after Ronnie Scott's, had set himself
up as a PR consultant (Brian Epstein took him on to work on
spreading the word about the Beatles). In April 1963 Andrew
went to see the Stones at the Crawdaddy. Andrew still has strong
memories of his visit to the Station Hotel. He'd been told he'd
find the entrance to the concert room at the back of the hotel, so
he made his way along a path, down an alley. On his right was the
Station Hotel, on his left the railway. Halfway down the pathway
he had to manoeuvre past a young couple in the midst of some
sort of argument, an attractive couple, he thought, the man 'thin
and waistless', in Andrew's words, the woman 'with brown hair
and flashing eyes'. Later he realised he'd chanced upon Mick
Jagger and Chrissie Shrimpton. He thinks they were having their
first fight, on their first date.

Andrew tells me that he remembers the Crawdaddy being

'hokey', and a long way from the venues, the well-cut clothes and the music he liked – not just a long way from Zoot Sims and Thelonious Monk but even the pop music he liked. 'I liked Leiber and Stoller, strings, the Drifters, that kind of r&b. I was not a big fan of the kind of r&b the Stones were playing. It was just one step away from skiffle, there was no way I could judge it. I had no criteria. But it was hokey, man. Three hundred middle-class students seizing something just to be different. Remember those student sweaters? Those Sixties films that came later with Hywel Bennett; that's what the audience looked like.'

You saw something though?

'I saw everything.'

Andrew insisted they should drop the apostrophe and name themselves the Rolling Stones. He also took it upon himself to remove Stewart from the band, reasoning that he was 'too normal' and that six was too many for a band in any case. With Andrew Loog Oldham hustling on their behalf, things started to move quickly. They secured a deal with Decca Records and, on 7 June 1963, in the middle of a run of gigs at the Scene, their debut single was released – a cover of Chuck Berry's 'Come On'. However, he'd followed Epstein's lead and, in order to help sell his band to the mainstream, he'd dressed them in a clean-cut style with matching jackets for their first TV appearance, on *Thank Your Lucky Stars*. Then he had a change of heart, put the matching jackets back in the wardrobe, and encouraged them to go back to their natural, casual, unkempt image, which he reckoned would make them distinctive and bring them attention.

On the back of the single they secured a gig at the Outlook Club in Middlesbrough on 13 July, sharing the billing with the Hollies, soon followed by that first headline show out of the Home Counties, on 10 August, booked by Ma Regan. As ever, Ma Regan had a couple of shows lined up for them at the Plaza Handsworth and at the Plaza Old Hill supported by the Redcaps.

Noddy Holder remembers the Redcaps as one of the best

bands on the local circuit, and they threw everything at the gig, sporting burgundy caps, burgundy suits and black ties, but that evening the Stones made them look sartorially and, by implication, culturally redundant.

Old Hill Plaza that evening was packed. The stage revolved with the Redcaps playing the last few bars of their final number and revealed a solitary drum kit. The Stones took to the stage one by one and delivered a stunning performance; aside from their energy and the confidence they'd gained from having made such a success of the Crawdaddy, the audience hadn't seen a group sporting long hair before. As local music fan Brian Hoggetts, who was at the Old Hill Plaza, recalls, 'We were mesmerised by it all – Bill Wyman playing the guitar vertical, Brian Jones never smiled. He just stood in one place all night. Charlie Watts bashing it out with a vacant look, with Jagger and Richards covering just about every part of the small stage. The end of the gig and the stage rotates with them playing out.'

On 11 May 1964, wishing to have lunch where they were staying, the Grand Hotel in Bristol, the Rolling Stones were refused a table because they weren't wearing jackets and ties. The press had a field day, the *Daily Express* carrying the story with the headline, 'The Rolling Stones gather no lunch'. But this kind of publicity was welcomed, even stoked, by Andrew Loog Oldham. It was all helping to define his group; unlike the Beatles, who were sold as four decent, lovable northern lads in suits, the Rolling Stones were the bad boys of pop. Oldham encouraged headlines such as the infamous 'Would You Let Your Daughter Marry A Rolling Stone?'

Although attention was often drawn to the difference between the image of the Stones and that of the Beatles – not least by Stones fans looking for street credibility – in private there was very little sign of a personal divide between the bands. Lennon and McCartney gifted one of their songs to the Stones, 'I Wanna Be Your Man', which became their second single. In the autumn of 1963 the Stones were off playing bigger shows around Britain in bigger venues, with their first headlining tour in January 1964, with support from the Ronettes.

By the beginning of 1964 things were beginning to take off for a third great British rock band, the Animals. Not only had they built a strong following in Newcastle but also a growing reputation in London, where they were rated by Alexis Korner and Graham Bond. Like other members of Newcastle's music in-crowd, the Animals frequented the Club A Go Go situated on the top floor in a building on Percy Street in Newcastle city centre, above a café used by Newcastle Corporation bus crews. Open by the end of 1962, the Club A Go Go was originally conceived as part casino, part live venue. It was owned by Mike Jeffery, who owned the Downbeat, and local businessman Ray Grehan, who was a sales manager at a company called Automaticket. When I meet up in Newcastle with Ronnie Barker of the local band the Junco Partners, he recalls the fall and rise of the venues: 'The Downbeat was on its last legs, and Club A Go Go took over.'

Arriving at the Club A Go Go, when you got up the stairs you had the choice of two rooms. One was the 'Jazz Lounge', which was licensed to sell alcohol and where gambling took place (roulette and chemin de fer). The other room was the 'Young Set', which was unlicensed and thus the place you'd find the switched-on, well-dressed sixth-formers and other local under-eighteens. The advantage of having two rooms was that bands could be asked to play two sets. On Saturdays the Jazz Lounge was open from 8 p.m. till 4 a.m.

Bryan Ferry had frequented the New Orleans Jazz Club and the Downbeat and soon graduated to the Club A Go Go. He remembers Myer Thomas who managed the club – a 'Sidney Greenstreet figure, a big, big man in a double-breasted suit' is how Ferry described him to writer Michael Bracewell. The Club A

Go Go attracted hot shots, said Ferry. 'Some quite hard men used to go there – like gangsters; dressed in mohair suits, with beautiful girls – the best-looking girls in Newcastle, quite tarty. It was really exciting – it felt really "it".'

In the first months Tony Henderson, who favoured jazz with Latin stylings, was resident in the Jazz Lounge. But within the first year, beat groups were booked, and blues artists like John Lee Hooker and young British rhythm & blues groups like the Graham Bond Organisation. The Animals became the resident attraction, playing sets in both rooms often three or four times a week. When they left for London, the Junco Partners took over as residents, playing for five guineas a night, and later there would be DJs too, including Joe Robertson. Ronnie Barker from the Junco Partners mentions him. 'He's a millionaire, very well known on the Newcastle scene. He was said to be a bit of a rogue.'

Weren't there some court cases, and he ended up living abroad? 'Aye, let's call him an "entrepreneur".'

The DJs would play from the stage, says Ronnie. 'They'd play a few records, it wasn't a big stage, so they were pushed over to the side; nothing like a DJ now, star of the bloody show! It was no big deal, it was just between the live music and sometimes a compere would get up and introduce the bands, old Myer might get up, usually there wasn't a big deal about it, you got up and started.'

Myer Thomas would be around to pay the bands at the end of the night. Cash, always. 'These places were run ad hoc,' says Ronnie. 'I doubt they'd pay much tax or anything, to be honest. Myer had a little office upstairs, on the same level as the club. He'd be sitting in there and he used to be drinking or something and at the end of the night he was incoherent. That's what I remember as a young guy: old Myer incoherent, counting out the five guineas.'

The standard practice in that era was when an American musician toured they'd have a group of local musicians backing them drawn from the area around each venue, usually the club's resident band. So a drummer like John Steel, who played in the Animals, would also when the time came play alongside Americans and other jazz stars like Tubby Hayes or Mike Carr, and maybe the next week he'd be backing bluesmen like John Lee Hooker and Sonny Boy Williamson.

Jazz and blues were the strengths of the Club A Go Go, and the Young Set in particular began to attract a lot of mods. In 1963 there were a number of venues – among them the Scene, the Marquee and Manchester's Twisted Wheel – which had no alcohol licence but attracted young fans of authentic blues and soul, many of them happy to eschew booze in favour of pills. As we've already seen with the Beatles in Hamburg, the mods weren't the exclusive users of amphetamines – it was widespread. The Young Set, though, didn't host all-nighters; venues that did tended to attract more pills.

A few weeks after playing alongside Sonny Boy Williamson on New Year's Eve 1963, the Animals took a decision to move from Newcastle to London, linking up with Giorgio Gomelsky and taking advantage of the industry figures who were championing their music. They'd not long left Newcastle when Don Arden offered them a support slot on a Chuck Berry tour. They took some time out in Newcastle and returned to the Club A Go Go to rehearse the set and refresh it with some new material. They decided to find a number with attitude but something of a counterpoint to the pilled-up energy of a lot of their repertoire; something slower, moodier. On tour, the Animals were getting a great reaction to 'House of the Rising Sun'. Eric Burdon later said, 'People were leaving the theatre singing it. We could hear them through the dressing-room window.'

So the Animals went straight down to London and recorded most of an LP, including 'The House of the Rising Sun', in about an hour and a half. They tried to capture it as they played it live, with as few takes as possible, not over-polish it, as guitarist Hilton

Valentine later recalled. 'The dynamics of the song was what the Animals used to do when we played – start off with a certain pace, move it up a few notches, really drive it – and then drop it right back down. And then build back to a crescendo at the end. I remember thinking, "This is going to be a Number One record".'

It's noticeable that the live experience was the primary experience, and the way the Animals developed and then recorded 'The House of the Rising Sun' wasn't out of the ordinary at that time. In blues, in jazz, in r&b, songs had their life onstage, and the aim of the studio recording was to capture this moment, this live, organic crackle. In later eras the reverse was often true: bands would work for weeks, years even, in the studio, devising and recording the songs, and then go out and tour the album to audiences expecting to hear the songs played as recorded.

The mini boom in rhythm & blues that could be traced back to those nights at Ealing Jazz Club and heard in the work of bands like the Stones, the Yardbirds and the Animals, also had a foothold in Belfast, at a mission for seamen (and before that, a Royal Irish Constabulary police station), which had been transformed into a new rhythm & blues venue called Club Rado – it would become better known as the Maritime Hotel. One of the prime movers behind the founding of Club Rado was Van Morrison, who'd just left a band called the Golden Eagles and was looking to make a fresh start in a new r&b-oriented group, Them. Them became one of the resident bands at the Maritime, all the while developing their sound, working on songs including the future classic 'Gloria'. The A&R man from Decca Records, Dick Rowe, who passed on the Beatles but signed the Rolling Stones, went to Belfast to see Them at the Maritime and recruited the band to his label.

Although the live scene in Northern Ireland was dominated by showbands – six- or seven-piece bands playing a mix of rock & roll and country & western standards, and cover versions of chart hits – there were also, by the time Them were signed, dozens of r&b and beat groups. There were gigs to be had at the Maritime, as well as other Belfast venues (including Sammy Houston's Jazz Club on Victoria Street). Nine miles away, in Lisburn, a venue called the Top Hat hosted live shows by the likes of Little Richard, Sandie Shaw, Roy Orbison and Brenda Lee.

There was a boom in the number of groups in Britain in the first years of the 1960s, but there was never enough room for more than a few to break into the big time. Sometimes, despite hard work and several years on the Ma Regan circuit, a break never came. Denny Laine & the Diplomats struggled to get a recording contract, which led to Denny leaving the band. In May 1964 he became the guitarist and vocalist of the newly founded Moody Blues. Within a year the group had a Number One hit – a version of the Bessie Banks single 'Go Now' – and were signed to Brian Epstein's management company. They were the first band of that era from the West Midlands to hit the big time.

By the middle of 1965 the young Robert Plant was being seen around the Plaza and elsewhere. He was lead vocalist in various bands, including the Crawling King Snakes. At one of their last appearances at the Plaza Ballroom in Old Hill Plant was approached by John Bonham, drummer in a band called Way of Life. Bonham had some advice for Plant: he announced that his band would benefit from having a drummer like him. It was the first conversation the two had.

Unbeknown to Bonham, though, Robert Plant was about to leave the Crawling King Snakes and join Listen, after another separate encounter at the Old Hill Plaza. A music fan deep into the scene, Plant on occasions would fill in with some DJing there. One Monday night in 1965 he'd been playing 'Land of a Thousand Dances' by Cannibal & the Headhunters and various Motown and Stax singles and got talking to Listen, who were the resident Monday night band, the 'N Betweens having moved on. During Listen's performance that evening, Plant asked if he could come up and sing, and the band's John Crutchley agreed. The arrangement continued. 'We started to look forward to Old Hill on a Monday,' Crutchley later recalled. 'Robert Plant would jump up and do "Everybody Needs Somebody" and "Smokestack Lightning".'

Meanwhile Noddy, who had officially left the Mavericks just before Christmas 1965 and then rehearsed with a couple of other bands, was considering an offer to join the 'N Betweens but needed to find a quick way to keep the cash flowing, so he asked his dad if he could borrow his van and began to roadie for Listen. Listen had just decided the young man from the Plaza should join the band and offered a permanent role to Robert Plant (or 'Planty' as Holder calls him). Noddy recalls: 'Planty was on the same circuit as we were, and when I wasn't gigging I used to roadie for them with my dad's window-cleaning van.'

As predicted by Hilton Valentine, the Animals scored a global hit with their rearranged cover version of 'The House of the Rising Sun'. It reached Number One in the American charts in September 1964, around the same time the Rolling Stones had their first Top Ten hit in the States ('Time Is on My Side'), although both bands were eclipsed by the Beatles, who had six different Number One hits in the USA in 1964. One of the changes ushered in by the Beatles was that they wrote their own songs, and did so, it was generally agreed, to a high standard. William Mann in, of all places, *The Times*, in 1963 lauded Lennon and McCartney as 'outstanding English composers', but what also made a difference was that America was listening to and loving them, and other British bands. We were into the so-called 'British invasion'. Not Paris, not New York; in 1965 the heart of popular culture was wherever the Beatles or the Stones were.

On 27 September 1965 an episode of the American music show *Hullabaloo* was broadcast featuring a live performance by the Animals. Near the end of every episode there was a segment of the show with a special set featuring 'go-go girl' dancers on podiums. This was too good an opportunity to miss, and the band played an existing song, 'Club A Go Go', inspired by their favourite Newcastle nightspot, written by Eric Burdon and released earlier in the year on the B-side of 'Don't Let Me Be Misunderstood'.

'Club A Go Go' is addressed to a girl-about-town whom the singer is dating, knowing she's also in love with the goings-on at the Club A Go Go, where there's a big shot she's carrying on with. He doesn't blame her for hanging out there: it's a place 'full of soul, heart and soul'. Sometimes he gives her money for the picture show, but then he thinks she probably spends it at the Club A Go Go. The song namechecks not just the club and not just John Lee Hooker, the Rolling Stones, Jimmy Reed and Sonny Boy Williamson, but Myer Thomas too. There's a phrase casually thrown in at the beginning of the second verse: 'You take too much though it's bound to get you down,' which over-alert listeners might pick up as a drug reference. When that line was delivered, Eric Burdon, live on *Hullabaloo*, put his finger up to the side of his nostril with a just-perceptible smirk.

We've seen the way that people in Britain have dreamed of music scenes in New York, Paris and Chicago, trying to get a taste of those mythical places in a home-town venue, including Eric Burdon himself at the New Orleans Jazz Club on Melbourne Street. First the Animals had recorded a song about New Orleans and made it their own, and now they were conjuring up a mythology of their own, disseminating a portrait of some thrilling in-crowd hangout in Newcastle upon Tyne that the millions of young Americans watching *Hullabaloo* could only dream of.

In March 1967 the Jimi Hendrix Experience played at Club A Go Go. The band's fee for the evening was £250 and there were two shows – an early evening one to the under-eighteens in the Young Set and one after midnight in the Jazz Lounge. Hendrix's connections with the Go Go are surprisingly strong. In August 1966 the Animals' bass player Chas Chandler was in New York and was told by music fan and model Linda Keith to check out

Jimi Hendrix playing at the Cafe Wha? He was blown away, and brought the singer over to England and became his manager, alongside Club A Go Go owner Mike Jeffery. Chandler – who lasted eighteen months or so before leaving Jeffery as sole manager – later went on to manage and produce Slade.

Noddy and his bandmates benefitted from Chandler's experiences with the Animals and with Hendrix. 'He pushed the idea of each of us having a character, a following – he saw the Beatles, and how that worked for them. He'd seen things from a band's point of view and from the management side.' A little later Chas Chandler's connections helped the band get gigs in America. Even when Slade were a chart act in Britain, touring abroad could be just as hard a slog as playing the pub function rooms with the Memphis Cutouts. 'They couldn't make head nor tail of us in America, especially when we first went out there,' says Noddy.

Back in the Black Country, in the last three or four years of the 1960s it was mostly the Motown and soul crowd who were Joe and Mary Regan's best customers. On 29 January 1966 'Little' Stevie Wonder played at the Old Hill Plaza, and the following years would witness appearances by Edwin Starr, Ben E. King and the Four Tops, as well as the biggest draws on the scene: Geno Washington & the Ram Jam Band. Subsequently you'd have appearances at the Old Hill Plaza by DJ entertainers like Emperor Rosko, or the Black Country equivalent, Barmy Barry (real name Barry Cary), who was a fixture throughout Staffordshire in the late 1960s into the 1970s at venues like Park Hall and the Lafayette (both in Wolverhampton), the Adelphi in West Bromwich, the Old Hill Plaza, and the Golden Torch in Tunstall. This was the era of lads drinking Ansells Mild and Bitter, and the girls Cherry B or Babycham or variations thereof, although some of the wilder women might have the sweet cider and Cherry B combination known as a 'leg-over'.

The Plaza remained the centre of the social scene in the area into the early 1970s. The venue benefitted from the unshakable local demand for somewhere half decent and local where you could get a drink or two, a dance, and turn some heads. I spoke to Billy Bagnall, a former lad-around-town, now in his sixties, who had one particular memory of his days at the Plaza he wanted to share: 'My mate's parents went to Majorca and bought him a jacket, a cream jacket, just a shade darker than cream. With no collar . . . a jacket with no collar. It was too big for him, wasn't it? So he gave it to me, and I when I walked into the Plaza I felt like a film star. Cream! No one could afford cream.'

In 1972 Ma Regan took the decision to close the Old Hill Plaza as a music venue and turn it into a bingo hall. Plaza Bingo suffered a fire in 1990, and the famous revolving stage was destroyed. Joe died in 2004, and Mary died four years later, aged ninety-four. Plaza Bingo then shut, and the building was bought in 2009 by Ashok Kumar and transformed into a banqueting and party venue. The main room, the Platinum Suite, is a favourite venue for Asian weddings. The Plaza in Handsworth has been refurbished and in parts rebuilt and is now a Sikh temple. The Ritz in King's Heath burned down in March 2013.

Old Hill's factories, around which communities congregated and thrived, failed to survive into our current era. The local Birmingham Sound Reproducers company benefitted from the demand for amplification equipment and turntables from album buyers and disco fans in the mid-1970s; in their best ever year, 1977, BSR's factories and tool rooms made parts for an incredible 85 per cent of all the world's turntables (including those for the best-selling Pioneer PL12D). But global economics began to work against them. The pound strengthened against the dollar in 1978, causing exports to America to slump at a time of increased competition from the Far East, and in 1983 their factory site in Old Hill closed. The ironworks Eliza Tinsley founded back in the mid-nineteenth century has also gone; the site, between Cradley Heath and Old Hill, is now a housing estate built by Barratt Homes.

The early 1980s were no kinder to Liverpool. When I first

went there to wander around Mathew Street it was 1981 and Pete Wylie was my guide. He took me to see where the Cavern had been. The original venue closed in 1973, after which construction work on the Merseyrail filled in the cellar. In 1981 the site of the Cavern was a car park, the Beatles were long gone and there was nothing to see.

The version of the Cavern that's open now was built in 1984 on the car park, occupying some of the same site and using some of the original bricks in a design resembling the original. This second version of the Cavern, which closed for a time from 1989, is now still booking live acts in the back room, and providing memorabilia and more photo opportunities for tourists. On the opposite side of Mathew Street there's a wall with bricks naming all the bands that played at the Cavern, from Merseybeat acts like the Big Three and the Beatles through to the Dutch group Focus, who were the last group to play in the original building. One of the acts to have played there was Gary Glitter, back when he was known as Paul Raven. In November 2008, as a result of a campaign in the wake of the singer's conviction for possession of child pornography and his deportation from Cambodia on child sexual abuse charges, the Gary Glitter brick was removed. However, subsequently, a brass plaque was erected adjacent to the brick display explaining that bricks honouring two former Cavern Club performers have been removed. The other missing brick was for another shamed music personality, Jonathan King. It's a bizarre bit of hocus-pocus, this attempt to edit history in order to present a less problematic version for any squeamish visitor, but the addition of a plaque trying to explain the removal of the bricks only serves to draw attention to the shenanigans.

As well as an ersatz version of the Cavern, also on Mathew Street is the site of a club that opened nearly twenty years after the Cavern – Eric's, which was operated by Roger Eagle, Ken Testi and Pete Fulwell. Pete Wylie is part of the Eric's generation; it was through the club that he found friends and a scene and formed the band Wah! Heat. Another graduate of Eric's is Jayne Casey, who went on to gain cult status in the late 1970s and early 1980s in bands like Big in Japan and Pink Military. For both of them, growing up in the late 1970s, Liverpool's Merseybeat past was suffocating; the Beatles cast a shadow under which not much could grow. So much so that Jayne remembers the advice given to her in 1977 by Roger Eagle: 'He told us never ever to listen to them.'

Other bands coming out of Eric's, like Orchestral Manoeuvres in the Dark (their first live performance was at Eric's in October 1978), Echo & the Bunnymen, Teardrop Explodes, Dead or Alive and others, made their mark twenty years after Merseybeat. It was as if the demolition of the Cavern had helped set the new generation free. They were to find their own role models, their own places to hang out, and to make their own culture.

CHAPTER FIVE

Pills, thrills, not keeping music live

Roger Eagle would have an involvement not just in Eric's but also in other significant venues in Liverpool and Manchester. By the end of the 1950s he'd left school, enjoyed the visceral pleasure of hearing rock & roll through a cinema sound system, and bought a motorbike. He'd driven his bike from Oxford down to London several times, visiting venues like Ken Colyer's club on Great Newport Street and Eel Pie. He'd enjoyed trad jazz, but hadn't fallen for skiffle. He'd begun to take a deep interest in music, tuning in to tracks like 'Peanuts' by Little Joe Cook & the Thrillers and rockabilly like the Jive-A-Tones 'Flirty Gertie' on Gus Goodwin's Radio Luxembourg show. Throughout Roger's life (he died in 1999) he was keen to discover music and share his passion and knowledge. He'd like to turn you on to something you may not have heard before. The title of his biography reflects this: it's called *Sit Down! Listen to This!*

Before the World Wide Web, searching for music was hard work. Access wasn't instant, and there weren't multiple libraries of music to trawl and download. Music took time and enthusiasm to discover, especially anything a bit different. It wasn't like it is now. One time Rolling Stones manager Andrew Loog Oldham put it to me like this: 'You couldn't walk into Tesco and walk out with a copy of "Paint It Black".'

In addition, radio and TV stations were limited, in number and variety. The BBC, particularly, played safe and was slow to change. If you wanted to hunt down something specialist or beyond the obvious, you'd tune into shows like Gus Goodwin's or the American Forces Network – a station set up to play music enjoyed by American troops stationed in Europe, which included specialist bebop and rhythm & blues shows. John Mayall would tape shows off the AFN using a reel-to-reel tape recorder; he was obsessed.

The unadventurousness of the general provision of music drove music fans to become inventive. They'd seek out venues with well-stocked juke boxes and switched-on DJs, or start their own. Gary Brooker (later a founder member of Procol Harum) in Southend had formed a group called the Paramounts. He started a club, Shades, in 1962, with no DJ, just a juke box stocked by local r&b enthusiast Tony Wilkinson. On at least one occasion they took a giant radio set into Shades. This was when they discovered Ray Charles was being broadcast live on French radio from Paris Olympia; 150 people turned up to listen to it.

The 1958 *Ray Charles at Newport* album captivated a certain section of the young, including Eric Burdon and Andrew Loog Oldham. It marked a moment when mods who'd been following modern jazz were beginning to hear something attractive in rhythm & blues. Their lifestyle still invariably included amphetamines and their look stayed sharp, but the favoured soundtrack of the mods was mutating.

The formula of a Saturday night – ballroom dancing to a jazz orchestra in the local dance hall – wasn't working in the way it had for thirty years. There were all the counter-attractions, the plethora of basement venues, self-organised events, coffee-bar dance clubs and new music choices. In addition, young people on a night out were beginning to accept and enjoy the idea of pre-recorded rather than live music. As we've seen in the 1950s, juke boxes were at the centre of a growth in all sorts of venues, formal and informal, free or relatively cheap, coffee bars and customised cellars like the Casbah. And by the early 1960s most youth clubs were expected to provide a gramophone and speakers and create enough of a vibe in a small room to get a crowd dancing.

Pre-recorded music was being heard in a variety of locations, with disc jockeys having an increasingly important part to play. Sound systems with record selectors like Duke Vin were entertaining audiences at house parties, town hall gatherings and community centres (the attractiveness of sound systems was boosted by the emergence of Jamaican ska, bluebeat and the early roots of reggae in the first years of the 1960s). After a few months, Mrs Best at the Casbah replaced the juke box with a Dansette. With the right amplification, promoters were hiring bigger spaces for disc-only events too – function rooms and village halls.

Much of this had been happening outside the control of the established music venues and promoters, which was why the Association of Ballrooms got together in 1959 to denounce the trend for disc-only nights. The Association of Ballrooms was being disingenuous, however. At the very moment they were bemoaning the new trend, the ballroom bosses at Mecca were hiring an expert to extend such events: a man called Jimmy Savile.

In the second half of the 1950s, aware of the success of Savile's record hops and disc-only events, and to enable them to absorb this new phenomenon, bosses at Mecca gave him jobs managing their venues, including the Ilford Palais. Despite the despicable nature of his crimes as a sex abuser that came to light after his death, it remains a fact that early in his career Savile was an influential figure who did much to establish how dance halls organised themselves and how DJs presented themselves. Savile moved from clubs to broadcasting when Decca executive and Radio

Luxembourg DJ Pat Campbell heard him play at the Locarno in Leeds and persuaded his radio bosses to give him a show. From there, he began to be employed by the BBC.

By the middle of the 1960s he was famous; if you'd asked record buyers in Britain to name a famous DJ, 99 per cent of them would probably have said Jimmy Savile. He was popular: in 1964 he was voted Best Disc Jockey in the *New Musical Express* Readers' Poll, and won that same *NME* award every subsequent year until 1972, when John Peel triumphed. You can't airbrush out his part in the history of nightclubs and music venues; that would be like pretending Gary Glitter never played at the Cavern.

In the beat group era DJs would be employed in a secondary role, in intervals between groups, and would be expected to compere the evening as well. Brian Rae's first experiences of DJing were at concert halls like Northwich Memorial Hall, playing records from the back of the stage in the intervals between groups. He had just a Dansette-style single deck that loaded several discs at a time and dropped them onto the turntable. He sat behind a trestle table, being very formal and announcing each record on the microphone, saying, 'Ladies and gentlemen, this is the new single by the Beatles,' and then trying to gauge it right so the records dropped correctly and the intro fitted.

At some other venues – including Mecca halls – the management would ask the sound technician or the lighting engineer to play records between bands, again without much fanfare (and nowhere near the stage; usually from the back of the hall hidden away near the projection box). When Jimmy Savile arrived at Ilford Palais he told them he wanted a small rostrum about three feet six inches high and the biggest speakers they'd got, one each side of the stage. On the rostrum he installed two linked record players so he could play one song straight after another.

Mecca managers were supposed to keep a low profile and wear

evening dress. In charge of things at Ilford Palais, Savile sported a two-tone haircut, with one side black and the other side white, and put himself spotlit, centre stage, playing records and entertaining the customers with banter and catchphrases. It all clicked, and Savile's mix of showbiz theatre and business acumen was a big hit with Mecca, so they moved him on to the Plaza on Oxford Street in Manchester. He was established there by the beginning of the 1960s.

Operators knew that a disc jockey's playlist could reflect changing tastes and be fine-tuned to suit or create an audience. A disc-only night was more than just a cheaper option; when the Musicians' Union complained to one venue operator that he wasn't employing enough live musicians, he was known to hire a band, and then when they arrived, he'd pay them to go away.

Thanks to the coming of age of the post-war baby boom generation, and full employment, the demand for leisure and dance clubs was expanding. Mecca invested in new venues, including the Coventry Locarno. The city had been heavily bombed during the Second World War but a recovery and redevelopment programme gathered momentum. The highlight of the process was the opening of the new Coventry Cathedral but also included the building of a swish new hotel, the Leofric, which opened in 1955. Later described by the *Coventry Telegraph* as 'a symbol of Britain's recovery after the Second World War', the Leofric included the Grosvenor Suite for functions and Ray's Bar, which would become a point of call on the way to a night out at the Locarno, frequented by men in smart suits and ladies in long dresses. The city of Coventry wasn't just recovering – it was prospering. Consumer culture was driving demand for the products of the local car manufacturing plants, and from the 1950s until the mid-1970s, Coventry had one of the highest standards of living anywhere in the country outside of the Home Counties; its population grew as the local jobs market strengthened.

The Coventry Locarno opened in August 1960, with its entrance at the base of a glass tower in the centre of Smithford Way, part of a new pedestrianised shopping precinct. The exciting, ultra-modern design reflected Coventry's confidence in the future, although the merits of the concrete and glass 'brutalist' style of architecture then in vogue are still debatable. The grand design and the presence of the glass caused one or two practical problems. While running through the precinct one afternoon, ten-year-old Ian Hambridge walked through a quarter-inch plate-glass window at the Locarno. Even though he escaped serious injury, to avoid further or worse accidents the management placed a large flower planter in front of the window. A year or so later, seven teenage boys were trapped in the lift halfway up the Locarno tower for five hours. Management served tea and biscuits to the anxious parents before the boys were freed.

A welcome problem for many dance hall operators was how to balance the continuing demand from customers still looking for old-time nights out with ballroom-style dance orchestras and the demand from the emerging younger audience. The older crowd tended to have better jobs and more money to spend at the bar, but wouldn't be out every week. The kids in their late teens were keener to find places to go but were less predictable in their tastes and large numbers of them would drive the bigger spenders elsewhere. They were also beginning to push against prevailing dress codes. In Edinburgh, the management of the Plaza at the corner of Morningside Road and Falcon Avenue found that mixing the old ways and the new generation could be problematic. Finally adapting the main ballroom to cater to the desire of the young to twist and shout the night away, they still hoped the clientele would adhere to the traditional modes of dress. When one youngster was turned away for wearing the latest roll-neck shirt, the newspapers sensed a scandal. 'It's a supposedly enlightened age,' complained the customer. The management issued a statement:

'People should remember it's a dance they're going to, not an après-ski affair.'

Such was the demand for leisure and dancing there seemed to be no limit to how far the night-time economy could expand. In Manchester, Mecca owned two popular venues barely 200 yards from each other – the Ritz and the Plaza. The Ritz had become a landmark building in the city (it features in the film version of Shelagh Delaney's *A Taste of Honey*). Phil Moss and his big band was the resident act for seventeen years. When Phil passed away, his friend the radio presenter Fred Fielder paid this tribute: 'People said he was responsible for half the population of Greater Manchester, because for the last dance of the evening the lights would go down, couples would have a kiss and cuddle on the dancefloor, end up going steady, then eventually get married and have children.'

Round the corner was the Plaza on Oxford Street, up steep steps, on the first floor. The Plaza features in Howard Jacobson's novel *No More Mr Nice Guy*; a character is thrilled by the 'city-lights eroticism' of a slow dance with a young lady but less thrilled to later find she had lifted his wallet from his pocket during their smooch.

The Mecca organisation played safe with its music policy and avoided chasing trends or alienating older audiences. However, when anything new came along, if there was money to be made, it would eventually find a place in the programming. For example, away from the weekends, Coventry Locarno featured one-off concerts by Shane Fenton (who became Alvin Stardust) and Screaming Lord Sutch. In the interval between bands a disc jockey was employed to play records from a double deck on the revolving stage.

The Locarno employed DJ Alan Mort, who was succeeded by Frank Pritchard; as was the custom, he doubled-up as compere. By 1963 Pritchard was extremely busy, as demand for disc-only sessions from the *Ready Steady Go!* generation rocketed. Mecca looked to win over the loyalty of the young by instituting under-eighteens disco nights. At Coventry Locarno these were on Tuesday nights and no alcohol was served – just coffee, tea or cold drinks. Alcohol-free Friday lunchtime sessions proved an attraction for office workers and shopgirls. The Friday night disco, meanwhile, remained popular through the 1960s, regularly drawing 2,000 people. In 1964 it's said that the disc jockey stopped playing 'Glad All Over' because everybody would get on the dancefloor and jump up and down so hard it was a danger to life and limb.

All sorts of clubs were going in a disc-only direction, including in London La Discotheque on Wardour Street, the Saddle Room on Park Lane and the Ad Lib above the Prince Charles Cinema on Leicester Place, although all three continued to feature live music too; at La Discotheque (formerly known as El Condor), Alexis Korner's Blues Incorporated were the resident band on Wednesday nights in 1962.

DJs were infiltrating venue after venue. In May 1962 the historic Hammersmith Palais launched a monthly disc-only night, and when, the following year, the Mecca Empire on Leicester Square opened, a resident seventeen-piece jazz orchestra featured every weekend, but every Monday evening there was a disc-only session with DJ Johnny Chapman. The Musicians' Union ramped up their opposition to these nights and the influence of DJs and in 1963 they launched a campaign with the slogan 'Keep Music Live' – with its familiar sticker, as seen on guitar cases ever since.

Mecca were keeping a tight rein on everything, not just the music but also the way staff presented themselves. Before doors opened at all Locarno ballrooms staff would gather on the dancefloor for an inspection to make sure they were clean and presentable (most of the staff wore uniforms); all of them, including the DJs, would have their fingernails checked for dirt. The music policy at weekends was expected to be similar in each and every Mecca hall. Winning formulas were milked, the pop charts reigned supreme, and spontaneity was discouraged.

This was the opposite of Roger Eagle's philosophy; he wanted to go beyond the obvious and find stuff people didn't know they liked. No generation has ever had uniform taste, and there was a small audience demanding something different. We've already met them – the kids who formed the scene the Rolling Stones came from, for example, and the Alexis Korner and Ray Charles fans; the cells of maverick characters scoffing at lightweights like Cliff Richard and Tommy Steele, namechecking blues heroes like Sonny Boy Williamson and clutching their Chuck Berry LPs.

The man who founded and ran the UK branch of the Chuck Berry Fan Club was Guy Stevens. As we'll see, Stevens would go on to have a profound effect on British music, the result of his DJ gigs at the Scene in Ham Yard. At the time he started at the Scene he was living in Leicester Square in what he later described as a 'one-room, no-water flat'. Nearby were a number of record shops, including Transat Imports, where Guy would spend hours hanging out, listening, buying. Like Roger Eagle, he was an enthusiast.

In 1962 Eagle had decided to leave his Oxford home and move to the big city. The Beatles would move to London to make a career, so too the Animals. Everyone did. Roger, however, moved to Manchester. He rode his motorbike up North without, it seems, much of a plan. What he found in Manchester was a change of scene and a job at the Kellogg's factory as a quality-control line inspector.

One of the first friends he made there was Roger Fairhurst. They'd meet up at Barry's Record Rendezvous or clubs or coffee bars, like the Cona on Tib Lane, where the open-house policy encouraged local music aficionados to take their latest finds and spin them on the in-house gramophone. A short walk to Albert

Square and right onto Brazennose Street, down on the right at No. 26, was the self-proclaimed 'beatnik-type' coffee bar, the Left Wing.

The Left Wing was relaunched early in 1963 as the Twisted Wheel. The owners, the Abadi brothers – five of them, including Ivor and Jack – had a basic vision and some experience (Jack Abadi, for example, was involved with Danny Betesh at the El Rio venue in Macclesfield). The Twisted Wheel became one of a generation of clubs descended from coffee bars. A coffee-bar dance club, offering music and dancing but still no alcohol, the Wheel became one of the defining venues of the era.

This 'dry' aspect was far from unique. The Mojo in Sheffield, opened by brothers Peter and Geoff Stringfellow in the former Dey's Ballroom on the junction of Burngreave Road and Barnsley Road, was another booze-free zone. For its first twenty-two years, the 100 Club also had no alcohol licence. The Marquee opened on 19 April 1958 at 165 Oxford Street and relocated to 90 Wardour Street in 1964. It finally obtained an alcohol licence in 1970.

The Wheel was far from being a glitzy venue. The decor was basic, determinedly so, although the Abadis collected wheels of various sorts to decorate the club. It was a basement: it had character, some black paint, some dark-red paint, a handful of bare lightbulbs – and an audience.

For people born in 1946 or 1947, during the baby boom in the immediate aftermath of the Second World War, still too young to visit licensed premises, clubs like the Twisted Wheel were perfect haunts. The Abadis were determined that the emphasis at the Wheel would be on dancing, opening four nights a week (Tuesday, Thursday, Friday and Saturday) from 7.30 p.m. until midnight.

Venues not serving alcohol were subject to fewer restrictions, and unlicensed premises, potentially, had unlimited opening hours. In order to gain even more autonomy, a membership scheme was launched at the Wheel and, within a year of opening, the 300-capacity club had a membership of 14,000. By this time, the weekly Saturday all-nighter sessions, from midnight until dawn, had been launched. In the early months of the club, Geoff Mullin had been employed as the DJ, playing before and after acts including local bands the Hollies and the Nashville Men from Oldham. But when the owners instigated all-night sessions every Saturday, Roger Eagle took the DJing job.

The Abadis were looking for someone with r&b knowledge, having heard from one of the El Rio crew that the recently opened Place in Hanley had got a good thing going with r&b and disc-only nights. They identified Roger as a prime candidate after they'd seen him endlessly hanging around the Left Wing with his bags of newly bought records. Once he was given the all-nighter job in September 1963, Roger pioneered a playlist of blues, r&b, bluebeat and soul, and took up a major role in the club, also having a hand in booking the acts – including the likes of John Lee Hooker, Screamin' Jay Hawkins and Sonny Boy Williamson – and organising the publicity as well.

Although there would be some tension between the venue owners and Roger – especially when it came to his more 'way out' ideas – they knew he was helping them create something that wasn't competing with the city's successful beat clubs like Oasis or the Jungfrau. Roger was one of the connoisseurs, on the lookout for good sounds, keen to play imports like the authentic r&b numbers rather than the UK cover versions. He wasn't shy with his opinions, to the point of falling out with anyone he considered was missing the point. He had a row with the Hollies, telling them their version of 'Searchin'' was lightweight, and berating them for recording and releasing a version after it had been nailed by the Coasters. 'It's already been done to perfection,' he told them, just after it had gone Top Twenty.

In many ways the Scene in Ham Yard was London's equivalent to the Twisted Wheel. We've visited the Scene in some of its previous incarnations. It was housed in the venue where Cy Laurie's all-night jazz raves took place and, before that, had been Club Eleven's first base. By the time the Scene first opened there in 1963, Soho had a confirmed and infamous reputation as an area of bohemian, late-night and even semi-legal activity. Within a few hundred yards of the Scene were strip clubs, gay clubs and late-night coffee bars. Among the bands that played in the early months of the Scene were the Rolling Stones in June and on 4 July (when the Beatles were in the audience).

The Scene and the Wheel featured live music, and many great bands played at both, but they are also both closely identified with the music tastes of the DJs – Roger Eagle at the Wheel and Guy Stevens at the Scene. Neither were showmen; they both eschewed the easy option with their music choices and music fans gravitated towards them. They didn't just demonstrate pioneering music taste, but also encouraged it. They both had an influence way beyond the four walls of their respective basement music venues.

At these two clubs, the future was being created, and it was to be influential. The Wheel turned out to be the birthplace of what, by the early 1970s, was being called Northern Soul. The relatively small size of these clubs was unimportant. If anything it gave them strength, the potential to be purist. They were inspirational. There are similarities with some of the unorthodox, maverick clubs discussed in later chapters – particularly the Rum Runner, Billy's and the Batcave – in the way the scenes that grew there were transmitted to a wider audience. They had a transformative effect on music but also on attitudes and clothes. Eric Clapton later recalled a group of guys at the Scene whom he eventually befriended. 'They wore a hybrid of American Ivy League and the Italian look, as personified by Marcello Mastroianni, so on one day they might be wearing sweatshirts with baggy trousers and loafers, on another maybe linen suits.

They seemed to be miles ahead of anyone else in terms of style. I found them fascinating.'

The Scene, and Guy Stevens, had a part to play in other careers, not only those of the Stones and Eric Clapton, but also the Who and the Small Faces (Stevens later went on to produce Procol Harum, Traffic and the Clash). The Scene is a venue now considered one of the key mod clubs. When Pete Townshend visited, he appreciated what he was witnessing, studied the looks, the dance moves and the music. 'The Scene was really where it was at, but there were only about fifteen people down there every night,' he said later. 'It was a focal point for the mod movement.'

Among the regulars was Dave McAleer, who went on to be a successful A&R man. A few years ago I met him round the corner from where the Scene used to be. As far as he can recall, the place was often full for live shows at the weekend, but he confirms Pete Townshend's story that the Monday night sessions featuring Guy Stevens were often sparsely attended. Stevens himself was low-key, and there was no sense of hero worship. 'I mean, I never looked on him as a DJ; I don't think we even knew what a DJ was. To us, he was just a guy playing r&b records.'

One of the attractions of disc-only nights for people with a real interest in music was the advantages records had over the ubiquitous live acts, many of whom, of course, fell well short of the Beatles and the Stones. Under an avalanche of four-piece acts, a rhythmically challenged drummer and a singer with the right trousers but a thin voice murdering songs like 'Hound Dog' and 'Long Tall Sally', DJs could stick with the original versions, the real deal. This was the argument Roger Eagle had applied when berating the Hollies. Dave McAleer agrees. 'Most of the live bands were crap. Most r&b fans didn't want to see British groups even if they were singing r&b covers; it would be, what's the point? We'd rather hear the real thing. We'd rather hear the records.'

Guy Stevens was a music fan, an evangelist for black American soul and r&b, and an avid record collector. DJing wasn't a branch of light entertainment to him. McAleer points out how different Stevens was to the likes of Jimmy Savile. 'He was quiet, and he was usually there on his own. He wasn't like a "personality" DJ at all, performing or leaping around.'

It's believed that Roger may have visited the Scene and even met Guy Stevens before he'd been invited to DJ at the Twisted Wheel. Certainly the two became friends and correspondents. They had much in common: they'd both been to boarding school, neither had much money-sense, and of course they had music in common – and they both got their DJ jobs thanks to the quality of their record collections.

Ronan O'Rahilly arrived in London from Ireland in 1961 and became friends with various people on the music scene including Alexis Korner and Giorgio Gomelsky. Gomelsky was running the Piccadilly Jazz Club from the same premises as Cy Laurie but was looking to move on. By 1963 O'Rahilly had taken over the venue and had renamed it the Scene Club. Most of the week's programming was given over to live music but, in time-honoured fashion, traditionally less busy nights were seen as opportunities to try something different, as O'Rahilly later explained. 'At that time in London there were only a tiny, tiny number of people who were into r&b. I knew Guy had a large record collection, so when I opened the Scene I offered him Monday nights.'

A 1963 advertisement for a Monday evening 'Rhythm & Blues Record Session' gives a flavour of what Guy Stevens was playing: 'Listen or dance to records by Bo Diddley, Chuck Berry, Jimmy Reed, John Lee Hooker, Howlin' Wolf, Muddy Waters, Fats Domino, Jerry Lee Lewis, Carl Perkins, Larry Williams, The Coasters and many other R and B artists.' Guy Stevens started with a focus on the blues but he'd also soon be playing jazz-tinged grooves by Jimmy Smith or Jimmy McGriff, or deeper soul songs like 'I Gotta Dance to Keep from Crying' by the Miracles and 'It's Alright' by the Impressions.

Mods had defined themselves by how they dressed, how they stood, how they walked. Their heroes were the likes of Miles Davis, Gerry Mulligan and Chet Baker, who played and dressed in a cool style. These modern jazz fans wore skinny ties, tight suits, short jackets, narrow trousers, and had a penchant for Italian and French designers. The next generation of mods, those who began frequenting the Scene, for example, maintained this sharp Continental look and the same attention to detail, but the music had moved on. They still liked to put distance between themselves and mainstream tastes but now their music heroes were likely to be black American acts, Ray Charles, Jimmy Smith, Tamla Motown.

The mods were looking outside of England for inspiration – they'd rather have frothy Italian coffee than dishwater English tea. They had begun to gravitate towards the Scene. You'd see them as you arrived in Ham Yard; they'd be hanging around in the shadows or idling near the scooters parked up nearby. Scooters were a thing, and the most coveted were the likes of a two-tone SX200 or any other Lambrettas, the Li 150, the TV175 perhaps, or if not a classic Lambretta, then maybe a NSU Prima D, made by a German manufacturer under licence from Lambretta.

They had musical differences, but others too; whereas the Mecca dance halls served alcohol, the nascent mod scene and the all-nighters were awash with amphetamines. It wasn't that the mods invented amphetamine use, but they took to the drug with enthusiasm, and the use of pills became another facet of the mod lifestyle. Jazz musicians who'd played in the same basement clubs where the mods now hung out had used amphetamines to stay awake, especially when they were playing three or four sets a night. Pills were also used by a wide selection of the general public in the early 1960s, many of them legally prescribed, some of which made their way onto the streets.

Most of the pills taken by mods and their nightlife companions were manufactured drugs, often bearing the manufacturer's name, SKF (Smith, Kline and French), rather than pills from illicit laboratories.

Guy Stevens, according to Dave McAleer, 'dressed like a student' and never sought to label himself a mod, but the desire of the mods to be seen somewhere semi-secret, to search out the best tunes, the original versions, black dance music, drew them to his disc-only nights. At the Scene, once past the scooters, customers would go downstairs, through a door wedged open with a brick into a bare room. The walls and floor were concrete; it was dark, too; this was before psychedelic light shows and strobes. The sound was reputed to be poor, the rumour being that the speakers had been liberated from a fairground. Andrew Loog Oldham described the Scene to me thus: 'Very basic. Dark, just a couple of lightbulbs and speed. There are certain drugs you don't have to take to be under the influence of it; speed was like a fog in the club, something that had taken over the room.'

The trade in pills in Soho was lucrative, and involved dodgy geezers in and around the environment, sometimes including those who ran the clubs, and usually gangs with various illegal interests. In Soho clubs like the Scene you could buy Drinamyl pills (the so-called 'purple hearts', which were actually blue and only slightly heart-shaped) for around 7d (3p), although – given that a common drug intake was probably three or four purple hearts near the beginning of the evening, topped up with a couple more every time energy levels flagged – they were usually bought in batches of five or ten. For a while, two cousins ran the door at the Scene and rigorously searched the customers who came in, confiscated pills, then passed them on to approved dealers who recycled them in the club. It's unsurprising that there would be a few casualties by the middle of the night, propping up the walls or draped outside, with staring eyes and foam flecks around their mouths.

The venue was relatively hard to find and attracted very few tourists, but many regulars. People with a special interest in the music would be invited – or invite themselves – back to Guy's flat. Steve Marriott hung out at the Scene; later he'd go on to play in the Small Faces and Humble Pie. Members of the Rolling Stones would sit in Guy's flat and listen to records by the likes of Jimmy Reed and Bobby Bland. Photographer David B. Thomson shared a flat with Brian Jones in Elm Park Mews and has always maintained it was as a result of Guy Stevens playing 'Time Is on My Side' by Irma Thomas that the Stones got the inspiration for including a version of the song on their second album.

Pete Meaden was an enthusiastic Drinamyl user and a believer in the mod life. He had a spell as a publicist working for Andrew Loog Oldham but they fell out when Meaden got too out of his head at a Rolling Stones reception. Meaden lived in a tiny flat in Monmouth Street but mod living, for him, meant being out and about, and noticed. He used to visit the Scene with another ace face, Phil the Greek. The Scene, he once said, was where 'the greatest records you can imagine were being played'.

Meaden began to work with the Who, taking Pete Townshend down to the Scene to introduce him to the music Guy Stevens was playing and the culture surrounding the venue. He was hoping Townshend would gain energy and take inspiration from there. He persuaded the Who to change their name to the High Numbers, pushed them towards a more overt mod image and encouraged them to play in a harder, edgier style. They'd visit other clubs too, places the mod faces talked about, like Klooks Kleek in West Hampstead and the Flamingo.

At the Flamingo, by then firmly established on Wardour Street, Rik Gunnell was hosting the all-nighters and had booked the relatively unknown Georgie Fame and His Blue Flames as resident band, a decision which turned out to be key to the venue's success. All-nighters took place on most Fridays and Saturdays and had a reputation for attracting a multiracial crowd; it was a particular favourite with black American GIs stationed at American military bases like Hillingdon and Ruislip, and visiting jazz musicians would also drop by.

The Flamingo became notorious in October 1962 as the site of a fight between Aloysius (Lucky) Gordon and Johnny Edgecombe, two West Indian boyfriends of the model and showgirl Christine Keeler. Investigations revealed that Miss Keeler was engaged in an affair with British Secretary of State for War John Profumo and was reported to be simultaneously involved with a Soviet naval attaché, creating a possible security risk and a scandal. The heaviness that sometimes disturbed the Flamingo didn't dissuade the occasional switched-on VIP from out of town from turning up: in June 1963 Muhammad Ali (then still known as Cassius Clay) paid a visit. Soon afterwards, though, a stabbing led to US military chiefs banning American servicemen from frequenting the venue, and rumours persisted that the Flamingo was involved in drug-dealing and prostitution.

For a short while early in 1963 the Rolling Stones had a Monday night residency there. Ian Samwell, who'd been hosting lunchtime disc-only sessions at the Lyceum since 1961, was one of the main resident DJs. Having built up his reputation via his sound system, Duke Vin also had some regular gigs at the Flamingo, playing r&b and ska. Georgie Fame began to build ska tunes into his band's repertoire, calling on the services of trombone player Rico Rodriguez, who'd moved to England from Jamaica in 1961. The mods enthused about ska and early bluebeat music and Caribbean culture in general; the smartness of the Jamaican performers in their sharkskin suits and pork-pie hats was appreciated by them, and Prince Buster became a hero, as did singer Jackie Edwards, who wrote 'Keep On Running', a hit for the Spencer Davis Group.

Another means to access ska and bluebeat in central London was at the Sunset Club on Carnaby Street, which Duke Vin's

friend Count Suckle took ownership of just before the boutique
boom there. Playing jazz and Caribbean music until seven o'clock
in the morning, it attracted a mixed crowd, with the black audience being predominantly Jamaican, but often including
African-American servicemen. The club was renamed the
Roaring Twenties.

This was how music trends and fashion spread, radiating out
from certain clubs. In August 1963, the TV show *Ready Steady
Go!* began broadcasting. The show's researchers and producers
would visit clubs looking for potential audience members. The
show's dancers, including Sandy Sarjeant, were all regulars at the
Scene. The music and the looks at the Scene one week would be
on *Ready Steady Go!* the next, and featuring in hundreds of suburban discotheques, dance halls and youth clubs the day after
that.

O'Rahilly was canny. He could see that what was happening in
his small basement club on a Monday night was rapidly becoming
peak-time and mainstream. In March 1964 he increased his music
business interests, launching Radio Caroline, an illegal radio station broadcasting from an ex-Danish passenger ferry off the coast
of Harwich. The first track played on Caroline was a Scene
favourite, Jimmy McGriff's 'Round Midnight'. Within three
weeks a Gallup survey estimated that the station had seven million
listeners.

Within a week or so of Radio Caroline's debut, the mod movement was in the public eye. The first generation of mods had
defined themselves against the trad jazz fans; the new wave of
mods were defining themselves against the rockers, and the split
developed into outright hostility and occasional violence. At
Easter 1964 during the Bank Holiday weekend there were skir-
mishes between mods and rockers at seaside resorts including
Brighton, Hastings and Margate. In May 1964 journalists from the
Sunday Mirror went undercover to a few mod clubs in Soho and
encountered pill-popping at the Flamingo and La Discotheque,

all-night partying, and 'the drug menace', which they said was sweeping Soho's 'all-night clubs and dives'.

Brighton became a centre of mod activity. Mods danced at the Florida Rooms, which was just a hundred yards from one of their favourite hangouts, the Zodiac coffee bar. Another venue where the mods would hear DJs spinning Tamla Motown (in among music by the Kinks and the Stones) was the Starlight Rooms (under the Montpelier Hotel, on the junction of Sillwood Street and Montpelier Road). Each of the two tribes had their chosen venues. You'd find mods at an all-night coffee bar called the Automat behind the Clock Tower, and rockers at a café near the King & Queen pub on Marlborough Place.

The High Numbers released a single 'Zoot Suit' with 'I'm the Face' on the flip side in July and a week or so later headlined a gig at the Florida Rooms at what was billed as an 'All Night Rave'. Meaden was relentless in his pursuit of what he considered to be the ideal demographic, and got the High Numbers a weekly residency at the Scene. However, two entrepreneurs, Kit Lambert and Chris Stamp, took over the management of the band, paid Pete Meaden off with £500, and the band reverted to calling themselves the Who. They wanted to attract a wider audience – apparently promoters were reporting that on seeing 'the High Numbers' on posters some customers were turning up expecting a bingo night.

The mods were locked into a fast-moving consumer culture; you'll still hear rueful ageing mods talking, half-bragging, about investing in a pair of shoes that cost a week's wages but were out of fashion the next day. The rockers were traditionalists, rode big British-made bikes, and wore leather jackets, jeans, long leather boots and heavy gloves. The rockers gave jazz and Motown a swerve; their heroes were Eddie Cochran and Gene Vincent. They didn't like anything too foreign-sounding. They weren't interested when some mods started branching out into a bit of Latin, like Cal Tjader or Ray Barretto.

The tabloid interest skewed definitions of mod, and tended to drive the cognoscenti elsewhere; clubs like the Last Chance Saloon prospered by playing rare soul to a more purist crowd. As far as Dave McAleer is concerned, this process of becoming conspicuous killed off modism: 'Mod was only interesting for me when it was something the man-on-the-street wasn't interested in and never heard of. By the time the mods and rockers began fighting on the beach it was all over, and it wasn't the real thing any more.'

Another point of difference among the many thousands of young kids who called themselves mods was their appreciation, or otherwise, of the Who. In some ways, the band created a third wave of mods, those who crushed into the Florida Rooms in Brighton to see them play (they played a series of gigs there in the run-up to Christmas 1964), for example, and those who were turned on to them during their amazing, career-changing residency at the Marquee.

In 1964 the Marquee still had a reputation predominantly as a jazz club, although it had moved through the trends and the times, presenting skiffle and then rhythm & blues. Harold Pendleton had booked Muddy Waters and in 1962 instituted rhythm & blues nights on a Thursday when Alexis Korner's Blues Incorporated had a residency. Late in 1963, however, Pendleton was given six months' notice to quit by the owners of the Academy Cinema, who had plans to turn his basement into a second cinema auditorium. Defying rumours of permanent closure, the Marquee moved to 90 Wardour Street in 1964, into a building that had previously been a Burberry warehouse. The Yardbirds had just started a residency at the venue and continued in the new premises (they recorded a show there that was later released as *Five Live Yardbirds*, their debut album). The stage was painted with red and white stripes, although the club was generally so dark some of the customers and even some bands never got much of a handle on the decor.

The Who had taken inspiration from the Scene, but with a change of management came a change of plan. The band withdrew from Wednesdays at the Scene and secured Tuesdays at the Marquee, from 24 November. They were booked for sixteen consecutive weeks, though seven extra were later added as the residency proved to be so successful. Tuesday was not the most auspicious night of the week but the Who took full advantage of the opportunity, notably by pushing the way live music was presented to a new level, including the marketing of the gigs. The band's management arranged for over a thousand fly-posters to be displayed all over London, designed by Brian Pike, picturing Townshend and making use of the slogan 'Maximum R&B', dreamed up by Kit Lambert. The band's name became a striking logo; there was an arrow pointing upwards from the 'o' in the Who's name. No one had hit the market with such a strong image before. The clever, artistic posters stood out in an era when most of those for other bands and venues looked no different to old variety or wrestling posters, just standard block typefaces.

Those weekly gigs at the Marquee through the winter are remembered fondly by Pete Townshend in his autobiography *Who I Am.* 'I remember wearing a chamois jacket, carrying a Rickenbacker guitar, coming up from the bowels of the earth at Piccadilly Circus train station feeling as though there was nothing else I'd rather be doing. I was an r&b musician with a date to play. It was a great adventure, and I was full of ideas.'

With just the poorly received High Numbers single to their (other) name, this was a complete relaunch. The Who-loving mods gloried in a band with a strong mod look and a repertoire that included Motown and James Brown covers, stuff they might have heard Guy Stevens play like 'I Gotta Dance to Keep from Crying'. In addition there was Keith Moon, with a target design on his T-shirt, building up an almighty sweat and stripping off then wringing out his shirt before kicking over his drums, plus the outpouring of energy from Daltrey and Townshend; The Who had a powerful in-your-face live show.

The Who were building a career on playing at the Marquee and elsewhere in the southeast of England, including at a series of all-night raves at Club Noreik, a bingo hall on Tottenham High Road. They also had a regular gig at the Railway Hotel in Harrow, where gigs were organised by Pete Townshend's friend Richard Barnes. It was, and remained, a popular mod hangout (in 1968 a young Kevin Rowland saw Geno Washington's rousing soul group perform there).

The Who's gigs outside the London area were relatively few. They didn't appear in Birmingham until 28 March 1965, around the time of the release of 'I Can't Explain', when they played at one of Ma Regan's venues (it was advertised that they would be at two of her venues, but it's thought they didn't show at the Ritz in King's Heath). Still they looked to embrace imaginative onstage presentation. A few weeks later, at a gig at the College of Art and Technology in Leicester, a local student projected his experimental films onto the group as they played.

Other promoters with access to several venues were giving the Who good gigs at this time, including Freddy Bannister, who ran nights in Bristol, Stourbridge and elsewhere. Their reputation as a great live band reached Paris, where they played at La Locomotive in November 1965, with Roger Vadim, Jane Fonda and Catherine Deneuve in the audience. They also received great support from *Ready Steady Go!*, including a headline slot on the 1965 Christmas special when they performed 'My Generation', which was followed on the show by an all-star *Cinderella* panto (Eric Burdon was the Fairy Godmother).

Mod schisms remained ongoing and definitions varied, but many resisted anything that wasn't Otis Redding, Tamla Motown, and 100 per cent authentic black American soul; generally, any support for British bands was limited to the Who and the Small Faces, although some mods went through a Yardbirds phase too.

By 1966 nightlife was entering into a rock/soul split. Venues tended to prioritise either but not both. And the popularity of disc-only nights grew in many dance halls, especially once the influence of Tamla Motown blossomed.

We've already seen the importance of black American dance music, from ragtime through New Orleans jazz and bebop, to blues and rhythm & blues morphing into rock & roll. The clean, driving upbeat singles released by Motown sounded glorious in clubs but also on radio and juke boxes, and blaring from fairgrounds. Rhythm & blues had a rawness. Motown gave this a bit of a tidy-up and polish, but with added sparkle and glam; it had a wide, cross-gender appeal.

For DJs the Motown sound was perfect. 'It was just the best dance music,' Brian Rae says, contrasting it to less hip sounds in the hit parade. 'Billy J. Kramer and stuff that was in the charts was too thin or it didn't have a constant dance beat, but with Motown you could keep the dancefloor going. It was the base of all club music.'

In 1965 Chubby Checker released a song called 'At the Discotheque'. The word had now achieved wider currency. The days of live bands exclusively providing the soundtrack for a night out were over. And not just nights out – daytime sessions were also proliferating. Tiles at 79–89 Oxford Street opened in April 1966. It was a basement discotheque, but it was also much more than that; attached to the club was an arcade of boutiques, a record stall and a beauty parlour.

The German TV show *Beat Club* filmed and broadcast a session from Tiles in August 1966. Sounds Incorporated, Cliff Bennett and The Rebel Rousers, and the Moody Blues were among the live attractions and resident DJ Clem Dalton also appeared. Clem had started his DJ career in Rochdale, before going to London and taking a job at Tiles. By the end of the year Tiles had become awash with pills, and attracted the close attention of the police.

The venue also attracted the attention of Tom Wolfe, who wrote about the lunchtime sessions there in an essay entitled 'The Noonday Underground' in which he describes the gathering of office girls, shop assistants and bank clerks. It would be as busy during the day as the night, sometimes more so. Wolfe writes about the particular aura surrounding Dalton: 'All these boys want to be DJs and they will do anything for a break,' he says.

Well before Tiles had opened, Guy Stevens had left the Scene, and he occasionally joined one of the other resident DJs at Tiles, Jeff Dexter, on the decks. Roger Eagle was also in the process of moving on, having already distanced himself from the mod movement. 1965 into 1966 could have been the time when he cashed in, but that's exactly what put him off the scene – if you heard the record at every club in town, you wouldn't hear it at the Wheel. Roger also edited the fanzine *R&B Scene,* which described itself as 'Britain's Leading Rhythm and Blues Magazine' and sold for a shilling. In the April 1965 issue he praised the Esquire Club in Sheffield, saying, 'Here's one club where the "mod" influence has not ruined the appreciation of r&b.' He feared dance fans were becoming too preoccupied with looking right and turning his favourite clubs into clichés.

Terry Thornton had opened the Esquire on 7 October 1962 on the second and third floors of an old flourmill and optical works on Leadmill Road in Sheffield. The venue had no alcohol licence, and daft decor that included a crocodile hanging from the ceiling, a blunderbuss and a skeleton wearing boots. The music policy started out featuring two nights of jazz and two nights of beat groups, and then nights appealing to fans of the twist, and then blues too. The Esquire hosted performances by John Lee Hooker, Howlin' Wolf, the Who, the Yardbirds and the Kinks. Thornton was a big fan of local singer Joe Cocker and he persevered, giving him gigs even though Cocker's drinking habits negatively affected his professionalism. Local guitarist Dave

Hawley – Richard Hawley's father – was also a regular performer (Richard's grandfather had been a music-hall performer with an act that included playing the violin behind his back while he stood on his head).

A second notable Sheffield venue in this era was the Mojo. After promoting shows at the Black Cat Club at St Aidan's Church on City Road in Sheffield, and the Beatles' appearance at the Azena Ballroom (the band's first appearance in the city), Peter Stringfellow had gone on to book the Rolling Stones at the City Hall in November 1963 (alongside Dave Berry and the Cruisers). With his brother Geoff, Peter Stringfellow opened the Mojo in an old Victorian house on Pitsmoor Road in February 1964. The Mojo positioned itself on the same circuit as the Twisted Wheel, playing host to the likes of the Graham Bond Organisation, the Spencer Davis Group, Steampacket, the Yardbirds, Wilson Pickett and the Who.

In 1965 the Twisted Wheel in Manchester moved from Brazennose Street across town to 6 Whitworth Street. In the manner of clubbing cognoscenti through all eras, many of Roger Eagle's fans are still adamant that the nights at the original venue were never surpassed, despite the fact that more lives would go on to be changed by the intensity and popularity of the Wheel in its Whitworth Street site, as we'll see in a later chapter. At its second location the music policy was more narrowly focused on up-tempo, rare soul, and attracted audiences from all over the North and even further afield.

Brian Rae would become a DJ at the new site. He'd been working at Lockers, the metal fabricators in Warrington. He also remembers people waiting eight deep all along the platform at Warrington Central station on a Saturday night getting the late trains to Liverpool or Manchester, such was the pull of the nightlife scene in those cities. Merseybeat was the prevailing sound in Liverpool, while in Manchester he'd heard of a small rare soul scene, and someone had told him about a song called 'Harlem Shuffle' that was being played by Roger Eagle, along with numbers of a similar quality. He was drawn to Manchester, and his destination was the Twisted Wheel. The first night he went there Solomon Burke was appearing.

Brian Rae had rightly recognised how important the Motown sound would be in filling the nation's dancefloors. Most people of the generation who were going out to dance halls regularly around 1967 and 1968 – from the Mecca in Basildon to the Locarno in Leeds – will recall that at some point there would be a fight either inside or outside the venue. And you'd always hear 'Reach Out' by the Four Tops.

In the 1960s, as well as maintaining, refitting and relaunching established venues, Mecca was actively investing in the construction of brand new dance halls. Coventry Locarno was an ambitious, landmark building – the centrepiece for a city-centre development including a pedestrianised shopping precinct. In the 1960s the landscape of so many of our cities was transformed by high-rise housing, ring roads and shopping centres. New nightclubs were often a major part of these huge projects, including the Bristol Locarno.

Like Coventry, Bristol was one of Britain's boom towns in the early 1960s. It had old trading traditions, with a centuries-old port that had been as active and lucrative as London's. The city's role in the slave trade had been the foundation of its prosperity; one of Bristol's most famous venues, Colston Hall, was funded by Edward Colston, who had accumulated massive wealth as a slave trader (aware of this connection some Bristol acts, including Massive Attack, refuse to perform there). In the 1960s shipbuilding in the Bristol docks still took place, but there was huge commercial expansion in the aeronautics industry and the city had a key role in developing Concorde.

Bristol Locarno was part of a £2m Mecca project that also included a dozen bars, an ice rink, bowling lanes, a casino, an

ABC cinema and a multistorey car park for the convenience of the centre's visitors. On a good day this could number 5,000 and in the mid-1960s Bristol, basking in the white heat of technology, had plenty of good days.

The opening night on 19 May 1966 was graced with a guest list of Bristol and West Country VIPs including local councillors, business chiefs, the region's top socialites, the Mecca top brass and Bristol's Lord Mayor and Lady Mayoress. Guests were thrilled by the ceiling illuminated by hundreds of tiny lights, the revolving stage, plastic palm trees and the polished expanse of dancefloor. Slinking their way through the crowds were half a dozen hostesses, including winners of the West Country heat of the Miss Great Britain contest in their bikinis. Drinks were served in the swish Le Club bar, and by waistcoated, bowler-hatted barmen in the Victorian bar. In the Bali Hai bar girls sporting Polynesian-style grass skirts distributed chunks of pineapple to the assembled dignitaries.

A formula emerged in the bigger Mecca halls. The young crowds, the students and the big live shows – plus any music the mainstream fans would consider noisy or leftfield – were consigned to midweek nights. One Thursday in July 1966 the Who played at the Bristol Locarno; the week after it was Solomon Burke, followed by Chris Farlowe and the Thunderbirds. Flyers for the regular Thursday night claimed, 'It's all happening' and promised a 'dee jay' every week.

By the middle of 1966, as we will see in the next chapter, we were at the beginning of a new era. Within a year, the Who would leave behind their aggressive power pop, their identification with mods, and write and record freeform, heavy tracks like 'I Can See for Miles'. Older clubs and venues throughout Britain, especially those with student populations, saw a mini-exodus to 'found spaces' like the Roundhouse and demands for new venues, and new kinds of psychedelic and underground music and entertainment (including light shows and 'happenings'). In Bristol, by the end of 1966, for example, the Bristol Troubadour had opened, which would go on to host the likes of Al Jones, Ian A. Anderson, John Renbourn, Bert Jansch and Al Stewart. The club helped spawn a scene and an alternative folk label, Village Thing. And Pink Floyd made their debut in Bristol at the 'Chinese R & B Jazz Club' in March 1967, at what was billed as an 'Easter Rave'.

In the next chapter we'll go back to the roots of the underground, the counter-culture. We'll trace the disparate influences that fed into this – the drugs, the beatniks, Bob Dylan. In his book *Give the Anarchist a Cigarette,* Mick Farren recounts what happened one Bank Holiday when he and his friends Paul and Beryl were sitting on Brighton seafront watching the mods stream past. Mick's crew weren't mods and they hadn't been rockers since at least 1961. They were a bit unkempt, with long hair, scruffy tight jeans, old army shirts and boots. Farren reckoned the three of them defied categorisation but they were asked to define themselves several times that day. Rockers asked if they were mods, mods asked if they were rockers, and to each and every interrogator Mick Farren replied, 'No, mate. We're beatniks'. Pressed for more clarification, he explained to the mods and rockers that he was a Bob Dylan fan. Little did his questioners know that they'd just met an early example of a third species that would one day fill major venues and large festival fields, but they appeared appeased. Farren writes of the 'strong sense of impending change' he felt witnessing a Bob Dylan gig in May 1965.

The arrival of the psychedelic underground wasn't a complete or overnight shift. It took time to germinate and it took time to make an impression on the general public. The Chinese R & B Jazz Club – an old blues night on Tuesdays at the Bristol Corn Exchange – was marginal in terms of the nightlife offered in the city at the time, but Pink Floyd's early gigs tended to draw people to them. Wherever they played – from the Technical College in

Canterbury to the Winter Gardens in Malvern – dispersed, disparate audiences coalesced, as they would when the Sex Pistols began touring.

In March 1966 you'd still only be seeing glimpses of these changes, reflected in the entertainment at the Marquee, for example. From March 1966, Bernard Stollman, a native New Yorker, began hosting Sunday afternoons at the venue, gatherings he called the 'Spontaneous Underground'. Stollman's publicity flyers promised 'poets, pop singers, hoods, Americans, homosexuals (because they make up 10% of the population), 20 clowns, jazz musicians, "one murderer", sculptors, politicians and some girls who defy description'. Among the various music acts who turned up and entertained the poets, sculptors and the rest was Donovan – who was then going through a sitars and congas phase – and a former assistant to Stockhausen, Cornelius Cardew, then appearing as part of the experimental group AMM. And, of course, Pink Floyd.

There were two or three Spontaneous Underground events each month in the spring and early summer of 1966. On 12 June Pink Floyd's future co-manager Peter Jenner, a lecturer at the London School of Economics, took a break from marking examination papers and got himself down to the Marquee. He was intrigued and then blown away by Pink Floyd playing just-recognisable versions of songs like 'Louie Louie', but distorted and realigned with feedback and echoes. Four months later Pink Floyd signed a management deal with Jenner and Andrew King. Several years later Jenner recalled the Marquee gig in an interview with rock magazine *ZigZag*. 'They were playing these very weird breaks; so weird that I couldn't even work out which instrument the sound was coming from. It was all very bizarre and just what I was looking for – a far out, electronic, freaky pop group.'

The Marquee is mentioned on David Bowie's 1967 debut album in a song called 'The London Boys', about flash clothes and taking pills. Events like the Spontaneous Underground were ush-ering in a new era, still defined by clothes and drugs, but not flash mod suits and purple hearts; on the way in was the counter-cul-ture era of long hair, unkempt hippies, freaks, headbands, bangles, frock coats, acid, grass, drop-outs, sit-ins, drug busts, Jimi Hendrix and Pink Floyd.

The venue on Eel Pie Island closed in 1967, although it briefly reopened as Colonel Barefoot's Rock Garden, where the likes of Black Sabbath and Genesis performed, and in 1977 Pete Townshend used the name Eel Pie for his publishing company. The Railway Hotel in Harrow burned down in 2000. The Esquire closed in 1967, although some of the same building later formed part of one of Sheffield's most significant clubs in recent decades, the Leadmill. The Station Hotel in Richmond, which housed Giorgio Gomelsky's Crawdaddy club, has had multiple makeovers and name changes and is now trading as One Kew Road, serving modern British food, apparently 'interwoven with some Mediterranean influences'.

Most of the bookings at the Marquee from 1968 onwards were made by John Gee. He had a rambling, oddball way of acting as compere and introducing bands. Jethro Tull and King Crimson were two of his favourite emerging acts (Jethro Tull wrote a song about him). He liked pushing boundaries; on one occasion Gilbert & George appeared. They sat, saying nothing, on either side of a table they'd placed centre stage.

Jimi Hendrix played the Marquee three times in 1967. From the moment the Who took up their residency, if not before, the Marquee had been cultivating many of music's various changes through the mid-1960s. According to *Uncut* magazine, 'For a few chaotic and historic years, the Marquee was the most important venue in Britain.' On 23 April 1968 the Who returned to play the venue to mark ten years of the club. There was even a birthday cake, and Keith Moon and Harold Pendleton were photographed wielding the cake knife. In 1970 John Gee retired, and Jack Barrie took over booking the bands (he'd previously managed a drinking club, La Chasse, just along Wardour Street from the Marquee). It remained an important live venue in the punk years and beyond but closed its doors at 90 Wardour Street in 1988. The site is now occupied by Soho Lofts, an exclusive block of flats. The original Marquee club at 165 Oxford Street has also been demolished, and a branch of the Santander bank now stands in its place.

CHAPTER SIX

Cosmonauts, light shows, Clapton takes acid

Mick Farren, the beatnik in Brighton, made his mark in the radical counter-culture in numerous ways. He wrote for the underground newspaper *International Times* and fronted the band the Deviants. He was a witness to and participant at numerous gigs, parties and happenings through the second half of the 1960s (including Jimi Hendrix's first gig at the Marquee). The cutting edge moved a long way from 'Love Me Do', not least in the work of the Beatles themselves. Things got psychedelic, the music got louder. Soft Machine was a band named after a William Burroughs novel. Along with Pink Floyd and others they provided the music at an event at the Roundhouse in 1966. Part-way through, they dragged a motorcycle onstage, revved up the engine and fed the roar through the PA. Things were getting experimental.

Wherever Pink Floyd played, out came the freaks. We'll track this activity at gatherings at the Roundhouse and Alexandra Palace, at clubs like 'UFO' and 'Middle Earth' and at venues around the country, including the Magic Village in Manchester where Pink Floyd played in June 1968, and Mothers, which was situated above a furniture store and a gentleman's outfitters in the Birmingham suburb of Erdington.

Given the proximity of art colleges, media and broadcasting outlets, boutiques, record labels, model agencies, PR companies, and the depth of its nightlife traditions, it's perhaps unsurprising that the area encompassing Soho and the West End of London continued to spawn several significant venues in the 60s, but it's less predictable that Erdington would feature a club that John Peel would declare was 'the best club in Britain' of its time. We'll hear about John Peel's visits to Mothers, including the night Mick Farren shared a moment of the intimate kind with Germaine Greer.

In the late 1950s, George Melly met Tommy Steele at a time when they were both successful figures in the music industry, but Melly didn't have a clue who Tommy Steele was. They had parallel lives, and Melly felt no compunction to keep tabs on the pop charts. Music has always had separate worlds, but what was different in the 60s was that the underground wilfully separated itself from the mainstream; it rejected and resisted the mainstream in all ways.

The mainstream could be angry or, at least, perplexed by underground counter-culture. It knew it was a world apart. Birmingham's *Evening Mail* explained the goings-on at Mothers: 'Though a huge slice of Birmingham's population do not even know of its existence, in the appropriate circles it is famed throughout the land. Mothers is more of a cult than a nightclub and has achieved an unrivalled reputation as a centre for underground music.'

The beatniks had no connection with beat groups; their heroes were American writers and poets including Jack Kerouac, Allen Ginsberg, William Burroughs and Gregory Corso. It was a scene in the mid-1960s that didn't have many music heroes or music venues. When Mick Farren sat on a wall in Brighton, he was part of a dispersed tribe of nonconformists with no space or place to call home. Most venues were doing well presenting beat groups and playing Motown, among them the Carlton Ballroom, which would later be home to Mothers. Beatniks were a rare species in Brighton and Birmingham, as elsewhere. Scruffy types weren't congregating in large numbers. Yet. Although for several years there had been moments when beatnik activity was publicised, including in one Sunday newspaper, which described beatniks as 'drug addicts and peddlers, degenerates who specialise in obscene orgies'.

The British media had been sensationalising conflicts between mods and rockers, and expected beatniks to invade the beaches too. In May 1966 the Newspaper Enterprise Association claimed British seaside resorts like Brighton and Blackpool were planning action against expected beatnik invasions. 'In some cases the police will meet trains and buses as they arrive from London and turn back the beatniks. The Cornish resort of St Ives has already set up a beatnik patrol.'

Mick Farren first saw Bob Dylan perform at the Royal Albert Hall in May 1965, at a time when Dylan was one of the few music heroes on the underground (or 'the rebel intelligentsia' as Farren liked to describe his circle of friends). It was a generation that felt like outsiders, enjoyed outsider status, but craved moments of community, relishing some years later their experiences at major events at the Roundhouse, the Isle of Wight Festival (Dylan headlined the second one) and then Pilton Pop, Folk & Blues Festival (which evolved into the Glastonbury Festival). Dylan's Albert Hall gig was one of the first occasions the dispersed tribe had gathered together.

Although its acoustics were derided, the Royal Albert Hall was, and remains, one of the best-looking venues in Britain, most famous perhaps for the annual series of promenade concerts which moved there in 1941. Although there's a lot more to the Proms than the Last Night, witnessing the Last Night's traditional couple of hours of patriotic music you'd struggle to imagine that on a number of occasions in the 60s the same space was filled with folkies, beatniks and acid freaks. In the years after those first Dylan appearances in May 1965, other artists who headlined at the venue include the Rolling Stones in 1966, Jimi Hendrix in 1967 and 1969, Cream in 1968 and Led Zeppelin in 1970.

That the 5,000-capacity Albert Hall was the venue for these shows was in part practical; there wasn't a great deal of choice, as many of the bigger venues now in London weren't operating in the mid-60s. One other was the Astoria Theatre in Finsbury Park, which hosted several momentous shows, including the Beach Boys, and had a capacity of around 3,000 (in 1971 it was converted into a full-time venue and renamed the Rainbow Theatre). Of course, neither the Rainbow nor the Royal Albert Hall has been a club or a venue with a focused music policy aimed at a particular audience. In recent years the Albert Hall has featured McFly, David Gray, Nitin Sawhney and the Bootleg Beatles.

The real Beatles were in their favoured vantage point, Grand Tier Box 12, taking a break from filming the movie *Help!*, when Bob Dylan took to the stage at the Royal Albert Hall, the same night Mick Farren witnessed. The Stones were there too. Both the Beatles and the Stones had been dropping Dylan's name in interviews. He was, it appears, some sort of a threat but also an inspiration. In the first half of 1965 the Stones appeared a little bit put out that they weren't an 'in' band any more, with Mick Jagger conceding in *Melody Maker*, 'I guess we were a little wild and far out two years ago but now we are a little more commercial. Dylan is the darling of the sweet young things now.'

The Beatles were lovable mop-tops who'd topped the charts with 'She Loves You' and were boxed in by light entertainment. A few weeks earlier they'd attended a *Mirror* newspaper event at the Royal Albert Hall headlined by Harry Secombe and hosted by Bruce Forsyth. Via Dylan and LSD they were lured into the underground. Dylan seems to have made more of an impression on them than any other act since they formed the Silver Beatles, since Elvis probably. He was admired for his edge, his literacy, the challenge he threw down.

By the time of his 1965 Albert Hall gig, Dylan had released his 'Subterranean Homesick Blues' single, the lead track on the *Bringing It All Back Home* album. It entered the UK Top Ten at the end of April 1965. His trip to England in spring of that year was a turning point in his career; the success of the tour transformed him from an emergent name on the folk circuit, attracting muso interest, to an international pop music superstar attracting mass interest. It would be the same for Jimi Hendrix a few years later – an enhanced reputation in England gave his career extra momentum back home in America (Dylan's 'Subterranean Homesick Blues' single only peaked at Number 39 in the USA). Breakthroughs were easier over here or, as one of Bob Dylan's biographers puts it, 'In a small country [he means England], excitement was like steam in a kettle.'

There were no significant music venues for the rebel intelligentsia, but the like-minded were beginning to gather, to find spaces, including Better Books on Charing Cross Road, which had a basement hosting happenings and art events, featuring the likes of Jeff Nuttall and his avant-garde troupe the People Show. One of the bookshop's managers was Barry Miles (known always as Miles); he'd track down small-press books, beat poetry from America and offbeat novels. Alternative bookshops were a valuable focus for counter-cultural activity. New York had Peace Eye bookstore, San Francisco had City Lights, and in Edinburgh Jim Haynes opened the Book Shop on George Square.

A month after the Dylan gig, an event entitled International Poetry Incarnation took place at the Albert Hall; not a music event, but a gathering of the likes of Jeff Nuttall, Scottish writer Alex Trocchi, Better Books, the magazine *New Departures*, Michael Horovitz, Miles and Pete Brown. Adrian Mitchell's anti-(Vietnam) war poem 'To Whom It May Concern' fired up the audience. The organisation was something of a shambles, but the event was blessed with the presence of Allen Ginsberg and the sense of energy and potential was undeniable. According to *International Times* contributor and counter-culture historian Jonathon Green, the Albert Hall poetry evening was 'the moment at which the nascent underground stood up to be counted'.

The British underground was in thrall to the Americans – the beats, the poets – and were inspired to follow their lead. Alex Trocchi was in the habit of calling himself and Burroughs 'cosmonauts of inner space'. The structures and reality of society itself were poisonous. Ginsberg imagined a better world: 'Everybody lost in a dream world of their own making.' (This was considered a good thing, by the way.)

Dylan returned a year later for two nights at the Albert Hall, but by this time he had embraced an electric sound, cutting his ties with many in the folk community, those who'd maybe picked up on his early work. The British folk movement felt close to Dylan; he'd always had a deep knowledge of American folk songs, but his repertoire of British standards was hugely enhanced over the weeks he spent around the Troubadour and with Martin Carthy over three years earlier. Carthy taught Dylan songs that would turn up, with a twist, on the *Freewheelin'* album. In the intervening three years, though, Dylan had moved on.

The controversy on the May 1966 tour is captured on a famous live bootleg recording which for years had been erroneously labelled as a recording from the Royal Albert Hall. One audience member shouts 'Judas!' telling Dylan he's never going to listen to him again. 'You're a liar,' Dylan spits back, and the band launch into 'Like a Rolling Stone'. This was music getting louder. The bootleg was actually recorded at Manchester's Free Trade Hall, a show attended by Chris 'CP' Lee. He remembers Dylan launching into 'Tell Me Momma'. 'It was like a B-52 taking off. I'd never heard anything, so loud in my life,' he once told me.

We are used to discussions about a generation gap but what was becoming clear in the 1960s were divisions within actual generations themselves; the different fads, the ideas, the outfits, the attitudes, the sub-divisions in the audiences in venues and clubs, including that schism between the acoustic folk fans and the electric long-haired tribe. Farren considered himself a 'freak', with a passion for embracing louder, visceral rock, and with a look too. 'People with whom I could empathise and identify,' he wrote in *Give the Anarchist a Cigarette*. Arrayed in thrift-shop capes, spray-painted wellington boots, Edwardian dresses and Victorian military jackets, they presented a DIY version of what, in twelve months, would be hawked on Carnaby Street and King's Road as 'flower power'.

There's film of the Rolling Stones playing at the Albert Hall during the autumn of 1966 catching them on the cusp of change too, as they embraced a darker, more unhinged sound – the likes of '19th Nervous Breakdown', for example. In the footage you can see how fashion was changing onstage and in the audience; generally far less buttoned-down than in the mod world, more free-flowing across all genders, more velvet, more satin, more tassles, more hair. Men with trailing scarves, bangles and eyeshadow, with the Stones a barometer and a motor for these changes. Incidents like the one at the Grand Hotel in Bristol when the Stones were thrown out of the restaurant were evidence of how their collar-length hair had become an issue, even more so when their TV appearances on the likes of *Thank Your Lucky Stars* and *Ready Steady Go!* increased. The end of national service for young men in 1960 contributed immeasurably to this freedom. Only ten years previously, those long tresses would be lopped off and erstwhile beatniks forced into drill and disciplined into respectability. Now they were free to roam and explore. Many of the Great British public found it hard to come to terms with their look. What were they? Nancy boys or delinquents? Or, heaven forbid, both?

Youth culture was near the beginning of a phase that would soon develop into dozens of dressed-up or dressed-down tribes. Pushed by Bowie, then embraced by punk, the use of dress for self-definition, even for protest, would become ubiquitous by the end of the 1970s. In the late 1960s, writer Angela Carter described clothes as 'our weapons, our challenges, our visible insults'.

It wasn't so much music, or politics, or clothes, but the use and acceptance of drugs that was the defining, deciding issue that split the mainstream and the underground. LSD became illegal in 1966, after a number of years of being available in London where, in Chelsea, Michael Hollingshead – the man who'd turned Timothy Leary onto acid – had established the World Psychedelic Centre, selling books, issuing pro-LSD manifestos, showing slides of sacred images and dispensing doses of acid in impregnated grapes.

There were high-profile British musicians among those turned on to LSD, as the drug and the attendant culture pushed music into new directions. According to a story told by Paul McCartney, in January or February 1965 John Lennon was served LSD in coffee by a dentist friend, and from that first experience onwards had a 'growing infatuation' with the substance. The Beatles' drug use and the *Sgt. Pepper's Lonely Hearts Club Band* album endeared them to Timothy Leary – LSD's infamous evangelist. He said the Beatles 'are the wisest, holiest, most effective avatars the human race has ever produced'. He wittered on about them at every opportunity. They were also 'prototypes of evolutionary agents sent by God with a mysterious power to create a new species'.

There had been the Spontaneous Underground events, which had briefly colonised the Marquee, and various one-off happenings, but there were very few dedicated, permanent spaces in which to demonstrate and encourage political or cultural alternatives. In 1966, though, Indica opened in Mason's Yard, next to the Scotch of St James club, founded by John Dunbar and Miles, with an art gallery in the basement, books on the ground floor (selling offbeat and cult novels, poetry, recordings of spoken-word performances by Ginsberg and Lenny Bruce, and a magazine rack that included import copies of underground newspapers and magazines from the USA; the likes of *East Village Other* and *LA Free Press*).

London soon had its own alternative publication, *International Times*, launched in October 1966. The magazine in its early months carried very little music content until Mick Farren intervened, concentrating instead on the bigger concerns of the cultural underground at that time – coverage and information about drugs and politics, and a listings service. John Hopkins (always known as Hoppy) was a member of the *International Times* editorial board and became a prime mover in the organising of a launch party for the magazine, for which he secured the use of the Roundhouse on Chalk Farm Road, just north of Camden Town, a former railway repair shed (built in 1847), then an improvised gin warehouse, with cracked brickwork, a gallery running around the circumference and still containing bits of Victorian machinery, washed up on the tide of history.

Playwright Arnold Wesker ran an arts scheme called Centre 42, which had started to use the Roundhouse in their search for 'a cultural hub', as Wesker described it. He said the Centre would 'by its approach and working destroy the mystique and snobbery associated with the arts'. The building's owner had given Wesker the Roundhouse, but no money to undertake the renovation and refurbishment of the building (there would be no proper renovation, at least during the lifetime of Centre 42, which was wound up in 1971, having only raised £150,000 of the £750,000 the project required). He was happy for the space to be rented out to *IT* for the evening. A stage was amateurishly erected and lights and movie clips were thrown onto sheets strung up on washing lines around the building.

Even though the place was a rusting ruin, the event locked into something new, something full of potential, and was mind-expanding in several ways. It built on the likes of the Spontaneous Underground but to an audience of thousands, presenting more than music, more than conventional gigs. There was body painting, a light show, and Soft Machine with their motorbike. It attracted a druggy crowd, a loose community, freaks, artists, anarchists, dandies, fops and fashion victims, with dope appearing to be the uniting factor. Onstage, Soft Machine and their motorcycle shenanigans were followed by Pink Floyd. Guests at the gathering included Paul McCartney, Mick Jagger and Marianne Faithfull. An Italian film crew came away with footage of topless women smearing themselves with paint.

There were other nights out, including the 'Zebra' club hosted at the Establishment (Soft Machine had a residency there during December 1966), and some kind of hippy ballet at the Electric Garden at 43 King Street in Covent Garden (there was an Electric Garden in Glasgow at a slightly later date, which was no formal relation, although it attracted a similar crowd and bands; Pink Floyd played there a number of times). The hippy ballet began with a curse-laden poem, then a communal dance to a distorted soundtrack. The team at *International Times* took against the Electric Garden, advising that it was 'an aggressively commercial scene run by hard cash gangsters'.

Ad hoc spaces became important, many of them short-lived, including All Saints Hall in Notting Hill, the site of live events staged to raise funds for the nearby Notting Hill Free School. Pete Jenner and Andrew King, who'd just become Pink Floyd's managers, were involved in shows there. Pink Floyd played at All Saints Hall, events for which Mark Boyle devised light shows. Also involved at All Saints Hall was Jack Braceland, who'd previously been responsible for running a nudist club in Watford.

Working with Joe Boyd – a tall American with some experience in the music business – Hoppy co-founded UFO, which was destined to become the most significant regular counter-culture music venue of the era. To stage UFO, Hopkins and Boyd hired the Blarney Club at 31 Tottenham Court Road, an old Irish dance club under a cinema, with a legal capacity of 600. Owned by a Mr Gannon, the hall had been known variously as the Carlton Dance Hall, Rector's and the Stork Club. Back in 1919 the Original Dixieland Jazz Band had featured there. UFO opened at the Blarney Club on 23 December 1966.

UFO was weekly, every Friday, not a one-off, and soon began to attract a crowd of regulars. You'd see them at other times floating around Portobello Road market, the Indica Bookshop, or at the Granny Takes a Trip boutique (opened at the beginning of the year on the King's Road). The venue became the home of a scene. The smell of incense and hash would waft up the stairs and, some nights, voluptuous prototype 'hippy chick' Suzy Creamcheese danced erotically at the side of the stage. Mark Boyle was responsible for most of the light shows; he'd be up above everybody on scaffolding burning chemicals in front of lenses to get particular effects. There was no DJ in any recognisable sense at UFO, but Jack Henry Moore was usually in residence, playing sounds with one deck and a reel-to-reel tape recorder, more in the manner of a freeform noise set than a discotheque. Sometimes Jeff Dexter would clock off from Tiles and attend, standing beside him and passing odd (literally) records to him to play.

Soon the number of regulars at UFO was into the several hundred, with chaos on the door. Most weeks in the first months, Pink Floyd played but, through the summer of 1967, the club also featured avant-garde jazz, Yoko Ono performances, poets including Brian Patten and Pete Brown, and a number of eccentric acts that may not have been appreciated by audiences in less mindaltered states, like the Bonzo Dog Doo Dah Band or, more particularly, Sam Spoons, who would perform, solo, on an electric trouser press.

Noting how hectic it was with not much being done to sort the chaos, after a few weeks Mick Farren found himself running the door at UFO. This involved explaining the nature of the night to Irish party people expecting the Blarney's usual jigs, reels and ballads, but mainly keeping the queue moving. At some clubs, like Studio 54 and on the opening nights at the Flamingo and the Cavern, queues were encouraged, but they were not always good news. A rabble of freaks jamming the pavement outside UFO would draw the attention of the police, and perhaps provoke harassment. In his memoir, Mick Farren doesn't register particularly fond memories of the customers – especially those who attempted to open a dialogue with him. Some would baulk at paying 10/- (50p) entrance fee to see a band like Pink Floyd. 'Don't freak me out with money, man,' they would say. When he gruffly ordered them to hurry on inside he'd get retorts like, 'You really need to do something about your ego, man.'

Down Shaftesbury Avenue and across Piccadilly Circus from UFO was the Scotch of St James in Mason's Yard. The Scotch had been opened in 1965 by Louis Brown and John Bloom and, along with the Ad Lib and the Cromwellian, became a favourite hangout for young rock & roll royalty like the Beatles, Eric Burdon and Keith Moon. The Scotch was one of the first venues Jimi Hendrix played in Britain. It was September 1966 and, escorted by Chas Chandler, Hendrix was on a seven-day tourist visa and couldn't do any official paid work, but that didn't stop him getting onstage and jamming when the opportunity arose. Kathy Etchingham was a DJ at the Cromwellian Club in Kensington for a while, and also at the Scotch of St James. She was at the Scotch that evening Hendrix turned up and, true to form, took to the stage to play some blues with the in-house band. Kathy and Jimi were something of an item from that night onwards.

On that same trip to London, Hendrix met Eric Clapton for the first time when Chas Chandler took him to a Cream concert at Central London Poly on Regent Street. During Cream's show, Hendrix joined them for a rendition of Howlin' Wolf's 'Killing Floor'. Clapton's first psychedelic experience was some months

later at the Speakeasy at a playback party for the Beatles *Sgt.
Pepper* album. Up until then he'd smoked a little dope; that was
the extent of his drug use. Micky Dolenz from the Monkees was
at the party and had taken it upon himself to dispense pills to
everybody, saying 'Love and peace, love and peace' while doing
so. It was STP, says Clapton: 'STP was like a quadruple-strength
dose of acid – within an hour or so I was saying, "Woah, what's
going on here?" Everybody was floating into one and everything
was floating or wreathed in flames. I remember being out of my
mind and thinking I was in the presence of giants, and we were all
going off somewhere together to another planet. The doors of
perception were wide open.'

In the first months of 1967 the nascent psychedelic scene in
Britain was being developed and mapped by Pink Floyd gigs.
They were building audiences in cities and medium-sized towns
around the country playing to *International Times* readers, college
kids and people who'd read lurid stories in the *Sunday People* on
the lookout for 'obscene orgies'; they helped build networks and
spread ideas and bring like minds together. When they weren't at
UFO, they were out on the road playing at student union events
at the University of Hull, Leicester College of Art and
Technology, St Catherine's College, Cambridge, and the canteen
at the London School of Economics, plus trips to Rotherham,
West Bromwich and Portsmouth.

In February 1967 Pink Floyd played at the Ricky Tick in
Windsor. The Ricky Tick events were run by music promoter
John Mansfield and his business partner Philip Hayward, who
took the name for their promotions from a book by Rudyard
Kipling about a mongoose called Rikki Tikki Tavi. The following night they played at the Ricky Tick in Hounslow, a venue that
also hosted gigs by Cream and Jimi Hendrix. Other Ricky Tick
venues could be found in Reading, Slough and Maidenhead, but
it was the one in the Windsor venue, at Clewer Mead – a rambling mansion by the River Thames on the outskirts of the

town – that was probably Ricky Tick's most successful venue. In Antonioni's 1966 film *Blowup*, the Yardbirds play at a venue that on the outside is the 100 Club on Oxford Street and inside is a replica of the Ricky Tick at Clewer Mead built at Pinewood Studios.

Pink Floyd's schedule through April was relentless, including engagements at the Britannia Rowing Club in Nottingham (later renamed the Boat Club) and the Floral Hall in Belfast (a beautiful modernist dance hall on the slopes of Cave Hill). Belfast was still thriving, with hundreds of bands and fifty or sixty clubs and venues in and around the city. After Them had success and moved to London, Taste (led by guitarist Rory Gallagher) were one of the Maritime's resident bands and the venue remained busy. Music lover and record collector Terri Hooley began getting work as a DJ there but was barred for making political speeches about the war in Vietnam.

At the same time as these live shows nationwide, Pink Floyd were reported to be beginning work on a half-hour-long film called *The Life Story of Percy the Ratcatcher*, as well as featuring on a series of all-nighter Saturdays at the Roundhouse. These occasions ran from 10 p.m. until dawn, with light shows. On 8 April Pink Floyd were joined by other entertainments including Earl Fuggle and the Electric Poets, dancers Sandy and Harda, and Sam Gopal, a tabla performer. Admission was 5/- (25p).

International Times was usually in a state of editorial crisis, subject to pressures from the police and financial woes. Hoppy decided to promote a festival to raise funds for the paper, specifically to fund a legal fight against the police after a raid on the *IT* offices. It was described as 'a giant benefit against fuzz action' and dubbed 'The 14-Hour Technicolor Dream'. The venue was the Alexandra Palace, which had been built almost a hundred years earlier between Muswell Hill and Wood Green in north London. Hoppy had seen the Rolling Stones play there with John Lee Hooker in 1964.

The doors to the 14-Hour Technicolor Dream on 29 April 1967 opened at 8 p.m., and the intention was for the entertainment and the event to last until 10 a.m. the next day. Pink Floyd, the Pretty Things, the Crazy World of Arthur Brown, the Move, the Deviants and Soft Machine were among the bands that played. In addition, there were jugglers, poets including Michael Horovitz, a reading by Alex Trocchi and a live performance by the Tribe of the Sacred Mushroom. The musical and other entertainment was set up on stages at either end of the hall, with a lighting gantry halfway along, cutting across the width of the building. Under the lighting, the music from both stages met and clashed. Mick Farren was one of a number of eyewitnesses who reported stoned hippies grooving to what he describes as 'a weird atonal cacophony'.

The gathering at Alexandra Palace demonstrated the sounds of the new movement, the fashions and the lightshows, and should also go down in history as the evening John Lennon didn't meet Yoko Ono. He was wandering round the event and elsewhere in the hall she was performing an art happening, employing a model and seating her on a stepladder illuminated by a spotlight, and then inviting people to cut the model's clothing with scissors. It's probable there were between seven and ten thousand people there, riding a helter skelter, watching the bands, losing their minds in the zone where distorted sounds clashed, smoking joints, dropping acid, floating around in a groovy haze. John and Yoko's paths didn't cross.

Pink Floyd had arranged to play as dawn broke, a plan which actually wasn't cosmic theatrics but based on a practical consideration. After playing at the Tabernacle in Stockport on the 28th, they had made their way to the Netherlands via London for the afternoon on the 29th, where they were filmed for a Dutch TV show, and then drove back from there, taking the ferry. Once back in London they took a short break at the management's HQ on Edbrooke Road before heading to Alexandra Palace. Pete Jenner, the band's manager, later recalled the Technicolor Dream: 'At least half the audience were doing acid. I was doing acid. We'd had to take a long drive to get there from a gig in Holland and I did the last bit of the drive in the van. We dropped in at home and I did some acid before we went, and by the time I got to Alexandra Palace, trying to drive the van was getting quite exciting.'

The band were probably just as exhausted as Pete Jenner was excited. Syd Barrett, in particular, was tired and tripping, although he seemed OK enough with his mirror-disc telecaster as the band played, dressed in flared trousers and satin shirts, the stage lit with a pink hue, dawn breaking through the windows. But acid use was shaking Syd apart.

Pink Floyd seemed always to be on the road. Early in May they were at a venue in Ainsdale on Merseyside called the Moulin Rouge. John Keenan was studying at the nearby Southport Art College and got involved in promoting events off campus. Prior to Pink Floyd, John had only promoted one show, featuring John Mayall's Bluesbreakers, Liverpool band the Mojos and his neighbour Max Lunt's band. He's forgotten the name of his neighbour's band but remembers the event lost £20. The Moulin Rouge in Ainsdale is now a Toby Inn.

Back at UFO, the club was often overcrowded, or at least near capacity, but was receiving unwanted attention from troublemakers and from the media, especially the *News of the World*. They sent a journalist to the venue from where he filed a report describing a 'weirdly-dressed' audience, listened to 'discordant music', 'tinkling cowbells' and 'obscene poetry'. The reporter claimed to have chanced upon people having sex and smoking cannabis. The paranoia of club operators and their customers wasn't only the result of journalists but undercover police and allies of the law enforcement agencies. *International Times* reported various sightings of 'a grass named Joe, thick-set, with large head'.

Encouraged so to do by the media, the police increased their pressure on Mr Gannon and threatened to close his premises, so Joe Boyd transferred UFO to the Roundhouse, although to some observers the Roundhouse was too big for something that had always thrived on its connections with the underground and drawn strength and its identity from being a minority, niche hangout.

There were alternatives, including Happening 44, founded by Jack Braceland. He converted a former strip club at 44 Gerrard Street into a psychedelic basement space, featuring a variety of entertainments: in the words of his advertising copy, 'rave groups, exotic entertainers. Movies, strobes, discs, groovy food'. Fairly typical of the acts that took to the stage were Shiva's Children, consisting of two underdressed hippy girls performing distorted ballet sequences while their gay friend Alan intoned and played bongos.

Tiles was still open in June 1967 and the programming included the 'Jeff Dexter light & sound show' presented on Tuesdays, but the venue was still mostly frequented by young mods who resisted some of the initiatives designed to attract the psychedelic underground, including a DJ set by John Peel. Peel had a show on Radio London called Perfumed Garden, with an eclectic content of poems, letters and talk, and a playlist championing a new generation of music – Captain Beefheart, Love, Pink Floyd, the Incredible String Band – but the show came to an end when the Marine Broadcasting Offences Act, which aimed to close pirate radio stations like Radio London and O'Rahilly's Radio Caroline, came into force. He continued to use the Perfumed Garden name for a column he contributed to *International Times* and also for various DJ engagements, but when Peel took the Perfumed Garden to Tiles on Sunday 24 September 1967 for the first of a scheduled run of Sundays, it was a disaster, with Peel and his friends and fans abused and threatened by some of the regulars. It turned out to be the club's last night; two days later it closed.

Three thousand people attended this grand ball at the Free Trade Hall, Manchester, in 1845.

Thomas Youdan (centre) built a huge music hall in Sheffield, featuring singers, daft competitions and performing dogs.

Charlie Chaplin and Harry Houdini performed at the City Varieties. It evolved from a music hall founded in 1865.

The Headrow entrance to the City Varieties in Leeds before the recent restoration and refurbishment.

The Ritz, Manchester (c.1925) with a sprung dancefloor. Now, just as well known for its sticky carpet.

The Streatham Locarno, 1939. Ruth Ellis worked here briefly (she was the last woman in Britain to be hanged, after killing her lover David Blakely in 1955).

A night out at the Dennistoun Palais in Glasgow (converted into a Fine Fare supermarket in 1962).

Cy Laurie entertaining dancers at his club in Ham Yard, 1954. He ran all-nighters, which George Melly's friends called 'raves'.

The Gateways – a lesbian nightclub on King's Road, London. The club and some of its regulars appear in the 1968 film *The Killing of Sister George*.

The Coventry Locarno, later known as Tiffany's (now Coventry Central Library); built in 1960 at the heart of a pedestrianised shopping scheme.

Roger Eagle's office at the Twisted Wheel, Brazennose Street, Manchester, June 1964; Roger with John Lee Hooker.

Entrance to the Scene Club on Ham Yard, December 1964. Amazing pleasures through that inauspicious doorway . . .

The Scene, December 1964. Described as 'a focal point for the mod movement' by Pete Townshend of the Who.

The Who filming for German TV at the Marquee club in May 1965.

Allen Ginsberg reading at the International Poetry Incarnation event at the Albert Hall, London (June 1965).

UFO on Tottenham Court Road. On the right, John 'Hoppy' Hopkins, one of the club's founders.

Who'd have thought? Black Sabbath plus DJ Pete Waterman.

DUNLOP (COVENTRY) APPRENTICES AND STUDENTS
ASSOCIATION

Proudly Present A DANCE
Featuring

THE BLACK SABBATH **PLUS THE 'GREGORIAN CHANT'**

with

all the LATEST and GREATEST DISCO SOUNDS provided by

PETE WATERMAN

in the GROSVENOR ROOM,   HOTEL LEOFRIC
26th. September, 1969   TICKETS 7s. - 6d.
Dancing 8 p.m. - 1 a.m.   Bar Till Midnight

'Shoop Shoop', a regular Thursday disco at the Golden Eagle, Birmingham, with DJ Mike Horseman (c.1977).

Front cover of the first issue of *International Times*, including news of the 14 Hour Technicolor Dream (Alexandra Palace, 29 April 1967).

UFO poster 1967. UFO was based at 31 Tottenham Court Rd, in an Irish club called The Blarney.

Poster advertising UFO nights at the Roundhouse, September 1967 (designed by Martin Sharp).

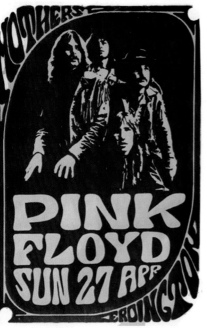

Pink Floyd at Mothers, Erdington (Birmingham), April 1969. DJ John Peel later said Mothers was 'for a few years the best club in Britain'.

Northern Soul fans on the dancefloor at Wigan Casino in 1975.

Northern Soul – an in-crowd and a movement like no other. Thirty years of Wigan Casino cloth badges.

Colin Curtis and Chris Burton on the site of the Golden Torch, Tunstall (Stoke). Photograph from 2013.

Membership card for the Timepiece, Liverpool, where DJ Les Spaine played modern soul and heavy funk.

The end of Tiles had come about following a meeting of its creditors. During the summer of 1967 various versions of the underground played at the Festival of the Flower Children, an open-air gig at Woburn Abbey, part-hosted by the owners of Tiles. It wasn't much more than a selection of post-mod groups, including the Alan Price Set and the Jeff Beck Group. Probably the most way-out act was Dantalian's Chariot, who included Zoot Money and Andy Summers (later of the Police) in their line-up; they performed in white robes, accompanied by a dazzling light show. The Peel fiasco was a sign of the times but it was the financial losses incurred by this mish-mash of a semi-psychedelic weekend that had forced Tiles to close.

Throughout the late 1960s into the 1970s, there were people willing to host anti-commercial events and happenings. On 4 June 1967 there was a 'be-in' with Yoko Ono on Hampstead Heath, with a mission, apparently, to share information on how to colour the clouds and find an imaginary snail (Yoko was organised enough to set up a wet-weather plan B – 'British Museum if it rains' explained the listing in *International Times*). Someone called Malcolm Luxury-Yot organised a Sunshine Fair in Sheffield featuring frolicking minstrels, magic and freak-outs.

It wasn't all sweetness and light shows, however. At UFO's new Roundhouse base, practical problems surfaced. One night skinheads broke in and created mayhem and on another occasion Miles was robbed of the takings. Mick Farren later recalled the struggles to keep aggro out and protection rackets at bay: 'The local protection racket gangsters would come round and say, "Nice place you've got here. Shame if it got smashed up." We were just a bunch of hippies and we really didn't know how to deal with it.'

Police harassment of the long-haired – under the pretext of drug enforcement – became a matter of routine. Middle Earth was busted in March 1968, with police rushing in, herding the boys up against one wall, girls up against the other. Everyone was searched, some people taken away. In his 'Perfumed Garden' column, John Peel urged support for Release, an organisation that had been founded the previous year by Caroline Coon and Rufus Harris and given funds from the proceeds of some of the first UFO events. Release set up a phone helpline offering legal advice to people arrested on drug-related charges.

It wasn't just the underground press spreading the word about long-haired counter-culture; networks were developing via venues, book shops, galleries and, of course, tabloid coverage helped fuel interest. Any time there's a new scene or an emerging music movement, the bastions of the previous eras suddenly face a battle to stay relevant. A former mod stronghold, the Birdcage in Portsmouth, closed despite a short-lived attempt to rebrand the venue as a hippy hangout called Brave New World. In Cheltenham, the Egg & Bacon milk bar, based above the Burton menswear store and beloved by mods, metamorphosed into the Blue Moon Club, featuring the likes of Jimi Hendrix and Mott the Hoople. In Sheffield, although most of the live acts remained soul-oriented at the Mojo, Peter Stringfellow gave the club's decor a flower-power makeover. The start of 1967 witnessed a Jimi Hendrix performance, but through the year the transitioning and juggling between the soul roots of the club and the psychedelic scene wasn't working and Stringfellow was losing interest. By the end of 1967, after some licensing hassles, the club had closed.

Despite the commercial success of *Sgt. Pepper* and other counter-culture interventions gaining a high public profile, long-hairs remained in a minority through the 1960s, apart from small towns with large university-student populations. Elsewhere the mod look continued to prevail (which meant, at various times, Ben Sherman and Brutus button-down shirts, Levi Sta-Prest or mohair trousers). Chris Burton at the Golden Torch in Tunstall had enjoyed three good years hosting beat groups, but from 1967 his takings took a dive. Only a few progressive rock acts pulled an audience at the venue, and his best nights were those featuring Barmy Barry, the bantering, one-deck, disc-only resident.

In Birmingham, the blues, folk and freak scenes in the area were being nurtured at the likes of the Whiskey on Navigation Street and the Elbow Room in Aston, where Band of Joy (featuring Robert Plant) had played in April 1967 and Fairport Convention and Spooky Tooth in February 1968. Traffic had come together there, jamming, and the Elbow Room DJs, among them Erskine Thomas and Micky Twitch, had built themselves a solid reputation playing blues and early psychedelia.

In Manchester, Roger Eagle hadn't lost his devotion to John Lee Hooker and Sonny Boy Williamson, but had found a new passion – Captain Beefheart & the Magic Band's *Safe as Milk* album, released in September 1967. Captain Beefheart's music was harsher than flower power, a kind of fractured blues. Roger incorporated this Beefheart influence into his events at a venue called the Blue Note, where he encouraged a young band of Manchester musicians called Jacko Ogg & the Head People to perform on a regular basis on Tuesday nights. CP Lee was part of the original line-up, as was drummer Bruce Mitchell (Bruce was known to take to the stage in a gorilla suit, and on occasion they'd randomly incorporate bagpipes in the set; their rhythm guitarist was North of England bagpipe champion). CP Lee reckons they were also the first Manchester band to use a light show. Dave Backhouse, wielding glass slides and revolving filters, soon established himself as Manchester's most in-demand light show operator.

Roger Eagle knew it was time for him to find a new club, a new space that the emerging generation could call their own, somewhere beyond one-offs and house parties and walks in the park, and he found a venue in the back streets of old Manchester at 11 Cromford Court, the former Jigsaw Club (which, in an even earlier era, had been the Manchester Cavern where Dave Lee Travis had been one of the resident DJs). The Magic Village opened on 9 March 1968, with a performance by Jacko Ogg & the Head People. The flyer announcing the opening proclaimed, 'This is Manchester's first new scene for five years – Be part of it!' (Roger was referring back to the opening of the Twisted Wheel in 1963). Dave Backhouse took charge of the light shows. Roger's first DJ playlist included Dylan, Frank Zappa and the Mothers of Invention, the Doors, Captain Beefheart, and the Velvet Underground & Nico. Early bookings included live appearances by Tyrannosaurus Rex, Jethro Tull, John Mayall and Tim Rose.

In an issue of *International Times* in May 1968, a correspondent called David Stringer sketched out the problems the underground was having building any networks or finding any focus in Manchester. Stringer suspends judgement on the Magic Village but despairs at the sense of imprisonment and inertia in the city: 'Everybody has been waiting for a mysterious someone else to lay the "golden egg" for them – which is natural in a society where the entertainer-entertained, boss-exploited, ruler-ruled, landlord-tenant relationships etc are taken for granted.'

For Roger a club wasn't a venue where random live bands played and random audiences gathered. He liked to create a community. The intention was for the Magic Village to be a bit of an arts centre, the kind of initiative David Stringer was hoping for, somewhere poets could perform, and films could be shown. Roger's movie plans were scuppered when it was realised that the low ceiling meant a projector wouldn't clear the heads of the audience, but undeterred Roger hired the nearby Houldsworth Hall in June 1968 for a showing of a film about Bob Dylan, *Dont Look Back* (there's some footage of Dylan soundchecking at the Free Trade Hall in the finished film).

On Saturday nights, the venue was open from 7 p.m. until 7 or 7.30 in the morning (it was alcohol-free). The Magic Village also went through phases of opening in the afternoons, just to give people somewhere to hang out.

Nicky Crewe was a fifteen-year-old convent schoolgirl who had developed a taste for music 'that wasn't mainstream or chart music' (in her words). She tells me that even before then, she'd found flower power appealing and intriguing. It had led her on a school trip to finding and buying a copy of *International Times* ('I absolutely devoured it, feeling a sense of recognition'). Her parents were in the Far East and she was staying with her best friend. They went searching for the Magic Village together: 'It was just like finding where I belonged. My parents would have been horrified because it was a dank cellar in a Dickensian-type courtyard.'

The Village was a cellar club, the walls used to run with water and the toilets were hideous. Inside there was a juke box, and Mike Don would set up selling alternative magazines including *IT*, *Gandalf's Garden*, *Friends*, *Oz* and local publications like *Grass Eye* and *Moul Express* (later rechristened *Mole Express*); he'd occasionally have to deal with water dripping onto his trestle table.

'We'd be hanging around [during] the day when other people weren't and for me it was the coffee bar aspect as much as the music venue aspect,' says Nicky. 'There were bands that I saw down there but for me it was hanging around during the day and meeting up with people and it was just amazing.'

You were very aware of how much more than music it was?

'Yes, it was a lifestyle and I was aware of it even at that age and that was interesting to me and I picked up on that. It was an intense period of time. People were talking about a lot of things, politics not just music, it was just fascinating and there was nobody telling me I shouldn't be going there or doing that.'

Brian Jackson, a regular attender, once described the Magic Village as a 'safe refuge for psychedelic people'. Roger Eagle and his team would do their best to help people not get busted, and there would be a sense of solidarity at the club. Freaks could find themselves targeted not just by the police but by members of the public taking against their look; CP Lee remembers 'navvies' chasing long-hairs down Market Street. Out touring, bands could also come up against the forces of reaction. The Deviants and Led Zeppelin shared a bill at Exeter Civic Hall in December 1968, which was disrupted by two dozen burly farmhands rioting. Led Zeppelin managed one and a half songs before retreating to the dressing room under a shower of beer glasses.

A safe and more lucrative circuit had developed at university and college unions, where there was a captive audience, more prone to growing their hair than the rest of the population, and with entertainment officers with a looser hold of budgets than most club owners. College gigs were money-spinners even for a middle-league rock band.

Students tended to give artists a warm welcome, but especially after the *événements* of May 1968 in Paris, student politics took a more hardline turn, and educational establishments became hotbeds of protests and sit-ins. On the college circuit various practices were being called into question by hardliners wary of perpetuating the entertainer–entertained relationship. For example, there was some ideological resistance to bands getting VIP treatment and student agitators of an anti-hierarchical bent were known to storm backstage areas and secure the crates of beer or any other food and drink, and, having liberated the band's rider, distribute it among the audience.

On Saturday 10 August 1968 in Birmingham the Deviants played the opening weekend at Mothers. Looking to move on from Motown and following their own interests and instincts, the management team at the Carlton Ballroom had decided to radically and permanently alter the booking policy and to rename the club Mothers, with the tagline 'The home of good sounds'. The club had a capacity in excess of 400, which was about the number that paid in on Sunday 15 September when Tyrannosaurus Rex appeared with DJ and compere support from John Peel. For a while, Peel made fortnightly appearances at Mothers, usually on

Fridays. The acts and the public mingled. And Peel would too, exchanging tips on forthcoming bands and releases; on his radio show he'd report back on what had happened on earlier visits.

Going to a club like Mothers wasn't about taking the easiest option; it was something of an adventure. After it had been open about six months or so, C.J. Stone got a sniff of something happening across town. Then a sixth-former, he went to explore. He didn't know what to expect or what to wear. The only youth cult that had made serious inroads into wider consciousness was mod, so Stone put on his best suit; a four-buttoned mod suit made for him by his grandfather. His mate Robert Russell sported a two-tone suit of shiny grey. Stone also had on a pair of brogues.

He was exhilarated but confused by what he saw. Lots of hair, beards, hippies, freaks. As he later described in the book *Fierce Dancing: Adventures in the Underground*, he struggled for a point of reference. 'No one else had suits on at all. They were in battered jeans with triangular, flowery vents to make them flared, with ragged patches all over them, which hung about the heels sucking up dirt. And some of them were wearing old stripey blazers or duffel coats two sizes too small. And bangles and beads and badges.'

The regular DJ was Erskine Thomas, who'd also been a DJ at a short-lived club called Midnight City (situated under the Moat House in Digbeth) as well as the Elbow Room. For some bands – the blues-influenced, underground progressive rock of the era – the club found and nurtured the perfect audience. Roy Harper played at Mothers half a dozen times between 1968 and 1970. 'That was the first club outside London that meant anything at all.'

You'd queue down a side alley, walk up the wooden stairs past Lenny the doorman, hear the music Erskine was playing and go into a room with a stage set up at the far end. There were posters on the walls and even the ceiling. Stone and his gaggle of friends became regulars, and he'd attend most Fridays and some Wednesdays.

John 'Ozzy' Osbourne, a trouble-making youth from Aston, had formed a band with the former guitarist in the Rockin' Chevrolets, Tony Iommi. Their band, Polka Tulk, was soon renamed Earth. In September 1968 they played 'Henry's Blues House', run by Jim Simpson every Tuesday at the Crown on Station Street in Birmingham (the same venue where the Ian Campbell Folk Group had recorded their live debut album). Earth then became Black Sabbath and performed several times at Mothers. C.J. Stone saw them play there, as well as Soft Machine and Blodwyn Pig. Afterwards he'd have curry and chips from a takeaway and then walk all the way home, which took hours.

As we'll see in the next chapter, mainstream city-centre night-clubs at the time were beginning to make promises of sophistication and cocktails, but Mothers was a world away. Anyone looking for glitz was sorely disappointed. Head-scratch-ing journalist Maurice Rotheroe – who'd concluded that Mothers was more of a cult than a nightclub – had visited one Sunday. There's no seating to speak of, he reported, aside from a few chairs in uneven rows near the stage and some tables and chairs near the bar. The audience sit on the floor during many of the shows, or stand. There's not much dancing to speak of. He spies a snack bar where pies can be bought for two shillings each. After concluding that the pies weren't the main attraction of Mothers, the journalist doesn't even attempt to explain the music. 'The pop-20 is deliberately excluded and the sounds you hear at Mothers are, its devotees claim, way ahead of their time.'

Mothers would also attract people from all over the Midlands, Wales and occasionally from London too, and local musicians would pop in on their nights off; John Bonham lived locally, Robert Plant, Stan Webb, and Ozzy Osbourne would also visit. Mick Farren recalled being invited by John Peel to accompany him from London to Birmingham to see the Who play there. Peel was friendly with Germaine Greer; she often stayed in his spare room in St John's Wood, when she wasn't teaching at the

University of Warwick or in Manchester (at the time she was presenting a Granada TV show called *Nice Time*). And she also took a ride up to Mothers with Peel that day in January 1969. They saw the Who at their most magnificent. It was the depths of winter, but a huge crowd packed in under the low ceiling generated an almighty heat; drummer Keith Moon collapsed at the end of 'Magic Bus' and was taken backstage and had water poured over his head. Peel dropped off Greer in Warwick and Farren got out of the car there as well, leaving Peel to drive the last hundred miles to London alone, but also marking the beginning of a Farren/Greer affair; they became something of a public couple on the scene.

Pink Floyd were at Mothers on 27 April 1969 when their set was recorded; some of the live material was later included on the *Ummagumma* album (together with tracks recorded at Manchester College of Commerce – now known as MMU – a week later). By this time the Mothers crew were also promoting gigs outside the venue, as word spread, the scene got bigger and there was enough demand and money around to bring over American acts. In May 1969 they presented the Mothers of Invention at Birmingham Town Hall.

At Mothers itself Black Sabbath had a fortnightly residency on Wednesdays through March and April 1970. They weren't a big draw, as the door price reflected: 4/- (20p) entrance fee to see Sabbath (the average admission at Mothers was around 15/- (75p). There were plenty of memorable nights – including the occasion the Principal Edwards Magic Theatre gave the audience kazoos and tambourines and led everyone a merry dance down Erdington High Street.

Early in 1970 the Principal Edwards Magic Theatre appeared as part of a bill in Manchester including Country Joe & the Fish and the Liverpool Scene at a gig in Houldsworth Hall promoted by Roger Eagle. Like the team at Mothers, he was branching out of his venue. By the beginning of 1970, Roger Eagle seems to have

decided to concentrate on Houldsworth Hall, and the Magic
Village tailed off. In the two years that the Village had been operating, the area of Manchester city centre around Cromford Court
and nearby New Brown Street had become a small enclave of
hippy-ish activity, with boutiques and a 'head shop' called On
The Eighth Day (purveyor of alternative magazines, joss sticks,
crafts, clothing, jewellery, bags and other hippy paraphernalia,
which soon moved to Oxford Road and evolved into a vegetar-
ian café). Roger went over to Liverpool and began to promote
shows at the Stadium, a boxing arena.

In Erdington, the lease on the space housing Mothers was
coming to a close and one of the managers, Phil Myatt, had
already set up more Town Hall shows, including gigs featuring
Love and Pentangle. A few months after the end of the Magic
Village, it was all over for Mothers too.

It's probably true to say that the most creative years of the
counter-culture were over; certainly there was widespread disillusionment politically, and as with any surge in new sounds and
styles, many of the pioneers had success which took them out of
the underground, or had faded, or had moved on. Nevertheless
most towns had established at least one venue sympathetic to the
long-hairs by the beginning of the 1970s. 'Friars' opened in June
1969 at the New Friarage Hall, then relocated first to Aylesbury's
Assembly Hall then (in 1975) to the Civic Centre. A small promotions company calling themselves Cherry Red began staging
regular events at the Malvern Winter Gardens (where Pink Floyd
had played in 1967). Their first show was July 1971 (when
Hawkwind headlined) and other artists Cherry Red promoted at
the venue included the Velvet Undergound in 1972.

Most towns and cities also supported at least one venue where
folk musicians played regularly. The Troubadour was still going
strong, and elsewhere in London Les Cousins, in the basement of
a restaurant in Greek Street, featured folk and blues (the likes of
John Martyn, Clive Palmer, Ralph McTell and Roy Harper all

appeared there). At the folk club held in the Red Rooster Café in Bow Street in Lisburn, Northern Ireland, the influence of Bob Dylan was matched by that of the Clancy Brothers and the Dubliners. Folkies met up on Thursday nights at the Green Moose Café in Liverpool's Brooks Alley; one the regular performers was singer-songwriter Willy Russell; he later became an acclaimed dramatist who has since realised how integral that small music venue was in his life and work. 'I now see that from having to do that gig every Thursday I was learning all kinds of things about the nature of performance, about audiences, about what will and won't work, about how overwriting can kill a song (or, indeed, a play or any other form for that matter). Although none of us knew it at the time, all those folk places, cafés, pubs, old cellars, were a fantastic training ground for all kinds of talent – it was a completely anti-commercial, anti music-establishment phenomenon.'

Folk was programmed alongside blues and other anti-commercial sounds; at venues including the Van Dike in Plymouth and the Granary in Bristol, for example. The Granary, on Queen Charlotte Street, was built in 1869 as a grain warehouse. Designed in a style that's been described as 'Ruskinian Venetian Gothic', its imposing frontage is red-brick, augmented by decorative black and white brick and limestone dressings. In 1979, Andor Gomme, in *Bristol, an Architectural History*, claimed that it is 'the most piquant and striking monument of the High Victorian age in Bristol ... as potent a symbol of the city as the cathedral or St Mary Redcliffe'. By 1979, though, its days as a granary were long gone. In 1968 the building – which had lain empty since the 1950s – became the home of a jazz club run by Ted Cowell under the guidance of the successful singer and clarinettist Acker Bilk. After a few months, midweek nights became available and some non-jazzers seized the opportunity to run nights they dubbed 'Plastic Dog', featuring progressive rock, folk and blues.

The Granary became a hub of activity. Plastic Dog spawned

Plastic Dog Graphics, a company of graphic designers responsible for producing posters and other promotional material for the gigs, and the monthly *Dogpress* magazine, which was distributed for free and carried listings of forthcoming events. Very much of its time, most issues had a 'groupie of the month' (*East Village Other* had a regular photo feature entitled 'Slum Goddess of the Lower East Side'). The use of photographs and drawings of naked women in the underground press was often challenged but persisted. The counter-culture was fragmenting, the world was changing. In 1973 the final issue of *Oz* included a piece by David Widgery that concluded, 'What finally knackered the underground was its complete inability to deal with women's liberation.'

Dogpress in December 1971 announced that DJ Ed 'Super-Ed' Newsom was leaving to go to London, although he later returned to Bristol and the Granary turntables. The longest-serving DJ was Al Read, one of Plastic Dog's founders. One of the directors through much of this time was Tony Bullimore, who, with his wife Lalel, had previously owned the Bamboo club in St Paul's, a favoured venue among Bristol's Afro-Caribbean community. Billing itself as 'Bristol's Premier West Indian Entertainment Centre', the Bamboo had hosted sound-system events, a restaurant, theatre, workshops, darts, dominoes, and live acts that even included Bob Marley and the Wailers, and Jimmy Cliff.

Deeper into the West Country, a number of the first festival-style events had been taking place, including the Bath Blues Festival in 1969. Twelve thousand people filled the Bath Recreation Ground to hear the likes of John Mayall, Fleetwood Mac, Taste and Liverpool Scene. Organised by Freddy Bannister, the compere was John Peel and the biggest impact was probably made by Led Zeppelin, just back from their second tour of the States. Planty had begun his life's work.

A year later the festival moved to a bigger site and was billed as the Bath Festival of Blues & Progressive Music, attracting tens of thousands of visitors over three days watching the likes of Frank

Zappa, the Byrds, Jefferson Airplane, Santana and Pink Floyd. Not only were such events in West Country fields a reflection of how big some of the international acts had become but, outdoors, far from a city, they also reflected a movement in the counter-culture away from the pressure and politics of urban protest and venues in derelict Victorian buildings, and towards dropping out in – and romanticising – rural Britain.

Michael Eavis, then in his mid-thirties, had inherited the family farm, Worthy Farm, in Pilton, Somerset. One of his neighbours told him about the Bath Festival of Blues & Progressive Music and he took a Sunday off to see what it was all about. Inspired, the very next day he decided to put on his own festival, even though he had no experience of organising such a thing. He recalls getting a phone call from what seemed like a friendly young man with a West Country accent much like his, offering the services of him and his friends as security for the festival. It was only later he realised they were Hell's Angels. He tried to put them off when they started demanding money from him and they ended up setting fire to one of his father's hay wagons.

Saturday 19 September was set as the date, and Eavis asked for a one-pound admission charge, which most people seemed happy to pay. Burned-out hay wagon notwithstanding, the Hell's Angels did their job. Fifteen hundred people attended the 1970 Pilton Pop, Folk & Blues Festival. Eavis incurred a loss of over £1,000 but resolved to repeat the festival the following year. In the interim he was approached by Andrew Kerr and Arabella Churchill (he describes them as 'glamorous hippies'; Arabella was the granddaughter of Winston Churchill). They persuaded Eavis to change the name to the Glastonbury Fayre.

The following year a film crew turned up at Glastonbury (the director was Nic Roeg but it was said he soon got bored and went off to another project). Several people got naked, including a bongo player and a guy riding a motorcycle. Linda Lewis had taken mescalin; she was singing alongside Terry Reid and dancing

with a tree. Arthur Brown's stage act, which involved setting fire
to himself during 'Fire', though a favourite of the freaks, was
notorious for setting off bad trips. He started playing and Linda
Lewis thought she was entering the gates of hell. A friend of the
organisers, called Rollo, was also freaked out by Arthur Brown,
started crying and took all his clothes off.

The second Isle of Wight Festival featured Dylan (the first was
headlined by Jefferson Airplane). The third, in 1970, included the
Who, Jimi Hendrix, Joni Mitchell, Leonard Cohen and other
big hitters. There were many free festivals in the era, but promoter
Ray Foulk had bands and invoices to pay, and to enforce paid
admission arranged for the site to be surrounded by walls of cor-
rugated iron and security guards with Alsatian dogs. Mick Farren
was among those who tore the fencing down. 'Commercial
overkill' is how he later described the festival, and was recorded as
saying, 'Rock's becoming an opiate designed to create docile consumers.'

By 1972, the keepers of the conscience of the underground
appeared to have given up on festivals as any kind of progressive
force. After the Great Western Express Festival at Bardney in
Lincolnshire, Richard Neville in *International Times* (issue 132) was
scathing. 'It was a Tory festival in the sense that it rehabilitated the
concept of hierarchies, superstardom, VIPs, and all the other paraphernalia of class society, which a genuine people's festival would
strive to dismantle.'

Mick Farren spent a lot of time in the second half of the 1970s
in Dingwalls in Camden – 'a long, narrow, live music and drinking joint' overseen by Howard Parker, a former DJ at the
Speakeasy who had also stage-managed bands, looked after both
Jimi Hendrix and Frank Zappa, and was renowned for his unflap-
pability and egalitarian attitude to club-goers. When Dingwalls
opened in Camden Lock, Parker became the club's creative director. At Dingwalls, Farren saw bands including Country Joe

McDonald and Johnny Thunders and the Heartbreakers, and Eric Clapton sitting in with Buddy Guy. He recalls seeing Guy Stevens drinking there, drunk and abusive. It was also the first place he saw Dr Feelgood. He felt it was his place, somewhere for 'the freaks who'd made it through'. Mick Farren died in July 2013, hours after having collapsed onstage during a performance by a reconstructed line-up of the Deviants at the Borderline Club in London.

Nicky Crewe started work at On The Eighth Day, where many of the Magic Village regulars congregated. It's still easy for her to recall the music she heard coming from the juke box when she was hanging out at the Village, like Bob Dylan's 'Crawl out Your Window', Jefferson Airplane's 'Crown of Creation' and Captain Beefheart & the Magic Band's 'Electricity'. She says the latter would be one of two songs that most sum up that period in her life: '"Alone Again Or" by Love, which is going to be my epitaph. And "Electricity", because that was equally influential on me, and one's kind of sad, and one's energising.'

The Granary closed in 1988. DJ Al Read was still playing 'Free Bird' and 'Stairway to Heaven' at the Friday-night rock disco well into the early 1980s. Tony Bullimore hit the national headlines in January 1997 while competing in a single-handed around-the-world boat race when his vessel capsized. The 55-year-old survived in an air pocket underneath the upside-down boat and was rescued some four days later by the Royal Australian Navy.

Earth officially changed their name to Black Sabbath in August 1969 and took their slum rock and mega-selling album tours to gigs in huge stadiums via Mothers. As Earth, they had been booked to play a few shows in the next month or so, and some promoters had to amend the tickets with the new name. They'd been booked to play at the Grosvenor Suite at the Hotel Leofric for a party hosted by Dunlop (Coventry) Apprentices and Students Association. The gig took place on 26 September 1969.

The amended ticket made mention of the other acts performing on the night, including the DJ, a straggly-haired Coventry youth who'd been promoting progressive rock nights at the Walsgrave pub and worked in a record shop. His name: Pete Waterman. Tickets for the party at the Grosvenor Suite in the Hotel Leofric featuring Black Sabbath and DJ Pete Waterman were 7/6 (37½p).

CHAPTER SEVEN

Soul power, Big Julie,
'You Make Me Feel (Mighty Real)'

The Abadi brothers moved the Twisted Wheel to a warren of rooms at the Piccadilly Station end of Whitworth Street after leaving the Wheel's original site on Brazennose Street. The first all-nighter at the new venue was on 18 September 1965 and featured the Spencer Davis Group. From 1963, at its Brazennose Street site, with Roger Eagle playing a leading role, the music policy had always been pioneering, rhythm & blues at the outset, and then predominantly soul music, but Roger grew restless and left, moving on to create a freak scene at the Magic Village.

Established at their second site on Whitworth Street, the Wheel was less eclectic without Roger, but continued to thrive in the second half of the 1960s, playing host to acts including the Who, Steampacket, Doris Troy and Irma Thomas, and finding a ready audience of all-nighter fans in the north Midlands and the north of England with their roots in mod, who resisted the lure of the psychedelic freak scene of the late 1960s. They kept the faith with short, sharp, black soul from northern cities of the USA – specifically the home of Motown, Detroit – but went beyond Motown to a deep passion for rare stuff from the mid-1960s that hadn't charted or had a UK release.

London-based journalist Dave Godin took a train up to an all-nighter at the Twisted Wheel late in 1970, on a night when Les Cokell was DJing. Once the doors were open sometime soon after 11 p.m., people gathered in the coffee bar on the ground floor then went downstairs, where lighting was provided by single bulbs, most of them situated behind the wheels, dim light filtered through the spokes. 'Such scarcity of illumination tends to have a widening effect on the pupils of the eyes,' reported Godin in the pages of *Blues & Soul*. He was taken with the dancing – acrobatic and quite unlike anything that would be tolerated at your average Mecca venue – and the devotion to the rarities. The music played didn't have any of the jazz or funk inflections of contemporary soul music that tended to find favour in London and the south of England. Godin in his report on the Twisted Wheel christened the scene 'Northern Soul'. A night out wasn't just a passing fancy. Godin puts it like this: 'Soul is more than just music, it is a lifestyle too.'

These soul fans, almost all of them white, were devoted to the music, almost all of it black. Fashions hadn't yet coalesced into a specific look as they did a little later in the Northern Soul scene – particularly at Wigan Casino – although Godin does note the prevalence of Ben Shermans in the crowd. The regulars were drawn by the music, the sense of adventure, the thrill of being night owls in a city that was asleep. I once had cause to make conversation with the Scottish writer James Kelman, who has always had something of a reputation for being hard-edged and glowering. He was neither of those when we started talking about what he did at the weekends during his time living in Manchester working as a labourer on local building sites in the late 1960s; his weekends spent at the Twisted Wheel were the highlight of Kelman's time in the city.

Across the north of England, there were one or two other post-mod rare soul scene venues like the Bin Lid in Dewsbury, Room at the Top in Wigan, the Bee Gee in Leeds and the Tin

Chicken in Castleford. The names were supposed to conjure a sense that the venues were as raw and authentic as the black American soul you'd hear there. None of them had anything along the lines of a Bali Hai bar, glamour, pineapple chunks or flashing lights.

The Abadis closed the Twisted Wheel just a few weeks after Godin's visit. They'd decided many months earlier they wanted to run a venue with an alcohol licence, as that was where the money was. The final all-nighter at the Twisted Wheel was on 30 January 1971 featuring Edwin Starr. The Abadis later reopened the venue as Placemate 7, with a plan to take the venue in a more commercial direction, and pitch to a smarter, monied crowd, who'd dress up, maybe have something to eat, and go out with the intention of drinking the bar dry. Placemate 7 had multiple bars making full use of the seven rooms in the building. Even tarted up, it was still a labyrinth of crumbling basement spaces under old warehouse buildings; maps were posted around the club to help visitors find their way round.

That era through the 1970s was replete with clubs aimed at an aspirational crowd. Venues would expect you to dress up; men in suits and ties, women in evening wear. The hemline lengths went from mini to maxi skirt. Sequins and sparkles were good, as were patterns, brooches, big earrings. Even at the end of the decade, 1970s dress codes requiring formal evening wear were being enforced, if not tightened. At Park Hall in Chorley denim was already banned for both sexes, and leather jackets; in 1979, suede jackets were added to the list.

At these nightclubs there might be roulette and cards, and often a cabaret element too, especially in the north of England, where the tradition of working men's clubs had set certain expectations for a night out, one of them being a comedian onstage – a 'turn' of some sort. At Placemate 7 the Abadis had hooked up with a business partner, William Morris, who was a specialist in booking cabaret acts (he owned a cabaret club in Stoke called Jollees). Live music might be provided by a chart-friendly act like the Dooleys (they lived in Worsley, on the outskirts of Manchester, having moved up from Essex in 1973 to be closer to the northern clubs where demand for their services was greatest).

Other attractions would include a disc jockey, who was usually also compere for the evening, but the most important components were booze and food, though the provision for eating out wasn't on anything like the scale it is today. For tens of thousands of people every week, the prospect of new outfits, a covers band, a disco, cabaret, laughter, booze and getting fed in a nightclub – even if the only thing on the menu was chicken in a basket – was a proper treat, and a more attractive experience than being in some chaotic basement club with water running down the walls, or sitting cross-legged in a room of long-haired folk fans above a pub somewhere.

In 1973 Barbarella's in Birmingham offered six bars, two restaurants, a grill bar, three 'stereo discos', and a cabaret. At Fagin's on Oxford Road in Manchester, live acts would be engaged for a week-long Monday to Saturday residency. In March 1973, for example, the Dooleys were there one week; a fortnight later it was Lonnie Donegan. Prices of admission ranged from 70p on Monday or Tuesday, 85p on Wednesday or Thursday, to £1.15 on Friday and Saturday.

Most towns had a discotheque/cabaret club. At the Nite Spot in Bedford in 1977 Saturday was cabaret night, with stars such as Ronnie Corbett and the Barron Knights (you were advised to book a table early, and reminded that men had to wear jackets and ties, and ladies in jeans would be refused entry). Thursdays and Fridays hosted live bands, like the Enid and U Boat, and Tuesdays and Wednesdays were disco nights (the £1 admission price included a 40p meal voucher).

A key element in the success of the Mecca dance halls in the 1920s and 1930s was that they delivered escape and sophistication, and many of the discotheques and nightclubs in the 1970s also appealed to a sense of aspiration. Sometimes, however, decor designed to enhance the glamour of the experience had unfortunate side effects. I'm thinking of the presence of ultraviolet lighting, the bane of many young lads in that era, as it showed up the dandruff on your shoulders and the fillings in your teeth.

Mecca bosses were aware that each generation needs its own space and that young people generally have some resistance to socialising where their parents had. They made haste to refurbish, reposition and, of course, rename some of the venues. A numbers of Locarnos were renamed Cat's Whiskers, including those in Burnley and Oldham. The Plaza on Oxford Street where Savile had presided was given a refit and rechristened Tiffany's, a name the Mecca organisation favoured for a number of its venues in the 1970s (Coventry Locarno became Tiffany's on Valentine's Day 1974). Tiffany's in Manchester for many of its early years was managed by Harold Hulley and Doreen Edwards, who kept a mynah bird in a cage on the stairs that harangued customers as they walked in, until someone taught the bird to swear and, after complaints, it was removed.

There was a flock of venues known as Cinderella Rockafella's (sometimes Cinderella Rockerfella's). Tiffany's in Edinburgh became a Cinderella Rockerfella's in about 1982. Among the many nationwide, you could find ones in Chester, Northampton, Guildford and Leeds. In Leeds, Cinderella's was an unglorified discotheque, but Rockafella's, next door, was for over-21s only, and appealed to locals who considered themselves a cut above their peers: footballers, wide boys with wide ties, dodgy gangster types and dolly birds.

In London, the private members' club Annabel's had been founded by Mark Birley in 1963 with the intention of providing a discotheque for the aristocracy. He named it after his wife (who left him a year later for the tycoon James Goldsmith). Aristotle Onassis and Jackie Kennedy visited and model Jerry Hall was a regular, as was Lord Lucan, until he disappeared in 1974. One of the prime celebrity haunts of the early 1970s was Tramps, which could count George Best among its fans. A generation of flamboyant footballers partied at Tramps (and, later, at Stringfellows) including the much-travelled Frank Worthington who had spells at eleven teams including Huddersfield Town, Bolton Wanderers, Birmingham City and Southampton, his favourite clubs though were Playboy, Tramps and Stringfellows.

Peter Stringfellow opened his venue in London in 1980. By that time he'd run clubs in Sheffield, Manchester and Leeds. Cinderella Rockafella's in Leeds was one of his pre-London projects. At his Leeds venue he employed girls in black leotards to staff the bar and provide a waitress service. Sophistication was the intention, though not always the outcome. Regulars at Cinderella's remember Mr Stringfellow encouraging good-looking girls to take to the stage to remove items of clothing, and if they did he'd reward them with a free bottle of bubbly. At Rockafella's the entertainment included appearances by Mike and Bernie Winters. In Cinderella's you could expect appearances by Paper Lace and Mud, and, like most mainstream clubs in that era, the girls danced round their handbags and the tempo would drop at the end of the night for a smoochy dance to 'When Will I See You Again?'

The Del Sol club in Manchester was another venue where the promise of sophistication in the name and advertising wasn't quite delivered. In the era it opened, Benidorm and the resorts on the Costa del Sol and Majorca and Marbella were all considered a refined holiday – an opportunity to see some sunshine, enjoy drinks with foreign names and return with holiday slides to show the neighbours, a doll in national costume, something glamorous to wear, a cream jacket perhaps, without a collar. At the Del Sol, you'd pay 5/- (25p) admission, which would include a plate of Lancashire hotpot, the compere Cedric murdering Frank Sinatra classics, and a performance by an exotic dancer called Big Julie.

In his autobiography *Blessed*, footballer George Best recounts a visit to the Del Sol club at a time when two of his friends were hoping they'd run a club together; he may have been drawn to the venue by the name, as Best loved his Spanish holidays. The Del Sol was grotty, though – 'a pigsty' (according to George) – but they decided to buy the venue, do it up and change the name, although a further cause for concern was that there was a police station on the same street; there's never been an era when clubbers would consider this a plus point. Nevertheless, with Malcolm ('Waggy') Wagner and Colin Burn (who owned Rubens, round the corner, the venue that had once housed the Oasis), Best took the plunge and bought the Del Sol at the end of 1973. They took it up-market and offered wine and cocktails. Best also came up with a new name for the club – Slack Alice – taken from a character who cropped up in routines by camp comedian Larry Grayson, whose repertoire included a number of popular catchphrases. As Best later explained, 'We could have hardly called a nightclub "Shut That Door".'

Half a mile away, down by the Manchester Ship Canal, the Pomona Palace had fallen into ruin in the 1880s after a fire, and the buildings and Pomona Gardens had closed; the ground they stood on became canalside docks, part of Manchester and Salford's ever-growing industrial power. But by the 1970s, nearing the tail-end of a different century, the docks were beginning to fall apart, as the area's industries waned. Into this wasteland, some life returned in January 1974 when a part-pub, part-nightclub opened. It was billed as providing 'luxurious and spacious surroundings with a difference'. The difference was that the venue was a ship, the *North Westward Ho*, which had been steered through the canal from the Irish Sea and berthed at Pomona Dock.

Other cities had discofied boats, including Clubship *Landfall* in Liverpool, a former Royal Navy vessel that had taken part in the Normandy landings, and the *Thekla*, which arrived in Bristol harbour in 1982 and has survived over thirty years as a floating live music venue. In 1983 the *Tuxedo Princess* became the first of two former car ferries that became floating nightclubs moored on the Gateshead side of the Tyne. Back then, according to Newcastle's *Evening Chronicle*, the *Tuxedo Princess* was 'a celebrity haunt helping build Newcastle's reputation as a party city'. Among the celebrities that haunted the *Princess* in the 1980s were DJ Noel Edmonds, comedian Freddie Starr, snooker player Steve Davis, singers Mick Hucknall and Nik Kershaw, and the cast of the TV series *Auf Wiedersehen, Pet*.

Most of the DJs at the various Cat's Whiskers, Tiffany's and Top Ranks took their cues from big-name, jive-talking performer DJs like Jimmy Savile or the Emperor Rosko. A few became local heroes, including Barmy Barry, who would play the chart hits, announce and back-announce the records he was playing, namecheck clubbers with a birthday, let people know when cars needed reparking, and encourage frivolity. But in some venues DJs with a less obviously commercial playlist had a foothold, and this was encouraged by some club-owners. They knew if they could introduce a more creative playlist, then perhaps they could give the venue a unique selling point in the area.

In Coventry, Pete Waterman moved on from his brief flirtation with progressive rock and immersed himself in soul music. He'd snared himself some DJ gigs at Coventry Locarno, comfortable on the microphone and happy to be earning some kind of living in the music business, playing a variety of music. Given half a chance, though, he liked to play rare soul; he would get hold of imports, numbers like 'Queen of Fools' by Barbara Mills.

We've already seen the hostility to the notion of DJs and discotheques from the likes of the Musicians' Union. As record labels like Motown, Stax and Atlantic continued to release records people wanted to dance to and DJs wanted to play, other institutions attacked the growth of interest in imported black American dance music, and the popularity of discotheques. In 1971, the PPL – the agency empowered to collect copyright fees on behalf of performing musicians – warned specifically against 'large quantities of soul records which presented particular problems in some kinds of discotheque use'.

Through the late 1960s, Mecca bosses had searched for ways to reach out to new and emerging audiences without alienating their loyal regulars, and perhaps give up some midweek evenings to beat scene kids or other younger, or weirder, customers. At Blackpool Mecca, soon after the closure of the Twisted Wheel, the Northern Soul scene was given a space to grow on a Saturday night. Blackpool Mecca, with its capacity of around 5,000, was divided into two levels. On the lower level they hosted standard Mecca fare, a straightforward live band playing covers, well-dressed singers, and DJs with plenty of patter and a tried-and-tested Top Twenty playlist. Up the stairs, the Highland Room on Saturday nights featured DJs Tony Jebb and Stuart Freeman playing rare soul. In August 1971 Dave Godin made a trip north again and, on his return, delivered a hyper-enthusiastic report on the Highland Room in *Blues & Soul*. This was a scene, in 1971 at least, pretty much ignored by the media and the record companies. As far as Godin was concerned, 'I think it shows how soul music has become the only true "underground" music in the country now.'

What's undeniable is that in the early years of the 1970s there were several tribes of music fans with antipathy to the mainstream, including the freaks with their underground magazines and the Northern Soul fans. There were also more-or-less self-contained networks of lovers of reggae, heavy metal and folk. Music choices dictated not just the state of your record collection, but what you wore, your attitudes, where you went drinking and dancing. The loosening of conformist pressures in the 60s was filtering through society, encouraging the young to follow paths of their own choosing, to feel empowered to seek out tribes and scenes away from what might be most obvious. For many of these scenes, underground was the chosen definition and destination; they didn't want to be discovered, let alone tamed.

The Highland Room wasn't an all-nighter – that wasn't Mecca's way of doing things – so the rare soul all-nighter fans were still looking for somewhere as potent as the Twisted Wheel where they could dance till dawn, fuelling their nights out with amphetamines. They were prepared to travel; as it turned out, the place many of them would travel to was Stoke-on-Trent. I made the journey myself one breezy March morning and met up with Chris Burton and Colin Curtis, two delightful men, honest guys with deep Staffordshire roots and a love of nightclubs and music venues, proud but still a little flummoxed how it had all come together for them at the Golden Torch.

Chris Burton had opened the Torch in 1964 in Tunstall, one of the six towns that make up the conurbation of Stoke-on-Trent. In the heart of a residential area, on Hose Street, there had once been a church on the site; the building had housed a skating rink and, for many years, a cinema. Chris had worked in the era of the ballrooms, promoting big bands led by the likes of Joe Loss and Eric Delaney, and then began promoting at the King's Hall in Stoke, where both the Beatles and the Rolling Stones played. The total cost of knocking the cinema down and rebuilding it was £27,000. 'As a young twenty-three-year-old I was probably earning too much money for my own good,' laughs Chris.

When the Torch first opened to the public, it was a neighbourhood beat club hosting a fairly predictable programme – the likes of Billy J. Kramer, and Wayne Fontana and the Mindbenders – but made good money, the 'three years of plenty' as Chris calls it. 'It was a band-oriented period; you'd have to have three groups a night. The band were the main feature, the DJs, dare I say it, were secondary.'

When pop culture took a psychedelic direction, the club suffered three years of famine – every week was a problem week, bills to pay, wages to find. 'I couldn't make it pay,' says Chris. 'You had the bigger places, in Hanley, the Mecca in Newcastle [under Lyme]; we had limitations. I thought it was the end of the Golden Torch's life, then Northern Soul came along.'

When Barmy Barry was there, he'd be playing a certain amount of soul – especially Motown – but it wasn't until 1969 that Chris Burton launched a dedicated rare soul night, after DJ Keith Minshull persuaded him to give him Friday nights. The rare soul scene took him by surprise. Keith rarely used the microphone, and the music was mostly unfamiliar even to Chris Burton, who'd been in the music industry for years: 'I remember the first one and thinking, what's this about?'

Then Colin Curtis came on board and they decided they should try Saturday all-nighters. Colin was living in Kidsgrove, running mobile discos in the area and DJing at the Crystal Ballroom in Newcastle-under-Lyme, which had been opened in an old billiard room by Eddie Fenton, who also owned a club with the most astonishing name in this era, perhaps any era: El Pussy.

It was in March 1972 that the all-nighters began, running from 8.30 p.m. on Saturday to 8.30 a.m. on Sunday ('Twelve hours of soulful tunes' the publicity promised). Keith Minshull and Colin were the resident DJs, but various guest DJs would play, such as Tony Jebb and Martyn Ellis (from the Pendulum in Manchester). In addition, an astonishing selection of live acts appeared at the Torch. During 1972 and 1973 you could have paid £1 for twelve hours of music, including Junior Walker live, or Sam & Dave, Edwin Starr and Major Lance. Chris's confusion had now become delight: 'I just could not believe the crowd, the amount of them, and the sheer enthusiasm. It was electrifying.'

When the Stylistics played Chris remembers they stayed at the

Sneyd Arms Hotel on Tower Square in Tunstall and he walked them in their lime-green suits through the terraced streets to the venue. Another memorable occasion was the time Dave Evison was DJing and a girl with a heavily lacquered hair-do asked him for a light for her cigarette – he obliged with a match, but in so doing set her hair on fire. Intervening as quickly as he could, he took the heat out of the situation by pouring beer over her head.

The success of the Torch came at the cost of a drop in numbers at the Highland Room, where the venue shut much earlier and Mecca's tight grip on proceedings held back the hedonists. When we start talking about the use of amphetamines on the Northern Soul scene, Colin looks me straight in the eye and tells me the drug use was less than at the Haçienda at the end of the 1980s.

Chris jumps in: 'This was the problem . . .' he says, and points across the road. Twenty-five feet away from where the queue would be there's a row of terraced houses. Within fifty yards of the entrance of the club in 1972, there were probably thirty homes, probably double that if you count the ones backing onto the site of the Torch. They'd tolerated beat group nights until midnight or one o'clock, but the change to all-nighters brought conflict over noise and parking. The queue would go all the way up the road. All night the zone around Hose Street would be alive, and busy, and noisy. In order to counteract complaints from the local residents about noise, Chris employed a number of them as cleaners. He points out which houses had family members with jobs at the Torch and confesses that he was never much concerned with the quality of their cleaning. The important thing was to ensure they had a stake in the club staying open.

By the beginning of 1973 the local police were logging an increasing number of drug-related incidents. One of the Torch's DJs had been busted by officers while on a break one night; they'd found him in possession of three tablets containing amphetamine and amylobarbitone. He was fined £50 and sentenced to six months' imprisonment, suspended for two years. In a separate incident, two girls aged sixteen and seventeen were seen taking tablets by a Drug Squad officer and placed under supervision orders. After such incidents, it was no surprise when the police objected to the renewal of the club's liquor and entertainment licences and the club closed at the beginning of March 1973.

The momentum behind Northern Soul was now very strong and the all-nighter scene didn't die off when the Torch closed. Six months later, at two o'clock in the morning of Sunday 23 September, the first all-nighter at Wigan Casino began. These weekly all-nighters lasted over seven years, and although, as we've seen, the Northern Soul scene was already established by the end of 1973, it was those seven years that codified the genre, gave it a huge audience, unique fashions, and so many of its mythologies.

The Twisted Wheel had been a warren of rooms with a stone floor; the Casino – a purpose-built ballroom, originally called the Empress – had a wooden dancefloor that encouraged the dancers to display back-flips, spins and other acrobatics. As at the Wheel, the all-nighters were alcohol-free and amphetamine use was prevalent; the most common pills included the Preludin-like Filon (introduced to the market as 'a dramatic aid to slimming'), Durophet ('black bombers') made by Rikers, and Dexedrine ('Dexies'). DJs later confirmed that the use of amphetamines by the crowd dictated a more frenetic pace to the night and created a demand for stompers at the expense of some of the slower or more subtle sides they might otherwise have played.

Wigan Casino has been celebrated and documented in numerous books and TV documentaries. In 2014 Elaine Constantine's film *Northern Soul* was released, encapsulating so much about the scene: the fashions (32-inch-wide baggies, vests or bowling shirts, badges and patches), the drugs, the sense of distance from mainstream music, and the desperation for a Saturday night fix of Northern Soul.

The founder of the all-nighters at Wigan was DJ Russ Winstanley, but live acts like Edwin Starr and Jackie Wilson were an occasional part of the programming and a special draw. Russ booked Richard Searling for some guest slots early in 1974, for a fee of twenty or twenty-five pounds (Richard can't quite recall) and then he became part of the regular DJ team. Richard had been a DJ at Va Va's on Great Moor Street in Bolton, which ran all-nighter sessions every Friday. Their advertising material additionally said, 'We also cater for trendy weddings'.

During the seven years when Wigan dominated the limelight, Northern Soul still had alternatives to Wigan, including all-nighters (and then all-dayers) at Cleethorpes Pier run by Mary and Colin Chapman, and the sessions at the Catacombs on Temple Street in Wolverhampton, where you'd still get progressive rock on Sundays and Mondays (Free played there, and Caravan), but from 1967 through to 1974 you'd have found DJs like Alan Smith, 'Farmer' Carl Dene, and Soul Sam playing some of the rarest r&b and soul played anywhere in the country.

Venue operators continued to look for ways to incorporate the smaller scenes without alienating the core audience. At the Coventry Locarno the management called Thursday nights 'Rockhouse' nights and booked live performances by the likes of Slade, Argent and Vinegar Joe. In Bristol the same year, 1972, several acts played at the Locarno under the banner of 'Electric Village'; these were held on Sunday nights and included an August Bank Holiday appearance by David Bowie (supported by Thin Lizzy). Bowie was gigging relentlessly in this period following the release of his album *The Rise and Fall of Ziggy Stardust and the Spiders From Mars* on 6 June 1972.

Bowie had given himself a makeover, created the Ziggy Stardust character, and released one of the most important albums of the decade, but when he embarked on a tour to promote it, shows weren't selling out. At the Free Trade Hall in Manchester there were 300 at most, and Newcastle City Hall on 2 June was half full (among the attendees, though, was Neil Tennant, later of the Pet Shop Boys). By the end of that month, though, his fortunes had changed for a number of reasons, including a turning point that demonstrated not just the power of the live gig, and the power of the moment, but the power of the moment memorialised: a photograph by Mick Rock.

At Oxford Town Hall on 17 June 1972 Mick Rock was taking photographs from the side of the stage. During 'Suffragette City', Bowie sank to his knees in front of guitarist Mick Ronson, grabbed his arse and began plucking at Ronson's guitar with his teeth. The photo of Bowie going down on Ronson's guitar was a high-impact image. Bowie understood that more than anyone and persuaded his manager Tony DeFries to run the photo as a full page in *Melody Maker*. Two weeks later Bowie appeared on *Top of the Pops* performing 'Star Man'. His tour took off, and the Ziggy Stardust shows became arguably the most celebrated live performances in the history of British rock music. Wherever Bowie was playing on any given evening, it was the centre of the music universe.

Bowie's shape-shifting reinvention and rock & roll androgyny drew on a few influences, including gay clubs he'd visited in London – although his wife, Angie, was a more regular frequenter of gay clubs and also took a significant role in styling her husband. The gay clubs and bars in the early 1970s formed another, usually hidden, underground scene, and for good reason. Legislation had been passed in 1967 decriminalising gay sex between consenting adults but 'coming out' was still unacceptable in many social circles. There's still violence and intimidation directed towards gay people but in the 1970s aggressive homophobia was more widespread; glittery guys in hot pants were accepted on *Top of the Pops*, but not out in public.

Alan Jones – who would later work for Malcolm McLaren and Vivienne Westwood at their shop on the King's Road – recalls there was no definable soundtrack to a night out at a gay venue in the early 1970s, not until disco became standard later in the decade, and then, later still, Hi-NRG. The default playlist was Motown medleys, but Alan remembers dancing to 'Paranoid' and revelled in the imaginative stylishness of the customers at the gay clubs and bars: 'Most of them would be wearing Alkasura,' Alan says. 'I used to have every single outfit Alkasura ever had, red corduroy jumpsuits, brilliant stuff. And people would be wearing those tucked into boots and there were little gold tops, and that's what I remember; people looking like that.'

Some areas, like Brighton, already had a reputation for gay-friendly venues. By the mid-1960s there were several gay-friendly pubs but these were generally low-key meeting places, sedate even. The first gay venue in Brighton with anything that could be described as a dancefloor was the Curtain Club in the basement of the Queens Hotel. Like a number of late-night premises at the time, the Curtain had what was called a 'supper club' licence, which entailed charging an entrance fee that secured a supper ticket, which you could then exchange for a plate of food. If customers ate on the premises, the club was entitled to serve alcohol and play music until 1 a.m.

The Curtain installed disco lights into one of the rooms, and dancing was encouraged, although under supervision. A monitor on duty would swoop on any gay couple that came close to touching each other on the dancefloor. Prosecutions of club managers for allowing close dancing were not unknown. In 1962 David Browne, the manager of the Kandy Lounge in Soho, was taken to court after plain-clothes police officers had apparently 'observed men dancing the twist with each other' (Browne preferred his surname to be pronounced 'Browné' and later became proprietor of the Downs Hotel in Hassocks).

In London, the Gateways club was a members-only cellar bar on the corner of King's Road and Bramerton Street in Chelsea. From its earliest days, owner Ted Ware encouraged a variety of people to use the venue, including the Chelsea Arts Club. In the 1950s pianist Chester Harriott was a performer, playing tunes made famous by the likes of Fats Waller (Chester's son Ainsley is a well-known TV chef).

The tolerant policy drew many lesbian regulars to the Gateways and in the early 1960s it formally declared itself women-only, a development that came after Ted's wife Gina took more of an interest in the club in the 1960s and installed an American lesbian by the name of Smithy as a co-manager. There was an untapped demand, as lesbians had few places to mix with any degree of free-dom. In many ways, women of all sexual persuasions were more marginalised in clubs and venues than they had been in the 1930s and 1940s. There were spoken and unspoken rules controlling their behaviour. It's difficult to believe now, but women wearing trousers were often still banned from many restaurants in the 1970s, while many pubs were risky places for women to visit unaccompanied by men.

In the 1960s more than a few queer bars operated in Soho, including the Mambo, the Apple, the Alibi and the Huntsman. In many ways the most significant was Le Duce on D'Arblay Street, owned by ex-policeman Bill Bryant and his partner Geoffrey Worthington. Le Duce was a basement where queer mods went to dance to bluebeat and Motown. There was no DJ, just a juke box and a fish tank. It's reported that there were a higher propor-tion of black girls who attended regularly and that the management turned away older (predatory) men. It was fashion-able, and made sense; the lyrics and the image of acts like the Supremes had a special appeal to the Le Duce audience.

Peter Burton was the manager from 1966 to 1968 and later recalled that the use of purple hearts and black bombers was even more relentless than at any straight mod club. The police raids were frequent though, and the fish in the tank kept dying because clubbers lobbed their pills into the water whenever the police arrived. He also saw various DIY ways to get high. A transvestite called Samantha was one of the habitués of Le Duce; she had a thing for sniffing her wig-cleaning fluid.

There were still several actively gay clubs in Soho in the mid-1970s, including the lesbian venue Louise's – which you entered through a red door at 61 Poland Street – but in the 1970s the queer scene also expanded in West London: Chelsea, Kensington High Street and Earls Court. One venue in particular, Yours or Mine on Kensington High Street – known more familiarly as the Sombrero (the exterior decor included a sombrero above the door) – was a place to be. Through the door you could make a reasonably grand entrance into the club down a sweeping staircase. There, DJ Rudi was set up in an arch often decorated with flowers. The Sombrero drew a crowd most evenings, even Sunday nights, and even though there was no other discernible nightlife in the vicinity. There was a coloured flashing Perspex dancefloor similar to the one later made famous in *Saturday Night Fever*. The club had a supper licence, with waiter service; the waiters would distribute plates of ham with potato salad. A glass of wine was 35p.

It was a popular hang-out, and not just for gay men. David Bowie visited, and Angie. There were often rumours that Mick Jagger was planning a visit. It's a sign of how strong some of the currents of sexual and gender experimentation were in that era that such a thing was possible; that the singer in the most famous rock band of the time might drop in for a pose and preen and a potato salad at a club described by one regular as 'very faggy indeed, gold chains and sprayed hair, little leather clutch bags, rich older queens and their younger pickings'.

Another gay club in London in the early 1970s was Chaguarama's, a former warehouse on Neal Street converted into a venue in 1970 by reggae producer Tony Ashfield. At that time the area was still busy with workers from the Covent Garden fruit and vegetable market, but there were shops and offices in the neighbourhood, and also prostitutes and rent boys and others involved in the sex trade. Chaguarama's had a struggle to stay profitable when some of the clientele disappeared after the fruit and vegetable market moved away, but it survived by becoming a gay club, with Norman Scott on DJ duties.

In 1974 Malcolm McLaren and Vivienne Westwood opened the latest incarnation of their boutique on King's Road, christening it SEX, a boutique with attitude. 'Specialists in rubberwear, glamourwear and stagewear', according to their business card. This is when Alan Jones arrived, joining the SEX gang. He particularly bonded with one of the other SEX staff, Jordan, who had arrived in London from a council estate in Seaford, Sussex, and with Alan would go to clubs like the Masquerade on Earls Court Road. Alan took to wearing stock from SEX on his nights out at one of his other favourite gay bars, the Catacombs in Earls Court, where DJ Chris Lucas threw down a great selection of tunes.

One man making things happen on the gay scene in London in the early 1970s was promoter Richard Scanes (usually known as Tricky Dicky). He would hire straight venues, pubs no one much used, and would host one-night-only, gay-only functions, a step on from bars with juke boxes, with more emphasis on dancing. Occasionally he would attempt larger gatherings, including one in 1975 underneath a hotel in Paddington that attracted 600 dancing queens.

In Birmingham there were covert meeting places for gay men going back to the 1950s and earlier, including the swimming baths on Kent Street. By the beginning of the 1970s there were two successful and competing gay clubs in the city. The Nightingale first opened in Camp Hill in 1969, before moving to near the Aston Villa ground. Later it moved to Thorp Street, where it helped establish the top end of Hurst Street as a focus for gay life, alongside gay-friendly pubs like the Jester and the Windmill. It was in this area where Jane Kahn and Patti Bell opened a boutique near the end of the 1970s, serving the way-out Bowie fans and Rum Runner regulars.

Birmingham's other major gay club in the 1970s had its roots at Guys, a former gay-friendly beatnik café co-owned by Keith Campbell and John Walters. Guys was in the Bull Ring market, very city centre, but for their next project Campbell and Walters opened the Grosvenor House Hotel at 326 Hagley Road, nearly two miles out of town. This was 1971. Neither the Nightingale nor Guys encouraged lesbians to attend the venues, but a dozen or more lesbians picketed Guys, which led to Tuesdays being relaunched as a mixed night, an arrangement that continued when the Grosvenor opened in 1971. The award-winning actress Noele Gordon, who starred in the long-running TV soap *Crossroads*, was a regular at the Grosvenor, often in the company of the entertainer Larry Grayson. In 1973 the pair announced their engagement, but observers who concluded it was unlikely the engagement would end in marriage were proved right.

The 1970s was a decade full of divisions and tensions, in politics, culture and out on the street. Among music fans involved in the established and emerging subcultures, the divide between rock music and disco in the 1970s was a particularly clear-cut example of the tribalism of that decade. DJs were everywhere, on radio and TV as well as in cabaret clubs and dance halls, but not everyone was convinced they were making a positive contribution to the culture. The standardised fare in discotheques was criticised for being formulaic or escapist. DJs also came in for criticism, being described by *Melody Maker* in 1975 as 'parasites'. British rock music was possibly not at its most creative at the time – lucrative, but not creative.

In 1975, ten years after Robert Plant and John Bonham had first met at Ma Regan's Plaza in Old Hill, Led Zeppelin were one of the biggest British rock bands, enjoying record-breaking album sales and proving a huge live draw, capable of filling all the major halls in Britain. During May 1975, they played five nights at Earls Court, attracting 15,000 people a night. Also in 1975 Yes played at QPR's football ground, Loftus Road, and Pink Floyd headlined a festival at Knebworth Park in Hertfordshire in July, attracting 80,000 people. In October the Who kicked off the first leg of their Who by Numbers tour at Bingley Hall just outside Stafford. It was a sign how big British rock music had become that bands that had once coveted a weekend slot at the Marquee were now playing big venues to satisfy demand for tickets. Bingley Hall was a 10,000-capacity shed owned by the Staffordshire Agricultural Society, purpose-built to accommodate penned farm animals.

In contrast to those mammoth events, in the early and mid-1970s live music was a feature of many pubs throughout the land – apart from in Northern Ireland. Record-shop owner Terri Hooley had been enthusiastically involved in the Belfast scene. 'The sixties for me was like a great big party which I thought would never end but by November of 1968 I knew it was over,' he later recalled. That month riots in Northern Ireland escalated, and decades of terrorism, killings and bombings began. 'When the troubles came it was a horrific time – the start of the seventies was the pits,' Terri says. On 17 June 1972, Lisburn's Top Hat Ballroom was destroyed by an IRA bomb. Nightlife collapsed, bands stopped touring. Terri got involved with the Music for Belfast campaign, trying in vain to persuade English bands to include a Belfast date on their tours.

Most of the active pub acts elsewhere were covers bands, but it was also easy to find pubs with a Sunday-night folk music session (the Blue Bell in Hull and the Three Cups in Chelmsford, for example) or a Friday biker-friendly heavy rock night. A number of pub bands specialising in recapturing the original spirit of rhythm & blues were active, particularly in London. In contrast to the big gigs and remote lifestyles of the Bingley Hall or Earls Court-type bands, these bands were reconnecting to the grassroots and, as we'll see, the pub rock scene had a role to play in the first stirrings of punk rock.

The 'parasites', meanwhile, were still enamoured of their rare soul. In Coventry in 1973 Pete Waterman launched a record shop, The Soul Hole. By 1974 he was filling the dancefloor at the Coventry Locarno with the likes of George McCrae's 'Rock Your Baby' and 'Love Train' by the O'Jays. In his shop he was selling tons of records by the O'Jays and other stuff on the Philadelphia International label. In March 1974 he saw the Three Degrees perform at a record company showcase at the Mayfair Hotel in London. He was impressed by their harmonies and their onstage confidence, and won over by their looks: 'The first thing that took our breath away was their see-through dresses,' he later wrote in Coventry's *Hobo* magazine.

By the early 1970s the idea of a disco as a place of delight and entertainment was established but, via songs like 'Love Train', mid-1970s disco became a sound too. 'Disco' was a genre, music made for the dancefloor, working and reworking certain sounds and formulas. Gamble and Huff, the Philadelphia producers behind the sound of songs like 'Love Train' and MFSB's 'Love is the Message', aimed straight at the dancefloor with lush strings, irresistible basslines and surging, usually life-affirming, choruses.

David Bowie was also in attendance at the Three Degrees gig and Pete claims they had a conversation about soul music, which is perfectly possible; it was in this era that Bowie began incorporating black American soul influences into his music. Despite the hostility of *Melody Maker*, black soul music played by parasites was inspiring British musicians, including Bowie, and especially during the making of his *Young Americans* album released in March 1975. The new sound worked well for Bowie. Near the end of

1975 he performed his single 'Fame' on the most important dance music show in the world, *Soul Train*.

Bowie would have been aware of the excited embrace of funk and disco in gay clubs but the flow of great dancefloor records being made in America in the mid-1970s was too strong to ignore wherever you were, even in the heartland of Northern Soul where the sound of Detroit in the mid-1960s still ruled. After the Torch closed, Colin Curtis was asked by a manager at Blackpool Mecca to take on the DJing job at the Highland Room. Colin and his DJ partner Ian Levine developed a playlist there, which evolved from old-style Northern Soul and embraced modern soul, disco and jazz funk. Curtis and Levine proved successful and ground-breaking, although some of the Northern Soul crowd vehemently rejected the new sounds.

'The Hustle' by Van McCoy and the Soul City Symphony was one of the big hits of the summer of 1975. The 100 Club had a Tuesday soul and funk night that was packing in the crowds; a young John Wardle (later Jah Wobble, of Public Image Limited) was a regular. Another young man about town at the time was Don Letts, who was working at Jean Machine on the King's Road and frequenting soul clubs. His big night out of the week was Monday nights at the Lyceum, where he remembers black and white kids dancing to soul and funk like James Brown, and the Ohio Players. He'd also be at places like upstairs at Ronnie Scott's, the Q Club on Praed Street (owned by Count Suckle) and the Lacy Lady in Ilford, where Chris Hill was the DJ.

Although Letts loved these soul nights out, in the mid-1970s he dropped away from the soul scene, as the messages he heard through sound systems like Jah Shaka, Moa Ambassa and Coxsone became more potent. Bob Marley's *Catch a Fire* had been a revelation to him, as had Big Youth's *Screaming Target* album. By 1975 he was immersed in the sound of dub and the words of the militant roots music champions like Big Youth, I-Roy and U-Roy.

In July 1975 Don went to see Bob Marley and the Wailers performing at the Lyceum, which he later described as 'the closest I have ever got to a religious experience'. Carrying a bag of weed with him, he followed Marley and his crew back to a hotel in Harrington Gardens, off Gloucester Road. Marley talked to the Rasta brethren through the night, shared Don's weed, and reasoned with him until sunrise.

Reggae was one of *the* sounds of the 1970s. Although, like every other underground scene, there were occasions when its profile in the mainstream took a leap – when a one-off single crashed into the charts (like 'Double Barrel' or 'Uptown Top Ranking') or thanks to the star quality of Bob Marley – most venues playing reggae were away from the high street.

The network of sound-system operators in the 1970s was nationwide, with particularly strong scenes in London, Bristol and Birmingham, and in the Leeds and Huddersfield area. Their audiences were not only devoted to the music but also had no desire to frequent mainstream clubs. Sound systems developed major followings and would travel the country, often with followers accompanying them, in order to 'do battle' with other sounds at community halls and other venues. In some respects there was little difference between some notable and permanent reggae clubs like the Four Aces in Dalston and community halls. The Four Aces operated as a valuable focus for its mainly Afro-Caribbean audience, hosting wedding parties, wakes, events for children and community meetings.

The record selectors at sound-system events and clubs like the Four Aces were among those who benefitted from the arrival of the twelve-inch single format in the mid-1970s. The broader dynamic range of the new format delivered clearer, heavier bass sounds. In addition to the instrumental and dub versions, which the seven-inch format had often carried, there was room for more and extended versions on the new format. From 1976 onwards reggae singles were often released with special 'discomix' versions, including 'Creation Time' by the Maytones and 'Keep on Moving' by Bob Marley and the Wailers.

The twelve-inch single format also led to developments in DJing technique, first in the disco clubs of New York; these included beat-matching and other tricks of the trade that weren't possible on the smaller seven-inch singles, which were less easy to manipulate. Club DJs in Britain though were becoming more important in the hit-making process. DJs who were playing pre-release or import copies of tracks were creating demand on dancefloors, irrespective of whether the tracks were getting any radio play. This would be a feature of the late 1980s rave era, but was in evidence in the mid-1970s. Donna Summer's 'Love to Love You Baby' became available on import and twelve-inch single late in 1975, and through sustained club play (and after some weeks in the American disco charts) the record had a British release, which, despite a BBC ban, went Top Five early in 1976.

'Love to Love You Baby' was a massive tune in the gay clubs, as post-Philly disco music locked into a spirit of gay liberation, with the latest soul, funk and proto-disco imports flooding the playlists of DJs like Tallulah (resident at Shanes in West Hampstead) and Chris Lucas at the Catacombs. It was becoming clear to Tricky Dicky that there was a demand for larger gay nights, and in 1976 he launched 'Bang' at the Sundowner on Charing Cross Road every Monday night, recruiting DJs including Gary London (the resident DJ at the Sundowner on straight nights), Tallulah and Norman Scott, with the atmosphere intensified by expensive and state-of-the-art venue lighting. The idea, the atmosphere and the music (new disco releases on import) pulled the crowd and Bang opened on Thursdays too.

Over the next year or two more large-scale high-profile gay clubs were launched, including the Embassy, owned by Jeremy Norman. The Embassy was an upmarket, avowedly glamorous, loud and proud club on Bond Street, with an onus on dancing and ideas imported from Studio 54, including state-of-the-art lighting and bus boys in short shorts. Fantasy Records filmed the video for Sylvester's 'You Make Me Feel (Mighty Real)' at the Embassy in 1978.

The practice of DJs beat-matching and mixing records rather than stop/starting records was also being imported from New York. Greg James at the Embassy (later resident DJ at the Warehouse in Leeds) was one of the first DJs in Britain to embrace the technique, along with others including James Hamilton and Graham Canter at Gullivers in Mayfair, and Steve Howlett (known as Froggy), who was probably Britain's most technically adept DJ at the beginning of the 1980s.

Larger events like Bang and the Embassy drew some of the gay crowd away from smaller venues, but the gay scene didn't move en masse to the new large clubs, partly because the compromises in the music policy inherent at a large venue had a tendency to lead to a less creative playlist, but an important factor other than music choice was that some gay customers preferred the less conspicuous clubs for reasons of discretion and privacy. Others were turned off by the increasingly straight crowd Embassy began to attract.

Crackers on Dean Street, Soho, was predominantly a gay club that on other occasions became a haven for aficionados of soul and funk. From 1973 onwards, the resident DJ at the venue was Mark Roman. Soon he was DJing every day except Thursday, and also had launched a Friday lunchtime session that began at twelve noon and ended at 2.30 p.m. In 1976 DJing duties on Friday lunchtimes were shared by George Power and Paul 'Trouble' Anderson. Admission was 50p.

The regulars at the Friday lunchtime sessions weren't into retro, fast-tempo Northern Soul, preferring modern soul, funk and a touch of jazz, but, like their Northern counterparts, they gloried in the exclusive finds of the DJs and loved to dance. They'd make their way to this small, dimly lit, dodgy basement disco, the tiny kitchen offering sandwiches at lunchtime, and scampi and chips in the evening. The girls would take their shoes to work so they could run out of the office to the club in double-quick time. Many of the young men there favoured tight jeans by Pepe or Fiorucci, loafers and sleeveless T-shirts.

Sunday evenings were another popular night among the soul and funk cognoscenti at Crackers. People discovered DJs and followed them, just as they would in the 1990s. Paul Murphy playing jazz fusion had a great reputation at the 100 Club and also at the Horseshoe pub on Tottenham Court Road (Paul DJ'd there with Baz Fe Jazz). Every DJ was on the lookout for surprising floor-fillers. George Power at Crackers would play Ryuichi Sakamoto's 'Riot in Lagos' and Manu Dibango's 'Goro City'.

Many of the Crackers crowd, and the regulars at Chris Hill's Goldmine and Lacy Lady nights, would tune into soul shows presented on radio by Robbie Vincent and Greg Edwards, and read magazines like *Blues & Soul*. Chris Hill had a big following. He'd built his reputation at the Goldmine on Canvey Island and made a success of the Lacy Lady. Hill had good ears (in 1975, for example, one of his big tunes was 'Fly Robin Fly' by Silver Convention, a Euro dance record that helped define the disco era), but the way he presented the music – alongside madcap antics and party games – irked and deterred many purists, although it certainly helped pull a commercial crowd towards funk and soul.

As the scene grew, Chris Hill and other DJs from the southeast of England who played music on a similar tip – the likes of Robbie Vincent, Greg Edwards, Chris Brown, Jeff Young, Tom Holland, Froggy and Sean French – were dubbed the Soul Mafia. They'd feature on the bill at soul all-dayers, and then soul weekenders. The weekenders would take place over three days at holiday camps, the first being Caister-on-Sea near Yarmouth in April 1979.

There was a clear preference for Northern Soul in the Midlands and the North, and for modern soul and funk in the South, but it wasn't a clear-cut geographic split; there were some major exceptions. For example, at the end of the 1970s soul fans in London also had an opportunity to hear some of the retro and rare rhythm & blues and Northern Soul when the 6Ts Rhythm and Soul Society was formed in August 1979 by Randy Cozens and Ady Croasdell. Among the venues they used was the Starlight Room in West Hampstead (which had been the Klooks Kleek club in the 1960s and earlier in the 1970s), before settling on a monthly residency at the 100 Club.

In the second half of the 1970s, the North wasn't only about Northern Soul, as the evolution of the music policy at the Highland Room at Blackpool Mecca demonstrates. One city in particular, Liverpool, eschewed the search for fast-paced rare 60s soul; instead, DJs like Les Spaine gave the city's soul scene a funkier, eclectic, contemporary groove. You'd hear Les at a club called the Pun, a little cellar venue on Seel Street which held just two or three hundred.

While he was at the Pun, Les began to pick up a following among black American servicemen, especially those stationed at the airbase at Burtonwood. They were attracted to the girls in the club – that's a given – but the servicemen also loved Les Spaine's selections. Ray Carrington, a white guy who owned the Timepiece on Fleet Street (it had previously been the Time and Place) asked Les if he would move there from the Pun, which he did, taking his black crowd with him, but also widening his audience.

The sparkling reputation for quality black music at the Timepiece created by Les was bolstered by fabulous live acts such as the Ohio Players, Heatwave and Chairmen of the Board. Just as they did for Wigan Casino, people travelled to be there, especially for the all-nighters and especially the young black kids from outlying areas. As with other significant clubs, at the Timepiece people were finding their music, their friends and their identity.

For the black community in Liverpool, it injected flashy, funky, Afro-American influence into a scene that had been predominantly Afro-Caribbean. The fashions were something to behold – big Afros, wide jeans, stacked heels.

At the Timepiece Les was playing to a crowd who knew their music, even more so on occasions when he was invited to play at airbases. He'd go over to Burtonwood midweek and DJ to the Americans, and get paid in dollars. Les opened a new bank account for all these wages, but after a short while the bank manager called him in to explain where he was getting all this money. It wasn't usual for some black guy from Liverpool to be walking into the bank every week with a bag of dollars.

Records Les championed – like Banbarra's 'Shack Up' – became so loved locally they even filtered into Liverpool's more commercial clubs. His work had a direct influence on one of the most innovative DJs of the 1980s and after, Greg Wilson, who'd been brought up in New Brighton, a seaside town that welcomed daytrippers from all over Merseyside. The nightlife in New Brighton had a strong reputation too, though not for being trendy. A club there, the Chelsea Reach, was later the subject of photographs by Tom Wood, published in 1989 as *Looking for Love*. The building has since been converted into apartments.

Greg's passion was black music but this involved searching for records and looking for the people and the networks that could sustain and expand his interests – magazines like *Blues & Soul* and *Black Echoes*. He'd also tune in to BBC Radio Merseyside every Monday night for the soul show presented by Terry Lennaine. Fan-boy Greg often sat in on the show and hung out at Terry's DJ events.

One evening Terry Lennaine took Greg to the Timepiece. This was 1976; they were two of the few white guys in the crowd. Impressed by the music and the vibe, Greg resolved to concentrate his DJing on finding and nurturing similar audiences. After some adventures DJing in Scandanavia, he took a slot at the Golden Guinea back in New Brighton (formerly known as the Kraal Club; the Beatles had played a gig there in 1961) and began building his reputation. From there he went on to a residency at Wigan Pier, then also Wednesdays at Legend on Princess Street in Manchester (easily, but not to be, confused with Legends on Whitworth Street). Legend is now called 5th Avenue; it's a massively successful student-oriented indie club, but when Greg ruled the roost he played electro, pioneering the sound in Manchester, and leading to a short residency at the Haçienda.

In theory, the 1965 Race Relations Act outlawed operating a colour bar in a pub or club, but in practice there were numerous loopholes and no easy redress. A full-scale overhaul of legislation in the 1976 Race Relations Act included the setting up of the Commission for Racial Equality. Suspicions remained, however, that many clubs operated a quota system, welcoming a small number of black people but denying entry to others once the quota had been reached.

In Manchester, black audiences gathered out of town in clubs like the Russell in inner-city Hulme. Half a mile further out, in nearby Moss Side, there were numerous 'blues' – all-night parties in private homes that brought problems for other residents. They often attracted the attentions of the police but some became almost semi-permanent, including two not far from each other on Barnhill Street and Broadfield Road. They provided somewhere to socialise and a way of raising money for the households that hosted them.

In addition, Moss Side had several clubs, including the Reno on Princess Street with a drinking club, the Nile, attached to it. The Reno was about as far from a clean, controlled mainstream nightclub as you can imagine but the music and the crowd were a great inner-city mix. In that era you'd get soul and reggae, young hustler-type black guys on the stairs selling weed, smartly turned-out old men playing dominoes, young women in small groups with great moves and wonderful outfits, old Irish women, drunks and DJs.

There were racist doors in most city centres, though. On one occasion Greg Wilson was playing in Liverpool and the club doormen complained to him about the way his music was attracting black kids. They'd been turning dozens away. 'The exact question I remember was, "What's with all the Sooties?" It was made quite clear that they held me personally responsible for the increase in black kids turning up at "their" door, and I was warned that this had to cease immediately. I quit that night.'

Racial discrimination at a Birmingham club called Pollyanna's came to light in November 1977 when someone from a local cosmetics company enquired about booking the venue for a Christmas party. The manager refused the reservation when he realised a large proportion of the invitees were black. Other incidents were reported over the following weeks and a protest group was set up that began to picket the club on Saturdays, only for the police to break it up and arrest nine of the protestors.

In April 1978 the group led a protest march from an anti-racist gig at Digbeth Civic Hall up to Pollyanna's. On flyers distributed by the Birmingham Action Committee Against Racism in Clubs – as the organisers called themselves – there were claims similar policies were in force at the Guilded Cage and Rebecca's. Finally the Commission for Racial Equality got involved and took the owners of Pollyanna's Birmingham to court. Pollyanna's closed in 1987.

All the confusion and conflicts surrounding the issue of race was played out at night. The black contribution to popular music – including but not limited to ragtime, bebop, rhythm & blues, soul and disco – has fuelled excitement at music venues in Britain for over a hundred years. In the 1970s and 1980s some of the same venues where dancefloors were being filled by music of black origin were turning away black customers. Trevor Nelson was turned away from the Goldmine, and Norman Jay and his friends were refused entry to the Lacy Lady on his 21st birthday. 'You never forget things like that,' he says.

On the other hand there was progress too, signs that the young were becoming more tolerant as a result of being together in clubs, listening to soul and funk, as well as the crossover appeal of Bob Marley, the success of racially diverse acts on the Two Tone label in the late 1970s, and the efforts of left-leaning pressure groups like Rock Against Racism. Evidence this was the case is provided by the response of far-right groups in Britain. In 1979, the youth magazine published by the BNP, *The Young Nationalist*, declared: 'Disco and its melting pot pseudo philosophy must be fought or Britain's streets will be full of black-worshipping soul boys.'

At the Catacombs in Wolverhampton white Northern Soul fans would dance their late nights away to 'Six By Six' by Earl Van Dyke, Barbara Randolph's 'I Got A Feeling' and Jackie Lee's 'Darkest Days'. Up the road, the Stylistics took their talents and their lime-green suits to Stoke, and the International Soul Club (based in Staffordshire) produced cloth badges depicting Black Power's clenched-fist salute. Some of this may have been naive, but potentially thousands of ISC members were flaunting the badges: a powerful statement in an area of the country where the National Front were making electoral gains, Enoch Powell was the MP representing Wolverhampton South West, and it was barely a generation since the controversy surrounding the Scala in Wolverhampton implementing a bar on black men.

The site of the Catacombs is now a red-brick office building called Molineux House. The Torch has disappeared. Blackpool Mecca became a Tiffany's, closed in the 1980s and was demolished in 2009. Wigan Casino has also been demolished. Sites key to Northern Soul have been lost but the scene has never disappeared, nor the affection with which its early days are remembered. In September 2013, BBC Two broadcast a short documentary film fronted by broadcaster Paul Mason during which he met and interviewed Fran Franklin (Fran sadly died in May 2014). She tells him she grew up in Muirhouse in Edinburgh, her mother was on her own bringing up four children and Fran spent most of the time being the big sister and doing all the chores. But when she became aware of the Northern scene, her mother encouraged her to go and seek it as an outlet. When Mason asks her what it felt like being black in an immensely white, working-class scene she says, 'For me it was like, I fit in, I've got a family. Every single person I ever met on the scene felt like my brother or sister.'

Peter Stringfellow opened the Millionaire Club in Manchester in 1976, where he achieved much success before finally moving on to London, where he opened his celebrity and model-filled nightclub in Covent Garden (the Millionaire Club was later known as the Wiggly Worm in the 1990s; it closed down after the venue was ram-raided during a night called 'Most Excellent').

In the 1990s, the *Tuxedo Princess* was used by the BBC to film scenes included in the TV drama *Our Friends in the North*. Tosker, the character played by Mark Strong, does up a boat and turns it into a floating nightclub with an Animals tribute act performing 'We've Gotta Get Out of this Place' on the opening night. In 2008 the boat was sent to Turkey to be scrapped, although the following year it was referred to by Maximo Park on their *Quicken the Heart* album, in a song mentioning a 'revolving dancefloor in the middle of the river'. Coventry Locarno also made it into a song. In Terry Hall's lyrics on the B-side of 'Ghost Town' by the Specials, Terry describes going out on a Friday night to the Locarno and returning home on a Saturday morning. He recounts a somewhat desultory experience that includes getting piss stains on his shoes.

Ian Levine, after leaving Blackpool Mecca, had a brief residency at Angels in Burnley and then became a key resident DJ at

Heaven near Charing Cross Station, opened by Jeremy Norman, the man behind the Embassy. Levine took Tuesday nights and his music tastes and beatmixing were part of the attraction of the venue, along with a massive sound system and a high-tech light-show. He later concentrated on production, recording 'So Many Men, So Little Time' with vocals by Miquel Brown in 1982 and the massive hit 'High Energy' by Evelyn Thomas in 1984, before going on to work with Take That, the Pet Shop Boys, Erasure, Amanda Lear and Dollar, among many others.

Les Cokell, DJ at the Twisted Wheel on the night Dave Godin visited, was later resident at the gay club Hero's on Ridgefield in Manchester; he died in a road traffic accident in 1998. Louise's on Poland Street is now a private members' club called Milk & Honey. The Timepiece in Liverpool later became the 147 Snooker Club and is now a nightclub called Envi, where recent entertainments have included drag queens, charity boxing matches and a personal appearance by the renowned psychic Derek Acorah.

Chaguarama's struggled through 1976. Late that year, and possibly as a last throw of the dice by the cash-strapped owner, or to sidestep a closure order that was hanging over the venue as a result of a petition by local residents, Chaguarama's had a name change to the Roxy. The owners issued new membership cards with 'Roxy Disco Club' printed on them. It appeared to make no difference to the venue's fortunes. Then, as we'll see, a new team arrived, looking for somewhere to host some gigs. A deal was done. Apart from building a stage, the other job that needed doing was crossing out the word 'Disco' on any of the membership cards that hadn't yet been distributed and writing 'Punk' on them instead.

CHAPTER EIGHT

*Secret gigs, home-butchered hair,
love action at the Roxy*

The Picture Theatre was a cinema opened in 1915 on Manor Park Road in Harlesden and was soon renamed the Picture Coliseum. In the mid-1970s it offered adult films and kung fu movies. In March 1977, the Clash, having just signed to CBS, hired the venue, invited three other bands on the bill and put tickets on sale; they were £1.50 and included admission to late-night kung fu movies after the gig. The venue later became a pub operated by JD Wetherspoon.

Reviewing the gig in *ZigZag* magazine, Kris Needs called the Coliseum 'the classic definition of a fleapit, all peeling paint and stained seats'. During the Clash's set, Needs described the crowd activity as 'a show in itself'. 'The crowd in front of the stage went potty, pogoing right up into the air, screaming the words, shaking themselves to death and falling into twitching heaps.' He was accurate enough, but the crowds were not so much shaking themselves to death as shaking themselves into life. Punk gigs were often an encouragement to get involved, make opportunities, participate.

Punk was another example of the tribalism of the 1970s. To its adherents, it was an antidote to the pseudo-glitz of disco, and a rejection of mainstream culture. Part of the thrill and attraction was that it tapped into a growing disdain for huge rock gigs at the likes of Earls Court and Bingley Hall. In June 1976, even before punk broke, Mick Farren – who had seen Gene Vincent at the Brighton Essoldo in 1960, Jimi Hendrix at the Marquee, and Pink Floyd at UFO – articulated the need to re-energise live music in a polemic in *New Musical Express*. The paper had been receiving letters from readers hostile to 'big-time, rock-pop, tax-exile, jet-set showbusiness' he reported. The hostility had been around for several months, if not years, but Farren now sensed some momentum, and claimed 'something seems to be happening'.

At the big gigs, according to Farren, 'The only role for the audience is that of uncomfortable observers.' To Farren, the gig-going experience at stadiums and football grounds was evidence of the determination of some artists, promoters and sections of the media 'to turn rock into a safe, establishment form of entertainment'. Some original thinking and innovative concepts were required, he suggested. It wasn't just a question of new music but also just as much how music was being staged and promoted. He hoped a new generation might reclaim and remake rock music. He made the prophetic observation that 'Putting the Beatles back together isn't going to be the salvation of rock'n'roll. Four kids playing to their contemporaries in a dirty cellar club might.'

Punk audiences and bands understood that gig-going wasn't a passive experience or spectator sport. Led Zeppelin, ELO or Fleetwood Mac might jet in and jet out to entertain a mega crowd but there would be no call to arms, no aftermath. As we'll see, however, after Pistols or Clash gigs ripples of activity invariably followed, and a gig was rarely just another gig. There's an apposite quote from Mick Jones of the Clash: 'The problem with those bands was that they left you as they found you. They did nothing to change you.'

In 1976 the people of Manchester and the surrounding area had four opportunities in their locality to see the Sex Pistols. Two were at the Lesser Free Trade Hall, a little all-seater theatre above the main hall where Bob Dylan going electric had precipitated the shout 'Judas' during a show in 1966. The first, on the evening of 4 June, was attended by Morrissey, among others, but so sparse was the audience he later described it as 'a front parlour affair'. Among those at the first Lesser Free Trade Hall show was Paul Welsh, who ran a fanzine, *Penetration*. 'They attack their numbers as if they were attacking a gang of thugs in a street fight, viciously,' he said of the Sex Pistols in his next issue (number 8, cover price 12p). Just over six weeks later the Pistols were back, and a larger crowd gathered.

The Sex Pistols were an entertainment, a sensation and a revolution. Part travelling circus, part art happening, they'd roll into a town near you and, apart from just a handful of occasions, trigger something, some moment of cultural subversion. An outrage to some, to others an empowering call to liberation. 'At last our prayers have been answered,' declared Paul in *Penetration*.

All venues provide somewhere to gather but, in addition, occasionally what happens between the four walls of a gig or club has the effect of being a catalyst. As we'll see, the two Sex Pistols gigs at the Lesser Free Trade Hall are testament to this, and testament to punk's most important ingredient, its sense of DIY culture. The first gig was staged by two fans of the Pistols, Howard Trafford and Peter McNeish. By the time the Pistols returned on 20 July those fans had formed a band: Buzzcocks.

In addition to Morrissey and those two Buzzcocks – who rechristened themselves Howard Devoto and Pete Shelley – other people who were said to have been at the first or second Sex Pistols gigs at the Free Trade Hall were future musicians, artists, journalists and photographers including Linder Sterling, Dick Witts, Paul Morley, Steve Shy, John the Postman, Mark E. Smith, Kevin Cummins, Peter Hook and Bernard Sumner. Tony Wilson is also rumoured to have been present. 'The seventies incarnation of the mythical Manchester scene developed from there,' says Richard Boon.

From the early days of the Sex Pistols through to the Clash's 'White Riot' tour, a gig with a bit of a buzz surrounding it would invariably lure the malcontents, the born performers and desperate poets out of the shadows and, in many cases, gave birth to a life, a gang, a band or a scene. Through the next chapters we will celebrate how punk and post-punk had this incendiary impact, activating scenes and cities, although we should be mindful that the reactions among fans of punk were many and various. One writer in Nottingham has a local angle on the Sex Pistols gig at the Boat Club in that city in August 1976: 'It's been said that when they played Manchester in the same year, everyone in the audience went out and formed bands. When they played Nottingham, alas, everybody went out to the chip shop and got the last bus home.'

By the mid-1970s there had been various scattered grassroots attempts to provide an alternative to the big rock shows, the Earls Court-type experiences. But there were two powerful precursors to punk – one of which was pub rock. In that era there were plenty of live music pubs, including cover bands on a Friday, perhaps, or folk sessions on a Sunday, or jazz trios maybe, or pubs that would host ceilidhs. By 1975 a particularly strong pub-rock scene in London had been created by various bands inspired by rhythm & blues, including the most celebrated of them, Dr Feelgood. In 1975 Dr Feelgood released two albums, and were soon way too big for the pub-rock circuit.

The 101ers, including founder member Joe Strummer, were another pub-rock band embedded in the London circuit. In May 1975 they took a weekly Thursday night residency at the Elgin pub on Ladbroke Grove, which they kept for nine months until January 1976 when complaints about noise pollution forced the landlord to switch to acoustic events only. They also played the function rooms of pubs like the Hope & Anchor in Islington and the Nashville in Kensington. From October 1975 the 101ers held down a joint residency on Tuesday nights at the Nashville with

Eddie & the Hot Rods, another group popular on the circuit. The Hot Rods had a neat choice of cover versions ('Wooly Bully', the Who's 'The Kids Are Alright') but there was something old-fashioned about the Hot Rods, which was both their power and their limit. They were imitating, rather than innovating, albeit with much energy.

The second precursor to punk was what was happening in New York in the mid-70s. Chris Charlesworth had reported for *Melody Maker* from New York in July 1974 at a time when the American economy was going into recession, with GDP falling and unemployment rising. New York was hard hit and areas now busy and full of expensive real estate were then falling into dereliction. His *Melody Maker* report namechecked the New York Dolls, Wayne County and Television, describing the 'scruffy late-night' venues they were playing in the city. 'Excitement, sweat, crude and simple music, and a "take-it-or-leave-it" attitude mingle together in this new generation of bands.'

Then there was Patti Smith. In June 1975 *NME* published a review of a gig featuring Television and Patti Smith penned by Charles Shaar Murray, a show which had taken place at one of those scruffy venues, CBGB ('an impossibly scuzzy little club' according to Murray). He was enthralled, ecstatic, proclaiming: 'Patti Smith embodied and equalled everybody that I've ever dug on a rock & roll stage,' and that Television 'represent an escape from the rollercoaster to oblivion into which rock is currently straightjacketed'.

Those nights at CBGB and Max's Kansas City sounded attractive, certainly more attractive than an evening in a cattle shed or a boxing stadium. Furthermore, the juxtaposition in New York of an economically broken city with a challenging, uncompromised creative excitement thanks to a small venue scene, seemed to encourage some British music press readers to believe that local scenes were also a possibility in Britain's post-industrial disaster zones, like Liverpool or Manchester.

Back in the 1920s jazz age, the nation had been in thrall to a version and perception of New York's shiny chrome and sophisticated modernity. This was so very different; a fascination with failure, ruin, artistic ambition, Warhol's Factory, Scorsese's *Mean Streets*. Punk in Britain would capture the same good rockin' energy of pub rock, but force a break with the past, and add artistic and cultural ambition. Joe Strummer went on to front the Clash, admitting in interviews that the limit of the ambition of the 101ers was the hope that the lads stood at the bar getting hammered on pints while the band played Chuck Berry cover versions and would come back the next week.

Sharing a retro impulse but finding a different way of expressing it were the teddy boys. Malcolm McLaren had been at Wembley in 1972, and stocked the requisite jackets and brothel-creepers in his shop Let It Rock, but opening SEX was a break with that, a new route. Intent on getting involved in the music industry, McLaren had been to New York and, enamoured of the New York Dolls, he tried to manage them, without much success. Nevertheless, he still hoped to find or create a band and in some way or other cause a sensation. SEX became the HQ for these activities. Alan Jones remembers the Sex Pistols congregating at the shop. 'It was all a bit of a shambles to begin with. But I always thought Johnny had something. He looked grungey even though the term wasn't used then, and he had these rotten green teeth and he had this old supermarket carrier bag he'd be dragging along with his belongings in. I used to love that.'

McLaren was adamant the Pistols weren't just going to be another pub-rock band to prop up the bill at the Hope & Anchor. He wanted to clearly differentiate his band from everything else at the time, so the Sex Pistols avoided the existing live venue circuit, and their first two shows, in November 1975, were at St Martin's School of Art and Central School of Art in Holborn, London.

In their early days the Sex Pistols would sometimes turn up unannounced and play. McLaren would just make stuff up to get the band onstage somewhere. For practical and financial reasons these performances would be at venues in London or within a short driving distance. As a result, the first stirrings of punk were in the London suburbs and the capital's satellite towns. These experiences inspired the Sex Pistols song 'Satellite'. 'It's the story of the travelling nonsense, around the satellite towns of London, and picking up enough money to survive for a day or two,' Lydon (aka Rotten) later explained. 'That's what built the Sex Pistols crowd. They came from all those godforsaken new towns: Milton Keynes, St Albans. As bad as it was in London for young people, they had nothing at all in the satellite towns. No social scene, nothing.'

In November 1975, as a result of Malcolm McLaren's habit of blagging dates, the Sex Pistols turned up at Hertfordshire College of Art and Design in St Albans and got themselves a gig. Shanne Bradley, then doing a foundation course at the art college, was in the audience. She was an inveterate gig-goer and unconventional teenager, and had a thing for dressing in daft clothes. When the Pistols played she was a bit of a sight in her customised outfit comprising an old ladies' salmon-pink corset from Oxfam and ripped tights. Inadvertently she had a haircut Johnny Rotten approved of: home-butchered hair, bright orange due to a henna/peroxide chemical reaction.

Subsequently, Shanne had a hand in booking the Sex Pistols for more gigs at the College of Art and Design. She also booked the Damned to perform after she'd seen them at the 100 Club, which was their first or second gig, and met their manager Andy Czezowski there. There's talk that they played the Nag's Head in High Wycombe just before, which would have made St Albans their third or perhaps – at the most – fourth gig. No one seems to know. There's so much urgency and chaos in the early days of punk, everyone getting stuck in, there's a lack of documentary evidence, aside from a few unreliable gig listings. No one was paying much attention.

As a result of this flawed record of events, various mythologies have thrived, particularly with regards to what happened at or who attended some of the landmark gigs of the era. There's even a book, *I Swear I Was There*, about the Pistols gigs at the Lesser Free Trade Hall, who was in the audience, and the impact of the Manchester gigs. There's a chapter in another book that discusses reasons why a Sex Pistols gig in Manchester on 1 October at Didsbury College – listed in many of the completist web pages and fan sites – didn't have the cultural impact of the other four in the city that year. The truth appears to be that the Sex Pistols didn't actually play there. If they were booked, they didn't show. This is according to conversations I've had with Steve Shy (the young man behind the fanzine *Shy Talk*), who went there with Paul Morley and saw a band called the Undead but no sight of the Pistols. Other histories claim the Sex Pistols never played in Liverpool . . . except, as we shall see, they did.

In the wake of gigs by the Pistols and the Damned at Hertfordshire College, St Albans became a regular stopping-off point for punk bands. In the first few months of 1977 *Antibof* appeared, a St Albans-based fanzine which mixed sideswipes at St Albans and 'the dozy morons who inhabit this place' with appeals to the populace to wake up to punk music. Phil Smee started a record label – Waldos Records – and began by releasing a seven-inch by the Bears and, later, singles by the likes of the Tea Set and Clive Pig. Much later Mr Smee designed the lettering for the Motörhead logo.

At that first Hertfordshire College Pistols gig Lydon took a shine to Shanne – he asked if she'd ever been to a shop called SEX, told her about a girl called Jordan who worked there and had a bold look, and suggested that she should go to London, meet up with him, and pay the shop a visit. It was an appropriate choice. There was no live music venue or nightclub at the time that could lay claim to be the headquarters of punk, but if you had home-butchered hair and a passion to find out what was afoot then SEX was a great hangout. In fact, SEX was Britain's first important punk venue.

Just along the King's Road from SEX, the Aquarius indoor market was mostly older stall-holders selling antiques, but one or two upstarts were also there, including Bernard Rhodes, who would later go on to manage the Clash; he had a stall selling screen-printed T-shirts among other things. When Acme Attractions opened in the basement of the Aquarius, the owner John Krevine asked Don Letts to work there. On one of his Monday nights out at the Lyceum he met Jeannette Lee, they started dating, and she began working at Acme with him. Acme became a place to hang out. Don blasted out reggae and there was a scooter in the basement.

After Don had got acquainted with Bob Marley after the Lyceum gig in 1975, Marley used to visit Acme to purchase weed whenever he was in London. Apart from weed, among Acme's other best-selling items in 1975/76 were winklepicker shoes and peg trousers that came in colours like shocking pink, but you'd also be able to get mohair jumpers like the one Johnny Rotten liked to wear, James Dean leather jackets and electric-blue zoot suits. Don began wearing one.

Viv Albertine, later of the Slits (Don Letts would briefly manage the band), was working at the beginning of December 1975 at Dingwalls, and dating Mick Jones of the Clash. She'd made friends with Rory Johnston, who told her that this band called the Sex Pistols managed by his mate Malcolm were playing at the Chelsea School of Art. 'They were people like me,' she told me just before the publication of her book *Clothes, Clothes, Clothes. Music, Music, Music. Boys, Boys, Boys.* 'They were in their ordinary north London clothes lounging about like all the north London boys I was at school with. There was no being what you're not. And Johnny Rotten leaning on the microphone, talking and snarling.'

Even though she says it's a 'corny' thing to admit, it was seeing the Sex Pistols that inspired a first jump into music. She believes there was something about that band, and that time, that gave birth to a sense of empowerment. Johnny stood out. 'Watching him, I could make that mental leap for the first time and imagine myself, how someone who couldn't really play or do anything, could be onstage. That I could just be myself.'

Four days after appearing at the Chelsea School of Art, the Sex Pistols played at Ravensbourne College, Chislehurst, Kent. This was the first Sex Pistols gig witnessed by eighteen-year-old Susan Ballion, who would later make her onstage debut at the 100 Club, take part in the infamous teatime Bill Grundy TV broadcast and release ten Top Thirty albums fronting Siouxsie and the Banshees. In 1975 Siouxsie was living in Bromley, another satellite town three miles from the gig in Chislehurst. She considered Bromley dull and conformist and hung out with a few artistic, exhibitionist types who felt the same way about their home town. Her little crew, which included Simon Barker, Berlin (real name Bertie Marshall) and Steve Spunker (aka Steve Severin), became known as the Bromley Contingent and would help shape and define punk – in its look, at least. On at least one occasion the Sex Pistols went over to Bromley to party at Berlin's house. He lived just two doors down from where Bowie had grown up and was a devotee of amphetamine sulphate. Speed was favoured by lots of people on that scene, including Johnny Rotten: 'I loved the stuff. I'm normally a very slow person and it made me more intense. I'm naturally paranoid and it made me feel better.' In retrospect, though, he added a caveat: 'You get bored with these things, the thrill wears off.'

Speed was an integral part of Northern Soul in this same period – a scene, like punk, based on three-minute, fast-paced singles. In 1976 Britain generally was experiencing new highs in the amount of drug use. Amyl nitrate was new, barbiturate use was increasing, marijuana and cannabis were now endemic in youth culture, and it wasn't just the hippies who were using pot and acid in 1975. John Lydon: 'We used to take acid at Louise's. It heightens the enjoyment.'

Early punk life in London hadn't revolved around a punk club, or regular venue, but for some the gap was filled by lesbian and gay clubs like Louise's on Poland Street. They were discreet, transgressive – places the first punks could go without attracting hostility. This link between gay venues and early punks would also be evident when the scene spiralled off into other cities. The Hosteria, where some of Birmingham's first punks hung out, was a wine bar with a gay clientele. In Manchester, a popular meeting spot for punks was the Ranch on Dale Street, a small basement room in Foo Foo's Palace, a club owned and run by the transvestite performer Foo Foo Lammar.

Once through the red door at Louise's, it was £3 to become a member, and Madame Louise was happy to welcome Siouxsie and the Bromley Contingent, the Pistols and their friends, and Steve Strange too. There was a dancefloor downstairs where a DJ played Diana Ross, Frank Sinatra and Bryan Ferry records. As with similar venues, licensing laws required food had to be served if patrons wanted to order alcohol. So, in slightly surreal fashion, Siouxsie and Johnny Rotten would sit down in the club with a vodka and orange and a paper plate of Spam and gherkins. On acid.

Meanwhile, struggling to find ways of gaining some profile and finding a label to release the Sex Pistols, McLaren's strategy of avoiding pub rock was trimmed and the band's name began appearing on adverts alongside pub-rock bands and at established venues. When the band supported Eddie & the Hot Rods at the Marquee on 12 February 1976, the Hot Rods claimed the Pistols had smashed up their gear and attacked their fans. The Marquee, unimpressed by the Pistols, never invited them back.

One advantage of playing established venues was that music journalists were more likely to attend. Neil Spencer was there at the Marquee, reporting for *NME*. He spoke to the Pistols afterwards and they gave him the classic quote: 'We're not into music, we're into chaos.' He reported that no one asked for an encore but they did one anyway. 'The Pistols looked completely unique,' he later recalled. 'Big mohair sweaters and spiky hair – absolutely nobody else looked like that. People were shouting abuse but what was novel was that the band screamed right back.'

Eight days later the Pistols supported Screaming Lord Sutch at the College of Art in High Wycombe; this was the show Ron Watts promoted, which led to their first 100 Club booking. Also in the High Wycombe audience were those two soon-to-be-Buzzcocks, Howard Trafford and Peter McNeish, and a former schoolmate of Howard's, Richard Boon (later Buzzcocks' manager) who was studying art at the University of Reading. When I interviewed him recently, Richard explained to me how the Sex Pistols came to his attention: 'Howard rang me and said, "Did you read that?" and I said, "Don't they sound interesting?"'

The three went to the High Wycombe show and then on to see them play in Welwyn the following day. 'Johnny was just utterly convincing in a remarkable way as a performer, like he almost hated performing, he hated the audience,' says Richard. 'There was a bunch of lads who sat across the front sneering and waving at their mates at the back and Johnny ran along the stage and tousled their hair at which point their mates at the back ran forward and pulled Johnny off the stage; there was a big scrum. Johnny crawled out and made his way back to the stage and said, "Well, that was no fun," and then they played "No Fun". It was astonishing and inspirational.'

You instantly wanted to become producers of culture rather than just consumers?

'Yes, it was a "let's do it" moment.'

Richard's first contribution to the ongoing activity was to set up a gig for the Sex Pistols at Reading University in a painting studio in the art department where he was studying. He had a very sympathetic tutor who said he'd consider the event a piece of work Richard could include in his ongoing assessed studies. The performance in May 1976 was witnessed by twenty art students.

The New York bands were gaining visibility; in April 1976 the Ramones released their debut album. The same month, the Sex Pistols were failing to fill a small, sleazy strip club called El Paradiso, on Brewer Street in London, a gig (dis)organised by Malcolm and Nils Stevenson. 'Nils was on the door and he was literally letting everyone in and shouting all these promises about girls, girls, strippers,' says Alan Jones. 'And all these people were getting thrown in through the door; he would take any money from anybody, so the audience was a mixture of punks and this very straight raincoat brigade who thought they were there to see some hot action.'

The Pistols continued playing a number of support slots, especially for Doctors of Madness, including two in the Northeast, at Middlesbrough Town Hall and Northallerton Sayers club. At the beginning of April 1976, the 101ers headlined the Nashville, the Pistols supported – and made an immediate impression on Joe Strummer. 'They were light years ahead of us,' he said later. When, after a gig the 101ers played at the Golden Lion on Fulham Road, Strummer was approached by Bernie Rhodes and Keith Levene and invited to meet a new band in the same orbit as the Sex Pistols, with a view to becoming the frontman, he accepted. The 101ers split after one last gig and within six weeks the new band, the Clash, were playing live. Having spent nine months at the Elgin playing Chuck Berry cover versions, Joe was now sporting a 'Chuck Berry is Dead' T-shirt.

Raw public violence was a feature of the mid-70s: trains were wrecked by football fans on the way to games on a Saturday afternoon, and provocative National Front marches often ended in battles between marchers and opponents, or between opponents and the police. The sorry history of racist attacks is described in my 2005 book *Not Abba*, as are the riots at the Notting Hill

Carnival, political extremism, confrontations between police and pickets, and punk and anti-punk violence. One Tuesday at the 100 Club in June 1976 Sid Vicious got into a row with *NME* journalist Nick Kent, who'd worked with Malcolm when the Pistols were first coming together but had fallen out of favour, particularly with John Lydon. Sid was walking past him, each time accidentally on purpose kicking his shins. When Nick Kent challenged him, Sid pulled out a bike chain and slashed at his head with it, drawing blood. Ron Watts jumped in and took Sid away.

Punk was continuing to sow seeds through the summer of 1976. On the day of her nineteenth birthday, 3 July 1976, Marianne Elliott-Said saw the Sex Pistols play at the Pier Pavilion in Hastings and the experience inspired her to become Poly Styrene and form X-Ray Spex. The following night in Sheffield approximately fifty people gathered to see the Pistols play in a pub on the corner of Snig Hill and Bank Street called the Black Swan (nicknamed the Mucky Duck by regulars and locals). On this occasion the Pistols were supported by the Clash (their first live appearance).

Less than three weeks after Hastings and Sheffield, the Sex Pistols returned to Manchester for a second gig at the Free Trade Hall, the first proper Buzzcocks gig. One of the people energised by the Sex Pistols was Tony Wilson, who arranged for the band to premiere their 'Anarchy in the UK' single on their debut TV appearance on his Granada TV show *So It Goes*. The Pistols were up in the Granada TV region a few times in that period, including at the Lodestar Blackburn (18 August) and at Quaintways in Chester (13 September). Quaintways was a venue on two floors, occasionally with bands, but was mostly a standard disco, with big weekends of excessive barley wine, fast-flowing Watneys Red Barrel and lots of 'Get Up and Boogie'.

By this time the Sex Pistols had begun to attract the attention of one or two individuals at major record labels including Polydor and EMI. When the 100 Club hosted the two-day punk festival in mid-September, which included the Pistols on the Monday and the Damned and Buzzcocks on the Tuesday, Richard Boon could sense there was a commercial imperative at work for Malcolm. 'It was a kind of shop-floor window for things that hadn't yet been produced.'

Those in attendance included Gaye Advert, Chrissie Hynde and Shane MacGowan. On the Monday Subway Sect made their onstage debut, and the Clash played, with a line-up that no longer included Keith Levene. On the second night Sid Vicious was carted off to Ashford Remand Centre. He still wasn't a Sex Pistol at the time, although the day before he'd performed with Siouxsie Sioux and he'd also rehearsed intermittently in a band alongside Viv Albertine through the middle of 1976. The band in question, the Flowers of Romance, never performed, or even wrote a song.

The profile of the Sex Pistols was on the rise. On 8 October they signed to EMI, a week later the *Sun* devoted a double-page spread to punk, and then BBC One's news magazine *Nationwide* picked up on the new music phenomenon. It was then that the Sex Pistols played their one and only gig in Liverpool, and it came courtesy of Roger Eagle.

By the beginning of 1976 Roger knew his time running shows at the Stadium were numbered, and was looking for a next move. There were dead spaces in city centres nationwide from Dean Street in Soho to Broad Street in Birmingham; acres and acres of derelict warehouses and workshops, the unloved debris of post-industrial Britain. You might find car repair workshops in old railway arches, but most of the dead spaces were usually only populated, if at all, by young and/or ex-hippy, pre-punk enterprises.

In Liverpool Roger Eagle had dealings with the road manager of the band Deaf School, Ken Testi. Deaf School rehearsed on Mathew Street in a rambling old building known as the Liverpool School of Dream, Drama and Pun, inhabited by stall-holders and drop-outs. Ex-art college student Bill Drummond had a work-shop underneath the building. Jayne Casey had a vintage clothes store on an upper floor. Close by on Mathew Street, the Cavern had closed and, at that time, there was no Beatles industry wooing the tourists. There were no tourists.

Roger and Ken got together to create Eric's over the road from the School of Dream etc., in a building belonging to one-time owner of the Cavern, Roy Adams, who had split the club into two, with a disco called Gatsby's on the ground floor accessed from Victoria Street, and the rock club Revolution accessed from Mathew Street. Roger and Ken had a name and an aim. The name, Eric's, was supposed to be a grumpy piss-take of the kind of names other club operators thought gave premises glamour: Annabel's or Sinatra's or, indeed, Gatsby's. In contrast to the bur-geoning number of chrome and sticky-carpeted discotheques, the aim at Eric's was to present live music, with the hope they could nurture a curious, creative audience for new or outsider music, with Roger Eagle booking the bands. Then a third person came on board: Pete Fulwell.

As any active promoter would, Roger talked up his project to people. One day he chanced upon Jayne Casey at her stall and thrust some invites in her hand. Jayne had worked in a few places earlier in her life, among them the hairdressing salon Cut Above the Rest. She had a little gang of friends, including Holly Johnson, Paul Rutherford and Pete Burns. In various ways they looked outlandish (Jayne shaved her head, Holly wore red tights, Pete wore high heels) and when they went into town they gen-erally attracted hostility and very few clubs welcomed them. But here was Roger turning up with a bunch of tickets for the first night. 'We couldn't get into clubs. Nobody would let us in,' says Jayne. 'A guy inviting us into his club was just amazing; somebody wanted us in a club!'

The first few gigs at Eric's were in the part of the building housing Gatsby's, the disco, so that's where the Runaways, the

Stranglers and the Sex Pistols all played. The Sex Pistols at Gatsby's/Eric's on 15 October 1976 was a low-key event with a tiny unimpressed audience which, on this occasion, left no impression, and certainly lacked the incendiary impact of the Manchester shows. A few days later the Eric's team took possession of the former Revolution in the basement space, decorated it with Roger's favourite colours (red and black) and gave Eric's a permanent home. The Stadium, which had hosted big gigs – among them a number of avant-garde and progressive acts – went back to hosting boxing bouts after Roger Eagle moved on. Eric's, meanwhile, would last three and a half years, and would become so loved in Liverpool that its closure precipitated a march through the city centre.

Eric's wasn't specifically conceived as a punk venue but its size and situation perfectly fitted the ethos of the new emerging scene. The programming wasn't exclusively punk either, and Roger's enthusiasm for reggae was reflected in shows featuring, for example, Dillinger in February 1978 and Tapper Zukie in April the same year. There had been a juke box at the Magic Village and he installed one at Eric's too, stocked with the records he was passionate about. The Damned weren't on the juke box, but 'Goin' to a Go Go' by Smokey Robinson and the Miracles was. Mick Hucknall played Eric's with his band Frantic Elevators (and recorded for the briefly flowering Eric's label); Hucknall remembers the juke box included 'A Night in Tunisia' by Charlie Parker.

Less than two months after their uncelebrated Liverpool debut, the Sex Pistols rise overground was complete after an appearance on the *Today* show on 1 December 1976 broadcast at peak family viewing time in the Thames TV region. The show was hosted by the Manchester-born former geologist Bill Grundy and hit tabloid front pages after a barrage of swearing from the Pistols. As a result of this and other sensationalised headlines, shows on the 'Anarchy' tour that didn't happen include those at the Top Rank in Cardiff, Birmingham Town Hall, and the City Hall in Sheffield. In

Caerphilly two Labour councillors failed in their attempt to ban the concert, but Christians and other concerned citizens picketed the venue (the Castle Cinema) and were said to exceed in number those who had paid to see the show; one of the attendees, however, was local boy Stephen Harrington, who would one day be better known as Steve Strange. The Lord Provost in Scotland banned the Sex Pistols, declaring, so legend has it, 'We have enough hooligans of our own in Glasgow without importing them from south of the border.'

Liverpool Council pulled the plug on the Pistols playing at the Stadium on 11 December after a campaign led by Councillor Doreen Jones, who told the *Liverpool Echo*, 'This is just the sort of thing from which the public needs to be protected.' A plan was hatched to put the show on at Eric's instead, but Roger and his colleagues were given no option but to abandon their plan after intense police pressure.

Buzzcocks were close to the centre of the growing activity in Manchester, and on 8 November played Band on the Wall, a former pub on the edge of what is now known as the Northern Quarter, which, as we learned in Chapter Two, was a thriving music venue by the 1930s. It was a venue favoured by bands connected with the Music Force collective of musicians and gig organisers in the early 1970s, by which time the platform had gone and a stage had been built. The Buzzcocks gig was reviewed in *NME*. 'They're producing the most significant musical output of any new British rock band,' the journalist declared. 'Where they're going to next is anyone's guess!'

Two days later, Buzzcocks played at the Electric Circus, a jump from one of Manchester's most historic venues to one of the scuzziest. Manchester's underground paper *Grass Eye* had organised nights in the early 1970s under the banner 'Electric Circus' at the Magic Village and Mr Smiths (booking the likes of Van der Graaf Generator and the Groundhogs). This new Electric Circus was at the former Palladium variety club in

Collyhurst and was run by progressive rock fans Allan Robinson and Graham Brooks as 'Manchester's latest and greatest rock venue' (or so it said on the logo on their letterhead).

The Electric Circus featured AC/DC in May 1976, but its fortunes were mixed and its finances precarious, so Robinson and Brooks began to allow punk gigs at the venue. You could walk there from the Ranch and it became the place to go to see punk, although only once a week; until the final month or so the venue owners only gave up their Sundays to punk, preferring heavy metal, prog and unpunk rock on other nights. When Buzzcocks played there on 10 November 1976 they were supported by Chelsea, and it was also when Pete Shelley met Ian Curtis for the first time.

After the two gigs in the summer at the Lesser Free Trade Hall and the non-gig at Didsbury College, the Sex Pistols played two further gigs in Manchester in 1976, in December, during the bands 'Anarchy' tour by which time, such was their reputation for being and attracting trouble, they were now banned from the Free Trade, as well as local hotels including the Midland in the city centre and the Belgrade in Stockport. Both gigs took place at the Electric Circus, on the 9th and the 19th of December.

Just as the Sex Pistols were finishing what was left of their dates on the 'Anarchy' tour, the first and perhaps only London club that could lay claim to being punk's headquarters was opening; the Roxy at 41–43 Neal Street in Covent Garden. There had been many landmark punk gigs in the capital – including the Pistols playing at the Screen on the Green, Islington – and the hit-and-run nature of the one-offs had given early punk some of its appeal and impact. The Roxy – although it came to a messy end, and dragged on way beyond its best-before date – for three or four months was somewhere that programmed punk relentlessly, creating a community of regulars, somewhere you could drop into, sell your fanzine, see a band, be part of a clan.

Shanne Bradley recalls: 'There were no other places like the early Roxy. It was tatty, with plenty of mirrors. It was wild, full of spontaneity, full of all sorts. Most of the audience were in bands or wished they were.'

The Roxy was the Roxy Disco Club, the old Chaguarama's. A group of friends, including Gene October – who was looking to find some rehearsal space for Chelsea – and Andy Czezowski were looking for a venue to host some punk gigs. They became interested in the venue in the late autumn of 1976, at which time Chaguarama's, owned by a Swiss-born barrister called Rene Albert, was more or less on its last legs. On a site visit there, they found a small upstairs reception room with a bar, with a dance-floor in the underlit basement surrounded by red leatherette bench seats and mirrors; it had a total capacity of around 150. Andy's offer to take up some quiet nights and promote some bands there was accepted and a date was set for the opening, 21 December. Generation X headlined and the Roxy was launched. On New Year's Day the Clash played. Andy's time managing the Damned had come to an end, but they still owed him some money so he cut a deal with them to play four Mondays for free. And they did, to nearly 300 people a night, way beyond the official capacity, putting the Roxy at the centre of things.

Andy Czezowski ran the Roxy with Sue Carrington; they took a decision to employ Don Letts to DJ. Andy had been round to Don's house in Forest Hill and seen the hundreds of records he owned and witnessed the vibe his reggae tunes created daytimes down in the Aquarius basement – he reckoned Don would be an asset to the club. This was still relatively early days in the punk era, so there weren't many punk records for him to play. Viv Albertine remembers everyone being strict about what music was acceptable and, aside from one or two groups like the MC5, rock's past was a no-go area, so Don Letts played reggae, dub. It proved to be a welcome break between the spikey, speedy punk playing live onstage. Some of his Rasta mates also worked at the Roxy, in various capacities. 'The punks couldn't roll their own spliffs,' says

Don. 'So the guys swiftly decided to sell ready-rolled ones behind the bar.'

As its notoriety spread, the Roxy began to attract some of the New York musicians who'd come to London to make themselves available for gigs – musicians like Wayne County and Johnny Thunders and the Heartbreakers. A number of accounts of those years describe an unfortunate downside to this. Don Letts is one eyewitness who suggests that the Heartbreakers and Nancy Spungen were responsible for introducing heroin into the British punk scene. Nancy also, of course, hooked up with Sid Vicious.

Viv Albertine was at the Roxy the night Nancy targeted Sid and remembers it well. 'She leaned out from behind a pillar and beckoned Sid to come towards her in the most theatrical cartoonish manner. She beckoned to Sid and I turned round to laugh with Sid at what she was doing and I saw him do this sheepish grin and trot off towards her. I couldn't believe it; it was like watching in slow motion.'

So this was another chapter opening in Sid's life story, the last chapter?

'Yes. They took heroin together that night and downhill he went. We were so anti all that kind of thing and I just saw him completely acquiesce.'

The Roxy wasn't a hot spot for romance, but a pattern of more primitive encounters developed. 'Blow jobs; that was the thing at the time,' says Viv. 'People weren't into having sex, they were into having blow jobs; the men were, I mean, the boys. I don't know if it was American influence or because everyone was so anti-emotions that blow jobs became the thing, the boys would be pestering you for blow jobs all the time . . .'

They wanted blow jobs in the Roxy toilets?

'In the toilets, yes, or if it wasn't that, it was people shooting up.' She pauses: 'I distinctly remember one night looking around and telling myself I must remember how boring this is, and not romanticise what it's like. You'd see the same people every time you went, the same people there, every time, the same conversations every week. The scene was so small, when the Heartbreakers came along it was an injection of something different, "injection" being the appropriate word, I guess.'

The turning point came at the end of March 1977 when the landlords attempted to sideline Andy. Rene started bringing other people in to book bands and make decisions, notably an ex-partner of his called Reiner. It was one of those occasions when club owners were watching club promoters fill their venue, and greedily and naively deciding to take back control, and it all goes horribly wrong. Andy Czezowski was physically ejected on 23 April 1977, just as Siouxsie and the Banshees were about to take to the stage. He never went back.

After Andy left, the quality of the bookings began to deteriorate, partly because Reiner didn't really understand the culture Andy had been operating in, and lacked his contacts, but also because most of the first wave of pioneers had become too popular to be booked into a small venue, so the programme was filled instead with second-division groups. In addition, many of the original crowd who'd been at the Roxy since its first weeks moved on. After the pioneers and the devotees had come the tourists, part-timers, pissheads and the sheep, and a number of people attaching themselves to what Don Letts calls 'the post-Grundy tabloid punk circus'.

Punk evolved from a revolution to a cliché in less time than it takes to scan-read a double-page spread on punk in a tabloid newspaper. Even before the 'Anarchy' tour, Buzzcocks singer Howard was already restless. In September 1976, Caroline Coon had reported: 'Devoto insists he is only in a rock band temporarily,' and by the end of the year he'd gone, left the band, uncomfortable with the direction punk was going in. Richard Boon recalls: 'I always thought that when Rotten said, "We want more bands like us," it was bands with the attitude not the style and the look, but you could just see the style and the look taking over in a very tabloid/Xerox way and so it's possible Howard was correct.'

A few weeks after their Roxy gig on New Year's Day, the Clash signed to the major label CBS. The first gig as a CBS band was at the Harlesden Coliseum on 11 March 1977, a gig the band arranged themselves, which also featured the Slits, Buzzcocks (their first gig after Howard's departure) and Subway Sect. This was the gig that was the subject of the lengthy report in *ZigZag* magazine by Kris Needs. Subway Sect played first, singer Vic Godard ending the set by stumbling backwards and falling over.

Viv Albertine was in the audience that evening in Harlesden and it was that gig that pushed her into joining the Slits. The band's drummer, Palmolive, had been in the Flowers of Romance, but Viv had previously turned down chances to join her in the Slits, partly because she was resistant to being in an all-girl band. 'When I saw them I was absolutely blown away by them. On stage Ari Up was utterly in her element, it all made sense. I went to the phone box the next day and rang them up, and that was it.'

On their 'White Riot' tour through May 1977, the Clash took support acts Buzzcocks, Subway Sect and the Slits round the country, although not every band played every date. Shows included St Albans City Hall, Nottingham Palais, Middlesbrough Rock Garden, Edinburgh Playhouse and Manchester's Electric Circus. The further north the Slits travelled the more rapturous the reception, remembers Viv, but the atmosphere could be dangerous too, tense, passionate and unpredictable. 'That you'd have to stop to fight someone in the front row because they were trying to pull Ari offstage and club them with the guitar was all part of the experience. It wasn't like, oh that was a bad night; every night was like that.'

The Slits didn't feature the night the 'White Riot' tour landed at Eric's but the band subsequently performed there several times, including 20 August 1977, 17 March 1978 and 6 January 1979.

On the latter date they also played a matinee show. Drawing on his experiences back in the early days of the alcohol-free Twisted Wheel and the daytime drop-in vibes of the Magic Village, Roger knew that he could embed Eric's further into the music consciousness of the city, and give bored kids a treat, by staging alcohol-free matinee shows. Thus, in this era, the Liverpool youth would get to enjoy 5 p.m. shows by the likes of the Rezillos, the Gang of Four and Iggy Pop (April 1979). In August 1979 Joy Division played a matinee show supported by Swell Maps (£1.10 members, £1.35 guests).

After a short while Roger, who liked to DJ as often as he could, realised that as promoter he needed to keep an eye on what was going on at the door and make sure backstage wasn't getting trashed by bands, so he brought in some youngsters to DJ in his absence; one of whom was Norman Killon. It wasn't unknown for former habitués of Revolution to turn up and hassle Norman to play hard rock, but Roger had strong views on the importance of Eric's having a strong identity, and wouldn't have anything on the juke box or played by the DJ that didn't fit his mission to educate and convert. On one occasion Norman buckled and played something by Free, but Roger was adamant there had to be a line drawn and Norman learned it was best for a DJ to ignore unhelpful requests, even if it meant, as it sometimes would, trad rockers shouting at him, 'Stop playing this crap!'

When the Clash played Eric's on 5 May 1977 the gig energised Liverpool as the Sex Pistols gigs at the Free Trade Hall had energised Manchester. Bill Drummond had been drinking with the ex-Cavern DJ Bob Wooler and Clive Langer from Deaf School. They'd been in the Grapes on Mathew Street and had then wandered up to Eric's. By the time the gig had finished Clive Langer had challenged Bill to get a band together, write some songs and, if he did, then Clive promised he'd join.

And so it came to pass; within weeks they took the name Big in Japan and Jayne Casey became the singer. In a flurry of personnel changes in the subsequent months, a young guitarist studying for his O levels, Ian Broudie, also joined the band, Holly Johnson joined and left and Peter Clarke – better known as Budgie – who'd been in the Spitfire Boys with Pete Burns, eventually became the drummer. In the words of Paddy Shennan, writing in the *Liverpool Echo*, Big in Japan were 'a supergroup with a difference – its members only became super after they left'.

Julian Cope had arrived in Liverpool. He was at the Clash gig at Eric's too, as was Ian McCulloch who was out celebrating his eighteenth birthday with his friend Pete Wylie. Pete Burns was dressed head to foot in PVC, his hair in a quiff that looked like it was made of molten vinyl. They all went on to be in groups, with each other and without, as Eric's became a hotbed of bands getting together and splitting up, rivalries growing, egos careering out of control. At Eric's it was, just as Mick Farren had hoped, 'kids playing to their contemporaries in a dirty cellar club'.

By May 1977, Don Letts had walked away from the Roxy, but not without having left something of a legacy. He'd picked up a Super-8 camera and reinvented himself as a film-maker, shooting footage at the club, including a backstage conversation between Siouxsie and Reiner about whether the Roxy was closing or not. As well as valuably documenting some of the activity there, he'd also helped cement a punk/reggae connection which manifested itself in many ways, from Johnny Rotten namechecking Dr Alimantado in interviews, to a young Ranking Roger (before he joined the Beat) entertaining punk fans at Barbarella's by toasting and MCing during the DJs' sets. Don's work also fed into the consciousness of Grant Marshall in Bristol, before Grant had become Daddy G and ten years before Massive Attack formed.

After the Roxy, Don was still hanging out with punk characters, like Johnny Rotten, Ari Up and Joe Strummer, all of whom, and others, would occasionally accompany him to the dark, weed-heavy Four Aces reggae club in Dalston. A month after the

Clash played at Eric's, Don took Joe Strummer to the Hammersmith Palais, to a reggae all-nighter featuring Dillinger, Leroy Smart and Delroy Wilson. This time it would be Strummer himself who'd find the gig-going experience feeding into his creativity. Having witnessed the Notting Hill riots in August 1976, and hungrily devoured the often revolutionary dub reggae Don Letts would play, Strummer expected that the vibe at the Hammersmith Palais all-nighter would be heavy and political but was disconcerted not to hear the incendiary voice of struggle. To him, it was a tame, relatively mainstream show. Out of this experience came one of the most memorable singles of that era, '(White Man) In Hammersmith Palais'.

The Pistols didn't attempt a full-scale tour in Britain in 1977, although in the last week of August and the first week of September they played a series of secret gigs. Without the internet and the instant messaging technology of today, secret gigs were easier to stage and harder to discover. Fans looked out for clues, and there were a number of false alarms, but among those shows that did happen were those at Wolverhampton Lafayette (the Pistols were billed as S.P.O.T.S., which stood for Sex Pistols On Tour Secretly), Doncaster Outlook (billed as the Tax Exiles), Middlesbrough Rock Garden (Acne Rabble) and Penzance Winter Gardens (Mystery Band of International Repute).

They played their last British gig (until they re-formed in 1996) in Huddersfield at a former cinema, built in an approximation of a Greek Revival style, which had opened in 1921. The cinema closed in June 1957, and in the 1960s became a ballroom and concert venue called the Sheridan Rooms (known affectionately as 'The Sheds'). The building was subsequently converted into a nightclub, Eros, later renamed Ivanhoe's.

Ivanhoe's welcomed the Sex Pistols on Christmas Day 1977. They played two shows, one in the evening with tickets £1.75, with proceeds going to help the striking firemen of Yorkshire. They played an afternoon show, too, which was a free show for kids. During the afternoon Johnny Rotten and Sid handed out cake and a food fight ensued. The DJ was running various competitions to win T-shirts and other Pistols artefacts, but also had a skateboard as a prize. Jez Scott took home the skateboard after winning the pogoing competition.

Three weeks later, on 14 January 1978, the Pistols completed their first (and last) tour of the USA at the Winterland in San Francisco, and the project fell apart. Later in 1978 Lydon went to Jamaica to scout for acts for a new reggae imprint at Virgin called Front Line, and invited Don Letts to film some of the trip (and Vivien Goldman of *Sounds* to cover it for the paper). Back in London he pulled together a new band, Public Image Limited, recruiting Jah Wobble and Keith Levene. This was May 1978. Levene later recalled that he actually thought the Sheffield Black Swan date in July 1976 would be his last gig with the Clash (he was out a few gigs later, after a Roundhouse show) and that one evening two years before he'd discussed one day forming a band with Rotten.

The Black Swan later metamorphosed into the Boardwalk, which played host to local Sheffield bands in the early twenty-first century; including the Arctic Monkeys, who entitled their first demo *Beneath the Boardwalk*. Ivanhoe's in Huddersfield closed in the early 1990s; the interior was redesigned and turned into a supermarket. Over in Chester, Quaintways is now known as Rosies, which has no apostrophe, but does a rock disco on a Tuesday and modern R&B most of the rest of the week (with semi-permanent offers on bottles of WKD).

As the Roxy deteriorated in the wake of Andy Czezowski's eviction, another promoter, John Miller, moved in on Crackers on Wardour Street, and, as the weekends and most other nights were doing just fine playing funk and disco, took Monday nights there, calling the venture the Vortex. His first night featured Buzzcocks, the Fall and John Cooper Clarke, and soon his punk rock gigs took over Tuesdays at Crackers too. Andy Czezowski continued in a career that took in band management and running venues, notably the Fridge in Brixton.

The site of the Roxy is now the flagship store for the swimwear brand Speedo. Shanne Bradley, who'd been at the Roxy from day one, formed the Nipple Erectors, recruiting Shane MacGowan (then known as 'Shane O'Hooligan'), guitarist Roger Towndrow and, as drummer, the gloriously named Arcane Vendetta from Ilford, who edited a fanzine, *These Things* (his real name was Adrian Fox). Several line-up changes ensued. Vendetta's place behind the drums was taken by Jon Moss, who later joined Boy George in Culture Club. By this time the band had been renamed the Nips.

Jeannette Lee started managing Public Image Limited, and then joined the band (she's the cover star on the sleeve of their *Flowers of Romance* album; the lack of activity by Viv and Sid's band wasn't going to waste a neat phrase). Jeannette went on to manage the likes of Scritti Politti, Spiritualized and Jarvis Cocker, and since 1987 she has played an integral role at Rough Trade Records.

It took the Slits a couple of years from forming to releasing music, although they recorded a number of John Peel sessions in the interim. In 1978 Palmolive left and was replaced by Budgie from Big in Japan (who later joined Siouxsie in the Banshees). Their debut album *Cut*, produced by Dennis Bovell, released in 1979, eschewed the edgy squall of punk and embraced reggae. They became allies of the Bristol band the Pop Group, who fused freewheeling funk, punk and dub reggae with avant-jazz.

Roger Eagle was a Pop Group fan; he thought they sounded like free jazz pioneer Cecil Taylor and passed a cassette round to some of his most discerning regulars. Bands outside London inspired by punk but not sounding like punk would be a feature of the next few years; Joy Division are another example. The Slits and the Pop Group released a joint seven-inch single and shared management for a while.

Hammersmith Palais was the venue chosen to host the last

show by the Slits on 30 November 1981. For their swansong, the band made an event of it, hand-picking the support acts – Carmel, and a troupe of nine modern dancers from the London Dance Theatre – and decorating the stage with a washing line hung with clothes.

At the Electric Circus, on the Bank Holiday at the end of August 1977, Warsaw supported the Rezillos on the Saturday and on the Sunday the headliners were the Adverts, along with 999 and a band billed as the Slugs. The club was packed, possibly as a result of a rumour spreading that 'the Slugs' were, secretly, the Sex Pistols, although it turned out not to be the case. *Bombsite* fanzine went down and reported back in a subsequent issue: 'The Electric Circus might be a dump but what a concert, the atmosphere was unbelievable.'

On the back of the very next Electric Circus flyer, however, Robinson and Brooks announced the club was closing 'Due to pressure from the Local Council and the Fire Service'. Within a year of Grundy, the Roxy had opened and closed, the Electric Circus had embraced punk and then closed; and just eighteen months after Grundy, the Pistols had broken up.

The final weekend shows of the Electric Circus were on 1 and 2 October 1977, and a short compilation was released by Virgin Records, which included songs by John Cooper Clarke and Joy Division. Joy Division also featured on the first release by Factory Records at the end of 1978. However, Factory didn't first come together as an organisation to be a record label, but as hosts of live music, at the Russell Club in Hulme. In the aftermath of punk the importance of small venues didn't disappear, as we'll see in the next chapter, when we pay visits to the 'Factory' nights in Hulme, the Limit in Sheffield and elsewhere, including John Keenan's 'F-Club' in Leeds.

John Keenan, after his flurry of activity in 1967 when he was at Southport Art College involved with shows at the Moulin Rouge in Ainsdale, hadn't continued promoting live music, but in 1977, while working freelance at Yorkshire TV, he became frustrated that Leeds appeared to be missing out on some of the bands around in the months after punk broke; he resolved to host some shows. He was twenty-eight, much older than the majority of punk fans and bands: 'I was the generation before them but this was a lot more interesting than the last ten years before it.'

John had a conversation with the management of the student union at the local Leeds Poly. It was the summer of 1977 and there weren't any students around, so the building was being underused. The management jumped at the chance to generate some business out of term-time, and John, with Graham Cardy, launched 'Stars of Today', a weekly punk night at the Poly, and booked the Vibrators, the Police, the Damned and, on 7 July, the Slits.

There was a good little scene building but come the new student term, John and Graham were told to leave. John decided to split with Graham but to continue promoting: 'I looked around and found an old cabaret club on Woodhouse Street called the Ace of Clubs, so I thought that I'll just do it myself, it's much easier to be in control and I thought, "How can I bring all the people that have been coming through the summer to the club?" so I formed a club and gave them discount as members.'

He'd distributed membership applications to the regulars on the last night at the Poly, declaring 'Let's get the F out of here', and had a book full of names and addresses, so he had some sort of database and soon had more than a few dozen members who all got F-Club cards. Between October and Christmas 1977 John presented shows at the Ace of Clubs featuring the Rezillos, Siouxsie and the Banshees, and X-Ray Spex. Although he'd split from Graham, he took with him Claire Shearsby who'd been the DJ at the Poly shows (we'll meet her in the next chapter DJing at Le Phonographique).

Ace of Clubs was an old cabaret club converted from and set among terraced houses. People like Diana Dors and Bob

Monkhouse and all the old-school comics had appeared there. They had a small stage and then an extra section that rose up from the front if required, but for the smaller bands John would put them on the small stage. One evening, a band played from Birmingham called the Killjoys, fronted by Kevin Rowland and featuring Gil Weston on bass (she was later in the band Girlschool). John remembers the mayhem. 'The punks were reaching out because there was a girl on bass in the band and she had fishnet stockings on and high heels and all these lads were reaching out for her legs and I remember seeing her kicking them in the face and quite a few of them retreated, bloodied, and I was, "Are you alright?" and they were like, "Yeah, yeah, fucking great, man," and they went back to get kicked in the face again.'

CHAPTER NINE

Posers, the Krays, a tribe called 'goth'

In the summer of 1977, Patrick Lilley was a seventeen-year-old Bowie fan in Birmingham who'd just started to dye his hair. He'd also decided to sell some records so he could run away from home. He had a vague idea he wanted to meet a rich older man: 'I think I was looking for decadence,' he tells me. 'I felt very isolated and alienated in my life, I was being bullied at school, big-time.'

When he went to the stalls at the Bull Ring market in the city centre to try to sell the records he met a boy who was interested in buying them who recommended that Patrick should visit the Hosteria wine bar on Hurst Street; because that's where people like him went. Patrick didn't quite know what he meant by 'people like him', but that weekend he applied more effort to his look, took the 113 bus into town and went to the Hosteria. There he met the first lesbians he'd ever encountered and the first gay man – Gay John – and felt he'd found what he was looking for: 'It was very bacchanalian and exotic.'

Patrick remembers some of the people he hung out with in Birmingham that summer of 1977, including Patti Bell who Patrick calls 'the queen punkette' (she dated local rocker Steve Gibbons and co-owned the Kahn & Bell boutique). Patrick remembers his first visit to a club called Barbarella's with his new-found friends, and another punk venue, Rebecca's. He met Martin Degville (later of Sigue Sigue Sputnik), who was into fashion and dressing outlandishly, and was often out after dark with Patti Bell and her set. Patrick had made his move to London in 1978, but his friends would be the core audience when the Rum Runner club was operating in its most celebrated era, the three years from 1979.

In that era the Rum Runner cast a spell on David Wright; although he was a couple of years younger than Patrick, had grown up in Balsall Common (over ten miles outside Birmingham), had never encountered anything there remotely bacchanalian, and he wasn't part of any in-crowd, he too became a Rum Runner regular. He remembers that when he walked in on his first visit the DJ was playing 'TVC15' by David Bowie.

'The music has stayed with me forever,' David says. He uses a word a couple of times to describe what he found at the Rum Runner: 'liberation'. Now, over three decades later, David organises monthly 'Only After Dark' events to celebrate that era, the club and that scene. It's in a disco room above a restaurant in Birmingham city centre and when I visit it's fairly crowded, maybe two hundred people there. The music powers the time machine. This is how it works, isn't it? Music has the power to take you back to a place, a time. Hearing 'Warm Leatherette' or 'Tainted Love', the Only After Dark crowd are transported back to the mirrored walls of the Rum Runner.

The part of Broad Street in Birmingham where the Rum Runner was once situated has changed beyond recognition. It was at No. 273, set back off the street, through a large gate (open at night) and along a short alley which dipped at a slight incline, with the club reception area off on the right. In the vicinity there's now a convention centre and a Hyatt Hotel. I've checked some old photographs, trying to get some sense of where things were. Just up the road there's now a Walkabout pub, but if you walk towards town past the Jimmy Spice restaurant, just as you draw alongside another bar, the Solomon Cutler, you're close to the entrance of the Rum Runner. From the Walkabout it's about fifteen yards away. Or twenty-five years.

The Rum Runner was a catalyst, where what happened next had wider significance. Duran Duran became one of the biggest bands in the first days of the MTV video age, hit-makers and millionaire pop stars; the band worked, rehearsed and performed there. I met John Taylor from Duran Duran on the occasion of the publication of his autobiography, and talked to him about the Rum Runner. He acknowledges how very different Duran Duran's career would have been if they hadn't made their base there. Looking at video footage of Duran Duran performing 'Planet Earth', filmed in the Rum Runner, what you see is mirrors and neon and lights and colours, sashaying dancers and a connection – a connection between the band, the space, the audience. John told me about his first visits there, listening to the resident DJ, Paul Anthony, before it all took off for Duran Duran: 'Our first exposure to it was all about glam, Bowie's soul period, lounge-lizard era Bryan Ferry, Grace Jones, disco from New York. We loved it, it felt like home.'

Like Patrick Lilley, John Taylor had previously been a regular at Barbarella's and Rebecca's. Both clubs were owned by the same family, the Fewtrells, an Irish family of ten children from Aston. Don and Eddie were the two Fewtrell brothers who were most involved in the club business, running Rebecca's (later called Boogie's) and Barbarella's, but also the Bermuda Club on Navigation Street, the Cedar Club on Constitution Hill, Abigail's, and Edward's No.7. The Fewtrells feature in plenty of tales from the shady side of Birmingham nightlife, but some of the stories also have a national dimension, including one concerning notorious London gangsters the Kray twins. Several cities have a version of a story that involves the Krays attempting to muscle in on the local clubs, only to be confronted at the train station and sent back to London.

The Fewtrells always claim to have resisted with violence any attempt by the Krays to expand their empire into Birmingham. The story is told in various versions. In one account, the Fewtrells were tipped off by the local police that the Krays were on their way; the Birmingham gang met their rivals at New Street Station and, after a major set-to, the Krays were banished from Brum. Eddie Fewtrell tells a different tale in his memoirs. According to Eddie, the twins recruited some local allies, including a man who worked at the local meat market and a doorman at Castaways, both of them maniacs with a long history of GBH. They came looking for him at the Bermuda Club, tooled up with multiple weapons. After backing off from his assailants, he jumped on a table, picked up a pint pot and hit one of them on the top of the head. He says the other three came at him and he did the same with them. They all dropped like flies.

The Krays were always interested in proceeds from gambling. In Bristol, the story goes that local bookies met them at Temple Meads station and sent them back to Paddington. As for Blackpool, British heavyweight boxing champion Brian London apparently had a hand in persuading Ronnie and Reggie to jump back on the train. In Newcastle, two film-makers made a DVD called *The Day the Krays Came to Town*, which includes contributions from various Tyneside hardmen who apparently had a role to play in sending the Krays packing, among them Kenny 'Panda' Anderson, and Ted 'Machine Gun' Kelly. A more mundane version was told to a local paper by a former manageress at the Club A Go Go. According to Jenny Clarke, the Kray twins arrived at the club one evening in 1964: 'They came into the club and we all spotted them. They soon left when they realised we didn't have any one-armed bandits.'

In addition to their apparent failure to make any headway in

Birmingham, Bristol, Blackpool or Newcastle, the Krays supposedly ran into Manchester's Quality Street Gang, were turned
around at Manchester Piccadilly and put back on the train to
London. One or more or all of these humiliations for the Krays
may well have happened, but you'd be forgiven for asking why the
twins would persist in wandering so far from their manor, wast-
ing train ticket after train ticket on a fruitless national tour. Unless
they both had free British Rail intercity season tickets it all sounds
a bit unlikely.

The Fewtrell-owned Barbarella's on Cumberland Street has
been replaced by an NCP car park attached to a gymnasium
owned by TV 'dragon' Duncan Bannatyne. The club hosted
many of the early punk gigs, including two by the Sex Pistols and
several by the Clash. John Taylor and fellow Duran Duran
member Nick Rhodes were childhood friends, sharing a first
gig-going experience when they went to Birmingham Town Hall
together in April 1974 to see Mick Ronson. By 1978 they'd
become regulars at Barbarella's, witnessing gigs by the likes of
Ultravox, Blondie and the Clash.

In the autumn of 1978 John Taylor began studying at
Birmingham Polytechnic and formed a band, Dada, with another
student, David Twist. In the spirit of the times, Dada mined electronic sounds. They didn't want to be punk, they wanted to be
part of what was coming next. John Taylor tells me: 'This was a
transition period. I got bored and not a little frightened by where
the purist punk scene was headed. I wasn't going to hang out with
skinheads spitting at Stiff Little Fingers.'

By the end of 1978 a number of songs had been released that
presaged a wave of new British music, electronica that sounded
good on the dancefloor, made by a generation inspired by punk
and David Bowie, including the seven-inch double A-side from
the Normal comprising 'Warm Leatherette' and 'TVOD', the
Human League track 'Being Boiled' and early work by Ultravox.
Points of reference included Bowie's *Low* album and Kraftwerk

(the *Trans-Europe Express* album and the single 'Showroom Dummies'). You might hear these new records on John Peel's radio show or see them talked about in one of the weekly broadsheet music papers of the era – *NME*, *Sounds*, *Melody Maker*. And you'd hear these records at new-wave discos and especially at clubs that had Roxy Music and Bowie fans.

Close to Manchester Cathedral was a club called Pips, spread over several rooms playing different genres of music. The so-called Roxy Room there was the subject of the BBC's *Omnibus* programme broadcast on 23 April 1977. It was one of many clubs in 1977 and 1978 that hosted nights for Bowie/Roxy fans, including Friday nights upstairs at the Adelphi pub in Leeds, and in London, most famously, Billy's.

Maureen Ward was in her mid-teens when she started going to Pips, and recalls how varied the looks were, and all beyond the obvious. She remembers a gang of girls in 1940s chic, Rita Hayworths with a look that managed to both impress and intimidate. Footage from Pips also reveals how androgynous the look could be at the Bowie/Roxy nights too. People like Martin Degville were brave; throughout history, suspicion of transgressive behaviour or uncertain gender has always been likely to provoke the mainstream population.

Even those at Bowie/Roxy nights not on the edge of fashion were often met by confusion and disbelief. The Fad Gadget number 'Back to Nature' is one of the songs that reminds Maureen Ward of her visits to Pips: 'I guess you had to be there, but this was very exciting to a sixteen-year-old hearing this very loud in Pips. Clubs weren't like they are now. They were much emptier. Maybe that's why this track felt so eerie, hypnotic, sinister even. And so was town when you stumbled out at 2.05 a.m. precisely and ran for the night bus back to Moston. That, or face a long, hostile walk home.'

When Dada split, John got together with Stephen Duffy (a fellow student at the Poly), Nick Rhodes and bass player Simon

Colley. Calling themselves Duran Duran (a variant of Durand Durand, the evil scientist in the film *Barbarella* – and thus a nod towards the club of that name), their first gigs were at tiny venues, including one in the puppet theatre at Cannon Hill Arts Centre and another, the Star Club, in a room above a pub on Essex Street where the band set up in front of the fireplace and no more than forty people could fit in at any one time. Stephen Duffy and Simon Colley moved on, so Nick and John continued to look for the right line-up and hustled for more gigs. Their plans were to avoid the well-worn and deadening local band circuit at venues like the Barrel Organ near Digbeth bus station where all the Brum rock bands played. These things mattered: venues have a place, a symbolic value. Round the corner from the Rum Runner was a successful venue called the Opposite Lock, but Duran Duran would have avoided playing there too; it was the kind of place a teacher at school might recommend.

So it was one Friday afternoon in February 1980 when Nick and John paid a daytime visit to the Rum Runner, looking for a gig. John had heard the club mentioned a few times, not always in a context that made it sound like an attractive proposition; it was known that, being close to the ATV (later Central) studios, stars and crew working on the likes of *Crossroads* and *The Golden Shot* would hang out there. However, he'd spotted a little poster glued on a lamppost on Hill Street advertising a Bowie night at the Rum Runner, so he hoped to find someone there who would give the Duran Duran demo tape a sympathetic ear.

The Rum Runner was one of a number of businesses run by the Berrow family. The venue had been active in the 1960s and 1970s (opening in 1964), but by the beginning of 1978 the club was only open three nights a week at the most and trade was poor. Ray Berrow, one of the club's original owners, had transferred his energies to a casino at the Grand Hotel and the Rum Runner was getting left behind; it was considered, in the words of Ray's son Paul, 'more of a nuisance than a viable business'. Paul and his brother Michael had worked there from a young age, learning the ropes, and they struck a deal with the family to be given the responsibility of relaunching the club. By the end of 1978 the brothers had been let loose to come up with new ideas, and took themselves off to New York to visit a number of clubs, especially Studio 54.

During 1978 the owners of Studio 54 looked at potential sites for a London version (including the New Victoria Theatre in Westminster) but never completed a deal. The New York venue was the most talked-about club in the world. The Berrows were inspired and returned from their trip to give the Rum Runner a makeover, musically and in every other way. The Bowie night started to pick up interest from the fashion crowd who enjoyed the music and appreciated a room full of mirrors; to underline the sense of exclusivity Studio 54 was renowned for, for a while a girl dressed in an iridescent blue plastic catsuit was employed to weed out anyone deemed unworthy.

David Wright remembers his first Rum Runner outfit included a 'grandad shirt', an approximate likeness of the one David Bowie wears on the front of the *Young Americans* album. He was dating a girl called Sarah who had a strong look, and David decided to wear make-up too – eyeliner, mascara, a little bit of eyeshadow and blusher. Given that Balsall Common was several miles from the club, there were transport complications requiring combinations of trains, taxis, buses.

Through the decades, centuries even, life after dark has been a search for something beyond the mundane, for escapism. Rising unemployment and collapsing industries were features of urban life in Britain through the late 1970s into the 1980s, especially in the first years of the Thatcher government, and in no city more than Liverpool. There was determined political resistance to the destruction of British industry, which in Liverpool led to the rise of the hard-core Militant tendency within the local Labour Party. But that wasn't the only response to the economic gloom in the city; madly dressed post-punk Bowie fans – who preferred the label 'Futurists' to 'New Romantics' – would gather on Thursday and Sunday nights at Cagney's (off London Road) and also found a home at Kirkland's wine bar (on Hardman Street).

Trying on outfits, trying on identities, hearing music daytime radio didn't play and surrounded by colour and neon, being out at Billy's, Cagney's or the Rum Runner was a chance to be somewhere else, to be *someone* else. David Wright was aware that the late 1970s could be dark and aggressive: 'Yes, that's what I remember about the Rum Runner, it was so far removed – especially from Birmingham, which as a city is very drab, well it is to me, it's a depressing place really; it certainly was back then. There was a cloud over us. And I remember the economic problems, the strikes, all coming through. In many ways it was escapism from the drudgery of everything that was going on. And the club was our little oasis totally removed from it.'

The Berrow brothers were ambitious, on the lookout for other opportunities. They gave Duran Duran a gig and shortly afterwards offered them rehearsal space at the venue too, and the band moved in. This was before Simon Le Bon joined them – he was recruited thanks to the network of friends the band made at the Rum Runner. His girlfriend, Fiona Kemp, worked behind the bar at the club and told him that Duran Duran needed a singer. The venue became their base, their hangout, and the Berrows became their management. The stories of the Rum Runner and Duran Duran were already intertwined and, as John tells me: 'If we hadn't made that short walk and knocked on the door of the Rum Runner, if we hadn't met Mike and Paul, who knows what that future might have looked like?'

One afternoon, the Berrows asked Nick Rhodes if he would consider joining the DJ team for one night a week. He took up the challenge, even though they were only offering him a midweek night and just £20 for the night's work. But he found a sound and nurtured a crowd, playing a mix of glam, punk and sounds from the new wave of electronic artists. Soon there were queues to the road and round the corner; Nick was given a small pay rise and offered Friday nights too. The club's regulars included Jane Kahn, Patti Bell, John Mulligan (co-founder of the band Fashion), Gay John, Whiskers, Slag Sue and Martin Degville. And, journeying from London, George O'Dowd (soon to be Boy George) visited occasionally, as did Peter Robinson (who was already Marilyn). This ultra-flamboyant crowd were a bit of a 'clique' according to David Wright and a touch standoffish. 'Posers', some of their detractors called them, and the posers gladly accepted the term.

As well as the Rum Runner's Bowie/Roxy nights there were also jazz funk and disco nights in the club, the music during the week feeding into Duran Duran's sound: songs like 'Are "Friends" Electric' and 'Good Times'. John Taylor also remembers other music thrown in at the Rum Runner, more Giorgio Moroder, singalongs like Frank Sinatra's 'New York, New York'. 'It all felt very cool to be a part of,' says John. 'But also raunchy. Let's face it, it was all about finding a darling for the evening.'

The Rum Runner had a key part to play in the career of Duran Duran but, unarguably, out of all the clubs in that era frequented by Bowie fans, androgynous types and the fashion crowd, the most significant was Billy's. Steve Strange and Rusty Egan approached the owner of Gossips, a Jamaican named Vince Howard, and offered to run Tuesday nights for him. Tuesdays isn't traditionally a busy night, so it made sense for the owner to give up his space to a couple of enthusiastic party animals who would work to bring in their friends and friends of their friends. Billy's opened in the autumn of 1978. There was always a soul-boy ingredient but also a punk one too. As with many of the similar Bowie/Roxy nights at other locations, the crowd were mainly suburban art-school students who had become disillusioned with punk but liked a challenge and channelled a punk spirit by gleefully customising their outfits. It was always more punk to wear something no one else was wearing than to buy garments off the peg.

The Billy's crowd took dressing-up to another level. One of the regulars was Nicola Tyson, then an eighteen-year-old student at the Chelsea School of Art, who has since gone on to make a career as a painter. She'd be at the venues most weeks, in among the other young people decked out in tuxedos and wing collars, mad hats, too much make-up, cummerbunds, customised T-shirts, diamanté brooches, taffeta gowns. On the first night of Billy's, Chris Sullivan's look included monocle and spats, Ollie O'Donnell was a tartan teddy boy, and Melissa Caplan went psychedelic. Robert Elms wore what he later called 'Chinese space-Cossack attire'. Nicola Tyson explains: 'There weren't really any rules, apart from push your look as far as you can. Invent yourself. Entertain.'

There wasn't often a Tuesday when the attendance went above a hundred, but among the core regulars were several who would later make a career and reputation in art, fashion and especially music, including George O'Dowd, Marilyn, Jeremy Healy (later of Haysi Fantayzee), Siobhan Fahey from Bananarama and Martin Degville down from Birmingham. Rusty Egan's music selections seemed spot-on but the role of the DJ had not yet been elevated to where it would be in the mid-1990s. At Billy's the stars were the crowd on the dancefloor.

As we discovered earlier, the building at 69 Dean Street where Billy's took place is now the Dean Street Townhouse, a 39-bedroom hotel and all-day dining room. When Billy's was operating in the Gossips basement in the late 1970s, where the Mandrake had been, the Gargoyle upstairs housed a strip club, which at various times was known as Nell Gwyn's. There were also revue shows, but none of this could keep the Gargoyle afloat and it soon closed its doors, by which time the buildings were listed Grade II. Word was spreading about Billy's, but it was still small fry, a tiny niche event on a Tuesday, and numbers were never going to be healthy given the glee with which Steve Strange turned away anyone he deemed less than sensational. And after just three months, Steve Strange and Rusty Egan appear to have had a falling-out with the owner of Gossips.

The scene moved on to Covent Garden, to the Blitz on Great Queen Street. There Steve Strange and Rusty Egan's weekly night lasted much longer than it had at Billy's, and generated more media attention. Among the Blitz crowd, many were destined for successful careers in fashion and millinery, including Melissa Caplan, Isabella Blow, Stephen Linard, Judith Frankland, David Holah, John Galliano and Stephen Jones. Although, it's true, some avoided the creative industries: Carl Teper went on to become an adjudicator for the Parking and Traffic Appeal Service.

From the Blitz club creativity took off, and change initiated. Fashion students got jobs, photographers were given commissions, bands got deals and released records, the music and the look and the lifestyle were propelled into the wider world. The strong visual component of the scene fed into two of the emerging and influential media, both visually oriented, hungry for images. The first was the newly launched style magazines *The Face* and *i-D*, which were deeply fashion-conscious, and on the lookout for innovators, futurists and posers. And the second was the rise of promotional videos.

The first key video to highlight the New Romantic scene was David Bowie's 'Ashes to Ashes'. Bowie always had an eye for the new and daring, and made a point of paying a visit to Billy's one week and inviting a handful of the club's regulars to join him on set the following day, including Darla Jane Gilroy and Judith Frankland. Bowie was dressed in the style of a Pierrot, and Steve Strange was featured as well. Strange was in awe: 'I had queued outside a record shop in Pontypool to buy his new album when I was thirteen, and now he wanted to work with me. When I was handing out flyers for Billy's I'd never thought something like that might happen.'

At the time Steve Strange was frontman in Visage with Blitz DJ Rusty Egan on drums, along with Rusty's fellow ex-Rich Kid Midge Ure, Barry Adamson, John McGeoch and Dave Formula from the band Magazine, plus the Ultravox keyboardist Billy Currie. Their first single, 'Tar', was released in September 1979 and was less than moderately successful. The follow-up, 'Fade to Grey', was released just after 'Ashes to Ashes' and was a huge hit. Another Blitz kid, Princess Julia, featured in the 'Fade to Grey' video; she went on to have a successful career as a model and then a DJ (she was a resident DJ at the ultra-flamboyant club night 'Kinky Gerlinky' in the 1990s).

Spandau Ballet also emerged from the Blitz scene. They considered themselves a white soul band, yet in an earlier incarnation, as the Makers, they'd played punk venues like the Roxy. Their live appearances at the Blitz in late 1979 and early 1980 positioned them at the forefront of what was happening at the club and they soon attracted positive coverage in the style magazines. Like Duran Duran in their early days, they were also careful in their choice of where to perform, preferring to play the Scala cinema and the Blitz rather than pubs or standard rock venues. The Spandau debut single 'To Cut a Long Story Short' was a British Top Five hit in the period between 'Ashes to Ashes' and 'Fade to Grey'.

At the Rum Runner, John Taylor and friends weren't much aware of what was going on around the country. 'At that moment all I cared about was Birmingham – Broad Street mostly, and the club and our friends who went there,' says John. But when journalist Betty Page first wrote in *Sounds* about Spandau Ballet and the Blitz in September 1980, John showed the article to the rest of the band. 'It sounded as if there was an exact mirror of our scene going on in London – the same impetus, the same impulses, and Spandau were their band as Duran were Brum's.'

Duran Duran tracked down Betty Page and invited her to visit them at the Rum Runner, which she did. This was their first national press. The phrase 'New Romantics', said to have been coined by Perry Haines, was used throughout her piece, as Betty Page drew the link between the Blitz and the Rum Runner and Spandau and Duran Duran. Haines later helped style Duran Duran. He'd co-founded *i-D* magazine earlier in 1980 and ran a night at Gossips after Billy's had closed.

One of the elements at Billy's, the Rum Runner and the Blitz that spread into the mainstream was androgyny. It was a remaking and reassertion of the gender-bending that David Bowie had displayed so conspicuously in the early 1970s, but that's not to say it didn't have major impact. When Boy George emerged with his first single 'Do You Really Want to Hurt Me?' there were people confused and disconcerted by his appearance, but there were also others, including those who would never have found their way to the Blitz, who were thrilled and empowered; via TV appearances, videos and photoshoots the Blitz had come to them. The second quarter of the 'Do You Really Want to Hurt Me?' video was filmed in the Gargoyle. Everyone but the Boy is dressed in a 1930s style.

Things were moving fast for Duran Duran. They'd recorded 'Planet Earth', a melodic, synthesizer-led single, pulsing with a Moroder-ish dancebeat. Their original version was tweaked and then released on 2 February 1981. Not only was it an immediate hit in the UK, but overseas too, going Top Ten in Australia. The lyric namechecks the new scene in the line 'Like some New Romantic looking for the TV sound'. Six months later, eighteen months after walking into the club's offices, John and Nick and the rest of Duran Duran were pop stars. Princess Diana, a flawed but nevertheless significant barometer of the nation's taste, would declare Duran Duran to be her favourite group.

Meanwhile at the Rum Runner, the Berrows had already opened up more space in the building and several other bands were rehearsing there, including Dexys Midnight Runners and the Beat (the latter filmed much of the video for the single

'Mirror in the Bathroom' in the club). The frontman of Dexys was Kevin Rowland, who was as preoccupied with clothes and the look of his band as any New Romantic. Dexys took to wearing a belligerent look, the antithesis of the gaudy flamboyance of the Rum Runner regulars – woolly hats, and black donkey jackets like a gang of New York dockers. They scored their first UK number one with 'Geno', inspired by Kevin's experiences watching a show by Geno Washington & the Ram Jam Band in 1968 at the Railway Hotel on Station Road in Harrow. Kevin was fourteen, he was hooked: 'The atmosphere was amazing. It felt great to be a part of it.'

After the demise of Blitz, a number of related club nights were started. Steve Strange, Rusty Egan and Chris Sullivan launched 'Hell' at Mandy's Club in Henrietta Street, Covent Garden, on Thursdays. Pursuing a more transgressive ethos, a mixed fetish night called 'Skin Two' opened one Monday at the end of January 1983, at Stallions in Falconberg Court, off Charing Cross Road, a gay bar with aquariums embedded in tree trunks as pillars. Hosts were ex-Blitz regulars David Claridge and Daniel James (a mask maker who specialised in latex-based creations), and guests on the opening night included John Sutcliffe – the boss of the rubber/bondage clothing range AtomAge – and the artist Allen Jones, best known for his forniphiliac sculptures. Entertainment on the opening evening included music provided by the club's first resident DJ, Chris Buxbaum, and a live performance by the model Sue Scadding, who shed clothes to a soundtrack of choral music.

The first days of Skin Two had links not just to Blitz, but to the Rum Runner too. Jane Kahn of Kahn & Bell was spotted on the opening night, and Bev Glick was also present – she was the 'Betty Page' who had championed Duran Duran in their early days. Claridge and James had attempted to limit media coverage but there were several journalists there, including Betty's then boyfriend Tony Mitchell, who wrote for *Sounds*, and also cultural

© Ray Stevenson

The venue now known as the 100 Club has presented live music since 1942. The Sex Pistols had a residency there in 1976.

Previously unseen photograph of Ian Curtis of Joy Division at the Factory/Russell Club, 11 April 1980; the last occasion Joy Division played in Manchester.

In the post-punk period the Limit in Sheffield – like Eric's in Liverpool and several venues nationwide – had great line-ups most weeks.

Rhona Mackay centre, Karen to her right, Katie to her left, and two other regulars at the Nite Club, Edinburgh, 1981.

Trojan, Nicola Bateman and Leigh Bowery at Bowery's Taboo club in 1985. To gain entry, 'Dress as though your life depends on it or don't bother,' Leigh Bowery said.

A haven for like minds. Sunday afternoon socialising at the Leadmill, Sheffield, 1986.

A building with an amazing nightlife history, on the corner of Dean Street and Meard Street in Soho. In 1982, it was trading as Gossips.

Mark Manning (a.k.a. Zodiac Mindwarp) and the bass player (and record producer) Youth, at Gossips, 1984.

Without the Dug Out, would we have had Massive Attack? Milo and Daddy G of the Wild Bunch DJing at the Dug Out, Bristol, 1984.

Bristol – home to many bass-heavy reggae sound systems in the 1980s especially, including the Enterprise Sound System (here, at St Paul's Carnival in 1986).

The Haçienda, 'Hot' night (Wednesdays), 1988. Acid house had arrived.

Laurent Garnier in the Haçienda DJ box, 1988. He picked up his love of techno and his first ever DJ gigs at the Manchester club.

Julie Stewart on the dancefloor at 'Jive Turkey' in Sheffield, late 1980s.

atrick Lilley (foreground) at Discotheque' at Busbys, in 1988, vith DJ Ben Wolff, one half of the Boilerhouse Boys.

James Barton, Andy Carroll and Darren Hughes, the founders of Cream 1992.

Eclipse, Coventry, flyer from August 1991. Guest DJs that month included Carl Cox, Stu Allan, Joey Beltram and Top Buzz.

A gathering of ravers and New Age travellers at a free festival at Castlemorton in May 1992 precipitated the Criminal Justice and Public Order Act 1994.

DJs Kemistry & Storm. Drum and bass pioneers. Kemistry (left) was killed in a road accident in the early morning of 25 April 1999.

The Rollins Band live at the Duchess of York in Leeds, August 1990.

January 1992. The early days of 'Trade', founded by Laurence Malice. It opened from 4 a.m. until 1 p.m. on Sundays at Turnmills, Clerkenwell Road, London.

'Return to the Source', a mid-1990s Goa-trance club that reunited in August 2014 for a 21st Anniversary Party at Electric, Brixton (formerly the Fridge).

Chloë Sevigny visited the Smiths/Morrissey disco at the Star & Garter in Manchester while she was filming in the city, August 2011.

Two customers entwined at Spiders, Hull, 2005.

Manchester's Twisted Wheel/ Legends club just after it had closed, with demolition imminent.

Hammersmith Palais opened in 1919 featuring an in-house band that proclaimed themselves 'musical anarchists'. It closed in 2007.

One of the great venues in contemporary Manchester – Albert Hall (converted from a Methodist hall buil in 1910).

historians Ted Polhemus and Lynn Procter who reviewed their Skin Two night out for the porn magazine *Fiesta*. Claridge had also arranged for a photographer to capture the scenes: Peter Ashworth.

There was also Le Kilt, which took place on Tuesday nights at 60 Greek Street and which in turn inspired Le Beat Route, which was on Friday nights in the basement of 17 Greek Street, where you'd hear old funk classics and new New York rap. We'll hear more of the legacy of the Blitz in later chapters. After Billy's, 69 Dean Street still had more to contribute to music history. In the summer of 1982, although the Gargoyle had stumbled to an igno-minious end, and the strippers had left the stage, the lift was still in operation and upstairs there was a new night run by Olli Wisdom and Jon Klein. They called this midweek gathering the Batcave. In its advertising it promised 'absolutely no funk'.

The Batcave was the beginning of the tribe called 'goth'. Every Wednesday the club was done up like it was Hallowe'en, bedecked with netting that was supposed to look like cobwebs. At the Batcave you'd be among Dave Vanian clones, dark-haired girls, ex-punk psychobillies, and a large number of whey-faced Bauhaus fans; you'd hear DJ Hamish MacDonald playing Siouxsie and the Banshees records, and the Cramps, and Eddie Cochran; and you'd also be treated to live music courtesy of bands includ-ing Specimen and Alien Sex Fiend. Nick Cave occasionally visited. Marc Almond met Lydia Lunch there, who'd just gone solo after starting out in Teenage Jesus & the Jerks. This was a while before she got the lead role in the film *Fingered*.

The Batcave moved on to a larger venue, the Subway in Leicester Square, and the DJ line-up was extended to include Anni Hogan of Marc and the Mambas. By this time it had helped define a movement, and most towns and cities had some kind of goth club, sometimes also overlapping with those labelled 'alter-native' and/or 'industrial'. In 1983 'Alice' was released on an EP by Sisters of Mercy, a band fronted by former F-Club regular

Andrew Eldritch. The Batcave certainly had its moment, but as
the 1980s progressed the part of the country that seemed to
believe in goth the most was Leeds, where life is shorter and the
skies are darker.

I once got a chance to ask novelist David Peace about the goth
scene in Leeds and the West Riding. David Peace had been a regular at Raffles in Wakefield, close to where he grew up. There, DJ
Electronic Glen would be playing Bowie, T. Rex, the Human
League and Gina X. He also paid a few visits to Le
Phonographique in the Merrion Centre in Leeds: 'The Phono
seemed to me, at least in 1982, to still be more for the old Bowie
crowd. To be honest, the music wasn't that different from the stuff
Electronic Glen was playing – although Raffles, at least at that
time, seemed to play more Cramps and Meteors, compared to the
Phono. So Raffles was that bit more macho and rougher.'

There's a line that can be traced from Bowie, not just to Billy's,
but to clubs like the Batcave. And in Leeds, few locals could resist
stomping glam riffs, says Peace: 'Goth in Leeds seemed to marry
the dressing-up of the Bowie nights and glam-metal stomp and
riffs. I remember some spectacular dancing going on around the
mirrored pillar in the centre of the dancefloor to "Alice" and
"Bela Lugosi's Dead"; all towering hair and flapping coats.'

The presence of local bands contributing to what was happening in the clubs gave goth in Leeds extra impact: bands like Sisters
of Mercy, ex-Sister Wayne Hussey's later band the Mission, and
the March Violets (all from Leeds), and the Southern Death Cult
from Bradford. There were landmark gigs by the Sisters at the
Warehouse in Leeds, and venues like the Hellfire Club in
Wakefield put on the March Violets, the Fall and the Meteors,
while a number of similar nights sprang up in places like
Dewsbury and Batley. The scene ended up with a huge reach, but
remained small-scale; being cut off from London gave it an
endearing insularity. It wasn't showbiz. At Le Phonographique
Claire Shearsby was the resident DJ. She lived above a chemist

with Andrew Eldritch of the Sisters of Mercy (along with Spiggy, their cat).

At the end of 1982, back in 69 Dean Street, the Batcave was one of a host of different club nights both up in the old Gargoyle space and downstairs at Gossips, run by different promoters with separate names for each different night, with differing DJs, music policies and clientele, including 'Gold Coast', a relatively short-lived night playing African highlife and afrobeat hosted by Christian Cotterill and Jo Hagan, and a Radio Invicta night on Fridays, hosted by Steve Walsh and others, including Lyndon T (they'd be playing quality jazz funk). The Saturday 'Roots Rockers' night featured David Rodigan and Tim Westwood, who would both take to bigger stages later in their careers. The most established of all these Gossips nights, having started in July 1980, was 'Gaz's Rockin Blues' hosted by Gaz Mayall, playing John Lee Hooker, Little Richard and reggae too.

I guess there aren't many artists who'd be happy to spend their career playing dives. John Taylor will look back fondly on gigs at the Star Club and elsewhere, but he'll be happy he hasn't spent a lifetime lugging equipment out of vans and up and down stairs, plugging into a cheap PA and playing to a small crowd, however clued-up or flamboyantly dressed that crowd might be. Once they'd broken out of clubs, Duran Duran loved playing Birmingham Odeon but in interviews with the band in 1981 they never hid their ambition to go even further: 'We want to be the biggest band in the world,' they'd say. And: 'We want to play Madison Square Garden by 1984.'

In the early 1960s a generation of bands emerged out of coffee bars and unwholesome basement beat clubs like the Cavern and moved on to headline Saturday nights in ballrooms and dance halls; but once more established, some groups had issues with the kinds of venues (and audiences) they played to. The Hollies found ballroom audiences too noisy and preferred to play in seated venues, theatres or cabaret clubs. In 1966 Graham Nash of the

Hollies expressed pleasure at the week-long engagement the band had fulfilled at a cabaret club called Mr Smiths in Manchester, where the band were able to perform slower, subtler numbers like 'Puff the Magic Dragon' and 'A Taste of Honey', and his bandmate Eric Haydock agreed: 'When we work in cabaret it's different altogether. Proper dressing rooms and lighting – and attentive audiences who have come along to listen and to applaud what they like.'

Duran Duran fulfilled their ambitions, playing two shows at Madison Square Garden in March 1984 at the height of their success. The same month, back in Britain, the miners' strike began. The portrayal of a high-gloss world of excess in a succession of Duran Duran videos while unemployment rose, CND marched and the Thatcher government and the miners clashed was an unfortunate, perhaps even damning, conjunction. But despite their ascent into the unreal world of pop stardom, Duran Duran never forgot their musical roots; on their world tour in 2008 they performed cover versions of Kraftwerk's 'Showroom Dummies', and the Normal's 'Warm Leatherette', both Rum Runner favourites. Walking through that doorway on Broad Street had opened a world, a life and a career for them.

The photographer at the opening night of Skin Two, Peter Ashworth, later in 1983 was responsible for the shot of Annie Lennox on the cover of the Eurythmics album *Touch* (and, in the early 1990s, the beautiful photo of Billy Mackenzie on the album *Outernational*). The model Sue Scadding, who had shed some clothes at the opening, has in recent years featured in advertisements for Amara hair products. Jacquie O'Sullivan was one of the original greeters on the door; she joined Bananarama when Siobhan Fahey left the band. Visitors to Skin Two in the early days included the 'robot' recording artists Tik and Tok and their friend Carole Caplin (who later became an adviser to Cherie and Tony Blair; she advised Cherie on style, and Tony on fitness).

As for the club's founder, David Claridge moved on from Skin

Two when a puppet he created, operated and voiced became a hot property on television. His creation was Roland Rat, who appeared – latex and fishnet free – regularly on *GMTV* (when he wasn't on TV, Claridge claimed the character lived beneath King's Cross railway station in the Ratcave). The tabloids almost derailed Roland Rat's rise to fame and fortune, however. On Saturday 27 August 1983 the *Sun* revealed the Rat's creator's link with what they called a 'kinky sex club'. They predicted a backlash against the man behind the lovable rodent, but none materialised. Claridge had handed over the running of Skin Two to his girl-friend Lesley Herbert a few weeks earlier, but provided a quote for the paper. 'It's all very embarrassing,' he said.

Four decades on from taking his records to sell at the Bull Ring, Patrick Lilley has made a life in music. After moving to London, he shared a squat with pre-Culture Club Boy George, and was Divine's publicist. He went on to work in PR and pro-motions in the early acid house days, and founded London's hugely successful club night 'Queer Nation' in 1990. He now runs 'Work', weekly since 2008, at various venues.

CHAPTER TEN

Tape machines, modern drugs, unknown pleasures

Among the stories, claims and competing mythologies of Britain's nightclubs and music venues there are a few recurring tales in addition to those featuring the Krays; one of which is the story of the night that Jimi Hendrix put his guitar through the ceiling. Online, and in print, there are a number of eyewitness reports of this happening at several different venues. It's said, for instance, that Hendrix put his guitar through the ceiling at the New Cellar Club in South Shields in February 1967. Sandie Brown from the local record shop, Saville Bros, was there and Sandie's words are quoted on a website dedicated to documenting Hendrix's visits to the Northeast. 'He rammed his guitar upwards, not necessarily intending to do any damage, it was accidental, but it brought down some plaster from the ceiling.'

Hendrix did the same a month later at Newcastle's Club A Go Go, ramming the head of the guitar through the plasterboard. Apparently actor/singer Jimmy Nail was in the audience and he saw the incident. 'I was in my mid-teens and used to go to the Club A Go Go which had a very low ceiling. Hendrix – I hadn't seen anything like it – leapt with the guitar and it went through a ceiling tile. But get this, he let it go and continued playing while it hung from the ceiling.'

Coincidentally, another future Geordie singing star, Sting, was also at Club A Go Go that same evening: 'I remember Hendrix creating a hole in the plaster ceiling above the stage with the head of his guitar, and then it was over. I lay in my bed that night with my ears ringing and my worldview significantly altered.'

The stories of being in a cool venue on a historic occasion are useful additions to the personal mythologies of Sting and Jimmy Nail, and why not believe they were there and the incident happened? It may also be possible that Hendrix's guitar actually damaged the ceiling a few months earlier at the Wellington Club in Dereham, a town in Norfolk, as one or two eyewitnesses report; one audience member at the Wellington claims Hendrix rammed the instrument into the ceiling because he was 'getting bored in the middle of one song'.

There was an incident in 1964 when Pete Townshend accidentally broke his guitar when it struck the low ceiling at the Railway Tavern in Harrow. Townshend followed this up with a deliberate act of vandalism, banging the guitar into the ceiling again and then the stage until his instrument was in bits. It was a turning point for him, and for how music was presented onstage. 'The old, conventional way of making music would never be the same,' he writes in his autobiography, *Who I Am*, describing the act of destruction as 'extraordinary, magical, surreal'.

Hendrix had studied the powerful onstage antics of Pete Townshend, and putting his guitar through the ceiling several times may or may not have happened and may or may not have been accidental or the result of boredom; it could have been a deliberate stunt. Certainly, Hendrix began to include the destruction and/or immolation of his guitar into his live performances. Townshend also recalls standing watching Hendrix smash up a guitar at the Monterey Pop Festival in 1967, and Cass Elliot of the Mamas and the Papas shouting, 'Hey, destroying guitars is your thing!' Townshend replied, 'It used to be. It belongs to Jimi now.'

That Sandie Brown from Saville Bros saw Hendrix is unsurprising. Hendrix was often in the Northeast, as his managers, Chas Chandler and Mike Jeffery, were based there. Jeffery sold the Club A Go Go though and moved the venue manager Myer Thomas out to Palma, Majorca, where Jeffery and a business partner, Keith Gibbon, had opened a nightclub called Sergeant Pepper's situated off the Plaza Gomila. This was 1968, and the Jimi Hendrix Experience played at the opening of the club. After the gig took place, *NME* writer Keith Altham reported, 'Hendrix literally brought the roof down on the opening night by the simple expedient of ramming the neck of his guitar up through the low ceiling tiles.'

Altham was doing PR for Hendrix and the club and wrote up the full story of Hendrix's trip in the paper. Inevitably perhaps, Jimi, the Experience and their entourage bumped into the biggest fan of Balearic holidays, George Best. According to Altham, Best was at the gig too ('mesmerised by the Experience's performance on stage'), but there's no mention of any of this in George Best's *Blessed*. Perhaps he'd forgotten his night out with the Jimi Hendrix Experience. Maybe Altham embellished the story a little, or even created it. There are some stories of nights out in Best's book but maybe his worldview wasn't as significantly altered by seeing a psychedelic rock icon destroying ceiling tiles as much as Sting's had been in Newcastle. The kind of stories Best does include in *Blessed* reveal different priorities to documenting rock history being made; like the time he describes going out with Mike Summerbee in Birmingham and finding a club 'crawling with women'.

Punk had reasserted the joy and value of experiencing live music in small venues. Basement spaces in out-of-the-way places and low-ceilinged venues were cool, and small-scale scenes and bands just starting out were to be supported, encouraged. There was participation, of various kinds, a swirl of activity; a girl selling a fanzine is the bass player in a band with a single out on a local label; the lads you see standing at the bar at the beginning of the night are the headline act.

The attractions of seeing bands made up of people you saw at gigs, hanging out at small venues a bus ride away, and feeling close and drawn to the action on the stage, were fuelling activity nationwide. Then there was the added pleasure of tracking down emerging bands – latching on to word of mouth triggered by fanzines or the weekly music papers, the occasional local radio show, and John Peel on Radio 1 – and ending up in a room full of like-minded music fans.

For some fortunate music fans embracing these excitements at Eric's, the Factory in Manchester, the Limit in Sheffield, the Nite Club or Valentino's in Edinburgh, the Bungalow Bar in Paisley, the Sandpiper in Nottingham back in the post-punk era – as now – some months or years later there could also be the satisfaction and a host of memories gained from having seen bands fresh, close-up and hungry, on their way to a career playing major halls and selling millions of albums. As we'll see, back then the denizens of small-scale gigs had opportunities to pay their £1.25 and get to see the likes of the Cure, New Order or U2.

Though I'm not sure how this theory can ever be tested, it's likely that more bands were formed in 1977 or 1978 than in any era since the beat-group boom years in the early 1960s. But in Northern Ireland, the troubles were still damaging live music; the only people out at night in Belfast and Derry city centres were the police and army patrols. The local youth stayed at home, although this had one intriguing result: it's said that 1 per cent of listeners to John Peel's Radio 1 show were from Northern Ireland. Punk and Peel began to make a difference. When Belfast band Highway Star discovered punk they changed their name to Stiff Little Fingers, dropped the Deep Purple cover versions from their set and wrote songs about the world around them. They recorded a single, 'Suspect Device', and Peel played it relentlessly. The interest in punk grew and soon punks started venturing out, bringing life back to pockets of the city.

The authorities had banned the Clash's first scheduled appearance in Northern Ireland (they'd been due to play the Ulster Hall on 20 October 1977), but punk was taking root, at the Harp Bar on Hill Street, for example. The Harp Bar's punk nights started in April 1978 (when Victim, supported by the Androids, performed). The establishing of non-sectarian spaces appealed to an old 60s idealist like Terri Hooley: 'Back then there were Protestant ghettoes and Catholic ghettoes and they were controlled by the paramilitaries,' he later explained. 'That's why the punks were my heroes – they were the first to say, "We're not part of your tribe". While the IRA and the UDA were keeping us ghettoised, it was a political statement to go down to the Harp Bar just to pogo and hear some great music.'

Terri Hooley, meanwhile, had expanded his interest in buying and selling records and set up Good Vibrations in a small derelict building on Great Victoria Street in Belfast. From that base he began promoting shows in various venues and launched a record label, releasing a Rudi single ('Big Time') and, subsequently, 'Teenage Kicks' by a Derry band called the Undertones, who had been resident at their home town's Casbah venue. On release, 'Teenage Kicks' struggled to make much impact until John Peel declared it 'wonderful' and featured it regularly.

The Undertones, like the vast majority of the bands formed in the wake of punk, made their way through the small-venue circuit. In March 1979 they had twelve dates in England in fourteen days, starting at the Norwich Boogie House where chaotic scenes included a fan suffering a broken leg and the police being called by the management to bring calm to the proceedings. Then the band moved on to the Factory in Manchester before playing Eric's in Liverpool on Saturday 3 March. At Eric's they played two sets, the first a 'matinee' at 6.30 p.m.

It was a fertile time for bands, and many that would later

become feted, iconic or stadium-filling were appearing in small venues nationwide, giving a generation of music lovers multiple chances to later lay claim to witnessing magical moments: the night Joy Division supported Dexys Midnight Runners and only seventy people were there, for example, or the night Blondie supported Television, the time Boy George sang with Bow Wow Wow, or when Terry Hall got arrested after a riot at a Specials gig. In Glasgow, Simple Minds (formerly known as Johnny & the Self-Abusers) had a Sunday-night residency at the tiny Mars Bar on Howard Street through the spring and summer of 1978, singer Jim Kerr, resplendent in a white jacket and make-up, taking the stage in front of the forty or so people there every week, the small room illuminated by the band's DIY light show (a revolving police blue light).

Post-punk's equivalent often-told story of paying seven shillings and sixpence to see Jimi Hendrix putting his guitar through the ceiling was paying £1.25 to see Bono split his leather trousers. There's footage of Glastonbury 2011 that appears to show the U2 frontman doing just that, as he has been for thirty years or more. One of the first occasions it's said to have happened was at the Limit in Sheffield on 13 November 1980.

The Limit had its fair share of memorable moments. Kraftwerk paid a visit to the club after they'd played Sheffield's City Hall but had to leave because a fight was about to break out. It was also where the B-52s made their debut appearance in England (July 1979). Over the following years the Limit played host to bands who were on their way to commercial success, including the Undertones, the Revillos, Wire, Simple Minds, the Police and Dire Straits. And many on their way to no commercial success or cult success whatsoever, some who managed a DIY record release, but many who disappeared – the likes of Alfalfa, the Crabs and Molodoy.

Of all the events Limit audiences could later lay claim to have witnessed, there are few as intriguing as the evening Def Leppard supported the Human League. It was 11 September 1978 and there wasn't much happening in the nightclubs and music venues of Sheffield; it was a Monday evening, not the most auspicious night of the week. In among the deserted streets of the city centre, the Limit wouldn't have got away with charging admission. It was free; free entry to see four local bands. Two of them, the Monitors and Graph, never troubled the charts (although watchers of alternative music around Sheffield thought that Graph had potential), but the other two bands that Monday evening at the Limit would go on to play arenas, and make hit albums. It was the first and only time the electro pop act and the heavy metal outfit shared a bill.

George Webster and Kevan Johnson, the two guys who opened the Limit in March 1978, were fans of the Eagles, and took the name of their venue from the song 'Take It to the Limit'. In the basement of a shopping precinct on West Street, the Limit was committed to live music seven days a week, although by October 1979 the club was hosting a new-wave disco every Wednesday (with half-price admission for students and nurses with appropriate NUS and NHS identity cards). Later it was widely regarded as a dive, but at the beginning it was decorated moderately ambitiously, the toilets were clean, and they even had tablecloths in the area where meals were served.

There was a sense that much of the music triggered by punk in various towns and cities was a communal enterprise. In Leeds, in their very early days, both the Mekons and the Gang of Four played at John Keenan's F-Club and shared rehearsal space. Clubs like Eric's weren't just spaces for bands to play. Music that didn't fit with mainstream expectations tended, of course, to attract people who had something different about them too, creating spaces with the potential for creative activity and collaboration.

In Nottingham, one of the established small venues, the Boat Club – where Pink Floyd had played when it was known as the Britannia Rowing Club (and, later, in 1971, Led Zeppelin, and, in 1976, the Sex Pistols) – booked mostly heavy rock and metal bands. Punks in Nottingham would travel to get their kicks; perhaps to the Grey Topper run by Alf Hyslop in the pit village of Jacksdale, or even to the Ajanta in Derby. But by the end of 1977 the Sandpiper in Nottingham was presenting shows by the likes of Penetration and Buzzcocks. Now an underground car park, the Sandpiper was the low-ceilinged basement of a warehouse. One regular, Steve Fisher, puts it like this: 'In the Sandpiper at least, the punk movement was a kickback against the disco scene that had overwhelmed all other sorts of popular music. However, most of the live music, but not all, was punk. The quality of the live bands went from tearfully bad to brilliant.'

These punk venues eschewed the draconian dress codes of high street discotheques and nightclubs. Although it might be supposed the punk 'look' of Mohican haircuts and bondage pants was popular, this just wasn't the case among post-punk audiences at the Limit or the F-Club or the Factory or Eric's. Girls had role models like Siouxsie Sioux, Debbie Harry, and the Raincoats, and would be out to see the Pop Group, Joy Division or Penetration wearing stilettos or maybe Converse or Doc Martens. Lads liked Doc Martens too, and at clubs like the Limit both lads and girls wore mohair jumpers, small badges and big shirts, and customised school blazers or finds from trips to army surplus stores for something khaki or grey, and to Salvation Army stores for overcoats.

The heyday of the Limit was probably 1978 to 1983. A typical venue might have random bands booked, but the Limit became known for a certain kind of band and a certain kind of audience. The programming was varied, though; it was the music the DJs played that created a regular crowd and an identity for the Limit. Midweek there would be disc-only nights and at weekends DJs playing after bands, or instead of bands, including DJ Paul Unwin who'd play the Skids' 'Into the Valley', Japan's 'Quiet Life' and 'Kick in the Eye' by Bauhaus. The Limit served watery Webster's beer. Soon the carpets began to absorb some of this beer, as did the dancefloor. The toilets were a disaster zone. Take a listen to Neil Young's 'Sail Away' lyric extolling 'dives'; he'd have felt right at home at the Limit, and seen its value.

Cherry Red continued promoting at the Winter Gardens in Malvern, featuring the likes of the Damned, the Stranglers and the Jam while offering support slots to local punk groups like the Tights. In the spirit of the times, Cherry Red decided to release a record by the Tights, the first step in what turned out to be Cherry Red's metamorphosis into a maverick independent record label. Eric's was still going strong in Liverpool. Over in Leeds, John Keenan was doing good work at his F-Club. In May 1978, a regular night at the Russell Club in Hulme, Manchester, was launched by some of the characters who'd go on to be integral to Manchester's subsequent music history, the Factory label, and the Haçienda.

Factory (Manchester), Eric's (Liverpool), the Limit (Sheffield), and the F-Club (Leeds); these four key venues were a reflection of and a contribution to the wealth of music happening in northern cities in the post-punk period. There was economic stagnation in those areas at that time with the collapse of manufacturing industries and rising unemployment but, if anything, this desperation motivated rather than destroyed creativity. And the struggles of British industry had one side effect which turned out to be a useful factor in the growth of music in these northern cities: as factories and workshops closed and warehouses emptied, unused buildings became a feature of cities, with no one much interested in them – there were no property developers snapping them up with a plan to build retail malls or apartment blocks – and they were left to rot, or to be populated by self-motivated mavericks who turned them into rehearsal rooms, recording studios, record shops and music venues.

How the lack of life opportunities in their locality pushed the young and disaffected towards music and other artistic expression has become a powerful narrative in the history of these cities, shaped by journalists at the time like Paul Morley and Jon Savage. The narrative had a ring of truth. Numerous musicians have talked about their desperation, including Martyn Ware of the Human League, here talking about Sheffield at the time: 'It was a place of great depression because of all the factory closures. Sheffield engendered a certain desperation to get on with something different and creative, because there wasn't a lot happening.'

Of all subcultures, Northern Soul was one of the strongest in Sheffield in the late 1970s, partly as a result of the legacy of mod clubs like the Mojo and the Esquire. There were also some mid-range live venues in the city, including the City Hall and the Top Rank (where the Damned played), but most of the city centre was a disco stronghold; outside of the centre was a network of working men's clubs where novelty acts, local crooners and covers bands playing unadventurous oldies and Top Forty hits made up the musical offering.

In 2012 the University of Sheffield produced a booklet, *Sheffield Music City*, in a neatly produced limited edition of 600 (describing itself as 'a beginner's guide to the futuristic, beautiful and strange music that our city has produced' and claiming, 'Culturally, Sheffield is as important as Salzburg'). Cabaret Voltaire feature prominently in *Sheffield Music City* as innovators and are described as key to music-making in the city. 'It's difficult to overstate how important Cabaret Voltaire were ... A band who had no idea how to play their instruments, so made records using found sounds, cut up and played through ex-army tape machines. Much of the sound that would later define the city.'

Richard H. Kirk of Cabaret Voltaire recalls you had to look hard in Sheffield in the mid-70s to find musical entertainment that wasn't mainstream, or obvious. Richard would frequent the Crazy Daisy, a basement club in an art deco building on the corner of York Street and High Street that hosted very popular glam nights. He also used to go to Shades on Ecclesall Road when they had student nights with DJs playing Roxy Music, although Shades was a club where you'd mostly hear soul and reggae. It was owned by Max Omare, who had moved to England from Nigeria. In 1971 Omare financed a record label, Shades Records, which released music by white reggae band the Inner Mind. When Richard was out dancing there, the upstairs was a casino, but after it was rebuilt in 1982 a shop was created on the ground floor and Napoleon's Casino replaced Shades in the basement.

Richard Kirk met Chris Watson, who had started using an oscillator, and together they'd listen to the tape loops and record randomly on tape recorders. By the end of 1974 Stephen Mallinder had joined them, and they'd borrowed a state-of-the-art synthesizer from Sheffield University's music department (an EMS VCS3). Richard bought a drum machine for £40 from a guy who'd been a losing contestant on *Opportunity Knocks*.

In May 1975 Cabaret Voltaire played their first gig courtesy of a University of Sheffield student organisation called Science for the People. Their set consisted of a rhythmic tape loop of a recording of a steamhammer, and Richard alternating playing guitar and playing clarinet. It wouldn't be the last time the Cabs encountered much confusion, and some hostility, from the student audience. It ended with a fight. Chris later recalled they gave as good as they got. 'To be fair, we did incite a lot of people. Richard throwing his guitar into the audience, I don't think that calmed people down.'

When I met Richard for a conversation about all this, it was mid-morning in the bar of the Sheffield venue the Harley, and time had lent some distance to what went on at early Cabaret Voltaire gigs. Richard seemed amused by his band's use of confrontation thirty-five or more years earlier: 'Confrontation was always important, I mean that was the whole point of starting

Cabaret Voltaire, just to wind people up like the Dadaists had done, you know, many, many years before us.' The band felt no obligation to conform to punk clichés, or indeed anything much. 'Even the fact we didn't have a drummer used to annoy people for some reason,' says Richard.

At the beginning of 1978 the live scene in Sheffield looked like it was going backwards; one of the city's best small music venues, the Black Swan, which had hosted the Sex Pistols and the first Clash gig, had closed. There were sparks of activity in the city, but they weren't being nurtured. One of the first things to bring some focus and put some momentum into what was happening in Sheffield was a fanzine called *Gun Rubber* run by Paul Bower. He championed the Cabs from his first issue, and his commitment to the cause increased when the Cabs recorded their first demo, including a number of songs with challenging titles like 'Baader Meinhof', 'Control Addict' and 'Do the Mussolini (Headkick)'. *Gun Rubber* gave a cassette of these tracks a rave review. 'Relief at last from the avalanche of so-called new wave. No thrashing two chords heavy metal riffs here to pogo to. Disco music for the 90s. Brilliant.'

Early Cabaret Voltaire shows were ad hoc, at various venues, including a pub called the Hallamshire, which became well known for small gigs. Another early one was in August 1977 promoted jointly with *Gun Rubber* at the Crucible's Studio, an annexe to the main theatre. In December 1977 they hired the Penthouse on Dixon Lane (the Penthouse was the last club Peter Stringfellow owned before leaving the city). The gig earned them their first national music press, Andy Gill in *NME*.

There was little sense of an infrastructure being built at this time in Sheffield, although a number of semi-derelict buildings were being used as rehearsal spaces. But in 1977 the city had regular venues for up-and-coming punk or new-wave bands and had no record labels of note. In Manchester, Richard Boon had set up New Hormones to release a Buzzcocks single, and although the band soon signed to United Artists Records, he maintained an office on Newton Street in Manchester. Richard had a reputation for good ideas and, with so much of the music industry based in London, was one of the few people with any kind of power base in the North, albeit a tiny, undercapitalised one. Cabaret Voltaire sent a letter and cassette to Richard Boon and a bond of mutual appreciation was established. The month the Limit opened, Cabaret Voltaire, at the invitation of Richard Boon, had a gig at Lyceum, bottom of a Buzzcocks bill that included the Slits and John Cooper Clarke. They were still finding the dominant audience reactions were hostility and/or disbelief, especially on the occasions the Cabs would leave the stage halfway through their set and stand in the audience just listening to the drum machine and tape loops playing.

We were still some months away from 'Warm Leatherette', and over a year from 'Are "Friends" Electric?' and 'New Muzick', but in Sheffield, at the end of 1977, Paul Bower had identified electronic, industrial, futuristic music close to home. He'd picked up on the Human League (before they'd even played a gig) and made a connection between their work and the Cabs. In the seventh issue of *Gun Rubber* he declared, 'There is a brand new wave round the corner and it's nothing to do with bondage pants and three nights at the Rainbow. Cabaret Voltaire and the Human League are part of that movement. Support them.'

The Human League had been formed out of a band called the Future, which included Martyn Ware and Ian Craig Marsh (Marsh had previously featured in a band called Musical Vomit). Ware was a fan of pop stuff, soul, Motown, but there was plenty of common ground; for example, both were obsessed with Brian Eno. They recruited singer Phil Oakey, who had esoteric tastes in music – contemporary jazz, and Frank Zappa – and a proper job, working as a porter at the Hallamshire Hospital on Glossop Road.

Human League started performing live in June 1978 and played at Limit for the first time on 25 July. They soon made their mark, recording a John Peel session that was broadcast on 11 August 1978 and included a version of 'Being Boiled'. They also supported the Rezillos at the Music Machine in London, where Charles Shaar Murray gave them an enthusiastic review in *NME*. 'They whack the shit out of NY's overrated Suicide simply by dint of intellectual rigour, superior imagination and a far more inspired use of stage non-presentation.'

With interest on radio, and positive national press, when it came to the Monday-night gig in September with Def Leppard, the Human League were in pole position to headline. Def Leppard had played their first proper gig at an end-of-term party at Westfield School in the Sheffield suburb of Mosborough only a few months earlier. They'd been writing and rehearsing for almost a year though, having found rehearsal space on the top floor of a semi-derelict spoon factory.

Every Friday Def Leppard met for several hours, mostly concentrating on perfecting cover versions of Thin Lizzy songs; they'd modelled their twin-guitar line-up on Thin Lizzy's. Bowie's 'Suffragette City' was also in their repertoire. There was much interest in heavy rock in this era in towns and cities but there weren't many local bands in Sheffield with the vision and desire to become the new Deep Purple, despite, potentially, a big audience; in May 1978 Black Sabbath chose to open their 'Never Say Die' tour at Sheffield City Hall (Van Halen were also on the bill).

The gig at the Limit was a meeting of extremes. The electronic, futuristic Human League clearly rejected rock traditions and were in love with new technology. Def Leppard, on the other hand, embodied heavy rock traditions to the max. By the time of the Limit gig they had amassed fifty minutes of original material, including 'Wasted' and 'World Beyond the Sky', but still liked to end their set with a version of 'Jailbreak' by Thin Lizzy. Def Leppard's singer was local lad Joe Elliott, who worked as a storekeeper at Osborn-Mushet Tools. At the Limit that Monday, he took to the stage stripped to the waist, with skin-tight loon pants and a huge wooden black cross hanging round his neck. Def Leppard had two lead guitar players; the Human League had none. The Human League made no attempt to hide the fact they were using tapes and pre-recorded sounds; the tape machine took centre stage. But they also had a strong look, although Phil Oakey's hair hadn't yet grown into its full splendour. A few weeks earlier, though, they'd begun to employ a Director of Visuals. Adrian Wright's role was to source films and slides, and to project them onto the stage as the band and the tapes played.

Another local lad, Stephen Singleton, had been to school with Joe Elliott but his tastes were more on the punk side of town. Crazy Daisy was his favourite hangout and the inspiration for his decision to form a band. 'It was the first place I was able to get into. I saw lots of the punk bands; they all had young snotty people in them and I thought, wow, maybe I can be in a band now. The whole punk explosion came along and it showed anybody could do anything.'

Singleton formed a band called Vice Versa and got a gig supporting Wire at the Outlook in Doncaster, then a gig at the Now Society supporting the Human League in July 1978. Singleton loved Cabaret Voltaire ('a huge influence') and was impressed by the Human League ('light years ahead of us in terms of presentation'): 'They were both from Sheffield. We'd been working away in isolation but this was revolutionary stuff. It gave us that impetus to go away and work hard.'

Martin Fry arrived in Sheffield from Manchester in 1978 to go to university there. After he saw a gig by Cabaret Voltaire and met musicians and others on the scene, he started a fanzine called *Modern Drugs*. He knew Stephen from Vice Versa, as they'd both worked in the Batchelors bean factory, and Fry also interviewed Vice Versa for *Modern Drugs*. A short while afterwards, Vice Versa lost keyboard player David Sydenham and Martin Fry ended up joining the band. Mark White from the band was impressed with Fry's leather coat, while Stephen liked that he was well read but also understood songs, ideas and structures and what could be achieved by aiming for intelligent, electronic dance music.

During the post-punk period, connections were being made, including between Manchester and Liverpool and between Sheffield and Manchester, in all sorts of ways, not all of them strictly musical. Richard Kirk remembers going over to Manchester a lot when punk came along. At one point he and Stephen Mallinder were going out with two sisters from Manchester. 'We used to go to the Ranch and Pips occasionally. There used to be a two o'clock train back to Sheffield so we'd often just nip over, you know, go for a night out there. Pips used to play great music. There was nothing like that in Sheffield, nothing at all at that point anyway.'

In Manchester plans grew for a new venue. The Electric Circus had closed, but a few gigs were being hosted at Rafters, a basement club in the building housing Fagin's, the cabaret club where the likes of the Dooleys had featured earlier in the decade. At Rafters in 1978 Friday and Saturday nights were given over to a successful soul and funk disco hosted by DJs Colin Curtis, John Grant and Mike Shaft. Mike was a respected name on the scene, and was then at the beginning of his extended time as a specialist and very influential black music DJ on the local commercial station Piccadilly Radio. He also played at Pips, and went on in the early 1980s to host the Main Event, Tuesday nights at Placemate 7 (the old Twisted Wheel club). He played outside Manchester too, including Videotech in Huddersfield (an old cinema, now a casino) and Angels in Burnley.

In April 1978, midweek, away from the soul and funk weekend, Rafters had witnessed one of Joy Division's most important early gigs, when they took part in the nationwide Stiff/Chiswick Challenge, a battle of the bands contest that had previously held heats in London, Liverpool and Glasgow. The winning artist was promised the chance to record for Stiff Records. Joy Division had already played the venue a handful of times and were picked to close the evening. Taking to the stage a long time after midnight in front of a dwindling crowd, they failed to win over either the judges of the competition or the *Sounds* reviewer, Mick Wall, who was scathing about their 'mock heroics', describing them as 'Iggy imitators acting out their sons-of-World-War-Two histrionics'.

However, two men in the audience *were* impressed. One of them was a DJ at Rafters, Rob Gretton, who'd seen them before, hanging out at the venue, and occasionally bothering him with music requests. He later recalled that 'they were smart, punky, but not scruffy; it was unusual. And the music was absolutely wonderful.' The other was Tony Wilson, who'd never met them previously but had been harassed earlier in the evening by Ian Curtis, who handed him a note requesting a slot on Granada TV. Wilson's show *So It Goes* had come to an end in December 1977, but there were still opportunities to show bands during the nightly news show *Granada Reports*.

Wilson had booked the Sex Pistols for their TV debut and had an abiding interest in the cultural power of music. Locally he was best known for his role as a TV presenter – the man off the telly. He'd go on, of course, to be a founder of Factory Records and co-owner of the Haçienda, but his first step into the music industry was becoming the manager of low-fi guitar virtuoso Vini Reilly aka the Durutti Column (a task he shared with local actor Alan Erasmus, who would go on to Factory and the Haçienda with Wilson). The Electric Circus had closed the previous October and Wilson and Erasmus were aware there were rumours that Rafters was closing too, and the two men decided to find a new venue and host a series of four gigs. If nothing else, the plan would give them the chance to provide the Durutti Column with a couple of gigs.

Following the Rafters show, Rob Gretton became Joy Division's manager and Tony Wilson got in touch to arrange for them to play at the new venue, which was on Royce Road in Hulme, just south of Manchester city centre. Wilson and Erasmus had booked Friday nights at the Russell Club, which was more usually a Caribbean club presenting sound systems like Blacka. They linked up with Roger Eagle, who of course had significant history in Manchester at the Twisted Wheel and the Magic Village, and had successfully established Eric's in Liverpool. There was talk of opportunities to bring artists to both the Factory and Eric's, potentially cutting costs. The local press announced that the Factory would present 'wayward sounds and noises inspired by the ideals of Tony Wilson and Roger Eagle'.

Erasmus later explained the choice of name for the venture. 'I was driving down a road and there was a big sign saying "Factory For Sale" standing out in neon. And I thought, Factory, that's the name, because a factory was a place where people work and create things, and I thought to myself, these are workers who are also musicians and they'll be creative. Factory was nothing to do with Andy Warhol because I didn't know at that time that Warhol had this building in New York called the Factory.'

The opening night, 19 May 1978, predictably featured the Durutti Column, with Jilted John also on the bill and, reflecting the Eric's connection, Margox & the Zinc (from Liverpool). A week later, the second Factory event offered Big in Japan, Manicured Noise and the Germs. Big in Japan were Roger Eagle's darlings; group members including Jayne Casey, Ian Broudie, Holly Johnson and also Bill Drummond all went on to all kinds of fame and infamy (this gig was possibly Holly Johnson's last in the band before he was sacked).

It wasn't just what happened next to Big in Japan that's of interest. It's noticeable too how a snapshot of people onstage at those first two nights at the Factory reveals a number of people with artistic careers ahead of them, even if their long-term artistic vocation turned out not to be in music. For example, the bass player in Manicured Noise – who took their name from a Buzzcocks flyer designed by Linder (Sterling) from Ludus – was Jeff Noon, who has become an acclaimed writer, responsible for novels including *Vurt* (which had scenes set in Hulme), *Pollen* and *Needle in the Groove*. Linder became a celebrated artist, feted with a retrospective at the Paris Museum of Modern Art in 2013. Jilted John two months later released a hit single on Manchester record label Rabid ('Gordon Is a Moron'). Jilted John, in real life, was the Sheffield-born aspiring actor Graham Fellows, who later went on to invent John Shuttleworth, a quaint, nerdy northern comic character. Margox was taken under Tony Wilson's wing and under her real name, Margi Clarke, became a Granada TV presenter before going on to act in films (including *Letter to Brezhnev*) as well as *Brookside* and *Coronation Street*. In 1985 Morrissey and Margi Clarke were filmed in conversation on *The Tube*. Morrissey afterwards described her as 'a wonderful creature'.

The third Factory night featured the Durutti Column and Cabaret Voltaire. Although the Cabs were yet to release a record they had maintained contact with Richard Boon and were being championed in the music press by the (then) Manchester-based journalist Jon Savage, who placed a feature on the band in *Sounds* following their support slot with Buzzcocks at the Lyceum. Chris Watson later recalled the Factory: 'It just had a brilliant atmosphere, and because it was a West Indian club they also had a great sound system.'

The fourth and last Factory night of the initial series featured Joy Division and the Tiller Boys. Apparently there were more people in the audience than on the stage, but not many more. The Tiller Boys included Pete Shelley in their line-up, on loan from the Buzzcocks and pursuing some sonic experimentation alongside Eric Random and Francis Cookson. The Tiller Boys not only provided more glorious moments featuring tape machines but also delivered a challenging mode of performance by stacking chairs across the front of the stage and going to the bar for a drink while the tape loops looped. Paul Morley was ecstatic, declaring the Tiller Boys 'a visionary alternative to support groups and DJs'.

By the middle of 1978 a generation of post-punk bands were gigging regularly, moving between key venues in various cities, building interest. Joy Division, the Durutti Column and Cabaret Voltaire made visits to Eric's in Liverpool, and to Leeds, where John Keenan was promoting his F-Club at the Cosmo club in Chapeltown from February 1978 (Howard Devoto's Magazine were the first band at his new venue). There was just about enough life in the scene for Factory to decide to return to the Russell after the initial series of gigs. Looking back at what was being booked in the key post-punk venues through the autumn of 1978, a number of names recur, including Siouxsie and the Banshees, and Penetration. On 20 October Cabaret Voltaire supported Joy Division at the Factory (four days later the same two shared the bill at the F-Club). On 17 November, Factory presented an almighty bill of the Human League, the Mekons and the Gang of Four.

Cabaret Voltaire had spent most of 1978 preparing to release a record, which included discussions with Richard Boon at New Hormones. Richard wanted to finance a Cabaret Voltaire record (and a Fall record), but didn't have the money or the time (Buzzcocks hits were in full flow), and the New Hormones label lapsed into temporary inactivity. The Cabs went to Rough Trade Records, who sealed the deal by buying the band a four-track Revox. Their 'Extended Play' single was released in October 1978, with a front-cover photo taken by Rod Siddall at the Crucible gig promoted by *Gun Rubber*.

The Factory nights at the Russell Club would come to an end

in the middle of 1979, by which time Tony and Alan had founded Factory Records too, with designer Peter Saville and record producer Martin Hannett joining as the other directors. The Russell and the Factory name would, however, continue to be used by other promoters, including Alan Wise (he also booked bands into the New Osborne club on Oldham Road, a ramshackle venue; the Cure played there in April 1980).

When it began, Factory Records didn't have much of a long- or even mid-term plan. There had originally been discussions with Roger Eagle about collaborating on a release with him, featuring Liverpool and Manchester bands, but in the end Roger wasn't part of the set-up and the first release was a sampler containing nine songs by four different artists. Two tracks by the Durutti Column were included and two from Joy Division. Wilson was turning out to be a committed Joy Division fan, and had answered the pleas made by Ian Curtis at Rafters by putting the band on TV; Joy Division performing 'Shadowplay' was broadcast on *Granada Reports* on 20 September 1978, the band's TV debut.

Factory wasn't conceived as being a local label: two Cabaret Voltaire tracks were included on the first sampler release, and 'Electricity' by the Liverpool band Orchestral Manoeuvres in the Dark was one of the first singles on the label. Other acts in the label's early catalogue of releases would include ESG from the South Bronx and Minny Pops from the Netherlands, but Factory made a tentative start. Joy Division spoke to a major label or two. No one quite knew the way forward; Buzzcocks had signed to United Artists but there was also talk of trying a different, independent route. It was part of a belief in the value of alternative ways of operating, being. In an interview in *NME* in January 1979, Ian Curtis expressed his hopes for Joy Division: 'We'd like to stay on the outside. We'd love it if Tony Wilson said he'd pay us to do an album on Factory. That would be great. We can't afford to do it ourselves, which we'd want. But you either stay outside the system or go in totally and try and change it.'

Factory did indeed pay for Joy Division to go into the studio with Martin Hannett; the result was *Unknown Pleasures*, released in June 1979. A few weeks later they travelled to Birmingham to support Dexys Midnight Runners at the Romulus Club on Hagley Road. On 8 September they appeared on the opening day of John Keenan's 'World's First Science Fiction Music Festival' (better known as 'Futurama'), staged at the Queen's Hall in Leeds, along with sixteen other bands, including Cabaret Voltaire, Orchestral Manoeuvres in the Dark, Public Image Limited and A Certain Ratio. Other Futurama festivals followed; the line-up in 1980 included Soft Cell, Siouxsie and the Banshees, Echo & the Bunnymen, and a number of Sheffield-based acts, including Clock DVA, I'm So Hollow, Artery and Vice Versa.

Vice Versa, with Martin Fry on keyboards, had founded their own independent record label called Neutron Records and released their first single, 'New Girls'. In the spirit of the times, it was very DIY, up to and including distribution of the record, as Stephen Singleton later explained: 'I remember going to the Limit nightclub and going up to people saying, "Pssst, do you want to buy one of these records?"'

After the release of the single and in the aftermath of more gigs playing alongside the likes of Clock DVA, Vice Versa were still having trouble with being written off as just another bunch of Human League impersonators, and felt the need to make some changes. Taking a swerve musically, and with Martin Fry moving to the centre of the stage on vocals, their songs started to embrace more soulful elements inspired by Chic, Earth, Wind & Fire, and Bowie's *Young Americans* album. They renamed themselves ABC. Their first gig as ABC was at Psalter Lane Art College in September 1980, their second at Penny's.

September 1980 was the month U2 first played at the Limit (they returned two months later). Six weeks before their first

Limit date, eyewitnesses claim Bono ripped his trousers jumping off the PA stack at London's Lyceum. His onstage antics were more than occasionally problematic. In May 1980, supporting the band Fashion at the Cedar Club in Birmingham where the audience numbered around 150, Bono jumped offstage and went into the audience. Caught up in the moment, the Edge and Adam Clayton followed him, inadvertently unplugging their guitar leads from out of the amps, leaving, for a tranquil minute or two, only Bono's microphone and Larry's drums audible.

On 5 June 1980, U2 played for John Keenan at the F-Club. The night before they'd been in Manchester at 'The Beach Club', an almost regular Tuesday night at Oozits, formerly known as the Picador (the first club owned by Manchester drag act Frank 'Foo Foo' Lammar). The Beach Club had been launched in April by a group of friends around the New Hormones label, and the *City Fun* fanzine, including, among many others, Richard Boon, Eric Random, Lindsay Wilson (Tony's wife) and Sue Cooper. It was a decrepit venue in a seedy area of Manchester, between Shudehill and Victoria Station, but it wasn't far from Pips. With the Factory having closed, Richard Boon hoped that creative, maverick types would gather there and a community would be created.

In Hulme there was an old cinema called the Aaben that programmed art-house and underground films, but in general it was difficult for adventurous Mancunians to access the likes of Kenneth Anger's *Scorpio Rising*, *Orphée*, *Eraserhead* or Kubrick's banned movie *A Clockwork Orange*, but Sue Cooper's father had good contacts in the film distribution industry and the Beach Club presented all these, and others, in a room on the floor below where the bands performed (it was usual for the band playing to choose the film for the evening). CP Lee had been around in the late 1960s, and the activities at the Beach Club sparked a degree of déjà vu. 'I remember thinking, Richard's doing what we used to do in the 1960s – put a band on with a film showing at the same time; dancers; just weird shit. It was great!'

Following the death of Ian Curtis in May 1980, the surviving members of Joy Division regrouped as New Order and played a number of low-key gigs; none of the band was even certain who should be the singer. Their first gig, on 30 July 1980, was at the Beach Club, billed as 'the No-Names'. In October, still unsure of their future direction, they played their first show with newly recruited keyboard player Gillian Gilbert at the Squat on Devas Street out near the University of Manchester.

In the wake of the Factory nights ending and the closure of the Beach Club, attention switched back to Rafters. In addition to hosting Friday and Saturday soul and funk nights, the club also hosted a number of gigs presented by various promoters. In August 1981, Ludus supported Depeche Mode, and Steven Morrissey attended, reporting for *Record Mirror*. In Morrissey's review he dismisses Depeche Mode as 'remarkably boring' and 'nonsense', an unimaginative boy band with nice hair attracting an audience 'possibly hand-picked for their tone deafness'. Ludus, he writes, were 'plainly wishing they were elsewhere . . . Linder was born singing and has more imagination than Depeche Mode could ever hope for.'

Elsewhere, Birmingham venues like Barbarella's, the Golden Eagle and the Fighting Cocks helped breed a scene that ranged from UB40 to Duran Duran and from Dexys Midnight Runners to the Au Pairs. In Nottingham, the Boat Club caught up with new sounds and styles, and bands featured there in the first few months of 1980 included Young Marble Giants, the Associates, the Fall, Killing Joke and Bow Wow Wow. And at the end of the year a new venue opened in Nottingham: Rock City.

Also in 1980, the Leadmill opened in Sheffield, on the ground floor of the building the Esquire had operated from in the 1960s. There was a political edge to it, as its official history makes clear: 'The opening of the Leadmill in 1980 was a response to the lack of cultural facilities in Sheffield and was set against the backdrop of a political and economic environment characterised by the beginning of Thatcherism.'

Sheffield's ABC released their first single, 'Tears Are Not Enough', in the autumn of 1981; it ended up going Top Twenty, as did all three other singles taken from their debut album *Lexicon of Love*. The Human League were also hit-making, with 'Don't You Want Me' topping the charts during Christmas 1981 and selling over 1.5m copies in the UK alone. But the line-up had undergone a radical transformation. Founder members Ian Craig Marsh and Martyn Ware had left the Human League in October 1980 but Phil Oakey retained the name and set out to put a band together in order to honour scheduled dates in Europe. Oakey was at the Crazy Daisy one Wednesday night when he spotted two teenage girls on the dancefloor, liked their look and their moves and signed them up. Joanne Catherall and Susan Ann Sulley have been in the Human League ever since. The Crazy Daisy became the Geisha Bar and then Legends nightclub, but closed in the mid-1990s. The building is still standing, however, and occasionally Susan Ann and Joanne meet camera crews there to tell the story of their historic encounter with Oakey.

In 1981 Rob Gretton and Tony Wilson went looking for a building to house a new venue. Not a borrowed venue like Factory at the Russell, but a new one, purpose-built, which the members of New Order and the directors of Factory Records would own. Martin Hannett was a dissenting voice; he thought that the monies coming in from record sales from New Order and the Joy Division back catalogue would be better spent buying state-of-the-art equipment to give the label an in-house studio. When it became clear the nightclub project would be pursued, Hannett left Factory.

The would-be club owners had a serious look at an old cinema on the corner of Oxford Road and Grosvenor Street, and a carpet warehouse just down the slope from Oxford Road

Station. Eventually they settled on an old yacht showroom, a cavernous warehouse across the road from disused railway arches and a rusting gasworks. They'd paint it mostly grey and call it the Haçienda.

The Beach Club had closed in a matter of a few months. It had made a contribution, for sure. If CP Lee was able to identify some antecedents in the late 1960s, the Beach Club also had some influence on clubs that followed, particularly the Haçienda, launched eighteen months later. When the Haçienda opened – with two big video screens and, in the early years, occasional film screenings – it described itself as a 'Club Disco Videotek Venue'.

With a capacity of 1,650, Factory were being ambitious on many levels, not least in the intention, laid out in the first flyer the Haçienda issued: as well as giving basic information on how to obtain membership (£5.25 per annum), the flyer declared the aim of the club was 'To restore a sense of place'. *City Fun* had been part of the collective who'd experienced the exciting but uphill struggles of running the Beach Club, and various writers in the fanzine were sceptical, even scornful of the idea that Factory could run, or fill, a big club.

If the fanzine crowd were sceptical, the majority of Mancunians were oblivious. There was no pent-up demand to go to a cavernous old yacht showroom on a Wednesday night and dance to Hewan Clarke playing amazing records like 'Don't Make Me Wait', as the management found out every Wednesday for months after the club opened. The decor wasn't what people were used to. The usual discotheque decor, like carpets and potted plastic palm trees, were nowhere to be seen. In imitation of the best New York clubs, DJs stopped talking between records.

The project and the design were very influenced by clubs New Order had visited in New York, especially Danceteria. The resident DJ there, Mark Kamins, was a big fan of New Order. In 1983 Mark took Larry Levan to see New Order play Paradise Garage. There was a lot of cross-fertilisation between the Factory Records crowd and New York in that period; New Order worked with producer Arthur Baker. Quando Quango worked with Mark Kamins. In December 1982 A Certain Ratio performed at the Danceteria, supported by Madonna. They all made friends with the New York booker and promoter Ruth Polsky.

The Danceteria was a magnet for interesting young creatives; Keith Haring would hang out there, the Beastie Boys too, before they were the Beastie Boys. Factory wanted some of that atmosphere in their club, for it to be a hangout. Mike Pickering always talks of how Rob Gretton was the prime mover behind the idea of the Haçienda. 'We just want to have somewhere to go,' Rob would say. Pickering was a co-founder of Quando Quango, a good friend of Rob's, and was entrusted with booking all the bands and the DJs when the Haçienda opened.

The Smiths played the third gig of their career at the Haçienda on 4 February 1983 supporting 52nd Street, a funk band signed to Factory. The first Smiths appearance in London was in March, supporting Sisters of Mercy. In the summer they played headline shows at the Fighting Cocks in Birmingham and the Midnight Express Club in Bournemouth, as well as a nicely organised little foray over the Pennines to play Leeds (Warehouse), and on to Hull and Newcastle. On 16 September 1983 they played at Moles in Bath. A few weeks earlier the Cure had chosen Moles as the venue for a special warm-up show before a trip to New York to play two nights at the Ritz. On New Year's Eve 1983 it was the turn of the Smiths to play New York, making their American debut at the Danceteria. Morrissey fell off the stage.

Back at the Haçienda, the failure of the endearing punk enthusiasm to match the grand ambition was beginning to take its toll. Mike Pickering: 'None of us who started working there had ever worked in a club or a venue before. But it was like one big party. I remember putting on Club Zoo with Teardrop Explodes and there were about a hundred people there and Julian [Cope] and everyone took acid and had this fucking mad party in the middle of it all. It was all very irresponsible.'

The DJs and the management hadn't found the music or the method to nurture a regular audience for the disc-only nights. The only one that worked was the Tuesday 'No Funk' night with John Tracy. His playlist appealed to the kind of crowd who'd visit the club to see gigs by the likes of the Birthday Party, although he'd throw lots of other things into the mix. John had come to the Haçienda after several successful years DJing in Sheffield. He'd DJ'd at a club called Penny's (on Arundel Gate, later called Isabella's) where he would play War's 'Galaxy', Japan, Grace Jones and – going way out on a limb – the likes of Lizzy Mercier Descloux's 'Mission Impossible'. In 1981 Paul Morley wrote a feature on ABC based around a visit to one of John's nights at Penny's. The playlist was a collection of all the influences ABC were absorbing and Morley enjoyed the evening, although what most impressed him about his night out with ABC at John's club was 'the best set of haircuts I've ever seen'.

John Tracy had gone on to pilot the first year of the Leadmill's Friday 'Videotech' night, but then moved all his efforts over to Manchester, and gigs at the Haçienda. The Leadmill remained a popular venue, and continued to go way beyond the provision of live music and DJs. At the beginning of 1985 it was open all day, 9 a.m. to 2 a.m. The venue received subsidies from Sheffield City Council and offered workshops, including some in music, acting, pottery and graphic design. There was a café, a theatre night on a Monday, and Sunday afternoons had become a popular part of the week. This was an era when nothing much happened on Sundays – there was no football, no shops – but alternative music types would gather at the club just to hang out, listen to music and read the papers.

During the mid-1980s, venues were a valuable means for alternative communities to build. In Birmingham, Mark 'Mack' MacDonald started a night called 'Sensateria', with cool psychedelic flyers and playlist. In Glasgow in the late 1980s, the 'Splash

One' nights took place at a crappy disco called Daddy Warbucks. Wire and Sonic Youth played there, as well as bands like the Shop Assistants and the Pastels. They both appeared to be uncommercial, their music choices a little far out, but they thrived; they nurtured pockets of interest away from the mainstream.

The Leadmill's varied programming incorporating all kinds of cultural interests was a reflection of the tendency in the mid-1980s to connect interest in music with other art, and the world. Post-punk music fans were often culturally and politically engaged, they shared that interest of Ian Curtis's of being outside the system somehow, and were interested in alternative culture and ideas. It was an era when *NME* would run a column called 'Portrait of the Artist as a Consumer' where the likes of Tracey Thorn, Morrissey or Pete Wylie would list their favourite books and films (Morrissey's included *The Killing of Sister George*) and other favourite things (which is how we learned that Blixa Bargeld from the Birthday Party was a fan of Ulrike Meinhof, and that Lydia Lunch liked *The Night Porter* and 'skinny boys with black hair'). In the same era Mark E. Smith worked with dancer Michael Clark.

There were a number of venues around the country that nurtured this sense of an alternative culture wider than music, including the 'Zap' in Brighton, launched by a team that hosted events at various venues including the Brighton Belle on Oriental Place and the upstairs of a pub called the Richmond. From November 1984 the Zap had its own building, two converted seafront arches on King's Road in Brighton, with a programme including live music, cabaret, comedy and club nights, and a mission statement declaring itself to be a 'club for artists, run by artists who understand performers and their needs'. Zap club events always had variety, with an avant-garde edge; the likes of the Wild Wigglers dance group, for example, and the appearance of writers such as John Giorno and Kathy Acker. Live performers in the first few years of the Zap included Marc Almond, James, 23 Skidoo, Hank Wangford and Nick Cave.

The core business of the Leadmill remained its music programme. Not just the bands, but the club night; according to an issue of *i-D* from the end of 1984, 'It seems that at some point or other everyone in Sheffield goes to The Leadmill.' That December, Pulp played there (two years earlier Jarvis Cocker had written and directed a Christmas pantomime at the venue). DJ Jools was particularly popular on Thursday nights playing Screaming Tony Baxter's 'Get Up Offa That Thing', 'Planet Claire', 'Shack Up', Sheffield acts like the Cabs and Chakk, and 23 Skidoo's 'Coup'. Her music policy was more eclectic than you'd get elsewhere in the city but in 1986 even some of the DJs who had always played lots of goth music started throwing Cameo's 'Word Up' into their sets, then the Beastie Boys. As we'll see in the next chapter, change was just around the corner.

Elsewhere in Sheffield there was a club called Genevieve's on Charter Square; it was pretty much a dodgy disco, and makes an appearance as such in Ken Loach's 1981 film *Looks and Smiles*. There was a second club hidden away behind Genevieve's called Mona Lisa's (later it became Scuba). Richard Barratt (better known as Parrot) had been a fan of John Tracy's DJing, particularly the way he incorporated alternative stuff with the likes of War and New York electro, but John was no longer DJing in Sheffield. Parrot was a bit bored of the Leadmill and the Limit and, together with some mates, including Matt Swift, went looking for a venue where they could start their own night, 'Jive Turkey'. Parrot loved Mona Lisa's: 'It was a proper little backdoor club which, at the time, had been unchanged since the 1970s, so it was all flock wallpaper. There were all these fantastic plastic screens up with bare-breasted Afro ladies looking fierce and righteous upon all the walls, with a big flashing star over a round dancefloor. It was as seedy as fuck. Just right.'

The plan was for Matt and Parrot and the others to take turns

DJing but Parrot became the main man on the decks, throwing down all kinds of quality music, from Northern Soul to electro, with bursts of Was (Not Was), New Order and Cabaret Voltaire. Richard H. Kirk was drawn to 'Jive Turkey'; it was his kind of club. There's footage of Cabaret Voltaire live at Mona Lisa's, first broadcast on BBC Two's *Whistle Test* on 17 December 1985.

The crew running Jive Turkey would be central in what was going to happen in Sheffield over the next few years and, of course, the Haçienda would evolve too, as electronic dance music began to dominate dancefloors. Other venues with their roots in the post-punk era – from the Zap in Brighton to the Leadmill in Sheffield – would be invaluable for the next generation of live bands: Pulp, the Stone Roses, Blur. John Keenan's shows continued, moving on from the Cosmo, and then Brannigans, through the 1980s and beyond to the Duchess of York on Vicar Lane in Leeds city centre. Nirvana played their first gig in Leeds in October 1989 at the Duchess of York and Kurt Cobain slept on a battered old sofa in an upstairs room. The Manic Street Preachers played there on 31 January 1991 (as did, five days later, the Afghan Whigs). Radiohead appeared at the Duchess of York in October 1992, and Oasis in October 1994.

In a number of towns and cities the post-punk generation had created alternative venues operating as a focus and a catalyst for independent, idiosyncratic action, some with low ceilings, some with dodgy toilets, some in a shady part of town. Derelict workshops, old warehouses and factories had turned into rehearsal rooms, venues and record shops. At a time of post-industrial malaise, dead spaces in towns and cities had been revived by the native creativity of local malcontents, musicians, promoters, fanzine editors, sympathetic venue owners, aspiring writers and actors, fashion and graphic designers, specialist radio shows and small label operators; out of desire or desperation. The point was to make something out of nothing. Customise your clothes, customise your life.

Venues, labels and an infrastructure of sorts had developed, as had a number of mythologies; the stories we tell ourselves to validate or shape the past and to direct or inspire the future. Punk had announced itself on screen with Bill Grundy with two 'shit's, one 'bastard', one 'fucker', one 'sod' and one 'fucking rotter'. Six or seven years later, in towns and cities throughout Britain, a small group of people had made their own culture, and left a legacy. They'd demonstrated a belief Richard Boon has articulated: 'Part of my, and that punk, rationale, was [to] make things happen,' he said. 'Make the place that you happen to be living in a place that you want to be living in.'

CHAPTER ELEVEN

The Wild Bunch, headless pigeons, a track with no name

Hyeonje Oh has never heard of Massive Attack and is a bit sceptical about the whole story I'm telling him. He owns the award-winning Surakhan restaurant on Park Row in Bristol, situated between a hairdressing salon called Hobbs and a pub called the White Harte. The Surakhan serves authentic Korean food. Mr Oh wasn't expecting someone to walk in off the street wanting to look in his basement. He's very polite and doesn't throw me out. He offers me a menu. Korean food, he tells me, is spicy – 'spicy tasty not spicy hot'.

His restaurant occupies the building that was once home to the Dug Out, a venue with an only occasionally charmed history, but in the early and mid-1980s earned its place as one of the most significant venues in our history, specifically as a result of the integral role it plays in the story of Massive Attack. Massive Attack's success and the work of other graduates from the Dug Out went on to encourage Bristol acts like Tricky and Portishead and fed into the work of the Mercury Music Prize-winning Roni Size/Reprazent.

The layout of the Dug Out changed during the 1980s with the addition of a video room, but customers from the late 1970s into the early 1980s recall queuing down a small corridor, and then descending into the basement. There was a back room. The music was mostly bass-heavy reggae, and the crowd a bohemian mixture of black and white, accomplished dancers and feisty girls, ex-punks and guys skinning up. Some nights would offer discounts to students and nurses. Regulars remember hearing stuff that wasn't reggae, like 'Jamaica Funk' and 'I Wonder If I Take You Home'. They remember ganja, Red Stripe, Jack Daniel's and Coke, a Space Invaders machine and murals on the wall courtesy of Delge.

Delge was Robert Del Naja, a Clash fan, useless at school but enthusiastic about the culture surrounding hip hop, especially graffiti. At times, he was too enthusiastic; after one graffiti spree in August 1984 he was charged with criminal damage. By this time he'd started hanging out at the Dug Out, in particular with a crew of DJs and MCs called Wild Bunch. He became part of the crew, they evolved into Massive Attack, and he was known as '3D'.

The Wild Bunch performed, played and partied at the Dug Out. At the outset, the Wild Bunch included Miles ('Milo') Johnson, Nellee Hooper and Grant Marshall ('Daddy G'), then Claude Williams and 3D, followed by Andrew Vowles ('Mushroom'). Grant had already started DJing at the Dug Out on Wednesday nights. Miles and Nellee had worked together DJing at parties around the Clifton area of Bristol and pre-Dug Out hangouts like the Prince's Court, just round the corner off Park Row.

There was a vibrant post-punk scene in Bristol. The Pop Group, fronted by Mark Stewart, had led the way with an unsettling but stunning mix of noise, dub, jazz, politics and punk. After their demise two former members, Gareth Sager and Bruce Smith, became part of Rip Rig & Panic; Neneh Cherry was the singer. Nellee Hooper played percussion with two local bands, Maximum Joy and Pigbag. As well as post-punk, Milo and Nellee liked Parliament and Lonnie Liston Smith. Milo met Grant Marshall in the Paradise Garage clothes store; Grant was the reggae specialist at a record shop called Revolver. Miles later recalled the first time the Wild Bunch played together was at the Green Rooms at the end of King Street. 'I didn't think being a DJ was a career back then, not at all, it was fun, and money was just a bonus not a goal.'

Delge was a useful addition to the Wild Bunch, not least because he knew how to design cool flyers, a useful asset in the competitive world of sound systems. Among the other sounds in Bristol at the time, and featuring at the annual St Paul's Carnival, were crews including City Rockers, Enterprise, the FBI Crew and the 3 Stripe Posse. In 1985 and 1986 the Wild Bunch made appearances at the Barnabas Centre and the Redhouse on Portland Square, but the Dug Out was their home. Dug Out regular Karl Harrington remembers how it rocked, but there was as much listening and grooving as outright dancing. 'There was always a very strong sweet smell of herb – no problem getting some there. You had to smoke herb to let that throbbing fuzzy bass do its thang! People who went to the Dug Out found their own sense of belonging and uniqueness; if it was a tad delusional, so what? There was a strong sense of "something happening" and whether you were a part of it or purely coasting, it left you with something that was original.'

In this chapter we'll visit some of the 1980s clubs where the future was formed, the Dug Out among them. Many nightlife histories have understandably concentrated on those 1980s clubs and venues that created the blueprint for the huge explosion of house, techno, ecstasy-driven clubs in the 1990s; the likes of the Haçienda and Shoom, the Clink Street parties, the Blackburn raves, the Trip and 'Spectrum'. It's understandable because, as we'll see, the pioneering acid house clubs had a transformative effect on music and fashion, changed the music industry, and established ecstasy as the drug of the 1990s. It's an intriguing story of how something that was originally a clear alternative to high street nightlife ended up *becoming* high street nightlife.

But those pioneering venues with a key role creating and establishing Britain's acid house scene weren't the only influential clubs of the 1980s. Through the 1990s and deep into the twenty-first century there have been further adventures in the sonic landscape developed by Massive Attack and their confrères in Bristol and elsewhere, with speaker-shuddering basslines, hip hop and herb-infected dynamics, and slower tempos. The Dug Out and the activities of Soul II Soul are both examples of ecstasy-free innovation in the mid-1980s, laying the ground work for the subsequent evolution of music in Britain: acid jazz, trip hop and chill out, from Mr Scruff to the Streets, through jungle, Wookie and dubstep to Dizzee Rascal, Holy Other and Four Tet.

Since the era of Duke Vin in the late 1950s we've seen how a Jamaican sound system was a primitive but potent way to get a party started. The New York hip hop crews which were established in the 1970s were a remodelled Afro-American version of Jamaican sound systems – with two turntables and a microphone plus breakdancers and graffiti artists – and were as much of a response to the pseudo-glitz of disco as punk.

Punk had stimulated a DIY sensibility throughout the music industry, inspiring a growth in independent record labels of all kinds. Networks of record distribution via independent retailers like Revolver were being established. Changing technology was making music-recording cheaper and quicker. We were entering an era in which DJs and producers took opportunities to make music quickly and get it distributed, often as white labels or one-offs.

Rob Smith and Ray Mighty of the 3 Stripe Posse produced two off-kilter down-tempo soulful hip hop cuts, both Burt Bacharach/Hal David covers: 'Anyone (Who Had A Heart)' and 'Walk On By'. Along similar lines, the Wild Bunch released 'Look of Love' on Fourth & Broadway with singer Shara Nelson and a raw, semi-industrial hip hop beat. This was 1987. After something of a falling-out, Nellee Hooper began working with Soul II Soul in London, one of the Wild Bunch (DJ Milo) moved to the States and three of the others (Mushroom, 3D and Daddy G) regrouped, took the name Massive Attack and, with production help from Smith and Mighty, cut the first Massive Attack single, 'Any Love'. Hip hop, reggae, funk, soul; the music they played melted into the music they made.

The Soul II Soul sound system had evolved out of the reggae sound Jah Rico, and was renamed by system operator Jazzie B, who was installing his rigs and hosting parties and events at a number of warehouses and other spaces, including Paddington Dome, under the arches near King's Cross railway station. He could see the culture of black music in Britain changing. He wanted to go beyond reggae and nurture a soul, funk and hip hop audience.

In 1986 Soul II Soul launched a regular Sunday-night gig at the Africa Centre at 38 King Street, Covent Garden – a building that had opened in 1964 as a meeting place for African and other overseas students. It had always attacted a wider African community too, particularly for its music events. Baaba Maal and Salif Keita both performed there and a long-established club night on Fridays called Limpopo featured Ugandan DJs who sourced and played tracks directly imported from Africa. The Soul II Soul nights also occasionally included live music but could always rely on DJs like Trevor 'Madhatter' Nelson, Norman Jay, Judge Jules and C.J. Mackintosh to provide a joyous mixture of party hip hop and classic funk.

In the mid-1980s there were several club nights of note in London, many of them hosted by graduates of Blitz. Among the regular weekly slots were Steve Strange and Rusty Egan's own nights at the Camden Palace, which rode the mass acceptance of the scene they'd helped to create. Among the one-offs were parties at Mayhem Studios in Battersea hosted by Chris Sullivan. The transgressive impulse stirred by Blitz stayed strong, and some promoters pushed the boundaries further, like David Claridge at the Skin Two fetish-themed nights at Stallions and the polysexual club night 'Taboo', launched by Leigh Bowery in January 1985 at Maximus, Leicester Square.

There's perhaps a degree of performance in the way people conduct themselves on a night out, and Taboo was extreme evidence of this. Customers didn't just wear mad outfits; they became new people. At Taboo, Leigh Bowery replaced the post-Blitz mainstream version of 'gender-bending' with something more hardcore and outsider. One of the ace faces at Taboo – a prominent character among all the other characters – was Bowery's friend Trojan; they'd met in November 1981 at Heaven. Trojan had extreme style.

Other graduates of Blitz, while eschewing the overtly sexual adventuring and flamboyant sartorial delights of Taboo or Skin Two, created a buzz with their musical offering. At Le Beat Route, DJ Steve Lewis, a former Crackers regular and a fan of Mark Roman, was playing electro funk on New York labels like Sleeping Bag and West End. When Le Beat Route closed some of its crowd moved to the 'Dirtbox', hosted by Phil Gray and Rob Milton (both Le Beat Route regulars), and Jay Strongman then became one of the resident DJs. The first Dirtbox event was in an old West Indian club above a chemist on Earls Court Road, and others followed at various found spaces throughout the middle years of the 1980s. Other one-offs in offbeat locations included Circus, promoted by Jeremy Healy and Patrick Lilley. Patrick had immersed himself in London's clubland since leaving Birmingham in the punk era. Jeremy Healy was known for his work in the band Haysi Fantayzee, but later became a high-profile DJ on the club circuit.

Warehouse all-nighters were also promoted by the fashion emporium Demob and run by Chris Sullivan and Chris Brick. Noel Watson was one of the regular Demob DJs. Noel knew the Bristol crew, including Sean Oliver from Rip Rig & Panic, who would DJ with Noel and his brother Maurice Watson in London.

Together, in 1982, they were running an illegal party for 300 people every Saturday in a disused school on Battlebridge Road at the back of King's Cross. Neneh Cherry and Andrea Oliver would run the bar; Jazzie B and Daddy G both visited. It was mostly hip hop; Maurice was an ace cutter, mixer and scratcher.

Chris Sullivan and Ollie O'Donnell opened the Wag Club in October 1982 in the venue formerly known as the Whiskey-A-Go-Go. They also installed Jay Strongman as resident DJ on Saturdays. Mondays became The Jazz Room with DJ Paul Murphy. A few months after that, flamboyant club operator Philip Sallon asked Jay Strongman to man the decks at 'The Mud Club', housed in a venue called Busbys on Charing Cross Road.

Away from the Wag, Gilles Peterson was beginning to make a name for himself playing jazz when he took over at the Electric Ballroom after Paul Murphy left. 'Family Funktion' and 'Shake 'n' FingerPop' warehouse parties included DJs Norman Jay, Judge Jules, Paul Anderson and Derek Boland (who was a rapper known as Derek B); they'd be playing rare groove, retro and reisssues, funk and soul to good crowds, and mixed races. The Fridge in Brixton, owned and run by the ex-Roxy promoters Susan Carrington and Andrew Czezowski, was one of the few legitimate clubs that captured the spirit and energy of the funk and soul warehouse parties (Soul II Soul presented some Africa Centre nights there). They'd first opened the Fridge at the small, but established, Brixton club the Ram Jam but eventually made their home at a converted 1913 cinema.

Away from London there was a lively jazz dance scene. Venues like Rock City in Nottingham would host all-dayers featuring DJs including Paul Murphy, Colin Curtis and Gilles Peterson playing very new and upfront jazz funk and Latin, but also retro-jazz. DJ Jonathan Woodliffe had played an active part in creating a scene at Rock City with a strong Friday funk, jazz and soul night, then a Saturday afternoon hip hop session where, among the young breakdancers and hip hop kids, you might have seen Goldie, who occasionally travelled over from Wolverhampton. On the jazz scene there were dance troupes and fusion crews, with moves that were more balletic than those of breakdancers, but sharing links to older jazz dance forms like lindy hop. Perhaps, too, it would even be possible to trace their moves back to 'breakdown dancing' in the nineteenth century, the style popularised by Dan Leno.

In Manchester there was a devoted jazz crowd at Colin Curtis's Tuesdays at Berlin at the bottom of King Street, including a dance troupe called the Jazz Defektors, who began making music and were signed to Factory Records. Factory had already signed Kalima, a jazz act that had evolved out of the Swamp Children; they played a gig at the Tropicana in Manchester in August 1984 alongside DJ Paul Murphy. An audience of boys in zoot suits and girls in pencil skirts would come out of the woodwork for nights like that – 'Jazz, Be-Bop & That Latin Beat' it was billed as – and to see acts like Sade and Blue Rondo à la Turk (a band founded by club impresario Chris Sullivan). One of the young promoters in Manchester at the time was John Kennedy. He booked Blue Rondo à la Turk to play a big show at the Ritz in October 1982 and offered the support slot to friends of his, the Smiths – their first-ever live appearance.

Although the Haçienda would go on to dominate the story of Manchester clubs it was primarily a live venue in its first four years. It drew a regular crowd of sorts for the gigs and the *i-D*-sponsored parties, but in many ways the smaller clubs were more fun as long as you knew which venues to pick on which nights. In addition to the jazz nights at Berlin and Cloud Nine, the goths at Devilles had a good thing going, the psychedelic Tuesdays at the Playpen with DJ Dave Booth were full, as were Greg Wilson's nights at Legend, where he was pushing the sound of New York electro. And further out of the city centre, two miles south in Moss Side, the Reno was still operating in tandem with the Nile, and stayed open for hours after the clubs in town shut. Like the

Dug Out, it was a place to score weed; you could buy enough for two spliffs for a pound.

By the mid-1980s one of the best-loved Reno DJs, Persian, had left the club, but the quality of the sounds were maintained by others including Hewan Clarke and Tomlin. In 1986 the Nile and the Reno were demolished by the council, leaving no trace of either (the site, on the corner of Princess Road and Moss Lane East, has never been redeveloped). Hewan had been an original Haçienda resident and was still very active, particularly in Moss Side. There's film of one dance he played at, at the Moss Side Community Centre in September 1986. The footage features a dance troupe called Foot Patrol, who'd established themselves on the jazz-fusion scene but developed moves specifically for early Chicago house.

The Foot Patrol footage is intriguing because received opinion has it that there was resistance to house from those who considered themselves soul and jazz fans. This was indeed usually the case, especially in London, but the resistance clearly wasn't universal. Jive Turkey in Sheffield also attracted jazz-fusion dancers who didn't leave the dancefloor when the DJs played early house. In 1986 and '87 Foot Patrol would visit the Haçienda, the floor clearing to make space for them when they went into their soft-shoe shuffles and lindy hops. One of their number, Samson, was a flamboyant dresser, a great athlete and a massive enthusiast for music.

Foot Patrol were most often found at the Haçienda on Mike Pickering's 'Nude' night on Fridays. Pickering was still booking the bands, although Quando Quango had come to an end. In September 1985 a Nude night featured Mike DJing with Andrew Berry and a Latin break courtesy of Simon Topping, a former member of A Certain Ratio. By mid-1986 Martin Prendergast had joined Pickering on the decks; both of them enjoyed the likes of Farley Jackmaster Funk's 'Love Can't Turn Around' and Adonis' 'No Way Back'.

When 'Love Can't Turn Around' was released in August 1986, in some quarters of London resistance was total. Although it got plenty of play in gay clubs, according to Mud Club DJ Mark Moore the trendy straight clubs in London were less enthusiastic, even hostile (he says the hip hop crowd thought the music was 'faggy'). Kiss FM DJ Steve Jackson told the TV documentary *Pump Up the Volume*, 'Most of the clubbers were into rare groove and hip hop. No one was used to that tempo and energy. It took a while, but up North everyone was into it, long before us.'

Manchester's embrace of electronic dance music strengthened. In some ways it was an easier transition. London had busy, established retro and rare groove clubs, strong fashions associated with the clubs, and press coverage – so why evolve? High-tempo dance music, though, had been a feature of Northern Soul and, the likes of Kalima notwithstanding, the Factory roster was full of bands who embraced drum machines and synthesisers, most notably New Order, who'd recorded the electronic dance classic 'Blue Monday' back in 1982 (described in a BBC Radio 2 documentary in 2005 as 'a crucial link between 70s disco and the dance/house boom that took off at the end of the 80s').

In its early years, the Haçienda hadn't much success in establishing DJ-only nights, with the exception of John Tracy's alternative nights, which drew three or four hundred most Tuesdays. The efforts of DJs including Hewan Clarke, Greg Wilson and Chad Jackson weren't rewarded with much of a regular crowd. One Saturday night I was looking after Sonic Youth on one of the first occasions they were in Manchester and they were aware of Factory, and Factory's New York connections (and vice versa), so we went into the Haçienda. There can't have been more than seventy-five people in there, and I remember the DJ played 'Ring My Bell' and we beat a hasty retreat.

Paul Mason arrived in January 1986 from Rock City in Nottingham and, with Paul Cons, instituted a new regime; they were responsible for the day-to-day running of the club and the promotion and marketing. Live music was clearly not making the Haçienda any money. Mason had employed DJs like Jonathan Woodliffe at Rock City, knew the potential of strong DJ nights to bring regular weekly cash into the club, and accelerated a switch into club nights. It turned out to be the right decision at the right time but it was made less for cultural than financial reasons. At that time having DJs playing was so much cheaper than booking bands; if Paul Mason and Paul Cons hadn't found a winning formula in 1986, Tony Wilson would have closed the club.

Then Mason and Cons came to hear me DJing a hundred yards down the road at Venue. Mason had some reservations about what I was playing, which was 'too art school' he said, but that was something I could live with. I loved Factory's ethos, and that their vision always seemed to involve a search for an alternative. I was invited to launch a Thursday 'Temperance Club' in May 1986. I started off playing New Order, hip hop, the Smiths and the Stooges. I'd dare myself to play tracks beyond the obvious, new releases from labels like On-U Sound, stuff that needed airing like Colourbox's 'The Official Colourbox World Cup Theme'. DJ Justin Robertson later talked about the lure and allure of the Haçienda even before the 'Madchester' moment went overground. 'I remember walking into this stark, industrial space. Dave Haslam was playing Shinehead, "Who the Cap Fit", which has this electronic backbeat that sounded incredible in there. I fell in love with the place. I started basing my entire life around going there. It was very stark but massively cool.'

Saturdays were more funky, and drew a slightly older crowd, including more *i-D* readers. I was partnered by Dean Johnson. Dean played specialist modern soul, jazz and reggae. One or either of us would play New York electro funk like D-Train's 'You're the One for Me'. I played hip hop and then hip-house. We were lucky in that we had an audience who understood and wanted music that wasn't just what they already knew. In the summer of 1987 'Pump up the Volume' by MARRS was released, a sample-heavy slice of electro, musically a bridge between hip hop and house, which filled our dancefloor and broke into the charts. But those records made even more sense on Nude night. Mike Pickering cleared the decks, literally, to fill his playlist with house. He also formed T-Coy with Simon Topping and keyboard player Richie Close, and released the ground-breaking electro/Latin/house single 'Carino'.

By the end of summer 1987 Jive Turkey in Sheffield had moved up several levels since their early weeks barely scraping enough money together to make their payments to Max Omare. Parrot's audience had no resistance to early house. In the first months Parrot played Northern Soul, early hip hop, electro pop and Cabaret Voltaire, but he grew into the resident DJ role and con-tinued chasing down music to play. 'The first house records had started to come out around that time so you'd be buying Chip E records thinking "What the fuck is this?" but it seemed to fit per-fectly with the vibe of the Cabs records. Then we started getting black kids coming down.'

One of the reasons Jive Turkey had progressed well was that the team had been strengthened. A group of young black dancers – the Footworkers – were really into the sounds Parrot was playing. They'd take to the floor dancing to Latin or minimal electronic sounds and one of them, Winston Hazel, became a regular at Jive Turkey and started DJing there. 'He always wanted to be a DJ,' says Parrot. 'And in terms of his attitude he was miles in front of me. And we carried on from there.'

Jive Turkey, in various locations and associated events under the banner 'Club Superman', continued to develop house music in Sheffield. Journalist Jon Savage visited one Friday in the autumn of 1988 when the club night was holding monthly events at the City Hall ballroom. Winston and Parrot were playing tracks like 'Hip Hop Salsa' by Bad Boy Orchestra. In his report in the *Observer*, Savage quoted Deno Thompson, a regular: 'The nice thing about coming here is that you get no hassle; the mix of types creates a more relaxed atmosphere.'

No doubt those of us in love with or involved with clubs and venues are right to focus on the power of music and to celebrate pioneering music promoters, venues, DJs and nightclub operators energising communities and refreshing or even revolutionising music, but there are often more prosaic reasons why certain clubs mark their difference from the competition and attract good audiences. In every era, for example, women are on the lookout for a hassle-free environment safe from predatory men. Some people are turned on by clubs with VIP rooms where footballers might gather, others go where the drinks are cheapest. Most people like a safe environment; such a thing was surprisingly hard to find in many cities in the mid-1980s and perhaps remains so. In his report Jon Savage heralds Jive Turkey's survival in the face of what he calls Sheffield's 'randomly violent club life'. In the mid-1980s if you found a discotheque where you knew there wouldn't be a fight, you'd definitely go back.

Stringent dress codes were no guarantee of a trouble-free night. Rotters, on Oxford Street in Manchester (on the site of what is now a multistorey NCP car park), requested all male patrons should wear a shirt, tie, dark trousers and shiny shoes. They were, it seems, under the misapprehension that a psycho becomes a pacifist by putting on a tie and shiny shoes. There was a chip shop up the road just before you got to the Odeon (now demolished). If the crowd from Rotters weren't fighting each other inside the club, or fighting the doormen outside the club, they'd find a reason to start fighting after 2 a.m. in the queue for chips.

Ironically, considering what was to happen in the club, the Haçienda in the mid-1980s was the safest club in Manchester city centre – and it had no dress code. It policed itself in that people who liked to battle it out at closing time were generally not likely to enjoy 'Let the Music Play', 'Bizarre Love Triangle' or 'Drop the Bomb'. But then when Nude night started at the Haçienda, the club decided to underline its position. 'I consciously reversed the dress code all the other clubs had,' says

Mike Pickering, 'Anyone who wore a shirt and tie, we wouldn't let in.'

Like other cities, Liverpool had its share of unsafe venues. In the mid-1980s, James Barton was stuck for places to go. Most of his mates were going to mainstream Top Forty clubs in town, including the upper floor of the building where Eric's had been. 'Gatsby's was one of those places . . . it always kicked off in there, someone glassed in the face with a pint pot or something, and that was just not my bag at all.'

James and I met to talk about his life up to and through the days when he was running Cream in Liverpool. He has always been into his music – in his teens he was blagging his way into the Royal Court to see the Jam. Then at some point, either outside the Royal Court or outside the Empire, he came across ticket touts and decided it was the perfect job. Even before he was eighteen he was working for one of Liverpool's most famous ticket touts and travelling across Europe following the likes of Prince and U2. On the 'in' he'd be selling tickets and on the 'out' he'd sell merchandise.

He heard about the State on Dale Street. James went there once, appreciated the music and the laser lightshow (and especially the fact there was no fighting), and he became a regular. He liked the alternative music night on a Thursday. He recalls you'd see members of Liverpool bands there. James would be in the other corner, though. 'That was the alternative crowd. Mine was a bit more scally, trainers, jeans. We were "casuals", that's the right word.' He stuck around at the State, got to know the DJs Steve Proctor, Andy Carroll and Mike Knowler as the music evolved, and the goth hits were relegated to the back of Andy Carroll's record collection. At the State in 1987, from Thursdays to Saturdays, you'd hear Public Enemy and then 'Pump up the Volume'.

If you were to draw a timeline for the ten months from the autumn of 1987 to mid-summer 1988 you'd track a steady rise in the production and profile of house music. The clubs playing the music started underground, mostly at venues off the radar. Radio shows playing the music were few, but included Jazzy M's *Jacking Zone* on the pirate station LWR, and Stu Allan on Piccadilly Radio (later known as Key 103). The music from 1987 onwards leaped forward as Chicago house garnered a harder-edged brother, Detroit techno. Then, by the end of 1987, the new sounds that had only been available on import were getting licensed to UK labels and appearing on compilations. All the while the music was challenging the other club scenes, but then, during the early months of 1988, it was clear that the arrival of ecstasy was making the big difference. This is the view of Sasha, one of the first high-profile DJs of the 1990s: 'I don't think the scene would have happened without it. The music was there, but the music fed off it. They went hand in hand.'

Ecstasy use changed clubs forever, as we'll see through and beyond the next chapter of our story. In London, one episode hastened the dawning of a new era, and that was a trip to Ibiza by a group of London DJs in the summer of 1987. Paul Oakenfold had met Trevor Fung on the soul scene and Fung had got him a DJ gig at Rumours, a wine bar in Covent Garden. In 1987 Oakenfold was working in club promotions, taking time out at the end of August 1987 to go to Ibiza to celebrate his twenty-sixth birthday, meeting up with Nicky Holloway, Steve Walsh, Johnnie Walker and Danny Rampling. Rampling was a painter and decorator who'd made a success of DJing in disco pubs in south London. Nicky Holloway had been organising parties and events, and had become one of the most energetic and prolific promoters in London, running events he called 'Special Branch' nights.

The lads went to a club called Nightlife in San Antonio where they bumped into two girls who Nicky Holloway recognised as Special Branch regulars. The girls suggested everyone should take some ecstasy and go on to Amnesia where, in the open air, they listened to Amnesia's resident DJ Alfredo. The experience under the stars made a deep impression. Alfredo's DJing, incorporating rock and disco, was the kind of mixture these London soul boys and funkateers hadn't heard before. The drug delivered an extra sense of warmth and communality. The lads came back with a mission to recreate that vibe at home in London.

Paul Oakenfold set up Ibiza reunion parties at Ziggy's wine bar in Streatham playing records by the Cure and Woodentops ('Why Why Why'), plus import dance records. The Project, as it was called, was held from 2 a.m. to 6 a.m. and lasted for five or six weeks. Carl Cox supplied the sound system. 'I loved the energy,' he said later. 'People dressing how they wanted to dress, dancing how they wanted to dance, sweating and not giving a shit what they looked like.'

Noel and Maurice Watson had worked with various people hosting hip hop and rare groove parties, and then they took Saturdays at the Astoria, establishing a night called 'Delirium', founded alongside Rob King, Nick Trulocke and Spencer Style. It started out as a hip hop night (the opening night, in September 1985, featured live performances from Run DMC, Beastie Boys and LL Cool J – admission was £5). There were films and light-shows, even a forty-foot helter-skelter on one occasion and, on others, mud wrestlers and girls dressed as Pink Panthers on high trapezes. Divine performed, as did Roxanne Shante, Whodini and Salt 'n' Pepa.

As the first house records made their way across from the States, Maurice was particularly keen to play them at the Astoria, but the rare groove and hip hop crowd were resistant. Eventually Maurice moved to New York and Noel, with promoter Rob King, took Delirium to the main room at Heaven and repositioned Delirium as a house music club. For the opening night Rob King brought over the Godfather of House, Frankie Knuckles, from Chicago. The music was right but the timing wasn't; it was always a struggle for them to make money doing Delirium and the night lasted less than a year, but during that year if you lived in London and were into house music, chances are you were at Delirium.

At this time the playlists of Paul Oakenfold and music favoured by the Balearic crowd he'd gathered at the Project was less dominated by house music than Delirium and some of the gay clubs in the capital, but the attitudes, the prevalence of ecstasy and the fashions were more indicative of what was becoming known as acid house. Oakenfold took the 300-capacity back room at Heaven in November 1987, calling the night 'Future'. Two friends, Lisa McKay and Nancy Turner, who had been enjoying summer in Ibiza for a couple of years, took the names Lisa Loud and Nancy Noise, and began DJing at Future. 'You weren't intimidated, you felt comfortable,' says Lisa. 'You weren't surrounded by inhibitions and barriers and bad attitude.'

Among all London clubs of this era, it's Shoom that's most often pinpointed as the one that knocked clubland off its axis and created the blueprint for acid house. It was started by Danny Rampling, along with his wife Jenni, at the end of 1987 in a fitness centre on Southwark Bridge Road, not far from London Bridge Station. The fitness centre didn't have much going for it, although the nature of the venue and the decor (or lack of it) at least ensured the experience of visiting the club night would be very different to visiting the Wag. But there was more. Rampling was also keen on creating a fun, looser atmosphere different to the trendy West End clubs, with an eclectic and Balearic soundtrack. It was full-on and loud. The strobe light was relentless, and a smoke machine pumped out strawberry-flavoured smoke. Mark Moore describes the club like this: 'There were these fresh-faced people completely mashed on drugs. It was just chaos; you never knew if the next DJ was actually going to make it for his set.'

Ecstasy, the 'hug drug' as it was known, was clearly having a big part to play; behaviour and attitudes were different from what people had previously experienced in clubland. A night at Shoom or Future wasn't about drinking, trying to chat-up girls; it was about dancing. The clothes the audiences wore – colourful tie-dye, loose T-shirts, Kickers and flares – played havoc with nightclub dress codes and proved a cultural jump too far for some of the established club big cheeses used to more fancy, individual, flamboyant dressers parading their cool rather than losing it. Other people loved what they experienced on their first visit to Shoom, as future member of the Beloved, Helena Marsh, later recalled: 'That first night was *the* defining, life-changing moment of my life. All my values, my opinions, everything changed.'

In March 1988 'RiP' (Rave in Peace) was launched in a warehouse on an abandoned Thames-side wharf on Clink Street, close to where the reconstructed *Golden Hind* is now on show. The DJs – including Kid Batchelor, 'Evil' Eddie Richards and Mr C – played unsparing, relentless house and techno to an edgier crowd than the one at Shoom. Ashley Beedle was a regular at the RiP parties and began to DJ in the back room of the venue. 'The sound was very much a very heavy black sound, very Chicago. There was a lot of ne'er-do-wells down there. A lot of football types, definitely. A lot of rude boys, black kids. But there was no trouble. I think a lot of that was to do with the pharmaceuticals that were going around . . .'

There was a definite change in the Haçienda around February 1988. By this time Graeme Park was DJing every Friday with Mike Pickering. At the Garage in Nottingham, Graeme's eclectic style had gained a very decent following and he introduced more house into his playlist. When Graeme moved on to the Haçienda, he was struck by how the playlist was similar, but the atmosphere was more chaotic. He soon realised this was mostly the result of the prevalence of ecstasy in the club. 'A packed club, everyone going absolutely crazy, but it was only like half past nine or something.'

It's worth remembering how secret and underground a lot of this activity was – and uncharted. There were no role models, no media coverage, no online videos; people didn't know how to dance to this music, and no one had laid down laws about what was cool and what wasn't – it was very liberating. In London, the guys who'd prided themselves on their regular attendance at hot-shot clubs had a big wake-up call. Readers inclined to be dismissive of the notion that acid house triggered a music and cultural revolution are urged to consider the significance of at least two developments. First, acid house challenged not just the notion of dress codes but the belief that an expensive jacket counted for anything. Terry Farley was an ex-Crackers regular who, with others, including Andy Weatherall, had a music, fashion and football fanzine called *Boy's Own*. He knew a character called Graham Ball who ran what Farley describes as 'very, very trendy clubs'. Then Mr Ball visited Shoom with some friends. 'They were in Gaultier suits one week and next minute they were, like, very spiritual and on one mate,' says Farley.

As Lisa Loud identified and enjoyed, one feature of these pioneering clubs was that the atmosphere appeared to be more female-friendly than many versions of nightlife. Many discotheques had the reputation of being so-called 'cattle markets'. Journalist John McCready later described the era like this: 'It wasn't like anything you'd ever experienced in a club before. At the Haçienda it was almost as if a generation breathed a sigh of relief, having been relieved of the pressure of the chase. The baggy clothes desexualised the whole environment.'

Perhaps all this and the relaxed style of dressing, as well as the lack of bad attitudes, were responsible for the second undeniable change in these years, other than the Gaultier-related one. I once had a conversation with Nile Rodgers about his first visits to Britain in the 1970s. Apart from recalling the terrible weather, and the weird regional accents, he recalled how in every club he went there were girls dancing round their handbags. Girls stopped dancing round their handbags at the acid house clubs; they danced on podiums, they danced on packed dancefloors, they danced facing the DJ, they danced queuing for the toilets, but they never danced round their handbags.

There had been numerous events like Dirtbox and Shake 'n' Fingerpop in found spaces and warehouses, but in early 1988 some of these events became specifically ecstasy-driven, including 'Hedonism' – illegal warehouse parties in a west London industrial estate, featuring DJs including Colin Faver and Slinkey. Norman Jay had done more than his fair share of house parties and warehouse gigs but he re-evaluated everything after a trip to Hedonism. 'It made a change to have a warehouse party that had no funky music. In one night, everything that went before it was gone, redundant.' Some months later he partnered Patrick Lilley and they launched 'High on Hope', which, at Dingwalls, featured quality US house DJs on their first visits to the UK, including Tony Humphries and Terry Hunter.

Paul Oakenfold and friends had been hosting Future in the back room of Heaven. Then, in April 1988, Paul took up an offer of a main-room night. It was daunting – a Monday night and a 1,000-plus capacity – but through the efforts of Oakenfold, Ian St Paul and Gary Haisman, Spectrum, as the night was called, was soon packed, pulling people not just from Future, but also Delirium on Thursdays. Oakenfold, arguably, was at his most creative as a DJ, taking chances, creating a night like no other. On one occasion all the lights were switched off and, with the club in darkness, he played an extract from Tchaikovsky's *1812 Overture*.

The Soul Mafia were still plying their trade in London and the Southeast and at soul weekenders. But at events like the Prestatyn Soul Weekender in April 1988 it became clear that the older generation of DJs like Chris Hill and Robbie Vincent didn't relate to the new era. Nicky Holloway, however, embraced it and his adventures as a club promoter continued. At the end of May 1988 he opened the Trip at the Astoria. His timing was just right. A year earlier, Noel and Maurice Watson had tried to convert the Astoria to house music but now, fuelled by features on acid house in *i-D* and *The Face*, crowds descended on the club, in dungarees, bandanas and smiley T-shirts.

The gap between the Haçienda as it had been and the Haçienda in the new era kept building week in, week out, and a new night was instigated on Wednesdays. 'Hot', launched in the second half of 1988, was the quintessential Summer of Love experience piloted by DJs Mike Pickering and Jon Dasilva. It was like a mini-midweek Ibiza, with a swimming pool next to the dance-floor, and bleepy Detroit techno, airhorns and thunderstorms and pianos filling the air.

Jon Dasilva also took Dean's place on Saturday nights. Park had joined Pickering. For a while in the middle of 1988 there were just the four of us who DJ'd every week at the club. From that time and for several years afterwards, there was only ever a handful of guest DJs at the Haçienda. Rather than booking them, Paul Cons was always looking at other ways of ramping up the excitement. Thinking a swimming pool in the club every Wednesday maybe wasn't enough, he would throw some random entertainment into the mix. On one occasion, Cons flew in a contortionist from New York and put her on the stage. It was a Saturday night. I had to stop the music for ten minutes while she tied herself in knots.

Over the last chapters we've had examples of music made by people inspired by nights out listening to DJs and bands, and we've seen how inspiration might lead to other vocations apart from music-making. When people are inspired to participate and create, then going to clubs moves from being a passive experience to an active one, and the culture takes off. Mark Moore was among those who understood this was important. In 1987 he was given an opportunity to write about the new era in the *Virgin Rock Yearbook*. 'Roll on the future when the new wave of British club-goers start turning out their own music.'

His prophecies were on the way to coming true. T-Coy had released 'Carino', and various collaborators in Sheffield, including the singer Ruth Joy, had a hit as Krush ('House Arrest'). Evil Eddie Richards and Mr C (calling themselves Myster E) released the single 'Page 67', which – befitting the deep vibe at their RiP parties on Clink Street – was a darker record than 'Carino' or 'House Arrest'. And then there was Mark Moore's own 'Theme From S-Express', which was Number One in April 1988.

In Manchester, a crew into hip hop and electro, calling themselves the Hit Squad, metamorphosed into 808 State, working as a trio: Martin Price of the Eastern Bloc record shop; Graham Massey, who was well known in the city as a member of Biting Tongues; and Gerald Simpson. In January 1988, taking their name from the Roland TR-808 drum machine, they recorded the album *Newbuild*, which included songs like 'Narcossa' and 'E Talk', followed by the profound and ground-breaking 'Pacific State' single. You can hear the influence of tracks like 'Open Our Eyes' by Marshall Jefferson, but 'Pacific State' manages to be both full-on and chilled-out; machine-soul with an emotional soprano saxophone melody.

Meanwhile, taking time away from his work with 808 State, Gerald, consciously working out ideas based on what he was hearing at the Haçienda, wrote and recorded 'Voodoo Ray'. One Wednesday night in the club, he gave Jon Dasilva a near-final mix on a cassette. Jon unleashed it peak-time; the crowd response was so instantly positive, even Gerald was taken aback. Released in a limited run and then later re-released, the single reached Number 12 in the UK charts. In 1995, Gerald remodelled some of the original samples to create 'Voodoo Rage' for his *Black Secret Technology* album, while also including the tracks 'The Nile' and 'The Reno' in homage to the Moss Side clubs.

By the end of the 1990s, we'd be used to clubbing hours being extended as a result of the liberalisation of licensing laws, but late-night opening at venues like the Reno were a rarity in the 1980s. Most clubs back then shut at two, with some in London maybe closing at three. But demand for after-hours events increased, along with frustration that high street clubs in most towns outside the major cities weren't embracing house music. In places in Lancashire like Blackburn, Nelson and Accrington there were abandoned warehouses and mill buildings – the remnants of the manufacturing industries that had once thrived in those towns – and from the end of 1988 some of these became settings for illegal rave parties, attracting people from the local towns but also the after-hours crowd from Manchester, Leeds and Liverpool. In Blackburn, ravers even descended on an old abbatoir.

These illegal raves came with plenty of risks, including to the organisers. Two young men who were particularly active in Blackburn were Tommy Smith and Tony Creft, who were soon hosting parties attended by five or even ten thousand people. The success of their events attracted the notice of professional crimi-nals, who tried to muscle in, and of course from the police. 'It was beyond the rule of law, beyond anything,' Drew Hemment, then a DJ, later recalled.

Illegal rave parties were becoming a feature of London nightlife too. 'Sunrise' was formed in 1988 by Tony Colston-Hayter and David Roberts. They ran parties dubbed 'Apocalypse Now' at Wembley Studios. One visitor was Paul Staines, who had a day job working for the right-wing Adam Smith Institute. 'The first E I took was at Apocalypse Now at Wembley Studios,' he later recalled. 'I thought it was fantastic, I was so out of it, so in love with everybody.'

In August 1988 the *Sun* ran an expose of Spectrum at Heaven, claiming, 'Junkies flaunt their craving by wearing T-shirts sold at the club bearing messages like "Drop Acid Not Bombs".' Oakenfold shut the club for a few weeks and then relaunched with a new name for the night – 'Land of Oz'. Media pressure didn't deter new warehouse party operators from getting in on the act, including Genesis, who began hosting warehouse parties in East London. Sunrise attracted 4,000 people to a rave in an old gasworks. The tabloid newspapers went into overdrive. Tintin

Chambers and Jeremy Taylor – the men behind the 'Energy' raves – were described by the *Sunday Mirror* as 'Evil Acid House Barons'. The *Star* revealed 'Plans To Flood Britain With Killer Pills'. Tony Colston-Hayter was dubbed 'Acid's Mr Big'.

Warehouse party operators were often able to stay a step or two ahead of the police, but only for a short while. It was the same for club promoters, as James Barton discovered. He'd become mates with John Kelly and together they organised a New Year's Eve party at a little club off Victoria Street called Nights Alive. It was a success, so Barton and Kelly decided to go weekly, renaming the venue the Underground. The Underground attracted the attention of the national press – John McCready wrote about it in *The Face* – but it also came to the notice of the police. Looking back, Barton concedes that he and his cohorts were a little reckless perhaps. 'There were too many drugs, it was all a bit vague on the ownership structure, and there were too many stay-behinds. We'd close the doors and carry on and we'd still be going at six o'clock in the morning playing music and the cops would be outside banging on the doors and we'd be like "Fuck 'em".'

A new police commander appeared on the scene, who changed the tactics. Faced with a club full of ravers locked in at 4.30 in the morning, he ordered his officers to rip the door off its hinges, closed down the club and revoked the licence. The police then threatened to bring criminal proceedings against the team, believing the Underground to be a front for drug-dealing, money-laundering and all kinds of gangster activity. 'They were sure there was more to it than met the eye,' says Barton. 'I was making around two hundred quid a week and spent most of it on bloody records and the rest on stupid-looking T-shirts and trousers. I think eventually the police realised we weren't part of some conspiracy, they were just like, "These guys are just bonkers, they're just dead-heads".'

The organisers of illegal raves in London during the first months of 1989 also found themselves subject to more stringent policing and many of the parties moved from inner-city areas to the countryside. Soon there were a number of regular events, among them Sunrise, 'Biology', Energy, 'Back to the Future', always with their locations kept secret until late in the day when meeting points would be arranged and word spread via pirate radio, mobile phones, BT messaging services and by word of mouth. On 24 June 1989 Sunrise promoted 'Midsummer Night's Dream' in an aircraft hangar at White Waltham Airfield near Maidenhead in Berkshire and over 10,000 people attended. Evil Eddie Richards, Judge Jules and Fabio were among the DJs, who played for ten hours, 10 p.m. to 10 a.m. The *Sun* on the following Monday claimed that ravers included 'youngsters so drugged-up they ripped the heads off pigeons!' Readers were told, '11,000 youngsters go drug crazy at Britain's biggest-ever Acid party'.

Not all the tabloids jumped in with fiction and sensation. For example, it's striking how different coverage of the event was in the *Mirror*, where journalist Linda Duff talked readers through the event. The 'Trippies [as she calls the revellers] hate discos. You won't find any girls in Dolcis cream stilettoes at an acid house party. There's no chatting up, and no dancing round handbags ... The drug ecstasy or "E" will keep the party rocking for the good ten hours that's required. Users say "E" makes them feel sexy, fit and carefree.'

At the Haçienda, Mike Pickering had been getting a Nude night crowd with a good racial mix, but as the ecstasy culture began to dominate, the black crowd drifted away. The chaos and euphoria intensified, and a night at the Haçienda became as unhinged as the door of the Underground. However, the liberal door policy, the prevalence of ecstasy and some of the other ingredients key to how the Haçienda became what one journalist has called 'the spiritual home of acid house in the UK' also contributed to its demise.

The police in Manchester were also paying close attention to rave clubs, especially following the death of Clare Leighton on 14 July 1989. Clare had borrowed an older girl's birth certificate to gain entry to the Haçienda, travelled from her home in Cannock, Staffordshire, with three friends, and took one of four pills her boyfriend had bought from a dealer in the club. She'd previously taken the drug two months earlier at the Haçienda but on this second occasion suffered an 'idiosyncratic reaction', collapsed, suffering massive internal bleeding, and died in hospital. The tragedy wasn't widely reported at the time, partly because, despite the club from Wednesday through to Saturday attracting over a thousand people every night, the goings-on at the Haçienda were underground, barely written about and far from public consciousness.

More media interest was generated following the inquest into Clare's death in December 1989, when the coroner recorded a verdict of death by misadventure. Coverage was greater, partly because the circumstances had become clear but also because between July and December the Haçienda's profile had risen as bands like the Stone Roses and Happy Mondays, closely associated with the scene in Manchester, were picking up radio and magazine interest, and both had made their *Top of the Pops* debut.

Police attention in Manchester city centre gave a boost to raves out on the surrounding hills and mill towns. 'Joy' at Stand Lees Farm, Rochdale, organised by Anthony and Chris Donnelly, took place in August 1989, followed six weeks later by 'Live the Dream' near Blackburn, which included a fairground, a chillout area and a number of DJs from London (including Paul Oakenfold and Nicky Holloway) with Manchester names like Jon Dasilva, Steve Williams and the Jam MCs. Raves were breaking down the traditional enmities between people from different cities; James Barton and John Kelly were also on the bill.

Word about Live the Dream was spread via pirate radio stations, including Fantasy FM and Centreforce. 'Freedom is a right not a privilege' announced the flyer, and 'We want to dance, so we are taking a chance'. The slogans captured both the idealism and the paranoia of that summer. Chief Superintendent Ken Tappenden of Kent Police had set up the Pay Party Unit in order to gather information about organisers and share this knowledge, and ideas and tactics, with other forces. Between the beginning of June and mid-September 1989 over a thousand raves were investigated by the Pay Party Unit. Tory MP Graham Bright pushed the Entertainments (Increased Penalties) Act through Parliament; the Act became law in 1990, with a range of penalties for organisers of unlicensed parties.

Matthew Collin, in his *Altered State: The Story of Ecstasy Culture and Acid House*, tells the story of the unravelling of Tommy Smith and Tony Creft's Blackburn raves. The first crunch came on 24 February 1990 at a party in Nelson, which 200 police raided, after which Smith and Creft decided to hold back from any further involvement in Lancashire. Five months later, Smith was involved in organising 'Love Decade' at an industrial warehouse in Gildersome, Yorkshire. Riot police with horses and dogs closed the event down, arrested over 800 people, confiscated Drew Hemment's records and charged DJ Rob Tissera with inciting a riot and what was described as the 'Dishonest Abstraction of Electricity'. He served three months in prison.

As the 1980s became the 1990s, the line between the perils of illegal raves and legal club nights were blurred in a few places, especially in Manchester. One club that was intense, druggier and darker than the Haçienda was the Thunderdome on Oldham Road. It had been known as the New Osborne, where Alan Wise had staged a gig by the Cure in 1980, but was originally a bingo hall. It was situated in a part of the city Darren Partington of 808 State describes as 'rough-arsed'. According to Darren, 'The Thunderdome was full of all sorts of lunatics, hooligans and vagabonds, but that didn't matter because everybody had come to dance.'

Various gangs infiltrated the Thunderdome, including the

notorious Cheetham Hill. But DJs like Steve Williams and Jay Wearden kept drawing capacity crowds. For a while Mike Pickering was a resident at a night called Hypnosis. 'It was great,' Pickering recalled in an interview with *Clash* magazine. 'I used to DJ and people used to come up and give me presents. I remember one night I got a mountain bike. Just came up and gave me it. I remember one night someone gave me an acid tab in my drink. That wasn't as nice.'

Konspiracy, under an adult book and video shop on the north side of Manchester's Corn Exchange, began featuring one-offs in the summer of 1989. Inspired by his early visits to the Haçienda, Justin Robertson had immersed himself in the culture. He DJ'd at Konspiracy on 1 August 1989 alongside John Tracy and Greg Fenton. Justin and Greg then launched 'Spice' there on Sunday nights. Chris Nelson, one half of the Jam MCs (with ex-Reno DJ Tomlin), became more involved, alongside Marino Morgan. Sasha was one of their regular DJs. He had made Manchester his home, and got many of his first gigs by taking slots Jon Dasilva was too busy to accept. As we shall see in the next chapter, Sasha would go on to make his name playing full-on, ravetastic house at clubs like Shelley's, but not every gig he did was on that tip. Early in 1990 he was playing a regular Wednesday gig at Konspiracy alongside dancers Foot Patrol with a playlist the flyers described as 'Jazz Soul Fusion'.

In May 1990, after months of surveillance, the police informed Paul Mason they were going to oppose a renewal of the Haçienda's licence at a hearing six or seven weeks later. The summer of 1990 then became the most intense period in the club's history. On the one hand, it was getting recognition not just from the British music press, but abroad too. In June 1990, Elektra Records financed a Haçienda DJ tour of America, the first time DJs from a British nightclub had toured the States. And yet, all the while, hanging over this was the threat that the club would be closed almost as soon as we returned home.

The management had secured the services of George Carmen QC, who the previous year had successfully defended the comedian Ken Dodd on charges of tax evasion. They'd also got support from Manchester City Council, having argued with some justification that, despite the problems, the Haçienda was a focus for a music scene bringing profile and positivity to the city.

Konspiracy was having similar problems. Within a few months of the club's launch, it was getting rougher, shadier, though busier. In this period, it wasn't just a case of avoiding the attentions of the police but trying to stay ahead of the gangsters. In *Altered State*, Matthew Collin compares the end of Konspiracy to the story of the Haçienda. 'Chris Nelson and Marino Morgan couldn't afford a lawyer of George Carmen's calibre and they didn't have the public profile to secure backing from the Council and the *NME*. They couldn't even control their own doormen or prevent Cheetham Hill gang leaders like the feared "White Tony" Johnson making Konspiracy their base.'

A year or so ago, I met with one of White Tony's associates. He didn't take his coat off, he drank tea, he was calmer than me. He described to me how the gangs that had controlled districts of Manchester, Salford and Cheetham Hill, earning from the supply of drugs and from protection rackets, began to move into town as clubs became busier and, specifically, when ecstasy use boomed. Gangs that had previously been involved with armed robberies and wages snatches, then found out how lucrative the ecstasy market was. He told me the key was not to be too greedy. He worked three or four dealers a night in Manchester, found them ecstasy from a contact in Amsterdam – a thousand, two thousand pills most weekends – divided them between the dealers and protected them while they dealt drugs in the clubs (mostly the Haçienda and Konspiracy); then they'd split the profits. The protection was easy; he carried firearms and a reputation (he'd been arrested and charged twice with murder, but the charges hadn't stuck). He says the best kids were from Beswick, Miles Platting, and a kid from Stoke. The kid from Stoke drove a grey hatchback up every Friday and Saturday. He could move Es like no one else, eight hundred a night, maybe. 'He was making good money and I was making good money. I could spend the evening in the Haçienda and earn two or three grand. From doing nothing.'

It was becoming clear to some of us that if the police didn't close the Haçienda, the violence would. The lucrative ecstasy market was creating a turf war. White Tony's associate was on course to make £100,000 from the Haçienda. 'Things were boiling up in the middle of 1990,' he says. 'The music scene, the crowd at the Haçienda; there was money to be made, and you saw all these guys swarming around, it was a buzz. People got caught up in it, the hysteria.'

Konspiracy closed, but on 23 July the Haçienda received a stay of execution and was granted six months to bring the availability of drugs on the premises and the associated violence to an end – which was easier said than done. The management discussed establishing a membership scheme – one had been in operation in the club's early years – hoping it would keep away undesirables. In addition, in the autumn of 1990, the doormen were asked to initiate a door policy on Thursdays, allowing entry only to NUS card-holders. The policy was abandoned the following week, but other changes were permanent, including stopping Nude night altogether. This was September 1990.

It sounds primitive and far-fetched, but before texts and emails you'd be used to communication by letter. In Tony Wilson's case, I'd write letters to him at his home address, and he used to write back. The change in the atmosphere and the various decisions being made to head off violent gangs contributed to my decision to leave the club. I expressed my exasperation in a letter to Tony. He replied, exasperated at my exasperation. 'Do you not think that the people who run the Haçienda hate every fucking minute of the way it is? Do you not think it is a constant argument at board level? Do you not think that whatever is happening it is to preserve this very special place for the people of Manchester? It's tough. Things happen. We have to get on with it.'

Unfortunately things got tougher, although the news at first seemed good; at the 3 January 1991 hearing, the magistrates noted there had been a 'positive change in direction' and renewed the Haçienda's licence; the club celebrated with a 'Thanksgiving' night featuring Electronic (featuring Bernard Sumner and Johnny Marr) playing live. Behind the scenes, though, pressure from the gangs was intensifying. Attempting to refuse admission to someone, members of staff were threatened with a gun. This was one of several nasty incidents. On 30 January Tony Wilson announced the club was closing voluntarily, with immediate effect. It had been a journey from innocence to experience. 'When we started up the club we had no idea that these were the sort of people we would have to deal with. It's the best club in the city, that's why they want to terrorise it,' said Tony at the time.

During the temporary closure, 'White Tony' Johnson had been killed in a gun attack and associates of the gang the police suspected of being behind the killing negotiated to take full control of the Haçienda door (no one has ever been successfully tried for the murder). The closure lasted just over three months, before the club reopened on 10 May.

The influence of the pioneers and their clubs was already spinning off in all directions, inspiring DJs and music-making. Paul Oakenfold remixed 'Wrote for Luck' by Happy Mondays and then co-produced their *Pills 'n' Thrills and Bellyaches* album. Terry Farley and Andy Weatherall from *Boy's Own* began to run their own parties and began a Boy's Own record label. Weatherall remixed 'Loaded' by Primal Scream and then co-produced their *Screamadelica* album. Drawing on experiences at Shoom, Helena Marsh, married to Jon Marsh of the Beloved, became part of the group and featured on the Beloved album *Conscience*, which included the single 'Sweet Harmony' – a Top Ten hit in January 1993.

A new generation of London club promoters was emerging. There was 'The Brain', for example, founded in 1989 by Sean McLusky and Mark 'Wigan' Williams on Wardour Street. As well as featuring DJs, it gave a stage to some emerging acts playing live, such as Orbital, the Shamen and Adamski, as well as DJs. McLusky later established 'Love Ranch' at Maximus on Leicester Square. Charlie Chester opened a record shop on Dean Street called Flying and then, hearing that Dean Thatcher and Brandon Block were going to launch a party out in Colnbrook, Berkshire, (near Heathrow Airport), he got involved with them and the club night 'Flying' was born. When it moved to the Soho Theatre Club, Flying really took off.

By the end of 1991, over in Leeds, the first night of 'Back to Basics' had been held at the Chocolate Factory, which was later renamed the Music Factory. Founded by Dave Beer and Ali Cook, Back to Basics would go on to be a legendary club night in Leeds. Tragically, though, Ali Cook was killed in a car crash in March 1993. According to an interview in *Jockey Slut* in August 1997, Dave Beer's first taste of acid house was at the Haçienda. 'At the time I didn't know where the records started or finished myself. We used to just go in there and get hammered and dance about all night. The beauty of it was that everybody was the star all of a sudden. There was no band, it was faceless music. And the facelessness of it, or the offyerfaceness of it, was perfect for me.'

In Sheffield, even when Jive Turkey came to an end its legacy was secure. One of the other important elements in Sheffield's fledgling dance music scene was the FON record shop. Steve Beckett and Rob Mitchell worked there and Winston Hazel joined them, building up an import dance section. Winston then went into music-making, linking up with his friend Robert Gordon, who had an Akai S1000 sampler and knew his way round a studio. Together they created a 'Track with No Name', credited to Forgemasters. The plan was to press 500 copies of the track. To help deliver this idea, Beckett, Mitchell and Robert

Gordon set up a label, Warp. Parrot and Richard H. Kirk from Cabaret Voltaire collaborated on a record for them: Sweet Exorcist's 'Testone'. The label's fifth release 'LFO' went Top Twenty in the UK singles chart in July 1990.

That Soul II Soul would one day record and release their own tunes was always on the cards. A demo of 'Fairplay' featuring Rose Windross led to a recording contract with 10 Records. At the time, Soul II Soul had a regular gig at the Fridge. They'd press up an acetate of songs they were working on and test them at these gigs. In 1989 they had massive commercial success with the singles 'Keep On Movin'' and 'Back to Life (However Do You Want Me)', both featuring Caron Wheeler on vocals. The songs were included on their debut album, which reached Number One in the UK charts and in the American R&B charts, where it went double platinum. The Fridge was where they first performed as a bona fide live act (there's even a plaque on the building commemorating this event).

Among the Bristol contingent, Smith & Mighty were signed to FFRR and worked with the Fresh Four to produce 'Wishing on a Star'. One of the Fresh Four, DJ Krust, later hooked up with Roni Size and in 1999 released the album *Coded Language* on Talkin' Loud, the label started by Gilles Peterson in 1990, which evolved from a night he hosted at Dingwalls. Neneh continued hanging with the Wild Bunch, namechecking them on her huge-selling 'Buffalo Stance' single and providing studio space for them during the recording of their album *Blue Lines*, released in April 1991.

Hyeonje and I sit in a back room on the ground floor of Surakhan and I start telling him about Mark Stewart – you must meet him, I tell him. Moving on from trying to explain Massive Attack, I give him a rundown of what Nellee Hooper's been up to in the last thirty years. I tell him about how Nellee served an apprenticeship here, in this building, and has gone on to pick up awards, including a Brit, a BAFTA and a Grammy, and to work with the likes of Björk, U2, No Doubt, Paloma Faith and Madonna.

Hyeonje knows about Madonna, we talk about 'Like a Virgin' and he tells me more about Korean food and his restaurant. Surakhan was established by Mr Oh and his wife four years or so ago. Before that it was a Thai restaurant, and before that a Chinese restaurant. He says he thinks the building has the same landlord as it did in the 1980s, a man from Hong Kong. It was the owners of the Chinese restaurant that stripped out the last of the club fixtures and fittings and gave the building a refurbishment, establishing the kitchen and new toilets.

Surakhan has a narrow frontage but it goes back a further distance than you'd imagine. Mr Oh takes me downstairs to the basement, a surprisingly big space, with plenty of headroom. I tell him Daddy G is tall, taller than me, and I make to recreate the scene, Daddy G DJing at the Dug Out, and I pretend to be Daddy G and – taking my cue from a photograph I'd seen – stand where I think the DJ box would have been, in a cramped space under the stairs. I suggest a Dug Out reunion should be organised. 'OK,' says Mr Oh, and laughs.

CHAPTER TWELVE

Police raids, the Prodigy in a bingo hall,
an MC in a cupboard

S helley's Laserdome was broken up and buried in 1994 during the building of the A50 in Longton, the southernmost of the six towns that make up Stoke-on-Trent. The demolition was the end of the story for the Laserdome, but it had lain empty since October 1992 after pressure from the local authorities and the police, concerned about the amount of drug use in the venue, forced it to close.

Every town has a venue, probably three or four, possibly more, where local lads gather in their dress code-approved apparel with not much more in mind than a piss-up and a punch-up. Shelley's had been one of those places, although there had been sporadic attempts to stage live music (the Fall played there in October 1985). But up until the middle of 1990, businessman John Matthews – who owned the venue – had never made much money, so he made Shelley's available to a new breed of clubbers and DJs: the ravers. Mr Matthews pitched in, doing what he could to make his venue acceptable to the clientele. 'If you go into a scene, you go all the way. We relaxed the dress restrictions – there was no need to wear a tie on a Friday, and trainers were quite acceptable.'

Shelley's became a prime example of a wave of ultra-hedonistic, full-on venues that emerged as electronic dance music and ecstasy spread nationwide, including Quadrant Park in Bootle (three miles from Liverpool city centre), the Sanctuary in Milton Keynes and the Eclipse in Coventry. Some of the subtlety of the early acid house scene was lost but the intensity didn't drop; at these venues you could expect lots of looping bleepiness like Psychotropic's 'Hypnosis' and the high-octane piano-driven Italo sound of tracks like 'Think About It' by DJ H feat. Stefy. In their rolling and unfolding euphoria, the crowds would respond with airhorns and whistles. There's a clip on YouTube of the moment a DJ plays 'Anthem' by N-Joi at Quadrant Park. It's bedlam.

In the era of the pioneers, no one knew that the dance music scene would have such huge monetary value and no one knew what a superstar DJ was. Among the changes in nightclubbing through the 1990s would be the increased status of DJs, including Tony Humphries, Sasha, Fabio and Grooverider, and Paul Oakenfold, and the rise of the profile of Pete Tong on the radio and Fatboy Slim in the charts. No one knew what a superclub was either. We discovered this during the 1990s via the likes of Cream, Ministry of Sound, 'Renaissance' and 'Manumission'.

By the mid-90s, nightclubs like Cream weren't just venues with flashing lights and dancing – they became 'brands' with major commercial clout. The clubs talked the talk. This is from a Cream press release in 2001: 'Cream now boasts one of the most instantly recognisable youth brands in the world's entertainment and leisure industries. The slick and innovative marketing campaigns devised by the club are a key factor in the brand's success.'

We've seen many times how the first signs of music revolutions are often to be found in nightclubs and venues. The first place to hear the music and meet its adherents, and the first place to glimpse the new look. We've seen how often a venue getting critical acclaim or helping achieve critical mass can go on to have a much wider impact. The rise of rave influenced our language. Top one, get sorted.

In the early days of his career, the late fashion designer Alexander McQueen would identify raves as one of his major influences, which McQ, the younger sibling of the Alexander McQueen men's line, still demonstrates. Journalists at *Women's Wear Daily* joyously described the spring 2015 collection from McQ as 'underground raves and travellers in layered looks with a lived-in feel'. And close to the other end of the garment trade, I remember a conversation with Anthony Donnelly, one of the two brothers who founded the clothing company Gio-Goi. Anthony and Christopher were raised in Benchill, Wythenshawe – a large council estate on Manchester's south side. They were the characters behind various activities on the scene including organising the raves 'Sweat It Out' in Manchester and Joy at Stand Lees Farm. Anthony told me their formative years were spent in the Haçienda: 'It was our university.'

The first days of Shelley's rave reincarnation had taken place in the summer of 1990 when a promotion team from Birmingham called Logical Promotions began to host weekly 'Sindrome' nights there every Saturday, attracting a local audience but also people travelling from Birmingham, Wolverhampton and Manchester. The venue came to the notice of a team of promoters in Manchester, who took over the Friday nights, calling them 'Delight'. Launching on the Friday of the Bank Holiday weekend in August 1990, the first Delight featured DJ Sasha.

At Shelley's Sasha was playing full-on piano anthems like FPI Project's 'Rich in Paradise' mixed with dancefloor favourites like Young MC's 'Know How'. 'It had a real innocent energy,' says Sasha. 'The big thing for me was holding the crowd back; they'd be gagging to hear a record they knew, and as soon as they did the whole place would go mental. From that point onwards I had to completely go for it. I knew that as soon as I put that one record on the airhorns would go off and that would be it, I'd have to completely hammer it.'

The Delight (Friday) nights and Sindrome (Saturday) nights ran concurrently for several months before 'Amnesia House' took over on Saturdays in February 1991. Local DJ Daz Willot was installed as resident. Rave was mutating into hardcore, and it was happening at Shelley's. The opening night featured an impressive line-up including Grooverider, Stu Allan, Doc Scott and a live PA by N-Joi.

Sasha left on 27 May 1991, partly out of frustration that the crowd resisted any deviation from the formula he'd developed. But the Delight nights continued in his absence; the new Friday residents were DJs Dave Seaman and Ralphy. Guest DJs would feature too, among them Frankie Knuckles and Laurent Garnier. Amnesia House was still a feature at Shelley's on Saturday nights until the Laserdome's licence was lost and the club opened for the last time on Saturday 31 October 1992.

Quadrant Park was another home of full-on rave madness. The resident DJ was Mike Knowler. The State had been closed at the end of 1989 after pressure from the police (although it was to reopen later in the 1990s), but Mike secured DJ work at Quadrant Park every Thursday, starting mid-January 1990. Making a success of this midweek gig, in March 1990 Mike was given the club's Friday and Saturday nights too.

James Barton and Andy Carroll got involved. Quadrant Park was the perfect place for an audience that liked to throw itself into an evening's entertainment with headless enthusiasm, a destination venue attracting people who'd picked up on rave culture in places like Formby, Southport and Preston. It went up yet another level near the end of 1990, when the venue obtained a six o'clock licence, and James and Andy took on the task of running the after-hours event; when the main club closed at 2 a.m. the back warehouse would open until the early hours of the morning. Barton and Carroll booked Sasha for this space (and other DJs, including Steve Williams). 'For a while it was really good,' says Barton. 'But a combination of numbers and everything meant it was madness, it was so huge, thousands and thousands of people. It was a struggle to keep it together and to keep the lunatics at bay because anything big means you're going to get an element in there.'

You couldn't buy alcohol in the venue but quite tasty fellas from Liverpool would turn up with crates of beer and just walk past the doormen. There would be thirteen- or fourteen-year-old scally kids waiting near the toilets on the lookout for hammered or vulnerable clubbers to demand cash with menaces from. The police had a presence in there, whether covert or not. 'They knew fully what was going on,' says James. 'The final straw for me at Quadrant Park was DJing one night and seeing a full-on fight moving right across the central area, a pitched battle, and I just thought, this is finished.'

James Barton had other things on his mind apart from Quadrant Park. His view was that Liverpool nightlife was still underachieving and yet to stake a claim to be part of this new, national scene. Whether it could be called house music or rave music or acid house, it was time for the city to ditch the ties and shiny shoes and get onboard. After the Underground he had high hopes for the 051, a venue just behind the Adelphi Hotel, but Barton lasted less than a year there before resigning. There were a few issues mostly with the venue owner, who had a different vision to James. 'The scallies and the nasty kids got in and turned it into something we'd never wanted, that was a shame. I'd got it on its feet. I'd booked them great DJs but they wanted to run it their way, another way.'

In other towns and cities a number of determined characters were establishing venues that had a different ethos and soundtrack to high street clubs and catered instead to the rave generation – like the Eclipse, an all-nighter in a former bingo hall in Coventry. The prime mover was Stuart Reid, a local lad whose brother-in-law was involved in the Amnesia organisation. He found an old Granada bingo hall on Lower Ford Street and spoke to the owner. 'It was difficult to speak to anyone regarding "acid house parties",' he later recalled. 'Everyone assumed you were all mad drug-taking lunatics and I think this guy did too, but the money was attractive to him, so we made a deal.'

Teaming up with Barry Edwards, Stuart opened the 1,500-capacity Eclipse, running through the night. There was no alcohol served and a private membership scheme was put into operation. These measures gave them plenty of autonomy and meant neither the council nor the police were able to step in and close the Eclipse, although they blocked every application made for a drinks licence. Local DJs Parks and Wilson were installed as resident DJs.

At the Haçienda in the late 1980s there hadn't been guest DJs; it was residents-based. Every week, the same DJs would play uninterrupted for five hours, 9 p.m. until 2 a.m. Continuity had its advantages. It also had the fortunate effect of keeping marketing costs down; there were no guest DJs, no acts, nothing to advertise, nothing to put on flyers, so few flyers were produced and there was virtually no press advertising. By 1991, at least away from the Haçienda, all this had changed, certainly among the other big clubs. Every self-respecting promoter was collecting a Filofax full of contacts and phone numbers for DJs and their agents. For their part, clubbers, while staying loyal to local or particular venues, were also looking out for, and following, the most talked-about DJ names. For example, 'Kaos' in Leeds booked Laurent Garnier for a night at Leeds Poly, and Leeds Warehouse went on to have some huge nights featuring Sasha and Steve Williams – for these guys, people would travel from all of Yorkshire and over the Pennines too.

Good residents and name guests – this became the prevailing model. In a reflection of how dance music was beginning to build an international network, the Belgian label R&S made a big impact in 1991 and the likes of Joey Beltram and Frank De Wulf guested at the Eclipse that year. In addition, several of the emergent live or semi-live acts performed short PA-style sets (two or three songs, usually, but not always, restricted to a DAT playback of their hit songs with live vocals or MCing). Among those who took to the stage at Eclipse were SL2, Altern 8, Leftfield, Moby and Shades of Rhythm. On one notable occasion, the first ever live appearance by the Prodigy took place there. Stuart remembers they were paid £60.

Despite occasional bargains, DJ fees were creeping up and the marketing spend was increasing. Stuart Reid took out advertisements in the dance music press; in 1992 this included *Mixmag* and *DJ* magazine. He used fly-poster crews and local flyering teams including Oracle and Turbo Promotions and, because he had instituted a membership list, he had addresses for the regulars, so worked on a primitive form of direct messaging, posting out a newsletter each month.

Pete Waterman was originally said to have dismissed rave music as 'blips and blops' but was won over, apparently, after hearing a track called 'Stakker Humanoid'. After his time DJing at the Coventry Locarno, Waterman had gone on to A&R, and music production with Matt Aitken and Mike Stock. Together they scored Number One singles by acts including Kylie Minogue and Rick Astley. By the end of the 1980s he was co-presenting a TV show called *The Hitman & Her* with Michaela Strachan late on Saturday nights into Sunday morning. Broadcast each week from a different venue, the show featured some of Waterman's own releases, including 'I'd Rather Jack' by the Reynolds Girls, as well as premiering new dance records and playing the current best-sellers, while Waterman and Strachan invited people onto the stage and the cameras panned across the clubbers at the Ritzy in Leeds or the Mall in Stockton-on-Tees doing their best to get their rave on.

Waterman made a trip back to Coventry in April 1992 when

The Hitman & Her descended on the Eclipse. There are suggestions that while filming there Michaela Strachan had a drink spiked with ecstasy, but there are also reports this happened to her when *The Hitman & Her* visited the Haçienda in January 1989. The 'Michaela Strachan getting spiked' story is Generation E's equivalent of Jimi Hendrix knocking a hole in a low ceiling.

By 1991 dance music was filling the charts, and the kind of sounds that just a year or two before would have been of limited interest were heard everywhere. In October 1991 Moby performed 'Go' on *Top of the Pops* – an almost lyric-less six minutes and thirty seconds of fast beats, atonal bleeps and melodic keyboard lines echoing the theme from *Twin Peaks*, plus thirty-seven shouts of 'go' and twenty-three of 'yeah'. Also in 1991 Pete Tong took to the airwaves on Radio 1, as presenter of *Essential Selection*, the station's first dedicated dance music show of the house music era.

There was an active dance music press but, as rave culture fragmented, in the northwest of England a string of particularly hectic, mostly working-class, rave nights opened with more in common with the Thunderdome or Shelley's than the Haçienda. They didn't, however, quite get their share of media coverage. When I spoke to her about how punk audiences differed in various parts of the country, Viv Albertine reckoned that the further north the Slits toured, the less restrained the crowds became. It often appeared the same was true in the rave era; at the Hippodrome in Middleton, Angels in Burnley, Legends in Warrington, and Maximes in Wigan, for example. The clubs were packed, sweat would be pouring off the ceiling and you'd hear Bug Kann & the Plastic Jam's 'Made in Two Minutes'.

DJ Welly made his reputation hosting the Pleasuredrome, down a side street in the middle of Farnworth in Bolton. Formerly known as Blighty's, the club was transformed from yet another half-empty regional discotheque – boys getting drunk, girls dancing round their handbags – to a rave venue packed with well over a thousand people every Saturday night. The Pleasuredrome was closed in 1992 after undercover police were sold drugs by bar staff.

DJ Welly became a resident at 'Life' at Bowlers Exhibition Centre, on Longbridge Road in Trafford Park, one of a number of rave venues on the edge of towns or hidden away on industrial estates. At Bowlers, tops-off hardcore raving survived through the 1990s, turning Welly, Stu Allan, Bowa, John Waddicker and others into cult DJs on the circuit. Another example is DJ Nipper. He'd guarantee a crowd, guesting at Shelley's, Konspiracy, Thunderdome, Bowlers or the Eclipse. Nipper also worked behind the counter at Eastern Bloc in Manchester and released a handful of tracks, including the extraordinary 'Nightmare Walking' under the name Kid Unknown, put out by Warp Records in 1992.

In 1991 there was a unique club in Manchester, hidden away behind the Central Library, just as sweaty as Bowlers, but with a clientele unlike anywhere else in the city. According to one regular at the No.1 on Central Street, Kath McDermott, the crowd were 'reprobates' – gay and gay-friendly. 'Rent boys, straight girls, queens, scallies, dykes and dealers,' she remembers. It was an old-fashioned basement club, more 70s naff than industrial chic, but it had a loud sound system and a DJ, Tim Lennox, who played quality ravey house every Saturday.

There was a successful women-only event at the Thompson's Arms on Sackville Street, Manchester, through the 1980s and clubs like Napoleon's, the Mineshaft, and the Archway, wine bars like Stuffed Olives, High Society, Hero's and Manhattan Sound, and pubs like the Rembrandt and the Union were either overtly gay venues or extremely gay-friendly. This activity was despite the best efforts of the homophobic Chief Constable of Greater

Manchester Police at the time, James Anderton, who saw indecency and subversion everywhere and subjected gay venues to clampdowns and raids. For him, policing was a moral crusade. Other police chiefs agreed. In 1981, Harold Salisbury, an ex-chief constable in Yorkshire, was asked which groups his force kept files on, and among those he listed as worthy of surveillance and disruption were 'The IRA, the PLO, anyone decrying marriage and family life or pushing drugs, homosexuals.'

The No.1 was the first stirrings of a new generation, the game-changer for gay clubs in the city. It was ecstasy-laden and house-music-loving. It wasn't poser-ish like Stuffed Olives or Hero's had been, and it wasn't a pick-up place; or, at least, the predatory aspect was diluted. In addition, although gay men and lesbians were aware they had common ground, they had rarely partied together, until the No.1. Freedom and friendliness is how Kath remembers it. 'Us girls would take our baggy T-shirts off and dance all night in our bra tops. Smiles as big as buses, hugs (lots of hugs).'

In some cities, there were signs that the 'hug drug' was not just breaking down barriers and creating more tolerance on dance-floors, but also on the street. The amount of lager-fuelled aggression that could mar nights out and city life in the 1970s and early 1980s diminished. Life after dark for gay men and lesbians became less hidden away, more open. As well as events at the No.1, gay nights playing upfront house music to a mixed clientele in Manchester included weekends at Paradise Factory (from 1993). The Thompson's Arms hosted the 'Strangeways' all-nighter, from 2.30 a.m. until 9.30 a.m. – 'the North's only queer nocturnal' – run by former Haçienda staffers Glenn and Brendon.

A feature of house music in the first years of the 1990s was the variety of styles. Many clubs rocked to big hands-in-the-air anthems. But in London, for example, Justin Berkmann was a fan of American garage – a style historians usually consider a more purist version of house, and trace back to Larry Levan and Paradise Garage (hence the name, 'garage'), which became associated with the likes of Frankie Knuckles in Chicago and Junior Vasquez and Tony Humphries in New York. Garage was a subgenre London clubbers had first heard at Delirium and High on Hope: American, disco-tinged and soulful rather than ravetastic, euphoric Italo.

In 1990 Berkmann met James Palumbo, son of Lord Peter Palumbo, who'd been schooled at Eton and then Oxford University. In 1990 James was working as a banker in Morgan Grenfell's property division, and despite having no background in music or clubs (but appreciating Berkmann's passionate descriptions of what could be achieved), he and his friend Humphrey Waterhouse decided to help finance a venue; they found a potential site in one of London's less salubrious areas, Elephant & Castle. Being away from built-up areas was something of an advantage when it came to obtaining a licence, as was the lack of alcohol sales on the premises. Ministry of Sound opened as a juice bar, open from midnight until ten o'clock in the morning. As a sign of their commitment to this purist sound, they persuaded Tony Humphries to become Ministry's first resident DJ. From its opening, though, the Ministry of Sound has always positioned itself as the respectable face of nightlife, and looked for a way to protect and exploit its name – much like the way the Mecca organisation steered themselves through the 1930s.

Tony Humphries became one of a number of American DJs who built an audience in the UK in the mid-1990s. Many of them were producers too, some responsible for early acid house classics, like Todd Terry. He'd play at clubs including 'Hard Times', which established its reputation in Mirfield in Yorkshire (Roger Sanchez was another Hard Times hero). In 1995 it moved to the Music Factory in Leeds where Todd Terry recorded a Hard Times compilation live. On one occasion DJ Erick Morillo appeared at Hard Times with his MC, the Mad

Stuntman (they had a number of hit records together as Reel 2 Real, featuring the Mad Stuntman chanting irresistibly vacuous phrases such as 'I like to move it, move it'). Afterwards, as dawn was about to break, Hard Times resident DJ Elliot Eastwick and his colleagues were halfway back to Manchester (where Elliot was based) when they realised the Mad Stuntman was still back at the club locked in a cupboard. They turned back and freed him. Ten years later, 'I Like to Move It' featured in the hit animation *Madagascar*. Twenty years later, the exact circumstances of how the Mad Stuntman came to be locked in a cupboard for several hours are still not clear.

A few artists were revered but in general clubbers weren't interested in acts with albums or careers; it was all about singles, remixes, DJs and clubs. So, attractively packaged DJ-curated and mixed compilations of records filling dancefloors branded by clubs was a neat match-up. The Ministry of Sound compilations and Sasha's mix albums for Renaissance were a souvenir for those who visited the particular venue, and a sampler for those who hadn't. And an earner for all concerned: Ministry of Sound compilation albums were capable of selling 500,000 copies.

At Heaven, on Thursday nights, the competing styles of purist and polished US garage and high-octane hardcore break-beat played itself out at a night called 'Rage' run by the Pure Organisation and launched in 1991. Rage started with Colin Faver and Trevor Fung playing US-flavoured house in the main room and Fabio and Grooverider in the upstairs Star Bar. Fabio and Grooverider had first worked together on the pirate radio station Phase One. They'd originally played hip hop and funk but, converting to house, they established a reputation for play-ing the toughest Detroit techno and breakbeat rave at warehouse parties and hardcore nights, mostly in London (although in 1991 Fabio played the Eclipse and Grooverider played at Shelley's).

With an ever-growing following, Fabio and Grooverider took over as Rage's main-room residents, playing to 2,000 people. They'd created a sensation around their DJing by incorporating swirly Belgian techno, speedier breakbeats, powerful basslines and minimal warehouse classics into a storm of sound that was a long way from the harmony-laden vocal house of radio-friendly tracks like 'Where Love Lives'. Fabio later recalled how instinctive their DJing was. 'We didn't have a clue what we were doing – we were just fuckin' around and doing what felt right.'

Fabio and Grooverider, along with music emerging from labels like Moving Shadow, were mapping out the path from hardcore rave and techno to both jungle and drum & bass. They were also attracting a multiracial crowd. The way they mashed up the genres encouraged a mix on the dancefloor, although the atmosphere could be heavy. Fabio later described Rage as 'scary sometimes'. There was an edge to the night, unpredictable electricity. 'You knew it could kick off at any moment, but in a weird way it just added to the intensity.'

Rage ended in 1994 but, as with other significant clubs, as well as providing intense nights out, it also inspired. Two Rage regulars were Kemistry and Storm, who met while at college in Northampton. Kemistry was in Sheffield for a while and got turned on to electronic music there. Kemistry and Storm went on to become two outstanding drum & bass DJs. Storm later paid tribute to the influence that Rage had. 'I'm not sure where we'd be without it. Rage was like a religion. We were all joined by this really emotional feeling that we were experiencing something new.'

In cities like London, Manchester, Sheffield and Liverpool, there's always been upfront music played somewhere, even if it's hard to track down, but in the early house era, people who'd often had to travel to big cities for their music fix established their own scene, an alternative to their local mainstream discos and to the big-city clubs.

To make something happen you didn't need a name DJ, just someone with some import twelve-inch singles, a sound system and some lights. And maybe a smoke machine. In Chester, for example, the DJ and impresario John Locke had the 'Blast Club' at High Society, a Georgian building on Love Street which had been Smarties in the late 1970s (when it hosted gigs by the Damned, the Pretenders and others); it's now the Forest House, a pub operated by JD Wetherspoon. The Blast Club evolved into a house music club from its alternative roots and by 1990 was attracting interested and interesting local people, including Charlotte Horne, Darren Hughes and Paul Roberts. Paul was making music, as part of K-Klass.

By 1992 a number of clubs rooted in the Midlands that helped define clubbing in their cities in the 1990s had launched, including 'Progress' in Derby and 'Wobble' in Birmingham, where DJ Phil Gifford would be joined by guests including Twitch & Brainstorm from 'Pure' in Edinburgh, Justin Robertson, Allister Whitehead and Dean Thatcher. Also in Birmingham, the Que Club had opened in a glorious former Methodist Hall, and 'Miss Moneypenny's' launched in the summer of 1993 at Bond's nightclub on Bond Street, near Constitutional Hill (other nights at Bond's included 'Oscillate'). In Nottingham, James Baillie at Venus became one of the legendary club promoters of the era; guest DJs like Allister Whitehead and Fatboy Slim used to plead to play at his venue, and among the most enthusiastic regulars was the actress Samantha Morton.

Cream had been born not long after James Barton had walked away from the 051. He'd become involved with managing K-Klass at the time they were looking to place their newly recorded dancefloor-filler 'Rhythm Is a Mystery' with a major label. Paul Roberts and Darren Hughes had both moved to Liverpool from Chester. Darren started hanging around, doing odd jobs and giving advice, says James. 'He was also one of the voices when we were doing the 051 telling us how it was. It's fucked, you need to leave, you're losing your reputation.' Darren also picked up on the dynamic between James and Andy Carroll. It was clear to everyone that Andy was strong in terms of music but less entrepreneurial, less of a 'doer', in James' words: 'Darren was a different animal. He was relentless in his pursuit of something whereas Andy was a bit *mañana*, "I'll do it tomorrow".' In October 1992, Carroll, Barton and Hughes launched a weekly event at Nation in Liverpool. Barton came up with the name. It was to be called Cream.

More than twenty years later, it seemed OK for me to ask some pertinent questions. Like, did they have a business plan?

'No.'

Did they have a legal agreement between the three of them?

'No. We came in as DJs and promoters on a door-split with the owners of the venue, Stuart Davenport and Len McMillan. We worked out creatively what we wanted; we hadn't worked out what we wanted business-wise. I wanted to get my old crowd back out; I wanted to reconnect with the early motivations for getting into all this.'

The room was 400-capacity and the team made it look and feel as good as they could. Darren's girlfriend and Paul Roberts' girlfriend were textile designers and they did prints for the walls and flowers were added to the club decor. 'House music with a party vibe' was the aim. Despite all their best efforts and fine theories, however, their guest DJ almost derailed the first week when Fabi Paras struggled to connect with the crowd. James thinks the music was too serious. 'He was in trouble,' is Barton's stark assessment. 'There was a pool table in the venue at the time and I remember sitting on the pool table and I remember Darren coming up to me and asking, "What shall we do?" I just said, "Go and fuckin' get him off." I wouldn't do it, I got Darren to do it and he dragged him off and Fabi wasn't happy.'

Paul Bleasdale went back on for the last hour and a half and the first night was deemed a reasonable success; 450 people had come through the doors. The following week, however, the numbers fell to 250. But that turned out to be the core crowd. From that point Cream built its reputation, with Andy, Paul Bleasdale and James Barton DJing most weeks. By the end of 1993 they'd moved up a level. They'd expanded into a bigger room and enjoyed a huge August Bank Holiday event, followed by a busy new student term and a very successful New Year's Eve.

If the various clubs discussed in the last chapter could claim to be creatively and musically pioneering, then Ministry of Sound and Cream have a claim to be commercially pioneering; they pursued other activities, other ancillary income streams. In its heyday, the Haçienda never released house music compilations, even though there was an extensive black market in cassettes of DJ sets and, of course, it was part-owned by a record company. The Haçienda missed other merchandising opportunities as well. In the 'Madchester' era, bands including James and Inspiral Carpets were selling thousands of T-shirts (it was said that both bands made more money selling merchandise than they did selling records) but at the Haçienda the discussions about whether and how the club should get round to doing some T-shirts dragged on and they were late to the market. Eventually a merchandise stall was set up just inside the club, and Factory and the Haçienda took a unit at the indoor market Afflecks Palace (which for some time was run by Fiona Allen, who went on to co-create the TV series *Smack the Pony* and to have acting roles in *Skins* and *Waterloo Road*).

Behind the scenes at Cream, James took the decision to tell Andy he was no longer part of the organisation. They'd met at the State, been through Quadrant Park together, and remained on good terms. Darren was still relentless, booking DJs. He found three or four big-name DJs every week for eight years. 'He lived, slept, dreamed it; he was all things Cream right through the week,' says James, of Darren. There was a lot of detail to attend to.

Image, too, was important for Cream, Renaissance, Ministry of Sound and the other big players, how everything was presented – the club decor, the look of the adverts, the albums and flyers.

Other venues, in contrast, were coming to an end. In 1993 the Eclipse decided to call it a day. The pressure of drug use in the club was one factor; police raids netted drugs of all kinds, and one young man, nineteen-year-old Christopher Doust, died after a night there (he'd bought drugs from a dealer outside). Another factor was the struggle to maintain credibility. The Eclipse had helped blaze a trail, but by 1993 most towns had some sort of dance club playing uplifting four-to-the-floor vocal house. Most clubbers could access the music – Radio 1 was championing 'Show Me Love', and the culture had gone mainstream. 'There were also people with better ideas,' says Stuart Reid. 'I had stood still and lost my way.'

Ministry of Sound and Cream started as clubs and then moved into releasing records. On the other hand, Metalheadz was first a label then became a club. It was inspired by Rage. One evening in Rage's early days, Kemistry took her boyfriend Goldie there. Storm tells the story: 'The night Goldie really "got it", we came back to our flat and he said, "Right, I want to make this music, you'll be the DJs, we'll have a label and a club, we'll make some T-shirts." That was our dream and that dream became the Metalheadz label.'

The first Metalheadz releases in 1994 had powerful basslines but a lustrous, even ethereal, sheen, and included artists such as Photek, DJ Peshay, Doc Scott and Wax Doctor. Then the label launched the weekly 'Metalheadz Sunday Sessions' club night at London's Blue Note on Hoxton Square in July 1995. It was a tiny dancefloor; the club was always packed, overflowing. Fabio had just started 'Speed' with LTJ Bukem at the Mars Bar in Charing Cross; he guested on the opening night. Goldie was very much the face of the night, his profile rising on the back of his debut album *Timeless*.

Tragically, Kemistry was killed in a road accident returning home from a gig in April 1999. Kemistry and Storm had become two of several female DJs who had good followings in the mid-1990s. There was Lisa Loud, who had moved on from the Future and was playing nationwide; Smokin' Jo with a key DJing residency at 'Trade' in the early 1990s (Trade, created by Laurence Malice, was a pioneering after-hours event opening from 4 a.m. until 1 p.m. on Sundays at Turnmills, a Farringdon venue owned by John Newman, the father of DJ Tall Paul); DJ Paulette, who made her mark at the Haçienda's 'Flesh' night; Anne Savage, big on the hard house scene in the 1990s (and half of the Tidy Girls, with Lisa Lashes); Andrea Parker, who attracted great critical acclaim for an album on the K7 label (she was later DJ for Radiohead on an American tour); and Charlotte Horne from Chester became DJ Lottie, and went on to feature at clubs including 'The Gallery' at Turnmills, 'Bugged Out' and 'Shindig', and to front shows on Radio 1. And that's a far from exclusive list.

The rave scene also attracted hooligans, hippies, students and druggies, and idealists and entrepreneurs cashing in. Spiral Tribe – who had been involved in warehouse raves in London until police action led them to relocate outside the capital and go on the move – were one of several itinerant sound systems plugged into the free party network. Another example, based in Nottingham, were DIY, who had a sound system they'd use to host free parties in the city and various club nights (including 'Bounce'). Then, outside Nottingham, they set up in rural locations usually: quarries, lay-bys, common ground on moors or in valleys. These sound systems often linked up with descendants of older counter-culture traditions represented by New Age travellers as well as, in Spiral Tribe's case, London's squatting community and the mid-1980s anarcho-punk scene represented by the likes of 'Club Dog', which had made its base at the George Robey on Seven Sisters Road, Finsbury Park (the venue was, briefly, the Powerhaus).

Spiral Tribe set up a system at the Stonehenge People's Free Festival, which took place in Longstock in 1991, and both DIY and Spiral Tribe were present at Castlemorton Common Festival in May 1992, a gathering of in excess of 20,000 New Age travellers, ravers and their sound systems, many of whom had been denied access to the annual Avon Free Festival near Bristol, which the police had halted. Many of those turned away made for Castlemorton in the Malvern Hills, Worcestershire. There, a free party lasted a full week, much to the consternation of the authorities and outrage in the media.

Castlemorton was in the minds of the legislators when the Criminal Justice and Public Order Act was being drafted; the Act targeted outdoor parties that played music 'wholly or predominantly characterised by the emission of a succession of repetitive beats'. But the Act wasn't a reaction to a certain kind of music, it was an attack on the lifestyles of the free party movement and on political dissent. Parts of the Act were clearly aimed at halting the anti-road-building movement and other ecologically minded travellers who had found common cause with the rave collectives.

The 'Megatripolis' nights on Thursdays at Heaven combined New Age ideology with rave culture. Megatripolis also promoted a number of parties at Bagley's in King's Cross and took a rented armoured car to a protest rally against the Criminal Justice Bill in July 1994, when around 30,000 ravers, eco-activists, squatters and travellers gathered in Trafalgar Square. There was a further rally in October 1994.

It could be argued, however, that by the time the Criminal Justice and Public Order Act came into force in November 1994, the days of big outdoor unlicensed raves, like Sunrise, were already numbered. Partly this was because of police harassment but also because ravers had found a focus at one or two permanent venues and at nights like Megatripolis and 'Megadog'; commercial festivals were also beginning to incorporate the energy of the rave scene (Orbital featured at

Glastonbury in June 1994). Not that causes espoused by the eco-activists, anarcho-punks and New Age travellers disappeared; they were that era's episode in the long revolution which has continued to more recent protest movements, like Stop the City, Reclaim the Streets and Occupy.

In December 1993, *Melody Maker* sent two reviewers to a Megadog event at the Rocket in London. They rejoiced in the multicoloured drapes and lightshows, the body-painters, the humanoids on stilts, and the mix of DJs and live acts. On the evening in question, Eat Static played, as did Transglobal Underground, with Psychick Warriors Ov Gaia playing from behind a roof-to-floor screen, which owed something to the 'ego-free' performances of the kind favoured by some acts in the 1960s. Megadog was like some post-ecstasy remix of blissed-out late 60s psychedelic happenings played out to thumping techno. The *Melody Maker* reviewers staggered out of the venue, proclaiming Megadog 'the very best club in the world'.

There was a strong tribal element to Megadog – a certain look, and a great sense of community. The events were a success too – the London events at the Rocket would attract upwards of 3,000 people. Thirty-three Megadog events also took place at Manchester Academy, a venue owned by the University of Manchester Students' Union, with some impressive line-ups assembled: during 1993, Orbital, the Drum Club, Aphex Twin, Banco De Gaia, Ultramarine and Underworld all featured at Manchester Megadog.

There were other psychedelic techno nights too. The original home of Megadog, the George Robey, hosted a club called 'The Far Side', firmly embedded in the squat/free-party scene. Flyers promised DJs 'spinning trippy trancey techno, delightfully deep house and pleasurable progressive for your entertainment'. And at least one flyer from 1994 also carried the slogan, 'Fight the Criminal Justice Bill'. The New Ardri was an old Irish club neatly placed between Manchester's universities and Hulme, an inner-city area which had become home to many squatters and artists. 'Pollen' took place at the New Ardri from 1992, and then 'Herbal Tea Party' took up residence there. Herbal Tea Party booked DJs including Sven Väth and Billy Nasty, and went hard on the visuals. Among its successes was reaching out and turning on many traditionalists who frequented rock clubs like Jilly's, introducing a new demographic to electronic dance music. On 21 June 1994 Orbital played live, with David Holmes the guest DJ. Holmes hailed from Belfast and, to this day, credits Terri Hooley and Good Vibrations as an inspiration. Like Hooley, Holmes got involved and made things happen. Among his activities were the 'Sugar Sweet' club night at Belfast Art College and recording as part of the Disco Evangelists.

By 1994, Ministry of Sound and Cream were established as two major superclub brands, but the likes of Goa-trance night 'Return to the Source' were determined to do things differently. Not every promoter wanted to be running a superclub and not every DJ chased superstar status. In January 1997 Andy Weatherall played a three-hour set at Herbal Tea Party. Weatherall had been among the pioneers – playing the top room at Shoom with his *Boy's Own* colleague Terry Farley – and continued making and playing music very much to his own agenda, leading not following. At the time of the Herbal Tea Party booking he was recording as Sabres of Paradise, having hosted the 'Sabresonic' club night for several years at Happy Jack's, London Bridge (which he once described to me as 'really substance-fuelled'). Every time a club took a step towards superclub status, a smaller club opened somewhere else offering a dissenting soundtrack.

'The Heavenly Social' is a good example of what could be enjoyed and achieved away from the superclubs. Studying in Manchester, the duo who would later become the Chemical Brothers – Tom Rowlands and Ed Simons – had hung out at the Haçienda, Most Excellent and Eastern Bloc. They loved the

Haçienda but wanted to do their own thing; they got involved in running 'Naked Under Leather' and played at various nights hosted by the magazine *Jockey Slut*. But Tom had always been making music, with a little studio of sorts set up in his student house. Tom and Ed began recording together as the Dust Brothers, and their recordings came to the notice of Heavenly Records based in London. Working and socialising in the capital with the Heavenly crew – Jeff Barrett, Martin Kelly, and Robin Turner – they collaborated on launching a Sunday evening, their first residency in London, in the basement of the Albany pub behind Warren Street tube station in October 1994. In retrospect, the Heavenly Social became a significant club, but according to Ed Simons the vision was that it would be 'very low key, or we thought it would be. The Albany probably fitted about a hundred and thirty people crammed in. It was similar to Naked Under Leather, putting a soundsystem downstairs, a couple of Technics just about balancing on a table.'

The facilities were a little different at Cream where the DJs each had a fully stocked minibar behind the DJ box, and nothing was low key. James Barton sees 1994–96 as the quintessential Cream era. By the end of the period, the club had moved into three rooms, and there were certain nights when there could be 3,500 people inside and another 2,000 outside. 'We weren't underground,' says James. 'What Cream represented was big, commercial, bright, colourful. That was the time when we'd announce our New Year's Eve parties and tickets would go on sale and we'd sell them all in a morning.'

Since her days at Eric's and fronting Big in Japan, Jayne Casey had continued making music (as Pink Military and Pink Industry) and worked at and with a number of Liverpool's cultural institutions, including the Bluecoat Gallery. She was aware how cultural activity could repopulate the spaces and rejuvenate the city. 'Jayne was the first to see the impact of what we were doing and the times we were living in,' says James.

Jayne studied some statistics provided by the local John Moores University and extrapolated from them that 70 per cent of applications to study there in 1996 had identified Cream as a key attraction of the city. 'Jayne said, "Your influence has extended beyond Saturday night,"' says James. 'We realised she was right. We never thought about student numbers. We never dreamed that we would be filling every hotel room in the city. In fact we never thought it would matter; why does it matter that the Holiday Inn, the Crown Plaza or whatever, that we fill their rooms for them? But it did matter, it does matter.'

Sometimes, when a business is at its most successful, it's also at its most vulnerable. The achievement of establishing Cream, the impact, the pressure, every Saturday, meant no escape and no rest for James, Darren and the team. 'To be honest we were being stretched a bit at this point, it was a bit crazy; we were stretched by the pace of change and what was going on.'

The 1990s were characterised by the astonishing market penetration of products like mobile phones, Microsoft Windows and Starbucks coffee shops, but the massive rise in the consumption of ecstasy is an even more remarkable example of booming sales and global spread in the decade. In the early and mid-1990s, there continued to be deaths connected with its use, at a rate of between eight and fifteen a year. Certain clubs became notorious: the Hangar 13 in Ayr suffered three ecstasy-related deaths during 1994 and was shut at the end of April 1995. Of all the ecstasy-related deaths during this period, one case became front-page news: that of Leah Betts in November 1995.

Leah Betts was only a very light user, but her last time wasn't the first time Leah had done ecstasy; she'd had Doves before, pills marked with a bird logo. Having had an ecstasy tablet at her eighteenth birthday party at her family home in Latchingdon in Essex, she began feeling unwell and drank lots of water. Overheating and dehydration were known risks of taking ecstasy, and she was following general advice. Unfortunately her water intake was far too extreme (at her inquest it was estimated that she'd drunk seven litres of water in a ninety-minute period), causing water intoxication and swelling in the brain, which led to her death. As a warning to others, her parents – Paul, a retired policeman, and stepmother Janet, a nurse – authorised the use of a photograph of Leah lying in a coma in the hospital.

The case was tragic, and triggered a huge debate in the media, much of it expressing horror that young people were putting themselves in danger, but there's no evidence ecstasy use dropped after Leah's death. In fact, by the end of the decade, it had surged, partly because the risks were known but considered by many users to be minimal (Professor David Nutt, an advisor on drugs policy to the UK government, was sacked for suggesting horse riding was a more dangerous pastime than taking E), and partly the result of a flood of good-quality pills known as Mitsubishi (they were embossed with the Mitsubishi logo). According to Dom Phillips in his book *Superstar DJs Here We Go!*, 'Drugs are cool, that is the problem. At least they are when you are twenty-one and feel indestructible.'

For Cream, the close relationship between house music and ecstasy was problematic. The issues that had almost destroyed the Haçienda in 1990 were now critical at Cream. Darren remarks: 'It became more and more a drug-dealer's paradise. As the gangs in Liverpool cottoned on to it, there was more money to be made and the bigger players got involved.'

James Barton knew his track record after the Underground and Quadrant Park didn't look amazing, but the Cream organisa-tion, with the help of Jayne Casey, worked on ways to avoid antagonising the police. At the Haçienda, Tony Wilson and Rob Gretton were music lovers and enthusiasts who had never expected that running a club was going to involve dealing with criminals wielding guns, but also, both were anti-authoritarian and libertarian and neither showed much eagerness to work with the police. The Manchester police wanted an easy life and would probably have closed every club in the town if they'd had their way. As a result, there was little common ground between the club and the police, especially when the Haçienda began employing a Salford door team the police were adamant had criminal connections. That was a move that looked like the club was selling out to the gangsters, doing a deal.

Cream decided to respond differently. They wanted the police to become their allies. James could see what was happening. 'We will come under pressure, we will have problems with gangs, we know we will, and we said, "We need you standing right next to us when it happens," and, guess what? They did. I don't think anyone at that time would have dreamed to have taken away the licence from the one big positive thing that was happening in the city.'

Liverpool was one of Europe's biggest centres for the international drugs trade in the mid-1990s, and wracked by drug-gang disputes. The murder of David Ungi in May 1995 sparked a gang war and almost fifty shooting incidents in the following twelve months, although most of these incidents were in neighbourhoods including Dingle and Kensington, with the trouble kept away from the city centre. James points out: 'Not only were Merseyside police sitting outside Cream on a Saturday night with guns but they were also outside McDonald's in the city centre. We had a tough chief constable who famously said, "You've got a gang, you've got guns, but we're a gang and we've got more guns." He made sure there was a visible deterrent on the street.'

The alliance between the club management and the police in the face of gang problems didn't mean the relationship was cosy. The police made sure the club were aware of their responsibilities as licensees, and undercover officers carried out extra-close surveillance at Cream for a ten-month period through and beyond the second half of 1995, leading to the arrest of a member of the security firm employed to operate the door, along with twenty-two other people. None of the Cream management was charged as police were satisfied they weren't in any way connected with the alleged drugs ring.

In the feverish atmosphere in and surrounding the club, Cream didn't quite control the chaos, but according to James they didn't have big problems ('A few threats,' he says). 'We made everyone aware that we were not interested in doing a deal,' says James. 'We'd hear about criminals, gangsters, or whatever, known troublemakers; we'd hear this person, that person, is out in town this weekend, and we'd make it known they weren't coming in. It was a siege mentality, we were standing up to them.'

You were protecting what you'd built for yourself, and the people of Liverpool?

'Yes, and the sad thing is that anything good attracts the shit and the shit eventually infect it and fuck it up.'

Police standing outside Cream with guns didn't dissuade clubbers from descending on the club in their thousands. According to James, it all appeared to add excitement, a dose of rebel chic, to proceedings. 'I remember [journalist] Ben Turner writing an article about turning the corner of Seel Street, seeing the police helicopter circling above the club and knowing this is the place; this is where the action is,' he says.

A lot happens when you're running a nightclub that the punters never know about.

'Yeah, so much! So much. But we always had a philosophy, whatever happens outside, inside the doors three thousand kids are having the night of their lives.'

CHAPTER THIRTEEN

Celebrities, more ecstasy, music is life

The first two years of the twenty-first century have been dubbed 'the acid house recession' by Dom Phillips, a former editor of *Mixmag*. In those years a boom in superclubs and superstar DJs turned to bust. Many of the rave pioneers had become the new establishment and, as such, were now ripe for mockery and rejection by the emerging generation; such are the cycles of revolution and reaction that power youth culture. In addition, nightclubs generally were struggling with changes to what was on offer after dark, as the liberalisation of licensing hours blurred the lines of demarcation between a bar and a club.

The Haçienda had been one of the first big club casualties when it closed in 1997. The numbers Cream was attracting, its ability to attract the name DJs and its profile all served to highlight that by the mid-1990s the Haçienda's sense of uniqueness had gone, as other clubs imitated or overtook it. There were still good times though, especially around 1993 and 1994 on a Saturday night with Graeme Park and Tom Wainwright installed in the DJ box. Another highpoint of the Haçienda in the 1990s was the weekly gay night Flesh founded by Paul Cons and Lucy Scher – the loudest, proudest gay club Manchester had ever experienced. The music was uplifting, the crowd both exhibitionist and friendly, and special events like the Miss Flesh contest and some of the other drag shows were unforgettable.

Kath McDermott, turned on to the notion of DJing by experiencing sets played by Tim Lennox at the No.1 club, became one of the Flesh residents along with, at various times, Paulette Constable, Dave Kendrick, Princess Julia and Guy Williams. A policy of positive discrimination was introduced. Flesh publicity material warned: 'The management reserve the right to refuse entry to known heterosexuals'. It was a great strategy. The glam gay night did what the metal detectors and huge bill for security staff seemed unable to do – it kept the gangsters away.

Nevertheless, the Haçienda's surrender of its place as a pioneer, plus ongoing problems with violence and the rising costs of security forced the final closure of the club in 1997. The last night turned out to be Saturday 28 June, with Elliot Eastwick and me DJing. It was packed that evening (one of a series of successful 'Freak' nights promoted by Paul Cons), but outside the club some dispute about who could and couldn't get in escalated, a car mounted the pavement, a mob from Salford and, it was said, from St Helens battled it out and then a doorman got a wheel brace slammed into his skull. If that wasn't bad enough, the trouble erupted in full view of a minibus of local councillors, licensing magistrates and police out on a research visit to Manchester's nightlife hotspots. On the following Monday the licence was revoked with immediate effect. The club had huge debts to the bank, the Inland Revenue and the brewery, and no viable options to retrieve the situation. Opened in 1982, it had lasted fifteen years, which – particularly in the context of some of the clubs around during and after the rave revolution (Shelley's, the Eclipse and Cream) – was maybe longer than could have been expected. Subsequently it was announced that the Haçienda would be demolished to make way for a block of apartments, and Tony Wilson expressed his disdain for any attempts to keep it open and turn it into a museum.

The Haçienda's role in the history of house music, the excitements of the Madchester era, and even the rejuvenation of the city, were fully fixed in the public mind. Like other significant clubs, it had acted as a catalyst. When it closed, a number of people inspired by the Haçienda were central to what was happening in Manchester and elsewhere – DJs, musicians, journalists, graphic designers, fashion designers, poets, promoters, photographers – and there are numerous examples of the club's legacy, the unfolding stories, including the rise of the Chemical Brothers.

Less than a year from the start of the Heavenly Social, Tom Rowlands and Ed Simons released their debut album *Exit Planet Dust*, which eventually sold over a million copies worldwide. The following year they released a compilation, *Live at the Social Volume 1* through Heavenly. It was the sound of joyful genre-hopping, drawing on the spirit of the music they'd heard when they'd first walked through the Haçienda doors and made the club their home, as well as evidence of the Social's influence on what became known as 'big beat' (later exemplified by Fatboy Slim's hits).

The Chemical Brothers were soon in high demand but discovered that on the club circuit they'd have to tailor their sets to the crowd. The eclectic approach they'd displayed in the early days at the Heavenly Social wouldn't transfer to the bigger rooms when people, whether or not they had MDMA coursing through their body, expected full-on euphoric house. 'We got thrown off the decks at Space in Ibiza, at nine in the morning,' says Ed. 'Everyone really wanted to go for it and we were playing Barry White records and stuff. So we learned pretty quickly that we had to rethink those kind of gigs. James and Darren put us on at the main room at Cream, the first time, and that's when we really had to step it up, and that's when we became as we are now, more full-on.'

Throughout this history we've seen instances of the composition and sound of the music people were writing and recording being inspired or deriving from what they heard and witnessed at clubs. The experiences, the sights, sounds and dynamics of the big-room dancefloors had an effect on the music the Chemical Brothers were making. One Saturday they went to Gatecrasher in Sheffield, where trance DJ Paul van Dyk was on the decks. 'The amount of energy there was phenomenal,' says Ed. 'When you see that kind of energy, of course it can seep through, and around "Hey Boy . . ." it did seep through into the production, that . . .'

He pauses, trying to find the right word for the sense of uplifting rush that polished trance encapsulated. Finally, he says, 'whoosh'. He says what seeped into the Chemical Brothers' sound at the time of 'Hey Boy Hey Girl' was 'the whoosh of what we heard being played there'. Released in 1999, the single 'Hey Boy Hey Girl' spent nearly three months in the UK charts. By this time they weren't just DJing, they had a live show too.

Live presentation of electronic dance music has gone a long way beyond the three-song PA circuit of 1991. Imaginative shows created by the Shamen, and the Megadog events, had demonstrated the potential for winning over a rock audience for acts with a full set, some stagecraft and a truck full of visuals. The Prodigy's career moved on a long way after their live debut in an old bingo hall in Coventry. Their second album, *Music for the Jilted Generation*, went to Number One in the UK album chart the week of release. Their third – which included the single 'Firestarter' – was released in 1997, the same year the band had a headlining slot at the Glastonbury Festival, having developed something of a crossover appeal to rock fans, and proving to be a strong live arena and festival act. They went on to headline Creamfields in 2006 and 2013.

In recent years, the Chemical Brothers have had headline slots at both Glastonbury and Creamfields. Ed Simons identifies Orbital's performance at Glastonbury in 1994 as a watershed moment, although he's aware there are some gig-goers still a little resistant to electronic dance music on major live stages and acts performing with elements pre-programmed, just as some people were aghast when Cabaret Voltaire turned up onstage without a drummer. Ed never thought he'd be a performer, but now embraces and enjoys the experience. 'What we took from rave culture was that idea that whatever you're doing, music or whatever, it's still about bringing people together, to feel that unity. I still think that's important.'

The success of clubs including Gatecrasher and Cream and, through 1999, the ubiquity of 'Hey Boy Hey Girl' – and its refrain 'superstar DJs here we go' – as well as the announcement of two big new club launches in London in the final months of 1999, were grounds for believing that dance music was still booming at the end of the 1990s. The big parties planned for Millennium Eve were being talked up by the dance music magazines of the time, which included *Mixmag*, *DJ*, *Muzik*, *Ministry* and *Jockey Slut*.

In September 1999 Home on Leicester Square opened in the heart of the West End. Darren Hughes fronted the club, but despite (or perhaps because of) a marketing campaign that drew such characters to the club as Chris Eubank, Paul Gascoigne and the guy who plays Ricky on the TV soap *EastEnders*, it didn't quite work out – it also triggered major changes at Cream. Originally, it had been a Cream project – a London venue for the Liverpool-based brand – but as the search for premises and negotiations with business partners began the process drove James and Darren apart. Eventually, in June 1998, Darren pulled out of Cream altogether, and set up Home with Ron McCulloch. He took Cream resident DJ Paul Oakenfold, who was hot property, topping the 'Best DJ in the World' poll in *DJ* magazine in 1998, as he would again in 1999. It's believed that every Saturday night Paul was being paid £20,000.

The other club launch in London in 1999 was Fabric, a three-room venue built near Smithfield Market, which owes its existence to Keith Reilly – the former owner of a CD and tape manufacturing business which he sold in 1989 – and Cameron Leslie. Fabric became a big club that wasn't a superclub by avoiding superstar DJs or Paul van Dyk and trance and euphoric breakdowns, and events sponsored by Lynx.

DJ fees for New Year's Eve at the turn of the millennium were astronomical. Judge Jules got paid £100,000 for playing Gatecrasher. Fatboy Slim pocketed £140,000 for four gigs in one night, and Shoom founder Danny Rampling took £50,000 for a gig in Cape Town. Promoters were paying these fees in the expectation of a big payday, but that isn't what transpired. In the face of terrible ticket sales, Geoff Oakes was forced to cancel a big Renaissance event at Trentham Gardens in Staffordshire and downsize to the Nottingham city centre club Media, in the process suffering a loss of £200,000. Cream's events in Brixton and Cardiff were poorly attended. Gatecrasher's New Year's Eve event in Sheffield was a disaster.

There was a sense of iconoclasm in the air, a backlash against the greed of DJs and superclubs, but the issue wasn't just the money, there was also a perception that what had started as a cultural revolution had become boring and conservative. *Ministry*, the monthly dance music magazine launched by Ministry of Sound, reflected dance music's retreat from any socially progressive ideals it might once have aspired to, invariably featuring drug surveys and pictures of DJs with their new cars inside the magazine, and bikini-clad girls on the front cover. It was as if the magazine had lost heart in the music.

The backlash affected more than just the superclubs and superstar DJs; several quality nights that had contributed a lot to the 1990s came to an end, including Pure in Edinburgh and Progress in Derby. In 2002 the Que Club in Birmingham closed (it reopened with a refit in 2007). In 2002 Trade at Turnmills came to an end, and Tall Paul of Turnmills admitted, 'The era of the superstar DJ and so-called superclub has come to a dramatic end.' Turnmills eventually closed in March 2008.

In 2002, three years after Darren Hughes' departure, Cream closed its weekly night, but revived its business by concentrating on occasional nights, and the annual Creamfields festival (which has survived and prospered). In the meantime, things weren't going well for Darren; Home on Leicester Square was losing its way and struggled financially. After eighteen months of trading, the venue was £11m in the red. Carrying all those losses, Home went into receivership in April 2001, although the timing of the move was triggered by an emergency meeting of Westminster Council ruling that the club should close with immediate effect after a police surveillance operation found 'open and serious Class A drug-dealing and usage'. Darren moved to Ibiza and relaunched Sundays at Space with a new organisation called We Love, and a new resident DJ: Sasha.

In June 2007, Gatecrasher in Sheffield, the club that had helped the Chemical Brothers to put some whoosh in 'Hey Boy Hey Girl', was destroyed in a fire believed to have started in the DJ box. But the best days were over for Gatecrasher, having lost the loyalty of its customers and its status as an industry leader even though it had expanded its operations, establishing new venues called Bed in Sheffield and Leeds. Gatecrasher hit serious financial trouble, and in April 2013 entered administration. The losses weren't small; the club owed £3.5m to 233 creditors including DJs, agents and printers, and £500,000 to the Inland Revenue. Bed in Leeds had already proved to be problematic. West Yorkshire Trading Standards had raided the club and confiscated over 600 litres of counterfeit vodka (tests revealed that the alcohol contained isopropanol, tertiary butanol and chloroform). Gatecrasher were fined £5,000.

Home never made it to its second birthday party, Gatecrasher turned into a bit of a mess, but Fabric survived, although not without some scares. Its adventurous music policy won enough loyalty to enable it to make it through the acid house recession. Instead of featuring the same name DJs playing the same formulaic sets, Fabric tended to concentrate on incorporating some of the more marginal, niche club scenes into its programming.

Through the late 1990s, away from the big main rooms at the major clubs, there had been a few signs that formulas were being challenged. The compilation *Live at the Social Volume 1* – including diverse tracks from the likes of Red Snapper and Cash Money – fed into a growing demand for eclectic DJs. Some of the DJs who had stepped off the circuit when acid house swept through the country made a return in the second half of the 1990s. Greg Wilson had stopped working and started selling some of his records, but found his place again with gigs including a guest slot at 'Yellow' at the Boardwalk in Manchester, and then, with more fanfare, at the Electric Chair at the Music Box. DJ Mr Scruff and others who would dig deep to find a selection of funk, breaks and soul, steering clear of the obvious, were rising in popularity.

This splintering had plenty of precedents. It was reminiscent of what had happened once the Mecca halls and the big dance orchestras dominated, only for self-organising music fans wanting to shake things up to find some basements in which to showcase weirder jazz. And in the aftermath of all-conquering disco music came the futurist nights, jazz funk and other small scenes through the 1980s.

The trend towards a fragmented nightclub scene picked up pace in the twenty-first century, especially once social media, podcasts and file-sharing gave routes to promoters, DJs and musicians, and others, to build networks outside the control of the major players. But even in the late 1990s, there were dozens of credible, rather than commercial, and marginal and small-scale club nights, each playing one or several underground genres, from deep house to breaks; Fabric made a point of booking DJs that represented that world.

At the Blue Note on Monday nights, Talvin Singh, together with promoter Sweety Kapoor, had established a night called

'Anokha', which Björk used to attend (Talvin had played percussion on her 1993 album *Debut*). Once at Anokha, Lee 'Scratch' Perry turned up and grabbed the microphone (people who were there remember it was fun but also remember that once he had the microphone he wouldn't relinquish it). In 1998 Singh released his solo debut album *OK*, which won him the Mercury Music Prize. His sound, tabla and other percussion, with drum & bass influence, was never going to be a superclub main-room sound, but it was perfect for Fabric.

Fabric was built on good first principles: not playing safe. Keith Reilly once explained the booking policy: 'There are certain styles of music we don't book because, quite frankly, you can hear them everywhere else.' He also recalled a moment that he thought summed up the loyalty and quality of the crowd – a Friday when Talvin Singh was performing. 'He lost a five-grand watch in the club. And someone handed it in. Talvin couldn't believe it.'

One of the genres that flourished away from the superclubs was UK garage, an intriguing hybrid sound incorporating drum & bass and house, big basslines, syncopated rhythms and sweet, soulful vocals that bubbled up through clubs in London like 'Twice As Nice' at the Colosseum in Vauxhall, 'Cookies & Cream', and 'Sun City'. Many of these were held on Sunday evenings, as this was the only night venues would hire out to what was then a fledgling scene.

The tougher end of UK garage – songs like So Solid Crew's 'Dilemma', Wookie's 'Storm' and the instrumental dub versions of hits like MJ Cole's 'Crazy Love' – fed into grime and dubstep, which emerged via the evolving playlist at club nights like 'FWD>>' on Thursday nights at Plastic People in Shoreditch, and larger parties like the 'DMZ' nights at Mass in Brixton.

Dubstep was primarily, but not only, a London sound. There were a number of significant nights elsewhere, including 'Subloaded' in Bristol and 'Murkage' in Manchester. Word spread online, via radio shows and podcasts from the likes of Rinse FM, and specialist BBC DJs including Gilles Peterson and Mary Anne Hobbs. Journalist Alex Needham described dubstep to American readers of the magazine *Interview* as 'less a party and more a sonic insurrection. Anyone who likes to experience music at mind-alteringly loud volumes should attend a dubstep night immediately. The latest sound to infect the London underground is a combination of skittering beats, ass-quaking bass lines and eerie atmospherics.'

The urge to do something different, the energy of young promoters and music fans, and various influences and innovations continually refresh the soundtrack to a Saturday night, but some of the most important changes in nightlife have come as a result of changes in the licensing trade and government legislation. In the second half of the 1990s, the divide between pubs and clubs began to break down. Previously, pubs were required to close at 11 p.m. and customers moved on to clubs if they wanted to dance or to continue to drink, but new style café bars, taking advantage of more relaxed regulations, were opening with DJs and designated dancefloors, free entry, and a bar open until 1 or 2 a.m. By the first decade of the twenty-first century, for many chains and independent club owners, this was having a destructive effect, even on clubs with a long history.

Eighty years after it had first opened at the Streatham Locarno, and after he'd been owner for fifteen years, ghost-buster Fred Batt closed Caesars and put it up for sale in 2010. Further changes to the Licensing Act (in force from November 2005) increased the hours that pubs and bars could stay open, and gave nightclubs the potential to open until dawn. Fred claimed that a proportion of his potential clientele were remaining in bars rather than moving on to Caesars. When developers bought the site and were granted permission to knock it down to build a residential and retail development, marking the end of eighty years of history at the Streatham Locarno, Batt put the contents of the club up for sale, everything from a statue of a chariot and four horses that used to adorn the entrance (and once featured in a Spice Girls video) to the gold-legged chairs and a stuffed Siberian tiger.

Despite the travails and nightclub closures during the last fifteen years, clubland has an ability to rejuvenate itself. There are always people inspired by new music, great nights out and full dance-floors, and some of them proved resourceful enough to contribute to the next wave. Take the story of Yousef Zaher from Crosby, Merseyside, and his 'Circus' night. 'Serious music and fun times' is the club's self-description.

One Friday at the beginning of the 1990s, aged sixteen, Yousef went over to Shelley's. He didn't get home until Tuesday and his mum asked him where he'd been. He told her the truth: he'd been to Stoke, and on to Derby and then Birmingham. Then Droitwich, and finally Gloucester (there was a girl involved, and she'd paid his train fare home). Just over ten years later, Yousef had a career as a DJ, had enjoyed a spell as a resident at Ministry of Sound, played regularly at Renaissance, and built a close rela-tionship with Cream. In 2002, together with Richard McGinnis, he launched his own night, Circus. Yousef at Circus has played alongside iconic DJs like Sven Väth, Loco Dice, Heidi, Laurent Garnier, MK and Derrick Carter. And with Sasha – the DJ whose work had sent him into ecstasy and to Gloucester all those years before.

A decade and a half on from that millennium moment, which signalled a backlash against superstar DJs, disc-only nights are even more prevalent. DJs are still everywhere, from playing vinyl in the tiny basement of a hipster bar, to major high street clubs like Tiger Tiger where you can dance yourself dizzy to a DJ on a laptop feeding the dancefloor with obvious chart hits. On the thriving underground house music scene, DJs like MK and Cajmere – who were first talked about in the early and mid-1990s – are, twenty years later, filling bigger halls with younger fans. In addition, new DJs have made their mark. This has led to powerful match-ups, across generations and continents; clubbers attending a recent season of events at the Warehouse Project in Manchester had the opportunity to hear veteran DJs like Andy Weatherall, Kerri Chandler (USA) and Laurent Garnier, as well as Tale of Us (Berlin), Nina Kraviz (Russia), Yousef and Ben Pearce.

It appears the backlash against the big-name commercial DJs around the turn of the millennium has turned out to be temporary. If some of the star names from then have slipped from favour, a new set of superstar DJs has emerged, pulling bigger crowds and earning even bigger fees than their 1990s counterparts. By 2014, the 'Best DJ in the World' annual poll by *DJ* magazine was dominated by the likes of Hardwell, Armin van Buuren, Tiësto, Steve Aoki and Calvin Harris. Among those featuring in the top five in 1999, Paul Oakenfold had dropped out of the top hundred, and Paul van Dyk was hanging on in at Number 38. The highest-placed female DJs were Nervo, twin-sister DJs (Olivia and Miriam) who started out their career as songwriters (they co-wrote 'When Love Takes Over', a hit for David Guetta).

One development over the last few decades is the blurring of roles that Nervo exemplify. Now, more big-name DJs are also music-makers (producers and/or songwriters); it's the same across the genres, and from the underground to the mainstream, from Dusky to Skrillex to David Guetta. DJs who play the records, make the records, many of them very successfully; invariably every single Calvin Harris releases, for example, goes to the top of the charts. His hit rate is phenomenal. And when he DJs, he pulls huge crowds and his fees reflect that. In the year to April 2014, Calvin Harris earned £39.7m, more than twice the amount earned by the second highest paid DJ of the year, David Guetta.

In addition, in a development it would be easy to regret, a lot of people with a public profile or celebrity status have turned into part-time DJs, including actors, TV presenters, and – at the top of the celebrity tree – Paris Hilton and Kim Kardashian. On 6 April

2013 celebrity DJ history was made at the Newcastle club Digital when customers paid £6 to hear the former Newcastle United centre forward Tino Asprilla DJing alongside Bez, the maracas player from Happy Mondays.

One type of club has remained impervious to recessions of all kinds and distant from the cutting edge of music: the members-only, VIP-heavy, expensive London clubs frequented by bankers, starlets, rich Russians and members of the royal family. Tramps on Jermyn Street in Mayfair, where George Best and Frank Worthington liked to party, was apparently favoured by Prince Andrew (Virginia Roberts, who claims to have been there with him in 2001, also alleges, 'Andrew was the most incredibly hideous dancer I had ever seen') but his nephews, William and Harry, preferred to be with a younger set at Boujis in South Kensington.

In June 2010 Anna Chapman was arrested on suspicion of working for a spy ring created by the Russian Federation's external intelligence agency, the SVR. She was a lovely-looking young lady who had been a regular at Boujis. This triggered a flurry of worry. Had she met the princes? Had there been a security leak? One journalist at the time, though, drew on her own several visits to Boujis and pointed out, 'The question perhaps shouldn't be, did Anna Chapman get to meet a prince, but if she had, other than their taste for vast quantities of alcohol and cheesy tunes, what information could she possibly have gleaned?'

Annabel's went for a relaunch in 2007 and pulled in some new members way beyond the aristocracy, including Russian oligarchs and models and others from the celebrity circuit. The sense that it had glitz and glamour beyond the wildest imagination of any commoner was undermined in the autumn of 2005 when Annabel's was revealed to have been the venue where Labour cabinet minister David Blunkett schmoozed a blonde estate agent, Sally Anderson, who engaged the services of PR agent Max Clifford and sold her story to the newspapers. Later it transpired some of the story she told the tabloids was erroneous and she was forced to apologise. 'He did not callously use me for sex and then abandon me as I claimed in the article,' Anderson said. Through and after Blunkett's crisis and the banking crisis, in a city with a rising number of billionaires, Annabel's has thrived. The business is worth in the region of £90m.

Through the last twenty years, there has been a plethora of musical trends and sub-genres, but one element of the rave era that's survived from the pioneering days in the late 1980s has been enthusiastic ecstasy use, although the quality of the drugs sold and their cost has been variable. In 2001, when the undercover police action that led to the closure of Home arrested a 'dealer' in possession of sixteen ecstasy pills, the retail value of such a haul was in the region of £50. The price of ecstasy had been dropping from highs of around £15 or £20 in 1988. By 2001 pills were around £3 each, and even that was subject to regional fluctuations (in some places in the north of England and Scotland you'd be getting three for a fiver). Three million British people have taken ecstasy on one occasion or more. Of the so-called 'club drugs', M-Cat (more properly known as mephedrone, but also known as 'meow meow') and ketamine usage continued to grow despite over a hundred recorded ketamine-related deaths in the last ten years and numerous reports of its propensity to destroy the bodies or unbalance the minds of users.

Given that we've followed several drug trails through our history – tinctures of laudanum in the early nineteenth century, sandwich shops selling drugs in Soho in the early twentieth century, heroin use among jazz musicians just after the Second World War, and speed in mod clubs like the Scene – it's unsurprising that there's drug use connected to life after dark in our current era. At the turn of the millennium, approximately 175,000 people a month were using ecstasy. With an excess of supply, the drug was easy to access and cheap to buy. Usage was increasing, as were ecstasy-related deaths. There were fifty-six ecstasy-related deaths in Britain in 2001 and seventy-two in 2002, more than three times the number in 1995, the year Leah Betts died. Since then, the annual number of deaths has stayed between thirty and sixty.

It remains illegal to make or sell ecstasy, so there's no regulation or mandatory testing of pills. Media reports of fatalities often talk of death by 'fake' ecstasy but all pills are fake to a greater or lesser degree; no one buys or sells pure ecstasy (the average street purity is 58 per cent). Pills sold as ecstasy can contain many other ingredients – some contain no MDMA at all – and users are vulnerable to poor-quality or adulterated pills. In 2013 there were five deaths in Merseyside and Derbyshire linked to the same batch of pills, which were found to contain mostly PMA (Paramethoxyamphetamine), which has different effects to ecstasy (less of a stimulant, more psychedelic) but crucially takes longer to kick in, which can lead to users taking more, with fatal results. In January 2015 four deaths were linked to red triangular pills with a Superman logo that were found to contain potentially lethal doses of PMMA (Paramethoxymethamphetamine); three of the deaths were in East Anglia.

In June 1971 American President Richard Nixon announced a 'war on drugs', pouring resources into drug control agencies and ignoring calls for any kind of legalisation. British politicians also like to use the phrase 'the war on drugs' to describe their strategy. But this war on drugs has done nothing to diminish the demand for ecstasy; instead there's a huge unregulated and uncontrolled industry supplying pills of variable or even fatal quality. And, mirroring the spread of speakeasies in prohibition-era America, the number of unlicensed raves remains high.

Unlicensed raves are an echo of that chant the supporters of Sam Lane at the Union Saloon in Shoreditch, east London, challenged the authorities with back in 1840: 'Freedom for the people's amusements'. They attract people looking to bypass traditional venues, dress codes, strict sound-level limits and restrictions on recreational drug use. Unlicensed raves take place in all parts of the country, and are often a haven for fans of music unplayed or undiscovered by high street clubs, although they can also be a dangerous, badly organised rip-off.

In May 2014 seven sound systems, 2,000 people and 400 vehicles turned up on a Bank Holiday Saturday at the South Downs beauty spot Devil's Dyke, near Brighton. The event went largely unnoticed and the police did little to prevent it, as a spokesman for Sussex Police explained: 'Officers have been on the site and the gathering is good-humoured though very noisy. At present the assessment is that it would not be possible or safe to close the event down, given the number of police officers available.'

The Devil's Dyke rave eventually attracted media coverage after a wandering mountain biker up on the South Downs on the Sunday morning chanced upon it and recorded video footage, which was then posted online. The press descended on the locality but although there were some concerned locals, not much controversy stirred. The *Daily Telegraph* spoke to 61-year-old resident Colin Warburton from Poynings, who said of the rave, 'It doesn't bother me one bit. To be honest I'd had a few drinks myself on Saturday, so when it started up I didn't really notice. As long as they're having a laugh up there then I'm OK with it.'

Meanwhile in British cities there are some areas where the recession has bitten hard, leaving buildings abandoned, while in other areas properties have been closed down prior to being demolished or redeveloped. These acres of unused buildings have given organisers of unlicensed raves a new lease of life. At a 'Project X' party in a disused building in Wapping in December 2013, a teenager was stabbed. In April 2014 another Project X party attracted over a thousand people to a 36-hour rave in a repossessed college building in east London.

As use of empty buildings for unlicensed raves appeared to be on the increase, warnings to secure potential sites were issued. A huge former Royal Mail delivery office in East Croydon had been closed to make way for flats but no preventative action was taken, and in June 2014 almost 2,000 people descended on the site. Missiles including furniture and fire extinguishers were thrown at police attending but, in an echo of incidents in the late 1980s and early 1990s, it was decided that the large numbers of party-goers precluded any drastic police action for fear of triggering severe public disorder; the police withdrew. One party-goer, fifteen-year-old Rio Andrew, died after reportedly drinking a cocktail of beer laced with ketamine (a nineteen-year-old was hospitalised after drinking from the same bottle). One of the alleged organisers was later arrested on suspicion of corporate manslaughter, money-laundering and fraud, and around thirty other people present at the rave were arrested for offences including violent disorder, criminal damage, possession of Class A drugs and affray.

Police clampdowns on licensed premises, meanwhile, were sporadic. But in May 2015 the iconic Glasgow club the Arches had its late licence revoked. In Liverpool, three licensed premises were raided in the space of just a few days in February 2015. Over a hundred police officers raided Garlands on Eberle Street in the early hours, arresting two people and discovering quantities of Class A and other drugs (including six bags of M-Cat, found behind the bar on the night of the raid). At a later court hearing police put forward undercover evidence of drug-dealing in the club and Garlands was ordered to shut for three months. The Lomax, on Cumberland Street, was also raided and issued with closure orders. A few days later, during a raid on a third venue, the Republik vodka bar on Bold Street, seven men were arrested.

For Jayne Casey, there's a frustration that even when customers in clubs know the scrutiny from the authorities and the pressure from the police they still continue to take, sell and pass drugs openly. 'It's very sad when you see a young kid's life ruined because he gets arrested for passing a drug to his mates. I've seen it many times. It's very easily avoided; people need to think about it. It's a two-way street . . . Ultimately if you buy your drugs from a club or take drugs openly, you are putting the club in jeopardy. Anyone who says they love their "local" club but continues to buy drugs from it, or takes drugs openly in it, needs to seriously check themselves.'

If evidence suggests ecstasy is not going away, then neither is dance music. In the three decades since acid house, a number of dance music genres have disappeared, only to percolate through the underground and emerge again, refashioned for a new generation. The revival of rave sounds, hardcore MCs and euphoric breakdowns in the music of Chase & Status and the renewed interest in deep house are two examples. Another genre that has recently re-emerged is disco, which over the last forty years has been diluted, exploited and then mocked and misrepresented. In recent years, disco has been back in favour, triumphantly led by a renaissance in the career of Nile Rodgers and Chic. In the summer of 2014 Chic took to the stage in front of 70,000 people at Bestival under the sparkly splendour of the largest mirrorball ever made, just over ten metres in diameter.

While the young crowd create new movements and adapt older ones, clubbers who first went out in the early acid house era have experienced a wave of anniversaries and reunions; twenty-five years since this, twenty years since that. But it's curious how quickly rave culture developed nostalgic tendencies. In the early 1990s, just as the flow of sub-genres and new releases accelerated, retro nights took off. In May 1992, at Shelley's, a whole eighteen months after the club had opened, Entropy promotions was running Friday nights with DJs Mickey Finn, Grooverider, Top Buzz and Carl Cox. The strapline on the flyers was 'Bring Back the Good Times'.

Among the pioneering DJs we've met in our history, Mike Pickering still DJs occasionally, but has had two further careers since his days piloting the Haçienda through the rave revolution: the founder of M-People, and ten years as an A&R man at Sony, where he has been responsible for signing Kasabian and Calvin

Harris. Sasha is never out of regular DJ work, performing world-wide from the Met in Brisbane to the Warung Beach Club in Brazil, House of Blues in Chicago, Sankey's in Manchester and Milk in Moscow. He's busier than most of his contemporaries, most of whom are now in their fifties, of course.

A number of clubs have been celebrated and memorialised in films. Piers Sanderson made a documentary about the Blackburn raves called *High on Hope*. Chris Good collected memories of Venus in Nottingham, Progress in Derby, and Turnmills in London (and elsewhere) in the film *One More*. The Haçienda featured prominently in Michael Winterbottom's 2002 film *24 Hour Party People* and in a documentary called *Do You Own the Dancefloor?* released in June 2015. An auction was held in 2000 when the Haçienda was demolished, and *Do You Own the Dancefloor?* interviews some of the people who bought pieces of Haçienda dancefloor or other items from the club, including an emergency exit sign, a urinal and the mirrorball.

It's endearing to see how attached people are to an object that reminds them of a landmark time in their life, as well as their pride in owning a little piece of Manchester music history, but one of the appeals of *Do You Own the Dancefloor?* is that the scattering of these cherished objects – widely distributed among fanatics, regulars and ex-employees – reflects the process by which significant venues leave a legacy of individual memories but also scatter their influence beyond the four walls of the building.

There are always memories and a legacy, even when well-loved venues have been transformed beyond recognition. Fury Murry's in Glasgow is now a lap-dancing club called Forbidden. The Place in Hanley now houses a swingers club called Adventures in Lust. The former Gardening Club in Covent Garden is an Apple Store. The Fforde Grene pub, where the Sex Pistols made their Leeds debut, is now an independently owned supermarket. Where Basement Jaxx hosted their 'Rooty' nights – the Telegraph on Brixton Hill – is now a Tesco Express.

Rafters in Manchester has also become a Tesco Express; the basement club where Colin Curtis and Mike Shaft played street soul, Tony Wilson first saw Joy Division play, and Morrissey was rude about Depeche Mode in the *Record Mirror*, was trading as the Music Box through and beyond the 1990s, hosting, among other nights, the monthly club night Electric Chair. In April 2010, however, owner John Bagnall decided to close the Music Box, claiming those changes to licensing legislation bound up with 24-hour drinking had had the same detrimental effect on his business as it had on Fred Batt's at the old Streatham Locarno. According to Mr Bagnall, late-night bars offering free admission and DJs – and a general reluctance of customers to pay admission to venues of any sort – had wrecked his finances. 'It's very sad. It's heartbreaking. The numbers are, over the last two or three years, 50 per cent down and we can't pay the bills any longer, the money's run out.'

In the meantime, however, the team behind one of the Music Box's strongest nights, Electric Chair, had helped launch 'HomoElectric' at Legends, the old Twisted Wheel/Placemate 7 venue on Whitworth Street. After its time as Placemate 7, the club had various names but through most of its last twenty-five years the former Twisted Wheel was a gay club. For a while from April 1988, part of the club housed a lesbian night, 'Radcliffe's'. Another part of the club was known as the Mineshaft where there were Sunday all-nighters (11 p.m. to 6 a.m.). According to adverts in 1989 in the magazine *Scene Out*, there was also a lunch served from 1 p.m. on Sundays. In October 1992 the Chemical Brothers (then the Dust Brothers) staged one of their Naked Under Leather nights there. In April 1994 the police raided the Mineshaft and made thirteen arrests; seven months later, the manager was convicted under the Disorderly Houses Act 1751 for allowing men to have sex with each other in a back room at the club.

Throughout the 1980s and 1990s, the club had very little refurbishment. It was happy to crumble while other parts of Manchester were being tidied up or torn down and turned into smooth-lined apartments, retail and office space, and mid-range hotels. In 1997 HomoElectric hosted an event in part of Legends, with a plan to do some irregular nights; after much success in the venue, it took over all the rooms and continued hosting one-offs and special events. A quarter of a mile away, the area around Canal Street had emerged as the centre of Manchester's gay village, an area replete with bars and clubs. But in the process of becoming regenerated, the gay village had, to some potential customers, been tamed with too many operators taking safe options and delivering a constricted, uncreative choice of nights out. Even a branch of the Slug and Lettuce pub chain settled on Canal Street.

Musically and in all other ways, HomoElectric looked to break the mould by setting up at the old Twisted Wheel. Other club nights established themselves there too, including 'Bollox', which also put an alternative twist on gay nights out. Luke Unabomber, one of HomoElectric's founders, later recalled why the HomoElectric team set up in an unregenerated part of town well away from the stag nights, theme bars, hen parties and the Slug and Lettuce. 'Where we did it meant that only good people came, because the venue was full of weird, dark corridors with stained walls, which weren't going to attract your middle-England, cul-de-sac fundamentalists who were worried by anything left of centre.'

In the early years of the twenty-first century, across Manchester, in equally unprepossessing surroundings, a midweek cabaret-cum-muso carnival called 'Club Suicide' operated in a grotty pub on Withy Grove called the John Willie Lees. Generally the clientele had been old men, off-duty bus drivers, skiving workers from the nearby Co-operative offices and – back when the area was busy with publishing houses and printworks – newspaper workers too. Club Suicide also took place at Charlie's on Harter Street, an odd Chinese karaoke bar. The club provided Patrick Wolf and M.I.A. with their first Manchester shows. Bill Campbell was a

Suicide regular: 'For me, the early Club Suicide nights at John Willie Lees reasserted a DIY, John Peel-esque spirit in Manchester, bringing together various generations of misfits, and giving them a new home. It reignited a sense of just-do-it in me personally and in the friends I made there.'

In addition to HomoElectric, other nights were also remaking and remodelling Manchester's LGBT club scene, among them 'Poptastic' and 'Club Brenda'. Poptastic mixed up the music – lots of indie – and Club Brenda incorporated eclectic music with stand-up, spoken-word and dramatic interventions from the likes of performance artists Fiona Bowker, Divine David and Chloe Poems. Jayne Compton, the driving force behind Club Brenda, went on to run the Switchflicker record label.

Boasting an eclectic music policy and a mix of performers, DJs, genders and sexualities, these nights challenged stereotypes but entertained too. On a mission, HomoElectric published a fanzine designed to complement the club night. It gave the people behind the night a chance to spread the word of their favourite music – anything from the New York Dolls to deep house – and their philosophy of avoiding airbrushed reality, fake tans and generic music. *The HomoElectric Chronicle* carried heartfelt polemics targeting personality-free celebrities and body fascism. Slogans adorned their flyers, including one in 2006: 'Music is life, gym is the coffin, be ugly'.

From Club Suicide to Club Brenda, via HomoElectric – this was some of the most impressive activity from Manchester's post-Haçienda generation, unencumbered by nostalgia, eclectic and uncommercial. That the venues they chose were out on the margins, in the underpopulated, undeveloped parts of the town, underlined their cultural distance from the mainstream, the distance too between their club and everything on Canal Street, or Paul Oakenfold on £20,000 a night, or the front covers of *Ministry*, or Annabel's with its caviar tartare fingers for £450 and £550 bottles of champagne, or the celebrities and princes inside

Boujis and the paparazzi outside. They were the sort of places Patrick Lilley was looking for in 1977 or like that Soho club in the 1920s described earlier in our history as a shrine of 'anti-convention and the home of talented rebels'. Abigail Ward of the Manchester District Music Archive says that Club Brenda in particular welcomed 'the outsiders, the strange ones'.

OUTRO

Michael Stipe's shoe, the cocktail from Hull,
worlds emerge

Hammersmith Palais, with a history going back to 1919, opened its doors for the last time in 2007. As the closure neared, two gigs were organised for the weekend of 31 March and 1 April; the first night featured Damon Albarn and Paul Simonon's band – the Good, the Bad & the Queen – with the Fall headlining the next night. The only beer available was Foster's. Mark E. Smith wore a suit and a crisp white shirt, and near the end of the Fall's set the last stage invader at the Hammersmith Palais made his entrance when Joe Ashworth from the Macclesfield band the Hot Bananas clambered out of the audience and danced around near Mark and then jumped back into the crowd. Joe Ashworth later left the Hot Bananas and formed the Magic Otters.

Hammersmith Palais was demolished in 2012. Everything eventually becomes history. There's no trace of Barbarella's or the Rum Runner in Birmingham, the Dug Out in Bristol or the Reno in Manchester or the Club A Go Go in Newcastle. The Hotel Leofric, where Pete Waterman DJ'd the night Black Sabbath played, closed in 2008 and became a Travelodge. The hotel was sold by Travelodge just five years later and the new owners converted the property into student flats. A block of student flats also now stands on the site of the Limit in Sheffield, which closed in January 1991. Bristol Locarno's ballroom was demolished in 1998 to make way for student accommodation, leaving only the ice-rink and the cinema. The cinema, though – which had closed in 1996 – was given a huge makeover and turned into a nightclub. It now houses the O2 Academy music venue. Of the original Bristol complex, only the ice-rink remains.

What of the clubs that have survived since opening in the early 1980s? The Leadmill has had to adapt, losing city council subsidies, dispensing with some of the artistic and cultural ideals it had when it was founded and, dictated by commercial pressures, now features a relatively straightforward programme of gigs and club nights with drinks promotions. Another survivor is the Escape in Brighton, although it's now trading as Audio, with a bar below and a club above. The Zap Club turned into Digital, then the Coliseum (it's now the Arch). In the 1980s, the Escape, along with the Zap, were two of a long line of important venues in Brighton, where the entertainments on offer were both a marker and a maker of cultural change.

Through many of the earlier chapters we've visited a number of major urban conurbations – with plenty of diversions to places including Stoke, Old Hill, St Albans and Wigan – and documented their range of nightlife, but for people in smaller towns life can seem restricted. There isn't so much variety. Local bands may not have anywhere to play, acts on national tours don't visit, and in the clubs it's likely no one has the inclination to go beyond the obvious.

In their time, venues like TJ's in Newport, Moles in Bath and the Forum in Tunbridge Wells have all been invaluable in their towns. Hull, City of Culture in 2017, has never had much of a reputation for its music scene; it's on the almost-forgotten edge of the country. The work of venues and promoters to attract touring bands there, and also to provide a platform for local talent, has been against all odds, and usually on a shoestring – important, but precarious. In the summer of 2012, the Lamp in Norfolk Street in Hull closed, having lost the goodwill of its bank.

In the context of the city's place economically and geographically, the ability of the Adelphi on De Grey Street to make things happen in Hull is worth celebrating. It began life as a working men's club, which was then opened as a music venue by Paul Jackson in 1984. Relatively rough and ready, the Adelphi is unlikely to win design awards or attract a glitzy crowd, but Paul is proud of the diversity of its music programming policy and its friendly reputation. 'We may not have the glossiest leaflets, or the biggest marketing budget,' he says. 'What we do have is far more important, and far more interesting than that. It was, and is, a meeting place for smart, talented and creative people, as well as being somewhere to see fantastic live performances from outside the mainstream.'

In the early 1990s, the Adelphi was one of several venues included on every half-decent emerging rock act's tour itinerary (others included the Windsor Old Trout, the Boardwalk in Manchester, King Tut's Wah Wah Hut in Glasgow, the Princess Charlotte in Leicester and John Keenan's Duchess of York in Leeds). Radiohead appeared at the Adelphi three times in 1992 and 1993. Shows at the Adelphi in more recent years have featured the likes of Courtney Barnett, Holy Orders, Paper Aeroplanes and Las Kellies, with some veterans making return visits, including Attila the Stockbroker and the Nightingales. At the most recent Nightingales show Paul Jackson was down the front shouting out the words to 'Real Gone Daddy'.

A thirty-minute walk from the Adelphi there's a goth nightclub that dates back to 1982; it's called Spiders, is open only on Saturday nights, sells cheap drinks – including an idiosyncratic range of cocktails (including their Tarantula: cider, Pernod, blackcurrant and ice) – and qualifies as one of Britain's most singular nightclubs. It carries a useful warning on its unrepentantly primitive website:

'WE DO NOT PLAY HOUSE — GARAGE — HIP-HOP — TRANCE. IF YOU LIKE THIS KIND OF MUSIC SPIDERS IS NOT FOR YOU'. On a Saturday at Spiders, the audience is treated to a rock disco featuring music from classic acts like the Rolling Stones, the Clash, Sisters of Mercy and the Doors.

Among the significant surviving clubs and venues with a thirty-year history, Rock City on Talbot Street in Nottingham is currently one of the most successful, hosting both live concerts and club nights. Among its celebrated gigs is an REM show at the venue in November 1984 that was broadcast on BBC Radio and later included in a list of the greatest hundred gigs of all time by Q magazine. Like the 100 Club, Rock City is something of a family affair; the current owner is George Akins who took over from his father (also called George). George Snr was relatively hands-off (he always employed a manager) but George Jnr is much more involved. Rock City has already made a few appearances in our history, notably when DJ Jonathan Woodliffe and others featured at hip hop and jazz funk nights and all-dayers. At the REM show, apparently the heel of one of Michael Stipe's shoes came off and he asked the crowd if anyone would swap shoes with him. A member of the crowd obliged; the fan got a broken shoe and Stipe finished the show. In another shoe-related incident, Stuart Adamson from Big Country once borrowed a pair of laces from Jonathan Woodliffe and never returned them. On another occasion, Joan Jett was sick in a bucket at the side of the stage just before she went on. The sightlines at Rock City are great; there's a balcony, and the one thing you learn to expect at a venue like this, with its layers of history – sticky floors.

Rock City, the Leadmill, the Adelphi and the 100 Club have survived downturns and recessions, but 2000 and 2001 witnessed the closure of a number of venues that had played a key role nurturing emerging music, including the Boardwalk in Manchester, Birmingham's Edwards No. 8 and the Duchess of York in Leeds. Although these closures were for a variety of reasons – Edwards

No. 8 was damaged in a fire, for example – a perception formed that the network of small music venues that had sustained post-punk and Britpop was in jeopardy.

All kinds of music industry business models were collapsing in the early years of the new millennium. As we've seen, there was a backlash against superstar DJs. Major labels were rarely signing new bands for large advances, and none were offering tour support to subsidise them on the road. Potential gig-goers were being drawn away by the counter-attractions of home entertainment, including video gaming. 'In the past three years we have profiled fifty venues, twenty of them are now extinct,' Crispin Parry of national pop-venues magazine *Circuit* told the *Guardian* in February 2000. He also suggested one of the reasons for this was that attending live music in small venues just wasn't as cool as it once was. 'Small gigs aren't as sexy as they used to be,' he said.

Live music since that time hasn't died though. Venues have come and gone and some currently in use aren't traditional pub-type venues (there's been an increase in the use of churches, for example). For many people the live experience might be confined to a festival or other major event, but emerging and established acts haven't been short of opportunities to play. Young bands get a foot on the ladder instigating their own shows, building an online presence, finding a local venue that might offer useful support slots or showcases, and hooking up with a sympathetic promoter.

A number of promoters in our current era have played integral roles in moving their local scene forward, including Arthur Tapp in Birmingham, John Rostron in Cardiff, Steve Revo at EVOL in Liverpool, Jason Dormon and Mark Davyd at the Forum in Tunbridge Wells, Phil Andrews at Moles in Bath, Mal Campbell at the Trades Club in Hebden Bridge, and Hey! Manchester and Now Wave in Manchester. Although they may end up as big as industry heavyweights like SJM, these promoters began, at least, as small, independent, under-capitalised companies, working with love and knowledge and providing a stage for bands who otherwise might have missed out. Where interest is minimal, they nurture an audience. Now Wave hosted a number of small-scale shows featuring the xx and Alt-J before they broke through; they've become a trusted brand, a signifier of a certain kind of taste.

Even if the talk in 2000 of gig-going not just dying but not being 'cool' was true, the situation started to change a little. One or two bands – definitely including the Strokes – created sparks that ignited renewed interest in guitar bands and gig-going. And the Libertines, before and after they signed to Rough Trade, played gigs galore with the Strokes and the Vines, but also became known for so-called 'guerrilla gigs'. This was late 2002 and into 2003. They'd announce a gig just a few hours beforehand, often by mass text, giving instructions to fans to meet at a given location. From there, the lucky few would be escorted to the venue – often somebody's home, their living room or basement. A number of performances took place at the flat bandmates Pete Doherty and Carl Barât rented together in Bethnal Green.

The determination to stage DIY gigs we witnessed on the 1950s jazz scene, and during and after punk, has never gone away, but the new millennium seemed to spur a younger generation to imagine and deliver new examples of self-organisation. Through 2002 a small collection of musicians and music fans calling themselves 'Helpyourself Manchester' began to build an informal network of ad hoc venues, enabling bands to play in people's living rooms and basements. To their devotees, these guerrilla gigs – bypassing promoters, agents and established venues – were authentic and exciting. The Libertines' shows would be crowded, chaotic, with no support act, no queues at the bar (in fact, no bar), and no 'online credit card plus booking fee' shenanigans. It was a development reminiscent of the chaotic excitement of early Jesus & Mary Chain gigs (I'm thinking particularly of a gig at the Ambulance Station, a squat, in November 1984), the audience packed tight, and a sense of history.

In June 2004, at almost the same time that at least one reviewer was complaining that 'a lacklustre Oasis performance fails to ignite fans at Glastonbury', a band called the Others hosted a gig on a Hammersmith & City line tube train. That month, *NME* featured the Libertines on the front cover. The Others played more guerrilla gigs, including one on the Abbey Road crossing made famous by the Beatles. The paper also picked up on an anti-establishment DIY scene in New Cross in southeast London headed by Art Brut, who were desperately seeking alternatives to arena bands and major-label ways of doing things. They were pissed off and iconoclastic, proclaiming, 'Popular culture no longer applies to me' in their song 'Bad Weekend'.

New technology was an aid to this activity; the online messageboards hosted by Helpyourself Manchester were key to spreading the word about their events. Art Brut were one of those bands who picked up early on what is now standard practice – the use of instant messaging. Guitarist Chris Chinchilla would announce short-notice guerrilla gigs with a post on the forum on the band's website and email information to fans. Chris later left the group, but in 2004 this was his take on things: 'Sometimes the music industry doesn't want to help, so you just do it any way you can. We use SMS, email, mailing lists, message boards, my Sony Ericsson T68i and technologies like MSN Messenger and iChat; then people pass details on to other people to spread the word.'

Those Libertines events appeared exciting, rebellious, different, vaguely or potentially illegal; all the key ingredients to create a sense of something new and, indeed, 'cool'. A small but significant music audience was making their own scenes, rendering obsolete all those who aspired to superstardom – musicians and DJs. All this helped create a renaissance in live music and new bands, in an era when the possibilities of the internet were suggesting new ways to socialise and share music without the need to leave the house.

With so much to enjoy in the online world, you can understand why people might have predicted fifteen years ago that by now we'd never need to go out again, and we could live our lives via computer and TV screens. But event organisers of all kinds have evidence that the appetite for live experiences has increased during this period. As well as pleasure in the ability to view streamed or recorded events on screen in a personal space, at a convenient time, there's also a demand for communal events that unfold in real time – what might be called 'primary experiences'. The huge growth in summer festivals reflects this. A festival weekend – or a week clubbing in Croatia or Ibiza – is an extreme going-out experience, a promise of a concentrated dose of sociability and good times.

In 2014 the Libertines reunited to play a Barclaycard-sponsored event in Hyde Park called British Summer Time. The band had first disbanded soon after their second album in 2004, and had briefly got back together for some shows in 2010. Hyde Park was a long way from the guerrilla gigs more than ten years earlier. Back then *NME* editor Conor McNicholas had declared, 'I really feel something big will come out of this.' The band had helped put life back into live music but it's possible that the Libertines headlining an all-day gig in a royal park alongside the Enemy and the View, sponsored by a credit card company (34.9 per cent APR) wasn't quite the revolution in music and culture *NME* had dreamed of.

Nurturing the next wave is important. Finding a way to encourage participation. Finding a space for something that's never going to fill an arena. All these things are valuable to a town or city's cultural life. Promoters like Chris Horkan from Hey! Manchester take a certain pride in getting in early on a band that goes on to break through but it's not just about that, it's also about seeing the significance of stuff that's marginal. 'Someone breaking through doesn't make them any better musically,' says Chris. 'Some of the artists I'm most excited about doing shows will play, and probably *always* will play, to fifty or a hundred people.'

There's a tendency to judge cultural significance only by scale, numbers, size or income generated, but this misses one of the lessons of the story of life after dark – how powerful a small and under-capitalised venture can be. It isn't just about clubs and venues. Cultural change starts away from the establishment and the big art institutions; it starts at the margins, unheralded. It's also clear that energised culture isn't neat and tidy. In the late 1940s the hip place, Club Eleven, was just a ramshackle basement room with lightbulbs. Those 'hokey' Rolling Stones fans in baggy pullovers swinging from the rafters at the Crawdaddy could see the future. The attendees on and off stage at the first Factory nights in Hulme were a rum bunch, many of whom would make their mark in the world in a hundred ways. Eric's helped trigger an explosion of bands in Liverpool, from a venue in a forgotten part of town.

How do we measure the cultural health of a town or city? Should opportunities for people to consume culture be matched by opportunities for citizens to produce and create? How do we feel about living somewhere with a number of cinema multiplexes but no inclination to provide provision for film-makers to make or screen films of their own? Or a city with breathtaking art galleries but no facilities for artist workshops or studios? Or somewhere with huge-capacity live music enormodomes that showcase the big acts but no grassroots music scene? Or a city that houses millionaires or even billionaires but doesn't have room for cheap spaces where people with ideas might gather, creativity take root, connections build – and, out of all that, a new world emerge?

It's still often the case that significant venues take root in the grim parts of a town that the developers of office blocks, apartments or retail malls would never touch. But this is the story that subsequently unfolds: the venue repopulates the area, attracts life and sparkle, and a bohemian cluster develops, which then attracts profile and positivity, and developers and commercialisation. The bohemian activity has brought life back into cheap buildings and the land gains in value. The independents and independently minded are driven out as developers bid to build chain hotels, retail malls or apartments. Their offers are attractive to landlords and usually also to city councils.

In June 2006, the highly regarded and much-loved Venue in Edinburgh closed after a quarter of a century hosting live music. Within five years other venues in the city were lost, including the Forest and Roxy Art House. In addition, the Bongo Club was told to leave its Edinburgh University-owned building to make way for offices. In February 2012, Kris Walker, promoter of 'Wasabi Disco' at Sneaky Pete's, told local magazine *The List*, 'Edinburgh's nightlife has suffered significantly since the millennium. It's seen venue after venue closed down or taken over and turned into a rugby-friendly soulless commode. Edinburgh is now in a state of fur coat and no knickers – a beautiful city with great history and a world-renowned arts festival yet provides next to nothing to support grassroots, counter-culture creative types and zero diversity for its long-suffering residents.'

In Liverpool, on Mathew Street, the original Eric's having long gone, there's now an unrelated music venue also calling itself Eric's. Across the road is the rebuilt Cavern. It's both a Beatles landmark and a Beatles theme park. I went there, saw a solo performer bang out a medley of Beatles hits to a half-empty room of people taking selfies, and fled. I reported back to a local, a man who runs events and a venue in another part of Liverpool, and he put me right: 'The tourists love it, it's lucrative. OK, it's not for you, but it works.'

By 2015 there was one issue that had become critical for small venues, related to the boom in the building of city-centre 'luxury' apartments: noise abatement. A noise abatement notice can be triggered by just one complaint and can lead to costly legal appeals, fines and revocation of a venue's licence. In Newport, Gwent, in 2013, Ashley Sicolo, the grandson of John Sicolo who'd run the legendary TJ's, was forced to close his venue, the

200 Club in Stow Hill. Big venues have been caught up in this too, including Ministry of Sound, which had moved to a dead space in Elephant & Castle but, from 2009, spent five years fighting the threat of closure after plans were unveiled to redevelop Eileen House, a tower block opposite the club's entrance.

You might think that if there is an established music venue and then someone moves into the area, that the new homeowner adapts to the surroundings, but that's not the case. Guildford's only independent, alternative live music venue, the Boileroom, was opened in 2006. After several years' trading, two people who moved into a rental property next door to the venue put in an application for their licence to be reviewed on the grounds of noise – fortunately the Boileroom survived. Brighton's Blind Tiger wasn't so lucky and shut in May 2014 after a person who'd moved into a flat a year earlier called the police and then the council. The venue had been a public house in the Victorian era, and had been hosting live music since the 1850s.

When the long-established Manchester venue Night & Day was threatened with closure after a noise abatement notice was issued in 2013, there was a suggestion that when the flats next door were built, the developer had neglected to install adequate soundproofing. Again, you might think that if a venue is already established in a location, developers moving in to build new homes are legally required to soundproof the homes, but that's not the case either. The problem this causes for small venues has been exacerbated in recent years, the government having dismantled many of the regulatory obstacles to converting empty offices into flats. Fortunately, Bristol Council was far-sighted enough to intervene when developers decided to convert an office block close to the Fleece and insisted the developers take a number of insulation measures.

If many of the changes in the last couple of decades – from the blurring of the lines between bars and clubs, to the smoking ban, and noise issues – have had a deleterious effect on some businesses, there are also plenty of reasons to remain positive. The spirit of self-organisation among music fans, musicians and DJs is still strong. The occasion in 1976 when Howard Trafford and Peter McNeish were instrumental in the staging of the two Sex Pistols gigs at Manchester Lesser Free Trade Hall is rightly celebrated for its transformative effect on that city's music scene, but music's history and, indeed, its present, is full of such episodes.

In the late 1990s Elbow were struggling to get anywhere, fighting even to keep the band together. Their brand of songwriting – thoughtful, semi-acoustic – didn't really fit with the spirit of the times; there seemed no room for them in a city in thrall to the swaggering laddism of Oasis and the euphoric house being played in the clubs. So what did Elbow do? With the help of a friend from Bury, Scott Alexander, they ran a Tuesday night in an Australian theme bar called Down Under – nights they dubbed 'Gecko'. Guy Garvey, lead singer of the band, says what went on most of the rest of the week there was 'dreadful, horrible', but Elbow and their friends had found a space.

Each week Elbow would be playing acoustic sets alongside like-minded acts, most Tuesdays to small crowds, maybe forty or fifty people. The fact some talented people were gravitating to the stage there was picked up by local musician and DJ Clint Boon, who told Guy he should record some of the activity at Gecko. Guy says somewhere there's video footage of one Tuesday which features sets from I Am Kloot, Badly Drawn Boy, Doves, Elbow and a band called Babel Tree. Success was just around the corner for most of them. All the while, Guy Garvey worked part-time behind the bar at the Roadhouse on Newton Street.

Talking to Guy about Gecko, he and I agreed that the camaraderie of those nights helped encourage and sustain the musicians, and the live stage gave them an opportunity to refine songs. I suggested that although the Lesser Free Trade Hall event is rightly celebrated, it's only a standout example of something that happens in all towns and cities with a half-healthy music scene; a poorly attended event in uninspiring surroundings might look like not very much at all, but if you fast-forward, clearly something was happening. It's a scene, it's significant, but it isn't acknowledged. Gecko was one of those moments, on a Tuesday night at an Australian theme bar on Peter Street. 'This is the first anyone's ever asked me about this,' Guy says. 'You don't realise you're on the inside of a scene until afterwards when someone marks it as that. As far as I am concerned, I'm still mates with all the same people. Some of us have been lucky since, some of us have had to work a bit harder, but, yes, you're right, we were in the middle of something special. We just didn't know it.'

The tradition of living for the weekend is built into our nation's DNA but it's noticeable how important nights at music venues and nightclubs have taken place away from Fridays and Saturdays when venue owners might be persuaded to try something a bit different, take a chance: Guy Stevens DJing on a Monday at the Scene; Billy's at Gossip's, like Gecko, on a Tuesday; and the punk festival at the 100 Club on a Sunday and Monday. Some of the best clubs in Manchester since the demise of the Haçienda have been midweek – including 'Tramp', Murkage and Club Suicide – and in London, Soul II Soul at the Africa Centre, the Heavenly Social, and the Metalheadz Sessions were all on Sundays.

The buoyant demand for literary and other sorts of festivals and for live music suggests that face-to-face, primary experiences and social occasions have virtues the virtual world lack. Furthermore, for anyone with an inclination to stage an event, nurturing and inviting an audience has never been easier, thanks to advances in electronic communication. Facebook has tended to make changes which have pushed promoters towards paying for enhanced reach, but thanks to social media the time and cost of connecting to an audience has dramatically reduced in the last twenty-five years. Back then, if you'd been in Liverpool, you might have glimpsed James Barton spreading the word about the Underground, hitting the streets, rucksack on his back, baseball cap, pair of Timberlands, dropping off handfuls of flyers and sticking posters on lamp-posts and walls. If you were in Coventry in 1992, and chanced upon Stuart Reid in the process of sending a newsletter to members of the Eclipse, in an era when a second-class stamp cost 18p, he might have told you that by the time he'd photocopied the newsletter, and bought envelopes and stamps, for every thousand members he then mailed out to the money he was spending was probably the equivalent cost of booking a decent guest DJ. Flyposters and hand-to-hand flyering still have a role to play, but so much is now instant, and online.

The range of events after dark remains huge. From small-scale gig venues like the Adelphi, to the enormodomes like the 21,000-capacity Manchester Arena, and from nightclub events featuring 'celebrity DJs' like Danny Dyer and those headlined by Calvin Harris and other *Mixmag* cover stars at the conspicuous, commercial end of dance music, to unlicensed raves and informal little enclaves of activity, basement bars, DJs playing seven-inch vinyl.

In the 1970s, as old-style dance hall activity was getting washed away by successive youth tribes and trends, the Barrowland Ballroom repositioned itself as primarily a live music venue as well as occasionally clearing the hall for roller discos. In the last thirty years acts that have graced the stage at Barrowlands include David Bowie, Coldplay, the Charlatans, Metallica, the Smiths and the Stone Roses. In 2014, it staged a successful ten-hour all-dayer called 'Barraloadasoul' featuring soul and mod classics played by DJs including Eddie Piller from Acid Jazz records, Dave Evison of the former Wigan Casino, and Yogi Haughton the man behind Scottish Soulful Weekender, an event that returned in 2015.

Recently at Barrowlands, the East End Social organisation has hosted tea dances featuring a sixteen-piece swing band with dance instructors, guest vocalists and cake. In London, Spitalfields Tea Dances are held on a Wednesday once a month. There's also an opportunity to quickstep back in time at the monthly *thé dansants* at the historic Palm Court at the Waldorf Hotel London for £49 per person (dancing to the five-piece band and an afternoon tea of finger sandwiches, freshly baked scones, cakes and a choice of teas, coffees or infusions included).

The Floral Hall in Belfast closed in the mid-1970s and was soon semi-derelict. The mirrorball that used to throw light on the waltzes and the quicksteps was taken down to feature in a show called *A Slice of Saturday Night* staged at the Arts Theatre on Botanic Avenue, but has since gone missing. In January 2015 a campaign was launched to save the empty Floral Hall from collapsing. Across town, the Ulster Historic Circle installed a blue plaque on the building on the site of the Maritime Hotel, honouring 'The birthplace of rhythm 'n' blues in Belfast' (it was unveiled in April 2010). A ten-minute walk away through the city, at the site of the former Harp Bar, a plaque celebrates the punk era in Belfast.

The Granary in Bristol, designated by English Heritage as a Grade II listed building, has been converted into apartments. Artefacts relating to another significant Bristol venue, the Bamboo Club, have been donated to Bristol Record Office by Tony Bullimore. This archive includes flyers, photos and the Bamboo Club minute book where membership rules are described. Suits and ties were obligatory for the men, and one entry explains: 'The Club management should use its discretion in deciding what disciplinary action should be taken when members or members' guests are heard swearing (English language or Jamaican style).'

The key role that Mothers and other West Midlands venues played in the story of rock and heavy metal was recognised in Birmingham Museum and Art Gallery's comprehensive 'Home of Metal' exhibition of 2011. Meanwhile, the online Manchester District Music Archive contains over 10,000 scanned artefacts (flyers, photographs, press cuttings, etc.), many of which relate to the 1,000-plus venues they have listed in the Greater Manchester area. Brighton & Hove Museum have a collection of oral history interviews with goths who describe the scene in Brighton in the 1980s.

When the Duchess of York in Leeds closed in 2000, the sofa Kurt Cobain had slept on was acquired by the National Centre for Popular Music, but its days as a museum piece were numbered, as the centre closed after just fifteen months. The old Duchess of York site is now occupied by a Hugo Boss store (the sofa seems to have disappeared). When David Tennant sold the Gargoyle he offered *The Red Studio* to the Tate for £400 (they declined, it was sold to an American collector and now hangs in New York's MOMA). A man called Ian Cape liberated a chair from Le Phonographique in Leeds and now describes it as his 'prized possession'. I guess someone somewhere near Nottingham owns a shoe that once belonged to Michael Stipe.

Most clubs close due to escalating operating costs or falling turnover, or both, but, as we have seen, there are many other causes – noise issues, or drug use or violence in the venue. As we've also seen, a present, pressing concern in cities throughout Britain is the enforced closure of clubs and venues as a result of redevelopment schemes. As Kris Walker suggests, there's been a money-driven slide towards increasingly homogeneous, sterile city centres. Not much for the misfits, but a ton of stuff for the cul-de-sac fundamentalists. Offbeat venues aren't being protected, and councils are unsympathetic when it comes to dealing with noise and other problematic issues. City councils and planning authorities are confused and defensive when faced with spaces that aren't fully monetised and controlled.

These issues became relevant when the fate of Legends was announced, the venue that had hosted the old Twisted Wheel/ Placemate 7, the outpost of unregenerated Manchester that Luke Unabomber from HomoElectric described as 'full of weird, dark corridors with stained walls'. In 2012 members of Manchester City Council's planning committee approved plans for Olympian Homes to build a budget hotel on the site, to be operated by the German hotel chain Motel One. This would entail the demolition of Legends. Over the next few months HomoElectric and other regular club nights had their goodbye shows or one-off last parties there before the wrecking ball arrived.

As with the disappearance of so many venues and clubs, the moment seemed to be more than just the demolition of the bricks and mortar. We've seen many examples of clubs embedded in our shared history and key to our sense of identity. As our cities develop, disintegrate or evolve, the loss of familiar landmarks has a dislocating effect. Even more so if it's the loss of buildings we have some emotional connection with, let alone the loss of a building that for many people symbolised the best days of their life and the best aspects of their city's music history, to be replaced by something as standard and culturally insignificant as a hotel. On the occasion of the announcement of the demolition, James Ketchell, chief executive of Music Heritage UK, said, 'Manchester has a proud musical heritage and for one of its iconic and historic venues to be demolished to make way for a budget hotel is, quite simply, appalling.'

A campaign flared, and there was plenty of media interest in the story. Most of the coverage of closure concentrated on the historical value of Legends in its five and a bit years as the Twisted Wheel up until 1971. There was also some focus on the name being revived by DJ Pete Roberts, who was running Twisted Wheel nights at the venue in 2012 on the last Thursday and the second Sunday of each month. There were far fewer mentions of its years as a gay club, the goings-on at the Mineshaft, or the fact the venue was used by the irregular gay, gay-friendly and misfit-friendly club nights HomoElectric and Bollox, a fetish club ('Club Lash') and a hardcore punk/metal night called 'Back to Hell'.

Of course, when a loved and significant building like the Twisted Wheel is threatened with closure and demolition, the default reaction is to plead for it to stay open, but it's not clear

Music Heritage UK or anyone else has viable alternative options. Should a venue deemed to be of historic interest benefit from a council grant or subsidy that other venues busting a gut and running on a shoestring have no access to? Should it be sold to a third party to do a Cavern to it and become, in this case, a nostalgic Northern Soul theme park? And why privilege its history as a Northern Soul venue when it had more years as a gay venue, including hitting the headlines when a police raid found men having sex in the toilets? An added complication remains; plenty of folk were of the view that the Twisted Wheel was never as good in Whitworth Street as it was in its early days, at its original home in Brazennose Street.

The Star & Garter, an atmospheric, down-at-heel pub venue behind Piccadilly Station in Manchester, had hosted Morrissey/Smiths discos, Club Brenda, a regular indie night called 'Smile', and numerous other regular and irregular maverick club nights and small-scale gigs. The area around the station was earmarked for development. Network Rail's plans and the three years of road closures the work would involve put the future of the business in jeopardy. In London, the area in and around Tottenham Court Road station is the site of an even bigger redevelopment plan, the Crossrail project.

The Astoria, close to the corner of Charing Cross Road and Oxford Street, at the northwestern edge of Soho, was an early victim of Crossrail (it closed in January 2009 and was subsequently demolished). A more recent victim was the 12 Bar Club on Denmark Street where the management were told to vacate the premises by January 2015. This was just a few months after the burlesque club and music venue Madame Jojo's in the heart of Soho was closed and plans for its demolition announced. At the same time, a gay bar, the Yard, situated opposite Madame Jojo's in a small courtyard just off Rupert Street, also came under threat. Campaign groups including the Music Venue Trust and Save Soho took up the cause of the 12 Bar. The Yard, too, began a fightback, underlining the historic importance of the building (Rupert Street dates back to the late seventeenth century, the building housing the Yard forming part of nineteenth-century stables).

In the context of anxieties about who runs our cities, and debates about how our cities should be, closed or under-threat venues of this kind have become a symbol of maverick, independent activity at loggerheads with the moneymen aiming to rinse every penny out of every site, and those powerful commercial forces in our society that are putting a squeeze on the counter-culture in a drive towards conformity. Alan McGee of Creation Records, who opened up his own live venue in a converted chapel in Talgarth in mid-Wales, became one of the 12 Bar Club's most vociferous supporters. He'd seen an early gig by the Libertines there in 1999 and paid a visit to the occupied space, proclaiming, 'We're facing a war on culture, fuelled by consumerism.'

While not denying that venues like the Star & Garter and the 12 Bar Club are irreplaceable, or the damaging effect wrought by the conformist and commercial forces, and also while applauding the petitions and the campaigners, it's also important to see some positives. Just as it was in the 1920s, the 1980s, and so many times in our history, it seems to be the case that in our current era, in big cities like London, Manchester, Liverpool and Birmingham there are enough resourceful people, motivated entrepreneurs and music fans to make their own version of Guy Garvey's Gecko heaven; enough people with the inspiration that powered the Cave of the Golden Calf, Eric's, Billy's and HomoElectric; and enough venues that will waive a hire fee on a Tuesday night, for example, or build relationships with promoters and bands to ensure that when venues close or club nights come to an end, new ones launch.

Furthermore, the mavericks and early adopters are one step ahead. There's usually a timelag between bohemian activity reaching its height and the moneymen moving in. Often pioneers have already gone to populate other areas. The area around Nation (Cream's venue) on Wolstenholme Square in Liverpool is currently a target for the redevelopers; it's become a musical and creative hub, especially since the Kazimier club opened there as well, but the most recent hotspot created by independently minded venues and businesses is down at the so-called 'Baltic Triangle' along the river to the south side of the city centre. As one Liverpool-based website puts it: 'Just a few years ago the Baltic Triangle was home only to disused and uninhabited warehouses and relics from Liverpool's industrial age; today it is emblematic of somewhat of a cultural renaissance that the city is undergoing.'

Similarly, Soho hasn't always been the sole centre of innovation and excitement after dark. You could argue the mavericks have already moved on in recent years to run live venues and clubs in areas like Shoreditch or Dalston. There have certainly been times when other areas of London have staked a claim to be the centre of the action. One or two venues in Camden were crucial to Britpop in the early and mid-1990s, for example, including a favoured hangout, the Good Mixer bar on Inverness Street, and the Laurel Tree, where promoter and DJ Paul Tunkin ran the 'Blow Up' club night (he launched it in October 1993 – by 1995 it was being described in *Melody Maker* as 'The Club That Changed The World').

In London, many live venues have been lost in the last ten years, including the Luminaire, but in the same period, gig-goers in the capital have been able to enjoy live music at a number of new venues including Islington Assembly Hall, the Lexington, Cafe Oto in Dalston, the Green Note in Camden, Indigo at the O2 (which has featured Gary Numan, Roy Ayers, PiL and Chic, among many others), and King's Place (with a regular Friday folk night). In addition, some older venues we visited earlier in this story now host live music after a break from doing so, including

Wilton's and the Roundhouse, which reopened in 2006 after a major overhaul.

Edinburgh, to an extent, has rebuilt its music infrastructure in the last few years, thanks to ambitious promoters programming intimate gig spaces like the Wee Red Bar in the grounds of Edinburgh College of Art, Sneaky Pete's on the Cowgate, and Bannerman's. The Bongo Club has relocated to a new home on the Cowgate, the Mash House is a new venture in an old church on Guthrie Street, and La Belle Angele reopened in 2014, twelve years after a serious fire. In addition, established venues like Voodoo Rooms and Cabaret Voltaire continue to operate, as does The Caves, a unique and atmospheric venue housed in a building formerly a collection of stone vaults dating back to the eighteenth century. After an open meeting of venues, promoters and the council at Usher Hall in November 2014, Councillor Norma Austin Hart, Vice Convener for Culture and Sport, agreed to look again at how the council could help, rather than hinder, the provision of live music venues. She also said: 'The meeting has highlighted the importance many people attach to music venues, which goes far beyond sentiment and is really around cultural enrichment.'

Culture changes, and that's good – women are now allowed into a dance hall wearing trousers, and most DJs have dispensed with the traditional 'smoocher' at the end of the night – and not just good but also inevitable (go out one Thursday and everyone's wearing flares, go out a year later and no one is – wait long enough and flares will return, and beards, and deep house). In Manchester clubs and venues have closed, but new spaces are in use too; over the last few years, music has been performed in a 100-capacity room at the International Anthony Burgess Foundation, as well as at a new venue, Gorilla, opposite the Ritz, which programmes imaginatively and is well run by the Trof organisation. Trof also operate one of Manchester's best new venues, Albert Hall, a wonderful new use for a derelict four-floor

building built by the Methodist Church in 1910. Manchester has
also seen recent enclaves of interesting activity out in the neighbourhoods, at various venues like Fallow in Fallowfield, Dulcimer
in Chorlton and Fuel in Withington. Young creatives are popu-
lating old warehouses and empty buildings in Salford, around
Chapel Street, clustering close to the pioneering arts lab and
music venue at Islington Mill (the brainchild of ex-Club Suicide
regular Bill Campbell).

The way music, clothes, people, inspiration and memories radi-
ate from a venue and take on a life of their own is some
consolation to those mourning the loss of the Twisted
Wheel/Legends. The erasing of all traces of the club came at a
time of renewed interest in Northern Soul. Even as the wrecking
ball tore into the Wheel, so much of the activity it supported had
moved on, its enduring influence clear. Young Northern Soul
dancer Levanna Mclean, for example, with over a million views
for her dancing down the street to a mash-up of Pharrell
Williams's 'Happy' and its inspiration, Velvet Hammer's late-70s
song, also titled 'Happy'. Around the same time, the Paul Mason
interview with Fran Franklin was broadcast and the final edit of
Elaine Constantine's *Northern Soul* film was completed.

Younger DJs carry the Northern Soul torch and keep the faith,
including the gloriously named Ashby-De-La-Soul crew, who
present a bi-monthly Northern Soul & Motown night in
Leicestershire, and the 'Black Bee Soul Club'. The Black Bee
takes place once a month at Kraak Gallery in Manchester.
Founders Paul Bailey and Sam McEwen attract an audience of
clubbers who weren't born when Northern Soul was at its height
in the 1970s, so the impulse isn't nostalgic; it's refreshing rather
than replicating what happened at the Twisted Wheel. The location of Kraak Gallery adds to the charm of Black Bee Soul Club
events.

Founded by the former Club Brenda promoter Jayne
Compton, Kraak Gallery has also played host to 'Witch*unt'

parties and to a couple of alt-queer nights, 'Drunk at Vogue' and 'Hot Space', in Manchester. It's the kind of place every city needs, an under-styled space a little like something you'd imagine finding in post-industrial New York circa 1980 or in a back street in Berlin. Kraak holds barely 150 people, but feeds the imagination and attracts the adventurous. Such spaces are so often fertile, as we've seen. The glories of the north of England's post-punk era emerged from just such rundown, crumbling, creative venues. Bailey and McEwen say they fell in love with Kraak, the venue's gritty vibe and the fact that it's hidden away, seventy yards from Stevenson Square but hard to find, with no passing trade. It's down a street no one can find, playing music the big clubs don't play, away from the eyes of the mainstream media.

Outside the big cities, where there's no critical mass, and fewer enthusiasts and entrepreneurs, small venues with a dissenting soundtrack threatened with closure may not be replaceable. These places tend to be dominated by large venues that don't have the desire or luxury to go beyond an obvious soundtrack and cheap drinks.

Choices are restricted in Preston, for example, where the loss of the Continental and the Ferret would be a blow to anyone who valued adventurous venues. In Southampton, Joiners is a small music venue on St Mary Street established in 1968. The Verve, the Arctic Monkeys and Friendly Fires all played gigs there in their early days. But the survival of the Joiners is precarious; in January 2013 the Vaccines played a fundraising gig there (in April the same year, Joiners was declared *NME*'s best small venue of the year). Without Joiners, the locals and students living in Southampton would still have the opportunity to visit Jesters on Bevois Valley Road, although it's possibly not such an attractive proposition, having recently been designated number one in an online feature describing the 'UK's worst nightclubs': 'A top tip is to make sure you're not wearing your favourite clothes as you will have snakebite over you by the end of the night,' said the reviewer, who happened upon a brawl within two minutes of entering the venue.

We all need to know there's an alternative. If you're stumbling towards an interest in maverick music or maverick culture, you're liberated if there's a venue where like minds gather, a venue that could open musical possibilities, and help you identify and define the person you are or the person you want to be.

The availability of spaces is important, but so is the role of the energised promoters who have taken possession of venues, and organised and hosted events, clubs and live music, those people we've met through our story like Denis Rose, Cy Laurie, Ma Regan, Roger Eagle, Steve Strange, Chris Burton and John Keenan; and, in the current era, EVOL and Now Wave, Jason Dormon and Mark Davyd at the Forum in Tunbridge Wells, and Phil Andrews at Moles in Bath.

Away from the high street, out on the under-capitalised, uncommercial periphery of clubland, point to anywhere on a map of Britain, from the Old Fire Station in Bournemouth to the Cafe Indiependent, Scunthorpe, and there'll be someone some-where organising a regular night playing irregular music. These characters are making something out of nothing, even if their impact doesn't match that of some of the maverick enterprises documented in our story – the Scene, for example, hidden away in Ham Yard, in among warehouses and old stables, off the beaten track. It's a model of how much potential a venue can have. From disc-only nights on a Monday attended by a few people leaning against the walls, as Guy Stevens played records by the Impressions and Jimmy Reed, the club became the quintessential mod hang-out and Stevens became an influence on the likes of Eric Clapton, Brian Jones and Pete Townshend. And the boss of the club founded Radio Caroline, and thus transformed British music radio.

Closing down doesn't mean an end to the story and influence of a venue. Laurent Garnier has had DJ residencies at the Ministry of Sound and the End in London, turned the Rex club in Paris into one of the techno meccas of the world, performed live accompanied by a full band at the prestigious Salle Pleyel in 2010, and runs his own Yeah! Festival in Provence, but his autobiography *Electrochoc* starts with his memory of his first visit to the Haçienda and hearing Mike Pickering playing 'Love Can't Turn Around'. Everything he has subsequently achieved – and the activity that, in turn, he's gone on to inspire, particularly in France – connects back to that life-changing moment.

Throughout this history we've seen and celebrated significant venues and the story of what happened next, their influence radiating; the trails lead on from Billy's and the Blitz, from Club A Go Go, the Dug Out, Crackers and Jive Turkey. People carrying objects from an auction and memories, and inspirations, ideas and relationships from clubs: Laurent Garnier, John Bonham and Robert Plant, Bryan Ferry, Viv Albertine, Tom Rowlands and Ed Simons, Samantha Morton and Patrick Lilley, for example.

New chapters get written. Sensateria in Birmingham had a playlist which inspired a number of musicians to take influence from the 60s psych aesthetic (Trish Keenan and James Cargill from Broadcast were regulars at the club night, which lasted ten years). Giorgio Gomelsky, who staged those Rolling Stones shows at the Crawdaddy, resurfaced in the early 1980s running Plugg on Fifteenth Street in New York City. Rob King went from promoting Delirium to becoming art director for François Hollande's presidential campaign in 2012. Warp Records, with a genesis closely bound up with Jive Turkey in Sheffield, suffered the death of co-founder Rob Mitchell in 2001, but has gone on to diversify into the production of videos and feature films including *Dead Man's Shoes*, *Four Lions*, *Submarine* and *Tyrannosaur*.

Sheffield is re-energised every September with the arrival of students; the growth in further education has helped nightlife in many British cities. There are, in addition, many small venues, nurturing new and emerging talent. The Plug on Matilda Street has a night called 'Propa Local' on the last Friday of every month, showcasing Sheffield-based bands, in addition to club nights and a range of live acts which, in the past, have included Bloc Party's Kele Okereke, Kate Tempest, and the Vaselines, plus guest DJs (including David Rodigan, and Mike Skinner of the Streets). In addition to the Plug, other Sheffield venues in the present day making a significant contribution include the Harley on Glossop Road. Sheffield holds a city-wide music festival every summer, Tramlines. The team at the Harley have an integral role in organising Tramlines, with the help of the city and the local musical community.

As we discovered in an earlier chapter, in the 1860s Thomas Youdan's Surrey Music Hall in Sheffield was the biggest building in the town, partly because the locals didn't get round to building a town hall until 1896, revealing an admirable sense of priorities and a reminder that the search for entertainment clearly runs deep in the city, as elsewhere. People still want to gather, listen to music, dance. And despite ecstasy, ketamine and nitrous oxide, alcohol is still the drug of choice.

Alcohol has downsides, of course; it's said to be a factor in 40,000 deaths a year and its contribution to nightlife street violence is horrifying. Not that the violence is a new thing, though; in his 1958 novel *Saturday Night and Sunday Morning*, Alan Sillitoe describes not only the lurch towards a beer-fuelled escape every weekend – 'Piled-up passions were exploded on a Saturday night, and the effect of a week's monotonous graft in the factory was swilled out of your system' – but accepts there's a price to pay (a punch-up and a hangover), calling Saturday nights out 'a violent preamble to a prostrate Sabbath'.

In the early 1840s, Friedrich Engels was remarking on the intemperance of the Manchester populace. 'I have rarely come out of Manchester on such an evening without meeting numbers of people staggering and seeing others lying in the gutter.' Manchester has undoubtedly changed much, but the drunken, thronging atmosphere of the city on a Saturday night in the current era would be recognisable to anyone who was out and about 150 or, indeed, 50 years ago.

The entertainments on offer, nationally, after dark, are testament to our nation's love for experiences beyond the mundane – light-shows, lasers, wrestling with an alligator, an American contortionist at the Haçienda, the Prodigy live in an old bingo hall, Jimi Hendrix playing in a club named after a mongoose, and Herr Schalkenbach's extraordinary Piano Orchestra Electro Moteur – as well as to the imagination of venue owners and promoters who've found or made special spaces, cared about some of the finer details too, the part of town, the height of the ceiling, the decor, the programming.

As we saw in an earlier chapter, in the wake of the closure of the Twisted Wheel in 1971, the focus for the Northern Soul scene moved on to the Golden Torch in Stoke, where a year of good times and intense chaos followed. After the demise of the Torch, DJ Colin Curtis moved on to continue a successful DJ career. Club owner Chris Burton, meanwhile, found himself selling satellite dishes; but selling satellite dishes wasn't his thing and he got stuck back into promoting events. He's now in his early seventies, still involved, still loves it.

The most recent time I met up with Chris, he was planning an event at the University of Keele featuring Northern Soul and r&b, in a variety of rooms (some starting at 9 p.m., running through until four or six in the morning) with some veteran DJs but also representatives of the younger generation, including Black Bee Soul Club and Stacie Stewart. Chris reeled off the names, talked up the idea, told me he'd also got a modern soul room, and – although the idea had met with some surprise – he'd added a ska/reggae room. He recommended I should check it out. 'You'd like it, Dave, it would be great to see you there.'

While the internet is abuzz with debate about venues closing and whether or not things were better back in the day, Chris

Burton cracks on, full of excitement about his upcoming event. I'm thinking: this man hosted a gig by the Rolling Stones over fifty years ago; he then ran a venue in Stoke so widely admired that a coach of clubbers from Manchester would travel down every week, and one Saturday back then he took a walk through the streets with the Stylistics. If this man can look forward to his next big night, then anyone can.

Those of us who've experienced amazing events reserve our right to be downcast when venues close and have an urge to celebrate them in some way – a blue plaque, a film, a display in a local museum, or online pages of memories – but it's also worth remembering that buildings come and go, but people make places. Our lives, our towns, our cities have been enriched by resourceful, reckless, entrepreneurial or desperate people who've not waited for something to happen, but have made something happen. And those people exist today, too; people who take their culture into their hands and create a space that's alive with a sense of possibility.

This activity in nightclubs and music venues has similarities with other spaces and places that can create a focus and act as a catalyst: maverick theatre groups like the Theatre Workshop, the 'head shops' of the 1960s, basement cafés, boutiques ranging from Bazaar to Kahn & Bell via SEX, and record shops like Good Vibrations in Belfast, Rough Trade in London, Probe in Liverpool, Revolver in Bristol, Black Market in London, Piccadilly Records and Eastern Bloc in Manchester. Or like indoor markets with second-hand stalls, or radical bookshops like Indica in London in the 1960s, and News From Nowhere, which has operated in Liverpool since 1 May 1974.

What we've witnessed through this history is what might be called 'the power of the cell'; how a tiny group of disaffected outsiders can create a sensation, or a movement, or even change the world. We've seen how important cultural activity invariably begins small-scale, maybe finding a focus in a grotty bar or a club or some barely selling magazine. And we've learned that, yes, the good life is out there somewhere. And that the best club in the world is the one that changes your life.

We've discovered how much excitement can be found lurking behind even the most inauspicious door. You don't have to be in London or Manchester. You don't need a red carpet or celebrity approval or even much cash. The nearest equivalent I can think of is that enduring idea of the secret garden, the midnight garden – the clock strikes thirteen and through a door a different world appears. That's the glory of a club or venue. You have a roller-coaster life, feel a little dragged down by the mundane things, spend hours, days, getting ready, and increasingly giddy with expectation. It could be a live band on a Tuesday or a semi-secret rave on a Saturday. You make your way to a venue, turn a corner, join a queue. Getting nearer to the entrance, you hear basslines, and taxis pulling up, and shouts in the street. You reach the front of the queue. Behind that door might be stimulation, intoxication, a cross-dresser, mad dancers, eye contact with your first love, enchantment, liberation, a new life. You just have to be lucky, or know where to look. The door opens, you step inside; you never want to leave.

ACKNOWLEDGEMENTS

Unless otherwise stated in the Notes, all direct quotes attributed to Patrick Lilley, David Wright, Maureen Ward, David Peace, Brian Rae, Richard Searling, Jeff Horton, Hyeonje Oh, Noddy Holder, Dave McAleer, CP Lee, Nicky Crewe, Ronnie Barker, Alan Jones, Jayne Casey, Pete Wylie, Andrew Loog Oldham, Chris Burton, Colin Curtis, Greg Wilson, Mike Pickering, Andrew Weatherall, Anthony Donnelly, Sasha, Ed Simons, Norman Jay, James Barton, Richard Boon, Richard H. Kirk, Chris Horkan, Kris Walker, John Keenan, Guy Garvey, Viv Albertine, and John Taylor are from email exchanges or interviews with the author.

Many thanks to three especially wonderful people: Catherine, Jack, and Raili. And to Matthew Hamilton at Aitken Alexander Associates, Kerri Sharp, Hannah Corbett, Dawn Burnett and Lewis Csizmazia at Simon & Schuster, Mike Jones, Andy Miller, Tracey Thorn, Jason Boardman, Elliot Eastwick, Sefton Mottley, Rachel George, Ursula and Philip, Nick Fraser, Tim Burgess, Andy Smith, Ade Dovey, Keith Patterson, Claire Turner, Richard Jones, Nathan McGough, Andrea Csanyi, Erik Rug, Lemn Sissay, John and Marian Haslam, KT Steggles, Guy Haslam, Greg Thorpe, Blacka Acoustics, Factory Records, Everything Everything, Christine Cort, Dave Pichilingi, the Art of Tea, Fuel, Folk, Thyme Out, Volta, and Fig & Sparrow.

SOURCES

Key Texts

Tony Bacon, *London Live* (Miller Freeman, 1999)

Lloyd Bradley, *Sounds Like London: 100 Years of Black Music in the Capital* (Serpent's Tail, 2013)

Robert Elms, *The Way We Wore: A Life in Threads* (Picador, 2005)

Mick Farren, *Give the Anarchist a Cigarette* (Jonathan Cape, 2001)

Simon Frith, Matt Brennan, Martin Cloonan & Emma Webster (eds), *The History of Live Music in Britain, Volume I: 1950–1967* (Ashgate, 2013)

Sheryl Garratt, *Adventures in Wonderland: A Decade of Club Culture* (Headline, 1998)

Jonathon Green, *All Dressed Up: The Sixties and the Counterculture* (Jonathan Cape, 1998)

Paolo Hewitt, *The Soul Stylists: Six Decades of Modernism – From Mods to Casuals* (Mainstream, 2000)

Phil Johnson, *Straight Outa Bristol* (Hodder & Stoughton, 1996)

Dagmar Kift, *The Victorian Music Hall: Culture, Class and Conflict* (Cambridge University Press, 1996)

Claire Langhamer, *Women's Leisure in England 1920–60* (Manchester University Press, 2000)

Shawn Levy, *Ready, Steady, Go! Swinging London & the Invention of Cool* (Fourth Estate, 2002)

Barry Miles, *London Calling: A Countercultural History of London since 1945* (Atlantic, 2010)

Helen Reddington, *The Lost Women of Rock Music: Female Musicians of the Punk Era* (Ashgate, 2007)

Mike Ritson & Stuart Russell, *The In Crowd* (Bee Cool Publishing, 1999)

Bill Sykes, *Sit Down! Listen to This! The Roger Eagle Story* (Empire, 2012)

Judith R. Walkowitz, *Nights Out: Live in Cosmopolitan London* (Yale University Press, 2012)

Recommended Websites

http://www.nickelinthemachine.com/
http://history-is-made-at-night.blogspot.co.uk
http://www.djhistory.com/
http://shapersofthe80s.com/
http://www.theskyliner.org/

Dave Haslam archive & news http://www.davehaslam.com

NOTES

Intro

p.viii   The review of Trevor Allen's novel describing the Hambone appeared in the *Catholic Herald*, 12 June 1953.

p.ix   Liam Gallagher, interviewed in the film *Do You Own the Dancefloor?*

pp.ix–x   'Strait-jacket masculinity'; Patrick Jones on BBC Radio Wales, 25 March 2011.

p.x   'On Saturday evenings, especially, when wages are paid'; Friedrich Engels, *The Condition of the Working Class in England* (1845: Panther, 1969), p.157.

p.xi   Aldo Rossi, *The Architecture of the City* (Opposition Books, 1984).

p.xiv   Stephen Tennant's 'prancing' gait is described by Philip Hoare in his book *Serious Pleasures: The Life of Stephen Tennant* (Hamish Hamilton, 1990), p.81.

Chapter One

p.2   'Flood-gates of vice and licentiousness'; discussed in Dagmar Kift, *The Victorian Music Hall: Culture, Class and Conflict* (Cambridge University Press, 1996), p.85.

p.4   The building that housed Evans's music and supper room was, over a century later, inhabited by Middle Earth, a psychedelic hotspot in the late 1960s.

p.6   'All in various stages of intoxication'; R.J. Broadbent, *Annals of the Liverpool Stage* (E. Howell, 1908), p.339.

p.7   Herr Schalkenbach's act in the 1870s was remembered to have been 'vastly impressive' in *The Spectator*, 17 February 1900.

pp.8-9   Thanks to Grace Dean at the City Varieties for permission to quote from her guided tour.

p.10   'The public houses and gin shops were roaring full'; Angus Bethune Reach, *Manchester & the Textile Districts in 1849* (1849; Helmshore Local History Society, 1972), p.61.

p.10   'Portable ecstasies'; Thomas De Quincey, *Confessions of an English Opium-Eater* (John Taylor, 1826), p.92.

p.12   'The display was very picturesque and made a great impression'; William E.A. Axon, *Annals of Manchester: A Chronological Record from the Earliest Times to the End of 1885* (Heywood, 1886), p.233.

p.13   For more on Mother Clap's (and the Samuel Stevens quote) see Rictor Norton, *Mother Clap's Molly House: Gay Subculture in England, 1700–1830* (Gay Men's Press, 1992).

p.14   Details of the raid on the drag ball at the Temperance Hall in Hulme from the *Observer*, 26 September 1880, and *Manchester Guardian*, 1 October 1880.

p.16   'Everyone is drunk. Those who are not singing are sprawling'; Sydney Smith, quoted in *The Pub & the People: A Worktown Study* (Faber, 2009), p.68.

p.16   'The War Office took steps to have the sketch "barred"'; Kift, p.41.

p.17   'Uninteresting bicycling by riders in curious dress'; J. Ewing Ritchie, *Days and Nights in London* (Tinsley Brothers, 1880), p.50.

p.18   'It is a curious thing'; J. Ewing Ritchie, p.62.

pp.19–20 'Guessing the number of pins or peas in a glass bottle'; *The Era*, 29 October 1897.

p.22   'Cried like a child'; Broadbent, p.353.

p.23   More on John-Joseph Hillier in Andrew Davies' *The Gangs of Manchester* (Milo Books, 2008), and for scuttlers see Dave Haslam, *Manchester, England* (Fourth Estate, 1999).

p.24   'She prostitutes herself for her own pleasure'; Henry Mayhew, *London Labour and the London Poor: A Cyclopædia of the Condition and Earnings of Those That Will Work, Those That Cannot Work, and Those That Will Not Work* (Griffin, Bohn, and Co., 1862), p.234.

pp.24–5 Brazen-faced women and shaggy-looking Germans are described in Mayhew, p.228.

p.25   'No virtuous woman ever enters this place'; Daniel Kirwan, *Palace and Hovel: Or, Phases of London Life* (Belnap & Bliss, 1870), p.477.

p.26   'A respectable, well-conducted house, frequented by low prostitutes'; Henry Mayhew, p.228.

p.26   Edward Colston was an eighteenth-century Bristol merchant with links to the slave trade. For this reason, Massive Attack have refused to play at the venue.

pp.30   'However crowded the room may be, as it was on the opening night, not the least inconvenience is felt from the heat'; *The Era*, 3 April 1859.

p. 32–33   The death of Thomas Bunn was reported in the Proceedings of the Central Criminal Court, 14 December 1863.

Chapter Two

p.34   'The dance halls we played in were dream palaces'; Eddie Harvey, quoted in Paolo Hewitt, *The Soul Stylists: Six Decades of Modernism – From Mods to Casuals* (Mainstream, 2000), p.25.

p.35   'A masculine woman or a feminine man'; Ethel Mannin's novel *Sounding Brass* (Jarrold's, 1925) p.239.

pp.35–6   Lord Rochester warned, 'Dancing has been known to lead to impurity of thought, desire, and practice.' See Allison Abra, *On With the Dance: Nation, Culture & Popular Dancing in Britain 1918–1945* (dissertation submitted to the University of Michigan, 2009), p.123.

p.38   'Filleted eel about to enter the stewing pot'; *The Encore*, April 1919.

p.38   'Doing its best to murder music'; *The Star*, April 1919.

p.38   'Bewildered by the weird discords'; *The Star*, April 1920.

p.38   'The syncopated frenzy'; J.B. Priestley, *The Edwardians* (Heinemann, 1970).

p.39   'Light-hearted and forgetful'; In *Testament of Youth* Vera Brittain writes: 'Already this was a different world from the one that I had known during four life-long years, a world in which people would be light-hearted and forgetful, in which themselves and their careers and their amusements would blot out political ideals and great national issues. And in that brightly lit, alien world I should have no part'; (Penguin Books, 1933) p.462.

p.40   For more on Soho in the era of Freddie Ford and Kate Meyrick see Marek Kohn, *Dope Girls: The Birth of the British Drug Underground* (Granta, 1992) and James Morton, *Gangland Soho* (Piatkus, 2008).

p.41   'An absolute sink of iniquity'; see James Morton, p.50.

p.44   The definitive work on the era's black jazz musicians, including Will Cook and Dan Kildare, is Tim Brooks' *Lost Sounds: Blacks & the Birth of the Recording Industry 1890–1919* (University of Illinois Press, 2004).

p.45   The police description of the sandwich shop's clientele as 'prostitutes and Continental undesirables' is quoted in Kohn, p.37.

p.45   Letter to Sir John Simon, reported in Kohn, p.32.

p.46   The 'list of abominations' is quoted in David Fowler, *The First Teenagers: The Lifestyle of Young Wage-earners in Interwar Britain* (Routledge, 1996), p.106.

p.46   'American peculiarities'; quoted in Jim Godbolt, *A History of Jazz in Britain 1919–50* (Quartet, 1984), p.3.

p.47   'The up-to-date dances'; quoted in Abra, p.86.

p.47   'The picking-up place'; the memories of Freda (assumed name), quoted in Claire Langhamer, *Women's Leisure in England 1920–60* (Manchester University Press, 2000), p.117.

p.48   'Preparing for a dance is half the fun to my mind'; quoted in Langhamer, p.65.

p.48   One of the characters in Ethel Mannin's novel *Sounding Brass* is described thus: 'Her life swung to the rhythm of the saxophone; her soul was Jazz … She was as bright as diamonds, and as hard', ibid. p.187.

p.48   'Frivolous, scantily-clad'; *Manchester Evening News*, 5 February 1920. Less than a week later, in the same newspaper, another opinion piece was headlined, 'Dance Music; has it a degrading tendency?' and concluded that, yes, on balance, it had (10 February).

p.49   'The majority of men much prefer a girl of modest disposition'; *Daily Express*, 23 February 1920.

p.49   'Partners are slow in coming forward'; see Abra, p.115.

pp.49–50   The story of the Kosmo Club emerged during the trial of the three club officials (reported in the *Glasgow Herald*, 1 December 1933).

p.50   'A woman's dancing skills trumped her looks at the dance hall'; see Judith R. Walkowitz, *Nights Out: Life in Cosmopolitan London* (Yale University Press, 2012), p.189.

p.50   'It was positively unsafe'; Phyllis Haylor and Alec Miller, quoted in Abra, p.66.

p.52   'The cultural directors of the nation'; see Tom Harrisson and Charles Madge, *Britain By Mass-Observation* (Harmondsworth, 1939), p.141.

p.53   'Women for ten shillings a bet walked naked through the rooms'; Mark Benney's memoir is quoted in Morton, pp.46–7.

p.55   Police surveillance at the Running Horse is described in Matt Houlbrook, *Queer London* (University of Chicago Press, 2006), p.77.

p.57   'The Royal dance hall in North London was known as the "Jewish" hall'; Abra, p.143.

p.57   For more on ceilidhs and other forms of female leisure activity, see Langhamer.

p.58   'You knew what kind of reputation'; Philomena Goodman in *Women, Sexuality & War* (Palgrave Macmillan, 2001), p.135.

p.60   '"Bop", "re-bop" or "be-bop"'; David Boulton, *Jazz in Britain* (Jazz Book Club, 1959), p.82.

p.61   'Bebop was like a clarion call'; Laurie Morgan, quoted in Pip Granger, *Up West: Voices from the Streets of Post-War London* (Corgi, 2009), p.297.

p.61   'Jazz was a serious music'; Humphrey Lyttelton, *I Play As I Please* (MacGibbon & Kee, 1954), p.122.

Chapter Three

p.67   'Young people – not necessarily jazz fans – began to desert the big dance halls'; Humphrey Lyttelton, *Second Chorus* (MacGibbon & Kee, 1958), p.56.

p.69   'The 600-strong line that stretched across two blocks'; Caroline Coon in *Melody Maker*, 2 October 1976.

pp.72–3   Don Rendell and Bill Le Sage's memories are recorded here: www.henrybebop.com/myclub11.htm.

p.74   'The sight of a teenage figure walking the streets'; quoted in Frith et al., *The History of Live Music in Britain, Volume I: 1950–1967 (Ashgate, 2013)*, p.126.

p.75   George Melly, *Owning Up* (Penguin, 2006).

p.76   'Give the poor cow a chance'; Elaine Delmar, quoted by Lucy O'Brien in Sarah Cooper (ed.), *Girls! Girls! Girls! Essays on Women and Music* (Cassell, 1995), p.77.

p.77   'To me it was just like being in a movie set'; Bryan Ferry, quoted in Michael Bracewell, *Roxy: The Band That Invented an Era* (Faber, 2007), p.46.

p.77   'Like a motorcycle gang without the motorcycles'; Eric Burdon, *Don't Let Me Be Misunderstood: A Memoir* (Da Capo Press, 2001), p.38.

p.78   'For the very first time you could see and hear this incredibly powerful music'; Roger Eagle, quoted in Bill Sykes, *Sit Down! Listen to This! The Roger Eagle Story* (Empire, 2012), p.12.

p.80   'An upstart generation'; Keith Waterhouse, quoted in Robert Sellers, *Don't Let the Bastards Grind You Down: How One Generation of British Actors Changed the World* (Arrow, 2012), p.335.

pp.80–1   'Pubs as old-fashioned'; Adrian Horn, *Juke Box Britain: Americanisation and Youth Culture, 1945–60* (Manchester University Press, 2009), p.181.

p.81   'Nobody bothered you'; Wally Whyton, quoted in Tony Bacon, *London Live* (Miller Freeman, 1999), p.25.

p.82   'No aim, no ambition, no belief'; Richard Hoggart, *The Uses of Literacy: Aspects of Working-Class Life* (Penguin, 1957), p.221.

p.84   'The most important agent and promoter based in northern England'; Frith et al., p.191.

p.85   'She single-handedly reinvigorated the idea of modern British fashion'; Shawn Levy, *Ready, Steady, Go! Swinging London & the Invention of Cool* (Fourth Estate, 2002), p.47.

p.85   'It was just amazing'; Dennis Hopper, quoted in Levy, p.9.

p.86   'Before that all you had was the same clothes your dad wore'; Ian McLagan, quoted in Levy, p.119.

p.90   'Its main ethos was uncommercial music'; Frith et al., p.111.

p.90   'The English can do the twist by moving only one leg'; Bob Dylan, quoted in Robert Shelton, *No Direction Home: the Life & Music of Bob Dylan* (Penguin, 1987), p.254.

p.91   'I couldn't find nowhere for a dance'; Duke Vin quote from Gus Berger's documentary film, *Duke Vin & the Birth of Ska* (2008).

p.91   H.S. Kingdon imposing a colour bar at the Locarno Dance Hall was reported in the *Norwood News*, 1 November 1929.

p.93   For more on record hops, Alan Freed, Jimmy Savile and early pioneering disc jockeys see Dave Haslam, *Adventures on the Wheels of Steel* (Fourth Estate, 2001).

p.93   'The first full-time rock & roll outfit in the country'; *Melody Maker*, 13 May 1956.

Chapter Four

p.103   'Danger money'; Jim McCartney, quoted in Bradford E. Loker, *History with the Beatles* (Dog Ear, 2009), p.45.

p.103   'Stank of disinfectant'; Gerry Marsden, quoted in Spencer Leigh's obituary of Alan Sytner, the *Independent*, 13 January 2006. Alan Sytner's assertion, 'I had terrible advice', from the same source.

p.104   'People know about the Cavern, but the Casbah was the place where all that started' and 'We were sitting with a cup of cappuccino trying to persuade Stuart to get this bass'; both McCartney quotes from *The Beatles Monthly*, September 2002.

p.106   'I rang him up from the Jacaranda'; Bob Wooler, quoted in Philip Norman, *Shout! The True Story of the Beatles* (Elm Tree Books, 1981), p.105.

p.106   'They thought we were from Hamburg'; John Lennon interview in *Playboy*, 28 October 1964.

p.107   Newspaper cutting related to the theft of 'Bern' Burnell's stage gear appears here: http://sladestory.blogspot.co.uk/2008/11/memphis-cutouts.html.

p.108   'A group of teddy boys started throwing coins'; McCartney quoted in the *Gloucester Citizen*, 27 November 2009.

p.111   'Ealing is obviously the foundation'; John Mayall in *Classic Blues* magazine, October 2012.

p.112   'Elite clique'; Chris Dreja in *Uncut* magazine, April 2013.

pp.112–3   'We weren't a pop band' (Bill Wyman) and 'They were playing with guts and conviction' (Giorgio Gomelsky); see Ian McPherson's website www.timeisonourside.com.

p.114   'Thin and waistless'; Andrew Loog Oldham in *Stoned: A Memoir of London in the 1960s* (St Martin's Press, 2000), p.186.

p.116 'We were mesmerised by it all'; Brian Hoggetts writes here: http://www.brumbeat.net/letters.htm.

p.118 'The best-looking girls in Newcastle, quite tarty'; Bryan Ferry quoted in Michael Bracewell, *Roxy: The Band that Invented an Era (Faber, 2007)* p.49.

p.119 'People were leaving the theatre singing it'; Eric Burdon interview in *Uncut* magazine, May 2009.

p.120 'I remember thinking, "This is going to be a Number One record"'; Hilton Valentine interview in *Uncut* magazine, May 2009.

p.120 One of the songs Van Morrison wrote and recorded after Them, once he'd gone solo, was 'Joe Harper Saturday Morning', which namechecks the caretaker at the Maritime.

p.122 'Robert Plant would jump up'; John Crutchley, quoted in Barney Hoskyns, *Led Zeppelin: The Oral History of the World's Greatest Rock Band* (John Wiley & Sons, 2012), p.44.

Chapter Five

p.132 'A symbol of Britain's recovery after the Second World War'; *Coventry Telegraph*, 9 April 2013.

p.133 'It's a supposedly enlightened age'; Edinburgh Plaza's dress-code debacle is reported in Elizabeth Casciani, *Oh, How We Danced! The History of Ballroom Dancing in Scotland* (Mercat Press, 1994), p.119.

p.134 'For the last dance of the evening the lights would go down'; Fred Fielder, quoted in the *Manchester Evening News*, 9 July 2007.

p.134 'City-lights eroticism'; Howard Jacobson, *No More Mr Nice Guy* (Jonathan Cape, 1998), p.160.

p.136 For much more on Guy Stevens, his time at the Scene and subsequently at Island Records, and also as a producer, see Dave Haslam, *Adventures on the Wheels of Steel* (Fourth Estate, 2001).

p.138 'It's already been done to perfection'; Roger Eagle, quoted in Sykes, *Sit Down! Listen to This! The Roger Eagle Story (Empire, 2012),* p.22.

p.139 'They wore a hybrid of American Ivy League and the Italian look'; Eric Clapton, *Clapton: The Autobiography* (Broadway Books, 2007), p.61.

p.140 'The Scene was really where it was at'; Pete Townshend quote in Geoffrey Giuliano, *Behind Blue Eyes: The Life of Pete Townshend* (Cooper Square, 2002), p.49.

p.141 'At that time in London there were only a tiny, tiny number of people who were into r&b'; O'Rahilly, quoted in *Mojo* magazine, August 1994.

p.142 For more on drug use among jazz (and other) musicians see Harry Shapiro, *Waiting for the Man: Story of Drugs and Popular Music* (Quartet, 1989).

p.144   'The greatest records you can imagine were being played'; Pete
        Meaden interview by Steve Turner, reproduced in Paolo Hewitt
        (ed.), *The Sharper Word: A Mod Anthology* (Helter Skelter, 1999),
        p.166.

p.146   There are a number of promoters and/or venues who have also
        run record labels. Count Suckle founded a record label, Q
        Records (a subsidiary of Trojan Records).

p.149   'There was nothing else I'd rather be doing'; Pete Townshend,
        Who I Am (HarperCollins, 2002), p.77.

p.152   'All these boys want to be DJs and they will do anything for a
        break'; Tom Wolfe, 'The Noonday Underground' in *The Pump
        House Gang* (Farrar, Straus & Giroux, 1968), p.108.

p.152   For more on the Esquire in Sheffield see Don Hale with Terry
        Thornton, *Club 60 & the Esquire: Sheffield Sounds in the 60s*
        (ALD, 2007).

p.156   'No, mate. We're beatniks'; Mick Farren, *Give the Anarchist a
        Cigarette* (Jonathan Cape, 2001), p.42.

p.157   'Weird breaks'; Pete Jenner in *ZigZag*, October 1972.

p.158   A photograph of the Railway Hotel in Harrow appears on the
        inside sleeve of the 1971 Who compilation album *Meaty Beaty
        Big and Bouncy*. Andy Neill & Matt Kent, *The Complete Chronicle
        of the Who* (Virgin, 2005) is full of useful Who-related material.

p.158   'For a few chaotic and historic years, the Marquee was the most
        important venue in Britain'; *Uncut*, May 2013.

Chapter Six

p.161   'The best club in Britain'; John Peel writing in the introduction
        to Kevin Duffy, *Mothers 1968–1971: the Home of Good Sounds*
        (Birmingham Library Services, 1977).

p.161   'In the appropriate circles it is famed throughout the land';
        Evening Mail, 12 March 1970.

p.162   'Drug addicts and peddlers, degenerates who specialise in
        obscene orgies'; the *People*, 24 July 1960.

p.162   'The rebel intelligentsia'; Mick Farren, *Give the Anarchist a
        Cigarette (Johnathan Cape, 2005)* p.18.

p.163   'Dylan is the darling of the sweet young things now'; *Melody
        Maker*, 22 May 1965.

p.164   'In a small country [he means England], excitement was like
        steam in a kettle'; Robert Shelton in *No Direction Home*
        (Penguin, 1986), p.288.

p.165   'The moment at which the nascent underground stood up to be
        counted'; Jonathon Green, *All Dressed Up: The Sixties and the
        Counterculture* (Jonathan Cape, 1998), p.128.

p.165   'Cosmonauts of inner space'; a phrase picked out by Burroughs in his introduction to Trocchi's *Man of Leisure* (Calder & Boyars, 1972), p.9.

p.165   Ginsberg imagined a better world: 'Everybody lost in a dream world of their own making', quoted in Barry Miles, *Allen Ginsberg: Beat Poet* (Virgin Publishing, 2000), p.63.

p.166   'People with whom I could empathise and identify'; Farren, p.61.

p.167   'Our weapons, our challenges, our visible insults'; Angela Carter in 'Notes for a Theory of Sixties Style', in *New Society* (1967), collected in Angela Carter, *Nothing Sacred: Selected Writings* (Virago, 1982).

p.167   Paul McCartney's recollections of LSD in coffee quoted in Green, p.195. Lennon's 'growing infatuation' with LSD also in Green, p.196.

p.167   'The wisest, holiest, most effective avatars the human race has ever produced'; Timothy Leary, quoted in Philip Norman, *Shout! The True Story of the Beatles (Elm Tree Books, 1981),* p.287.

p.169   'An aggressively commercial scene'; *International Times*, 2 June 1967.

p.172   'STP was like a quadruple-strength dose of acid'; Eric Clapton in an interview with Nigel Williamson quoted in Christopher Hjort and Charles Horton, *Strange Brew: Eric Clapton and the British Blues Boom 1965–1970* (Jawbone, 2007).

p.174   'A weird atonal cacophony'; Farren, p.120.

p.175   'At least half the audience were doing acid. I was doing acid'; Peter Jenner, quoted in Jonathon Green, *Days In The Life: Voices from the English Underground, 1961–1971* (Pimlico, 1998).

p.175   'A grass named Joe, thick-set, with large head'; *International Times*, 2 June 1967.

p.180   David Stringer in *International Times*, 31 May 1968.

p.181   'Safe refuge for psychedelic people'; Brian Jackson, quoted in Bill Sykes, *Sit Down! Listen to This! The Roger Eagle Story (Empire, 2012),* p.106.

p.183   'No one else had suits on at all'; C.J. Stone, *Fierce Dancing: Adventures in the Underground.* (Faber & Faber, 1996).

p.183   'That was the first club outside London that meant anything at all'; Roy Harper, quoted here: http://www.birminghammusic-archive.com/carlton-ballroom/.

p.187   'I was learning all kinds of things about the nature of performance'; Willy Russell, writing here: http://www.willy russell.com/music.html.

p.187   Andor Gomme, quoted in Andrew Foyle, *Bristol* (Pevsner Architectural Guides: City Guides, Yale University Press, 2004), p.155.

p.190   'A long, narrow, live-music and drinking joint'; Farren, p.358.

Chapter Seven

p.194   For more on the Twisted Wheel and Northern Soul, see David Nowell, *Too Darn Soulful – the Story of Northern Soul* (Robson Books, 1999).

p.194   'Such scarcity of illumination tends to have a widening effect on the pupils of the eyes'; Dave Godin, *Blues & Soul*, issue 50 (January 1971).

p.199   'We could have hardly called a nightclub "Shut That Door"'; George Best, *Blessed: The Autobiography* (Ebury, 2002), p.221.

p.199   Clubship *Landfall* in Liverpool was moored first at Canning Half-Tide Dock, and then the Collingwood on Regent Road. It then became a favoured lunchtime haunt, before evolving into a club with an over-25s policy. After a brief time as a club, it was left to rot for two decades before sinking at its berth in Birkenhead in 2010. In November 2014 it was refloated as part of a plan to take it to a museum in Portsmouth.

p.200   'A celebrity haunt helping build Newcastle's reputation as a party city'; Newcastle's *Evening Chronicle*, 7 December 2007.

p.201   'Soul music has become the only true "underground" music in the country now'; Dave Godin, *Blues & Soul*, issue 67 (September 1971).

p.210   'Very faggy indeed'; Bertie Marshall, *Berlin Bromley* (SAF, 2006), p.99.

p.213   'A great big party'; Terri Hooley, quoted here: http://news.bbc.co.uk/1/hi/northern_ireland/7797071.stm.

p.216   'The closest I have ever got to a religious experience'; Don Letts, *Culture Clash: Dread Meets Punk Rockers* (SAF, 2007), p.74.

p.218   More on Crackers in Roberts Elms, *The Way We Wore* (Picador, 2005).

p.219   For more on jazz, jazz funk etc. see Mark 'Snowboy' Cotgrove, *From Jazz Funk & Fusion to Acid Jazz: the History of the UK Jazz Dance Scene* (Chaser Publications, 2009).

Chapter Eight

p.227   'The classic definition of a fleapit, all peeling paint and stained seats'; Kris Needs in *ZigZag* magazine, June 1977.

p.228   'Something seems to be happening'; Mick Farren in *NME*, 19 June 1976.

p.228   'The problem with those bands was that they left you as they found you'; *Uncut* magazine, October 2004.

p.229   'A front parlour affair'; Morrissey, quoted in Jon Savage, *England's Dreaming The Sex Pistols & Punk Rock (Faber & Faber, 1991)*, p.176.

p.229   'The seventies incarnation'; Richard Boon, quoted in Johnny

Rogan, *Morrissey and Marr: The Severed Alliance* (Omnibus, 1992), p.126.

p.230   'When they played Nottingham, alas, everybody went out to the chip shop'; claim made online: http://www.left lion.co.uk, 1 May 2005.

p.231   Chris Charlesworth in *Melody Maker*, 20 July 1974.

p.231   Charles Shaar Murray, *NME*, 7 June 1975.

p.233   'It's the story of the travelling nonsense'; John Lydon, quoted in the sleevenotes for Sex Pistols, *SexBox 1* (3 CD box set, Virgin Records, 2002).

p.234   The book in which there's a chapter discussing the Sex Pistols gig at Didsbury College which didn't happen is Ian Inglis (ed.), *Performance & Popular Music: History, Place & Time* (Ashgate, 2006).

p.236   'I'm normally a very slow person and it made me more intense'; John Lydon, quoted in Jon Savage, ibid. p.191.

p.237   'We used to take acid at Louise's'; John Lydon, quoted in Jon Savage, ibid, p.187.

p.238   'Absolutely nobody else looked like that'; Neil Spencer, quoted: http://www.geocities.ws/kutie_jones/earlygigs.html.

p.239   'They were light years ahead of us'; Strummer, quoted: http://www.geocities.ws/kutie_jones/earlygigs.html.

p.242   For more about Jayne Casey, Cut Above the Rest and her gang of friends, see Dave Haslam, *Not Abba: the Real Story of the 1970s* (Fourth Estate, 2005).

p.244   'Where they're going to next is anyone's guess!'; Buzzcocks review in *NME*, 27 November 1976.

pp.245–6 'There were no other places like the early Roxy'; quote from an interview with Shanne Bradley on the website http://www.punk77.co.uk/. In the *Leveller* magazine in March 1978 Poly Styrene of X-Ray Spex had this to say about the Roxy: 'When the Roxy opened it was somewhere any new band could play. If it hadn't been for the Roxy, we probably wouldn't have formed the band.'

pp.246–7 'The punks couldn't roll their own spliffs'; Don Letts, *Culture Clash (SAF, 2007)*,p.95.

p.248   'The post-Grundy tabloid punk circus'; Letts, p.96.

p.251   'A supergroup with a difference – its members only became super after they left'; Paddy Shennan, *Liverpool Echo*, 20 September 2003.

Chapter Nine

p.259   The 'Only After Dark' events are monthly, and have taken place at various venues in Birmingham. At the time of writing they take place at the Apres Bar, Summer Row.

p.261 'Eddie Fewtrell tells a different tale in his memoirs'; Eddie Fewtrell with Shirley Thompson, *King of Clubs: The Eddie Fewtrell Story* (Brewin Books, 2007).

p.261 Jenny Clarke's memories of the Kray Twins at the Club A Go Go were reported in 1992 in the local *Chronicle* newspaper. The article is posted on Roger Smith's excellent website documenting venues in the Northeast through the 1960s; http://www.readysteadygone.co.uk.

p.264 'In the words of Ray's son Paul'; in an email to the author.

p.265 Report on Studio 54's aborted plans to open a London venue in *NME*, 17 June 1978.

p.268 Robert Elms recalls his 'Chinese space-Cossack attire' in Robert Elms, *The Way We Wore: A Life in Threads* (Picador, 2005), p.183.

p.268 'Invent yourself. Entertain'; Nicola Tyson, quoted in the *Guardian* (online), 25 January 2013.

p.269 'I had queued'; Steve Strange, in an interview carried on the website www.theblitzkids.com.

p.272 Confirmation of the details of the Geno Washington gig from Kevin Rowland in an email to the author.

p.273 *Fingered*, film by Richard Kern, 1986.

p.276 'Attentive audiences'; Eric Haydock, quoted in Simon Frith et al., *The History of live music in Britain, Volume I: 1950–1967 (Ashgale, 2013)*,p.181.

Chapter Ten

p.278 'He rammed his guitar upwards, not necessarily intending to do any damage'; Sandie's words are quoted on a website dedicated to documenting Hendrix's visits to the Northeast: http:// www.hendrixnortheast.pwp.blueyonder.co.uk/hendrix/.

p.278 Jimmy Nail told his Hendrix story in January 1999 on the occasion of the release of the film *Still Crazy*.

p.279 'I remember Hendrix creating a hole in the plaster ceiling'; Sting, *Broken Music: A Memoir* (Dial Press, 2003), p.85.

p.279 Ian Vargeson was in the audience at the Wellington and discusses Hendrix 'getting bored in the middle of one song' here: http://norfolksamericanconnections.com/people-g-m/jimi-hendrix/.

p.279 'The old, conventional way of making music would never be the same'; Pete Townshend, Who I Am (HarperCollins, 2002),p.4.

p.280 The Jimi Hendrix and George Best in Majorca story by Keith Altham appears in *NME*, 27 July 1968.

p.280 'Crawling with women'; George Best, Blessed (Edbury, 2002), p.199.

p.282   'The punks were my heroes'; Terri Hooley interview in *Sydney Morning Herald*, 3 June 2014.

p.284   For more on the Limit, Human League, Cabaret Voltaire etc. see Martin Lilleker, *Beats Working for a Living: the Story of Popular Music in Sheffield 1973–1984* (Juma, 2005).

p.285   Steve Fisher recounts his Sandpiper memories here: http://www.smfpics.com/backcat/sandpiper/.

p.287   'It was a place of great depression because of all the factory closures'; Martyn Ware, quoted in Lilleker, p.94.

p.288   'To be fair, we did incite a lot of people'; Chris Watson, quoted in Lilleker, p.23.

p.291   'They whack the shit out of NY's overrated Suicide'; Charles Shaar Murray in *NME*, 29 August 1978.

p.292   'The whole punk explosion came along and it showed anybody could do anything'; Stephen Singleton, quoted in Lilleker, p.94.

p.294   'Iggy imitators acting out their sons-of-World-War-Two histrionics' and the quote from Rob Gretton ('smart, punky, but not scruffy') are from James Nice, *Shadowplayers: the Rise and Fall of Factory Records* (Aurum, 2010), pp.33–4.

p.295   'There was a big sign'; Alan Erasmus is quoted in FAC 229, a *Music Week* supplement, 15 July 1989.

p.296   'Because it was a West Indian club they also had a great sound system'; Chris Watson, quoted in Nice, p.38.

pp.298–9 'We'd like to stay on the outside'; Ian Curtis in *NME*, 13 January 1979.

p.299   'Do you want to buy one of these records?'; Stephen Singleton quote from http://www.sheffieldvision.com.

p.301   'Remarkably boring'; Morrissey in *Record Mirror*, 22 August 1981.

p.305   'The best set of haircuts I've ever seen'; Paul Morley, *The Face*, August 1981.

p.307   'It was a proper little backdoor club which, at the time, had been unchanged since the 1970s, so it was all flock wallpaper'; DJ Parrot quoted here: http://www.djhistory.com/ interviews/dj-parrot.

p.309   'A place that you want to be living in'; Richard Boon in *Sublime: Manchester Music and Design 1976–1992* (Cornerhouse, 1992).

Chapter Eleven

p.310   For more on the Bristol scene in the 1980s see Phil Johnson, *Straight Outa Bristol* (Hodder & Stoughton, 1996).

p.312   'I didn't think being a DJ was a career back then'; Milo interview in Chris Burton and Gary Thompson, *Art and Sound of the Bristol Underground* (Tangent Books, 2009) p.94.

p.312   'People who went to the Dug Out found their own sense of

belonging'; Karl Harrington comment here: www.electric
pavilion.org/dugout/blog.

p.315   For more on clubs including the Dirtbox see Sheryl Garratt,
Adventures in Wonderland: A Decade of Club Culture (Headline,
1998). For more on all forms of DJing and club nights from the
early 1960s onwards see Bill Brewster and Frank Broughton,
Last Night a DJ Saved My Life (Headline, 1999).

p.320   'I remember walking into this stark, industrial space'; DJ Justin
Robertson is quoted in Richard Norris, *Paul Oakenfold: The
Authorised Biography* (Bantam, 2007), p.156.

p.321   'Then we started getting black kids coming down'; DJ Parrot
quoted here: http://www.djhistory.com/interviews/dj-parrot.

p.325   'I loved the energy'; Carl Cox in Garratt, p.107.

p.326   'You weren't intimidated, you felt comfortable'; Lisa Loud in
Garratt, p.109.

p.326   'There were these fresh-faced people completely mashed on
drugs'; Mark Moore, quoted in Sean Bidder, *Pump Up the
Volume* (Channel 4 Books, 2001), p.102.

p.327   'That first night was *the* defining, life-changing moment
of my life'; Helena Marsh, quoted in Garratt, p.114.

p.327   'The sound was very much a very heavy black sound'; Ashley
Beedle quote here: http://blog.scottsmenswear.com/rip-par-
ties-at-clink-st/.

p.327   'A packed club, everyone going absolutely crazy, but it was only
like half past nine or something'; Graeme Park in an interview
with Raili Haslam.

p.328   Terry Farley talking about Graham Ball in Bidder, p.103.

p.328   'It wasn't like anything you'd ever experienced in a club before';
John McCready, quoted in the *Observer*, 20 April 2008.

p.329   'In one night, everything that went before it was gone, redundant'; Norman Jay, quoted in Garratt, p.122. Later Norman Jay
was a prime mover in the 'High on Hope' night. On one occasion he put on En Vogue, who played for free as long as it was
unannounced. 'Hold On' was just about to break. When they
performed, the crowd went berserk. Thankfully Norman had
hired extra security. En Vogue had to be smuggled out of the
back door.

p.332   Paul Staines recalls his first E in Matthew Collin, *Altered State:
The Story of Ecstasy Culture and Acid House* (Serpent's Tail, 2009),
p.105. Staines now runs the Guido Fawkes blog site.

p.334   'You won't find any girls in Dolcis cream stilettoes at an acid
house party'; Linda Duff, *Daily Mirror*, 29 June 1989.

p.335   'Idiosyncratic reaction'; quote from the coroner reported in the
Daily Mail, 9 December 1989.

pp.336–7   Quote from Mike Pickering about an acid tab and Darren Partington describing the area around the Thunderdome as 'rough-arsed' both from *Clash* magazine, September 2008.

p.340   'When we started up the club, we had no idea that these were the sort of people we would have to deal with'; Tony Wilson, quoted in *NME*, 9 February 1991.

Chapter Twelve

p.344   'There was no need to wear a tie on a Friday, and trainers were quite acceptable'; Mr Matthews, quoted in the *Evening Sentinel*, 19 June 1992.

p.345   For more on the history of DJing and the rise of the 'superstar DJs' see: Ulf Poschardt, *DJ Culture* (Quartet, 1998); Dave Haslam, *Adventures on the Wheels of Steel: the Rise of the Superstar DJs* (Fourth Estate, 2001); and Dom Phillips, *Superstar DJs Here We Go!* (Ebury, 2009).

p.349   The quotes by Stuart Reid in this chapter are from an interview on the http://www.kmag.co.uk website.

p.352   'Reprobates' and other Kath McDermott quotes are from the 'Queer Noise' section of the website www.mdmarchive.co.uk.

p.356   Fabio and Storm quotes about Rage from http://www.dj mag.com/node/7168.

p.357   James Ballie's Venus on Stanford Street was housed in a venue formerly known by other names, including the Dungeon, and – during a phase as a gay club – Shades. As Baillie later said, 'Venus was the place that bridged the gap between the North/South divide and brought the whole Balearic network together' (interview here: http://dalstonsuperstore.com).

p.363   The Megadog review in *Melody Maker*, 11 December 1993, credits two reviewers: Zane and Push.

p.364   'Substance-fuelled'; Andrew Weatherall an onstage conversation with the author at Beacons festival, August 2014.

p.367   'Drugs are cool, that is the problem. At least they are when you are twenty-one and feel indestructible'; Phillips, p.315.

p.367   'It became more and more a drug-dealer's paradise'; Darren Hughes, quoted in Phillips, p.234.

Chapter Thirteen

p.370   'The acid house recession'; Dom Phillips, Superstar DJs Here We Go! (Edbury, 2009), p.353.

p.375   'The era of the superstar DJ and so-called superclub has come to a dramatic end'; *Evening Standard*, 7 November 2002.

p.378   Keith Reilly talking about Fabric and recounting the story of Talvin Singh's watch from an interview in *Jockey Slut* in October

2000. Later, Fabric's owners opened a second venue, a 2,600–capacity music venue, Matter, located at the O2 Arena in Greenwich, but Matter ran into financial trouble and caused a hiccup at Fabric, which was placed in administration for a short while in 2010.

p.379   Alex Needham here: http://www.interviewmagazine.com/music/the-london-dubstep-scene/#_.

p.382   'Andrew was the most incredibly hideous dancer'; Virginia Roberts in diary extracts published on http://radaronline.com/.

p.382   'The question perhaps, shouldn't be, did Anna Chapman get to meet a prince'; Olivia Cole writing on the http://www.thedailybeast.com site.

p.383   'He did not callously use me for sex'; Sally Anderson, quoted in the *Guardian*, 19 February 2014.

p.385   'Officers have been on the site and the gathering is good humoured though very noisy'; quote from Sussex Police, reported in the *Mirror*, 26 May 2014.

p.385   'It doesn't bother me one bit'; *Daily Telegraph*, 26 May 2014.

p.386   After the raids on Garlands, the Lomax and Republik, Chief Superintendent Jon Ward, from Merseyside Police, said the raids and closures were linked, all part of 'An investigation targeting irresponsible licensed premises where violence and contributory factors, such as drugs and excess alcohol, have caused issues.'

p.389   Mr Bagnall explaining the closure of the Music Box, *Manchester Evening News*, 28 April 2010.

p.390   Luke Unabomber's 'dark corridors with stained walls' quote is from an interview posted on www.skiddle.com on 24 October 2012.

p.391   'The early Club Suicide nights at John Willie Lees reasserted a DIY, John Peel-esque spirit in Manchester'; Bill Campbell quote from www.skiddle.com (posted 13 July 2013).

p.391   The full champagne list at Annabel's is here: http://www.annabels.co.uk/sites/default/files/food-and-drinks/champagne-menu.pdf.

p.392   Abigail Ward quote from *Strange Trees* (Switchflicker, 2009), p.2.

Outro

p.393   The last act to play the Hammersmith Palais were Groove Armada, some six weeks after the Fall.

p.395   'We may not have the glossiest leaflets, or the biggest marketing budget'; see the Adelphi website: http://www.theadelphi.com/.

p.399   'You just do it any way you can'; Chris Chinchilla quote is from an interview posted on www.wired.com, August 2004.

p.402 'Edinburgh's nightlife has suffered significantly since the millennium'; Kris Walker in *The List*, 28 February 2012.

p.408 Ian Cape confesses to liberating a chair from Le Phonographique in Leeds on the club's Facebook page.

p.409 'For one of its iconic and historic venues to be demolished to make way for a budget hotel is, quite simply, appalling'; James Ketchell, quoted on the website http://www.mancunian matters.co.uk/, 3 August 2012.

p.411 'We're facing a war on culture, fuelled by consumerism'; Alan McGee, quoted in *NME*, 9 February 2015.

p.412 'Just a few years ago the Baltic Triangle'; http://independent-liverpool.co.uk/blogs/a-moment-with-baltic-creative/.

p.412 'The Club That Changed The World'; *Melody Maker*, 18 March 1995.

p.413 The words of Councillor Norma Austin Hart reported here: http://www.theedinburghreporter.co.uk (25 November 2014). Subsequently Kris Walker told me the outlook for grassroots culture has improved: 'Edinburgh, whilst hardly Berlin, has really improved since *The List* article'; (email to the author, January 2015).

p.415 The top tip for surviving a night at Jesters (Southampton) is in a review carried on the website www.omgmad.com.

p.418 'Piled-up passions were exploded on a Saturday night'; Alan Sillitoe, *Saturday Night and Sunday Morning* (W.H. Allen, 1958), p.9.

p.418 'Numbers of people staggering and seeing others lying in the gutter'; Friedrich Engels, *The Condition of the Working Class in England* (1845: Panther, 1969), p.157.

p.420 Mick Farren wrote that 'stumbling into Indica was like a ticket to the magic kingdom'; Give The Anarchist a Cigarette (Jonathan Cape, 2001), p.84.

INDEX

(venues whose names begin with figures are placed as if spelled out)

A Certain Ratio, 299, 304
Abadi brothers, 137, 138, 193, 195–6
Abbott, Myra, 90
ABC (formerly Vice Versa, *q.v.*), 299, 302, 305
Abigail's, Birmingham, 260
AC/DC, 245
Ace of Clubs, Leeds, 256–7
Ad Lib, London, 135, 171
Adamski, 341
Adamson, Barry, 270
Adamson, Stuart, 396
Adelphi, Hull, 395
Adelphi, Leeds, 263
Adelphi, West Bromwich, 124
Adventures in Lust, Hanley, 388
Advert, Gaye, 241
Adverts, 255
Afghan Whigs, 308
Africa Centre, London, viii, 314, 405
Aitken, Matt, 350
Ajanta, Derby, 285
Akins, George Jr, 396
Akins, George Sr, 396
Alan Price Set, 177
Albarn, Damon, 393
Albert Hall, London, *see* Royal Albert Hall
Albert Hall, Manchester, 413–14
Albertine, Viv, 235–6, 241, 246, 247–8, 249, 351, 417
Alex Harvey and His Beat Band, 107
Alexander, Scott, 404
Alexandra, Manchester, 10–11
Alexandra Music Hall, Canterbury, 2
Alexandra Music Hall, Sheffield, 22
Alexandra Palace, London, 173–4
Alhambra, Nelson, 40
Ali, Muhammad, ix, 145
Alibi, London, 209

Alien Sex Fiend, 273
All Caribbean Steel Band, 84
All Saints Hall, London, 169
Allan, Stu, 347, 352
Allen, Fiona, 359
Allen, Trevor, viii
Almond, Marc, xiii, 273, 307
Altern 8, 350
Ambrose, Bert, 51
AMM, 157
Amnesia House, Longton, 347
Amnesia, Ibiza, 324–5
Anderson, Ian A., 156
Anderson, Paul 'Trouble', 218, 316
Andrews, Phil, 416
Androids, 282
Angels, Burnley, 225, 293, 351
Animals, 77, 89, 100, 101, 117, 118, 119–20, 122–3, 136, 225
Annabel's, London, 197, 382–3
Anokha, London, 378
Aphex Twin, 363
Apocalypse Now, London, 332
Arch, Brighton, 394
Archway, Manchester, 352
Arctic Monkeys, 253, 415
Argent, 206
Argyll Rooms, London, 25–6
Art Brut, 399
Artery, 299
Ashby-De-La-Soul, 414
Ashfield, Tony, 210–11
Ashworth, Joe, 393
Asprilla, Tino, 382
Associates, 301
Astley, Rick, 350
Astoria, London, 62, 325, 329, 410
Astoria (aka the Rainbow), Finsbury Park, 163
Au Pairs, 301

Audio, Brighton, 394
Azena Ballroom, Sheffield, 109

B-52s, 283
Back to Basics, Leeds, 341
Back to the Future, London, 334
Back to Hell, Manchester, 409
Backhouse, Dave, 179, 180
Bagley's, London, 362
Bagnall, Billy, 125
Bagnall, John, 389
Bailey, James, 357
Bailey, Paul, 414, 415
Baker, Arthur, 304
Baker, Chet, 86, 142
Baldry, Long John, 111
Ball, Graham, 328
Balmbra's, Newcastle, 6
Bamboo, Bristol, 188, 407
Bananarama, 268, 276
Banco De Gaia, 363
Band of Joy, 179
Band on the Wall, Manchester, 57, 244
Bang, London, 62, 217, 218
Bannerman's Edinburgh, 413
Bannister, Freddy, 150, 188
Barbarella's, Birmingham, 196, 259, 260, 262, 301, 393
Barber, Chris, 79
Bargeld, Blixa, 306
Barker, Ronnie, 117, 118
Barker, Simon, 236
Barmy Barry, 124, 179, 200
Barnum, P.T., 19
Barratt, Richard, see Parrot
Barrel Organ, Digbeth, 264
Barrett, Jeff, 365
Barrett, Syd, 175 (see also Pink Floyd)
Barrie, Jack, 159
Barron Knights, 196
Barrowland, Glasgow, ix, 34, 51, 58, 62, 406
Barton, James, 52, 323, 333, 335, 347–8, 357–9, 365–9 passim, 405
Batcave, London, xiii, xvi, 139, 273–4, 275
Batchelor, Kid, 327
Batt, Fred, 63–4, 379–80, 389
Bay Hotel, Sunderland, 94
Beach Boys, 163
Beach Club, Manchester, 300–1, 303
Beastie Boys, 304, 307, 325
Beat, 251, 271–2

Beatles (formerly Quarry Men, q.v.), 62, 63, 89, 96, 101, 103–9, 110, 113–14, 116, 122, 126, 127, 136, 153, 160, 163–4, 167, 171
beatniks, 74, 95, 105, 137, 156, 161–2
Beckett, Steve, 341–2
Bed, Leeds, 376
Bed, Sheffield, 376
Bee Gee, Leeds, 194
Beedle, Ashley, 327
Beer, Dave, 341
Bell, Patti, 258, 259, 267
Beloved, 327, 340
Beltram, Joey, 350
Benson, Ivy, 59
Berkmann, Justin, 353–4
Berlin, 236
Berlin, Manchester, 317
Bermuda, Birmingham, 260, 261
Berrow, Michael, 265, 266
Berrow, Paul, 264–5, 266
Berrow, Ray, 264
Berry, Andrew, 318
Berry, Chuck, 105, 119, 136, 141, 232
Berry, Dave, 153
Best, George, 198, 199, 280, 382
Best, Mona, 104, 105, 130
Best, Pete, 89, 104, 105
Bestival, 387
Betesh, Danny, 84, 137
Better Books, 164
Betts, Leah, 366–7
Bez, 382
Big in Japan, 127, 254, 250–1, 295, 365
Big Three, 104, 126
Big Youth, 215
Bilk, Acker, 187
Billy's, London, xi, xii, xv, 83, 139, 263, 267–9, 271, 405, 417
Bin Lid, Dewsbury, 194
Bingley Hall, 213
Biology, London, 334
Birdcage, Portsmouth, 178
Birley, Mark, 197
Birmingham Odeon, 275
Birmingham Sound Reproducers, 100, 125
Birthday Party, 305, 306
Björk, 378
Black Bee Soul Club, 414, 419
Black Cat Club, Sheffield, 153
Black Market, 420

Black Sabbath, 94, 100, 158, 184, 185, 191–2, 291, 393
Black Swan, Sheffield, 240, 253, 289
Black & White Milk Bar, London, 58
The Black and White Minstrel Show, 29
Blackpool Mecca, 201, 215, 224, 225
Blake, Cyril, 56
Blake, George 'Happy', 56
Bland, Bobby, 144
Blarney Club, London, 171
Blast, Chester, 357
Bleasdale, Paul, 358–9
Blind Tiger, Brighton, 403
Blitz, London, xii, 83, 269, 270, 271, 314, 417
Blodwyn Pig, 184
Blondie, 262, 283
Bloom, John, 171
Blue Bell, Hull, 213
Blue Lantern, London, 54
Blue Moon, Cheltenham, 178
Blue Note, London, 360, 377–8
Blue Note, Manchester, 179
Blue Rondo à la Turk, 317
Blues Incorporated, 94, 111, 135, 148
Bluesbreakers, 111, 175
Boardwalk, Manchester, 377, 395
Boardwalk, Sheffield, 253
Boat Club, Nottingham, 173, 230, 284–5, 301
Bob Marley and the Wailers, 188, 216
Boileroom, Guildford, 403
Boland, Derek, 316
Bollox, Manchester, 390, 409
Bolton Palais, ix, 34, 36, 63
Bond, Graham, 117
Bond's, Birmingham, 357
Bongo, Edinburgh, 402, 413
Bonham, John, 100, 121, 184, 212–13, 417 (see also Led Zeppelin)
Bono, 283, 300
Bonzo Dog Doo Dah Band, 170
Boodle's, London, 11
Boogie's, Birmingham, 260
Book Shop, Edinburgh, 164
Boon, Clint, 404
Boon, Richard, 229, 238–9, 241, 248–9, 289–90, 297, 300, 309
Booth, Dave, 317
Bootleg Beatles, 163
Borderline Club, London, 191
Boujis, London, 382
Bounce, Nottingham, 361

Bow Wow Wow, 283, 301
Bowery, Leigh, 315
Bowie, Angie, 207, 210
Bowie, David, 157, 167, 206–7, 210, 214–15, 262, 265, 269, 274, 406
Boy George, xiii, 254, 267, 271, 277, 283
Boyd, Joe, 169–70, 176
Boyle, Mark, 170
Braceland, Jack, 176
Bradley, Shanne, 233, 234, 245–6, 254
Brain, London, 341
Brannigans, Leeds, 308
Bread Basket, London, 81
Brick, Chris, 315
Brighton Essoldo, 228
Britannia Panopticon, Glasgow, 3
British Queen, London, 26
Bromley Contingent, 236, 237
Brooker, Gary, 129
Broudie, Ian, 251, 295
Brown, Chris, 219
Brown, James, 149, 215
Brown, Joe, 81
Brown, Louis, 171
Brown, Miquel, 226
Brown, Pete, 164, 170
Browne, David, 208
Bruce, Lenny, 168
Bryant, Bill, 209
Budgie, see Clarke, Peter 'Budgie'
Bukem, LTJ, 360
Bullimore, Lalel, 188
Bullimore, Tony, 188, 191, 407
Bungalow Bar, Paisley, 281
Bunn, Thomas, 32–3
Burdon, Eric, 77, 82, 89, 123, 150, 171 (see also Animals)
Burgess, Guy, xiv
Burke, Solomon, 155
Burn, Colin, 199
Burnell, Bern, 107
Burns, Pete, 242, 251
Burra, Edward, xvi
Burroughs, William, 161, 165
Burton, Chris, 178–9, 202–4, 416, 419–20
Burton, Peter, 209–10
Buster, Prince, 145
Buxbaum, Chris, 272
Buzzcocks, 68, 229, 238, 240, 241, 244, 249, 253, 285, 289–90, 297, 298
Byrds, 189

Cabaret Voltaire, 287, 288–90, 292, 296, 297, 298, 299, 307, 308, 342, 374, 413
Caesars, Streatham, 63–4, 379–80
Café de Paris, London, 40, 57–8, 62
Cafe Oto, London, 412
Cagney's, Liverpool, 266
Cajmere, 380
Calvert, Leon, 72
Cambridge Music Hall, Toxteth, 18
Camden Palace, London, 314
Campbell, Bill, 414
Campbell, Ian, 90
Campbell, Keith, 212
Campbell, Pat, 131
Canal Street, Manchester, 390
Canter, Graham, 218
Canterbury Arms, London, 5
Cape, Ian, 408
Caplan, Melissa, 268, 269
Captain Beefheart, 176, 179, 191
Caravan, 206
Cardew, Cornelius, 157
Cardy, Graham, 256
Carlton Ballroom, Birmingham, 161–2, 182
Carlton Club, London, 11
Carmel, 255
Carmen, George, 338
Carr, Mike, 82, 119
Carrington, Ray, 220
Carrington, Sue, 246, 316
Carroll, Andy, 323, 347, 358–9
Carter, Derrick, 315
Carthy, Martin, 90
Casbah, Derry, 282
Casbah, Liverpool, 104–5, 130
Casey, Jayne, 127, 242, 250, 295, 365–6, 367, 386–7
Casino, Manchester, 23
Castle Cinema, Caerphilly, 244
Catacombs, London, 211, 217
Catacombs, Wolverhampton, 206, 224
Catatonia, 69
Catherall, Joanne, 302
Cat's Whiskers, Burnley, 197
Cat's Whiskers, Oldham, 197
Cat's Whiskers, Streatham, 63 (see also Locarno, Streatham)
Cave, Nick, 273, 307
Cave of the Golden Calf, London, 42–3, 62
Cavern, Liverpool, ix, 88–9, 101, 103–4, 105, 106, 126, 242, 402
Caves, Edinburgh, 413
Cecil, Malcolm, 82, 94
Cedar, Birmingham, 260, 300
Chaguarama's, London, 210–11, 226, 246
Chairman of the Board, 220
Chakk, 307
Chambers, Tintin, 332–3
Chandler, Chas, 89, 123–4, 171, 280 (see also Animals)
Chandler, Kerri, 381
Chapman, Anna, 382
Chapman, Colin, 206
Chapman, Johnny, 135
Chapman, Mary, 206
Charlatans, 406
Charles, Ray, 129, 136, 142
Charlesworth, Chris, 231
Charlie's Manchester, 390
Chase & Status, 387
Checker, Chubby, 151
Chelsea, 245, 246
Chelsea Reach, New Brighton, 221
Chelsea School of Art, 235, 236
Chemical Brothers (formerly Dust Brothers, q.v.), 364, 372–4, 389
Cherry, Neneh, 311, 316, 342
Chester, Charlie, 341
Chic, 299, 387
Chinchilla, Chris, 399
Chinese R&B Jazz Club, Bristol, 156
Chisnall, Arthur, 111
Chris Farlowe and the Thunderbirds, 155
Churchill, Arabella, 189
Cinderella Dance Club, London, 58
Cinderella Rockafella's, Leeds, 198
Cinderella Rockerfella's, Edinburgh, 197
Circus, Liverpool, 380
Circus, London, 315
Ciro's, London, 40, 42, 44–5, 51, 62
City Hall, Sheffield, 287, 321
City Rockers, 312
City Varieties, Leeds, 3–4, 7–9, 16, 28–30, 93
Clancy Brothers, 187
Clapton, Eric, 111, 139–40, 171–2, 191, 416
Claridge, David, 272, 273, 276–7, 314–15
Clarke, Hewan, 303, 318, 319
Clarke, John Cooper, 253, 255, 290
Clarke, Margi, 296

Clarke, Peter 'Budgie', 251, 254
Clash, 63, 68, 140, 227, 228, 230, 232, 235, 239, 240, 241, 246, 249, 250, 251, 262, 282
Clayton, Adam, 300
Cleethorpes Pier, 206
Cliff Bennett and the Rebel Rousers, 151
Cliff, Jimmy, 188
Clock DVA, 299
Close, Ritchie, 321
Cloud Nine, Manchester, 317
Club A Go Go, Newcastle, 84, 94, 101, 117–19, 123–4, 261, 278–9, 280, 393, 417
Club Brenda, Manchester, 391, 392, 410
Club Dog, London, 361
Club Eleven, London, 71–2, 73, 74, 83, 139, 401
Club Lash, Manchester, 409
Club Noreik, London, 150
Club 60, Sheffield, 95
Club Suicide, Manchester, 390–1, 405
Club Zoo, 304
Clubship Landfall, Liverpool, 199
Coasters, 138, 141
Cobain, Kurt, x, 308, 408
Cocker, Jarvis, 254, 307 (see also Pulp)
Cocker, Joe, 152
Cohen, Leonard, 190
Cokell, Les, 194, 226
Coldplay, 406
Cole, Gracie, 59
Cole, Nat King, 74, 76
Coleman, Emil, 51
Coliseum, London, 227, 249, 378
College of Art, High Wycombe, 238
Colley, Simon, 263–4
Collin, Matthew, 336, 338
Colston Hall, Bristol, 26, 154
Colston-Hayter, Tony, 332, 333
Colyer, Ken, 66, 71, 79, 111, 113
Comets, 78
Compton, Jayne, 414
Cons, Paul, 319, 320, 330, 370, 371
Constable, Paulette, 371
Continental, Preston, 415
Cook, Ali, 341
Cookies & Cream, London, 378
Cookson, Francis, 297
Cooper, Alice, 66
Cooper, Sue, 300
Cope, Julian, 251, 304
Corbett, Ronnie, 196

Corea, Chick, 102
Cornershop, 69
Corso, Gregory, 161
Cosmo, Leeds, 297, 308
Cotterill, Chris, 275
Country Joe & the Fish, 185
County, Wayne, 231, 247
Cousins, Les, 186
Cowell, Ted, 187
Cox, Carl, 325, 387
Cozens, Randy, 220
Crackers, London, 218–19, 253, 417
Crane River Jazz Band, 71
Crawdaddy, Richmond, 101, 112–15, 158, 401, 417
Crawling King Snakes, 121
Crazy Daisy, Sheffield, 287–8, 292, 302
Crazy World of Arthur Brown, 174, 190
Cream (band), 163, 171, 172
Cream, Liverpool, 365–9 passim, 323, 345, 357–9, 359–60, 364, 367, 370, 372, 374–6, 412
Creamfields, 373, 376
Creft, Tony, 332, 336
Crewe, Nicky, 181, 191
Croasdell, Ady, 69, 220
Crombie, Tony, 72, 93–4
Cromwellian, London, 171
Crown Bar, Edinburgh, 90
Crown, Birmingham, 90
Crucible studio, Sheffield, 289
Cruisers, 153
Crutchley, John, 121–2
Crystal Ballroom, Newcastle-under-Lyme, 203
Culture Club, 254
Cure, 281, 298, 304, 336
Currie, Billy, 270 (see also Ultravox)
Curtain Club, Brighton, 208
Curtis, Colin, 202, 203, 204, 215, 293, 316, 317, 389, 419
Curtis, Ian, 245, 294, 298–9, 301
Czezowski, Andy, 233, 246, 248, 253–4, 316

Dada, 262, 263
Daddy Warbucks, Glasgow, 306
Daddy G, 251, 311–12, 314, 316, 343
Dalton, Clem, 151–2
Daltrey, Roger, 150
Damned, 65, 68, 234, 241, 243, 246, 256, 286, 287, 357
Danceteria, New York, 303, 304

Dane Tempest & the Atoms, 110
Dankworth, Johnny, 60, 71, 74
Dantalion's Chariot, 177
Dasilva, Jon, 330, 331, 335, 337
Dave Hunt R&B Band, 112
Davenport, Stuart, 358
Davies, Cyril, 94, 96, 111
Davies, Ray, 112
Davis, Miles, 72, 83, 86, 102, 142
Davis, Spencer, 90
Davis, Steve, 200
Davyd, Mark, 416
Day's Concert Hall, Birmingham, 17
De Quincey, Thomas, 10–11
De Wulf, Frank, 350
Dead Kennedys, 62
Dead or Alive, 127
Deaf School, 241
Dean Street Townhouse, London,
    xii–xiii, xv, 268
Def Leppard, 283–4, 291–2
DeFries, Tony, 207
Degville, Martin, 259, 263, 267, 268
Del Naga, Robert 'Delge', see 3D
Del Sol, Manchester, 198–9
Delaney, Shelagh, 84
Delight, Longton, 346, 347
Delirium, London, 325–6, 329, 354, 417
Delmar, Elaine, 75–6
Dene, 'Farmer' Carl, 206
Dennistoun Palais, Glasgow, 36
Denny Laine & the Diplomats, 110, 121
Depeche Mode, 301
Deviants, 160, 174, 182, 191
Devilles, Manchester, 317
Devoto, Howard, 229, 238, 248 (see also
    Buzzcocks)
Dexter, Jeff, 152, 170, 176
Dexys Midnight Runners, 271–2, 283,
    299, 301
Diamond, Johnny, 19
Diddley, Bo, 141
Didsbury College, 234
Digbeth Civic Hall, 223
Digital, Brighton, 394
Digital, Newcastle, 382
Dillinger, 243, 252
Dingwalls, London, 190–1, 235, 329
Dire Straits, 283
Dirtbox, London, 315, 329
Disco Evangelists, 364
Divine, 277, 325
Dixielanders, 61, 67

DIY, 361, 362
Dr Feelgood, 191, 230
Doctors of Madness, 239
Dolenz, Micky, 172
Dollar, 226
Domino, Fats, 91, 141
Don, Mike, 181
Donegan, Lonnie, 79–80, 196
Donnelly, Anthony, 335, 346
Donnelly, Chris, 335, 346
Donovan, 157
Dooleys, 196
Dormon, Jason, 416
Down Under, Manchester, 404
Downbeat Club, Newcastle, 82, 84, 89,
    117
Dreja, Chris, 111–12
Drum Club, 363
Drummond, Bill, 242, 250, 295
Drunk at Vogue, Manchester, 415
Dubliners, 187
Duchess of York, Leeds, 308, 395, 396,
    408
Duffy, Stephen, 263–4
Dug Out, Bristol, viii, 310–11, 312, 313,
    343, 393, 417
Dulcimer, Manchester, 414
Dunbar, John, 167
Duran Duran, 260, 262, 264, 266, 267,
    270–1, 275, 276, 301
Durutti Column, 294–5, 296, 297, 298
Dust Brothers (later Chemical Brothers,
    q.v.), 365, 389
Dutton, Lyn, 71–2
Dyer, Danny, 406
Dylan, Bob, 90, 156, 162, 163–4, 165,
    180, 190, 191, 229

Eagle, Roger, 78, 95, 126, 127, 128, 136,
    138, 139, 140, 141, 152, 154,
    179–80, 185–6, 193, 241–2, 250,
    254, 295, 298, 416
Ealing Jazz Club, 96, 111–12, 113
Earl Fuggle and the Electric Poets, 173
Earth (later Black Sabbath, q.v.), 184, 191
Earth, Wind & Fire, 299
Eastern Bloc, Manchester, 352, 364, 420
Eastwick, Elliot, 355, 371
Eat Static, 363
Eavis, Michael, 189
Echo & the Bunnymen, 127, 299
Eclipse, Coventry, 345, 348–9, 350, 351,
    352, 355, 360, 406

ecstasy, 326, 329, 334, 338, 345, 366–7, 383–4
Eddie & the Hot Rods, 231, 237
Edge, 300
Edgecombe, Johnny, 145
Edinburgh Playhouse, 249
Edmonds, Noel, 200
The Edwardians (Priestley), 38–9
Edwards, Barry, 349
Edwards, Doreen, 197
Edwards, Greg, 219
Edwards, Jackie, 145
Edwards No. 7, Birmingham, 260
Edwards No. 8, Birmingham, 396–7
Eel Pie Island Hotel, 111, 112
Egan, Rusty, xii, 267, 268, 269, 270, 272, 314
808 State, 331
El Paradiso, London, 239
El Rio, Macclesfield, 84, 137
Elbow, 404
Elbow Room, Aston, 179
Eldritch, Andrew, 274, 275
Electric Ballroom, 316
Electric Chair, Manchester, 377, 389
Electric Circus, Manchester, 244–5, 249, 255, 293, 294
Electric Garden, Glasgow, 169
Electric Garden, London, 169
Electric Light Orchestra, 100
Electric Village, Bristol, 206
Electronic, 340
Electronic Glen, 274
Elgin, London, 230, 239
Elliott, Joe, 291–2
Ellis, Martyn, 203
Elms, Robert, 268
Embassy Club, London, 51, 217–18
Emerson Lake and Palmer, 100
Emperor Rosko, 124, 200
End, London, 417
Enemy, 400
Energy, London, 334
English Stage Company, 80
Enid, 196
Eno, Brian, 290
Enterprise, 312
Envi, Liverpool, 226
Epstein, Brian, 107–8, 110, 114, 121
Erasmus, Alan, 294–5, 298
Erasure, 226
Eric's, Liverpool, viii, 126–7, 242–3, 244, 249–51, 281, 282, 286, 295, 401, 402

Escape, Brighton, 394
Esquire, Sheffield, 96, 152, 158, 287
Establishment, London, 169
Etchington, Kathy, 171
Eubank, Chris, 367
Eurythmics, 276
Evison, Dave, 204, 406
EVOL, Liverpool, 397, 416
Exeter Civic Hall, 182
Expresso Bongo, Morley, 84

F-Club, Leeds, 284, 286, 297, 300
Fabio, 334, 345, 355–6, 360
Fabric, London, 374–5, 376–7, 378
Factory (club), Manchester, 281, 282, 295–8, 401
Factory Records, 255, 286, 294, 298, 302, 304, 317, 319
Fagin's, Manchester, 196, 293
Fahey, Siobhan, 268, 276
Fairhurst, Roger, 136
Fairley, Alan, 52
Fairport Convention, 90, 179
Faith, Adam, 81, 105
Faithfull, Marianne, 169
Fall, 253, 274, 301, 344, 393
Fallow, Manchester, 414
Falstaff, London, 53
Fame, Georgie, 144
Family Funktion, London, 316
Far Side, London, 363
Farina, Richard, 90
Farley, Terry, 328, 364
Farlowe, Chris, 155
Farren, Mick, 156, 160, 161, 162, 168, 170–1, 174, 177, 184–5, 190–1, 228, 251
Fashion, 300
Fatboy Slim, 345, 357, 372, 375
Faver, Colin, 329, 355
FBI Crew, 312
Feldman, Joe, 70
Feldman, Monty, 70
Feldman, Robert, 70
Feldman, Victor, 70, 83
Feldman's, London (later 100 Club), *see* 100 Club, London
Fellows, Graham, 296
Fenton, Greg, 337
Fenton, Shane, 134
Ferret, Preston, 415
Ferry, Bryan, 76–7, 94, 117–18, 417
Fewtrell, Don, 260–1

Fewtrell, Eddie, 260–1
Fforde Green, Leeds, 388
5th Avenue, Manchester, 222
52nd Street, 304
Fighting Cocks, Birmingham, 301, 304
Finn, Mickey, 387
Fitzgerald, Ella, 85
Flamingo, London, 56, 77, 85, 144–5, 146
Fleece, Bristol, 403
Fleetwood Mac, 188
Flesh, at the Haçienda, Manchester, 370–1 (see also Haçienda)
Floral Hall, Belfast, 173, 407
Florida Rooms, Brighton, 75, 147, 148
Flowers of Romance, 241, 249
Flying, London, 341
Focus, 126
FON, Sheffield, 341
Foo Foo's Palace, Manchester, 237
Foot Patrol, 318, 337
Footworkers, 321
Forbidden, Glasgow, 388
Forest, Edinburgh, 402
Formula, Dave, 270
Forsyth, Bruce, 163
43 Gerrard Street, Soho, 41, 54
Forum, Tunbridge Wells, 394, 397, 416
Foulk, Ray, 190
Four Aces, Dalston, 216, 251
Four Tops, 124, 154
14-Hour Technicolor Dream, 173–4
Franklin, Fran, 225, 414
Frantic Elevators, 243
Free, 206
Free Trade Hall, Manchester, 12, 180, 207, 240
Freed, Alan, 93
French, Sean, 219
Fresh Four, 342
Friars, Aylesbury, 186
Fridge, London, 254, 316, 342
Friendly Fires, 415
Fry, Martin, 292–3, 299
Fuel, Manchester, 414
Fullado, London, 61
Fulwell, Pete, 126, 242
Fung, Trevor, 324, 355
Fury Murry's, Glasgow, 388
Futurama, Leeds, 299
Future, London, 326–7, 329
FWD>>, London, 378

Gaiety Music Hall, 2

Gallagher, Liam, ix
Gallagher, Rory, 173
Gang of Four, 250, 284, 297
Gardening Club, London, 388
Gargoyle, London, xiii–xiv, xvi, 268, 271, 273, 275, 408
Garnier, Laurent, 315, 347, 349, 381, 416–17
Garry, Len, 89
Garvey, Guy, 404–5
Gascoigne, Paul, 367
Gatecrasher, Sheffield, 373, 375, 376
Gateways, London, 209
Gatsby's, Liverpool, 242–3, 323
Gaumont, Coventry, 79
Gaumont State, Kilburn, 79
Gaumont, Wolverhampton, 110
gay venues/nights, 13–14, 54–5, 62, 207–12, 217–18, 237, 352–3, 370–1, 389, 390–1, 408–9, 410–11
Gecko, Manchester, 404–5
Gee, John, 158–9
Geisha Bar, Sheffield, 302
Generation X, 246
Genesis, 158
Genevieve's, Sheffield, 307
Geno Washington & the Ram Jam Band, 124, 272
Gentle, Johnny, 107
George & Dragon, Manchester, 57
George Robey, London, 361, 363
Georgie Fame & His Blue Flames, 144
Germs, 295
Gerry and the Pacemakers, 103
Getz, Stan, 102
Gibbon, Keith, 280
Gibbons, Steve, 258
Gifford, Phil, 357
Gilbert, Gillian, 301
Gill, Andy, 289
Gillespie, Dizzy, 60, 67, 72
Ginsberg, Allen, 161, 165, 168
Glitter, Gary, 81, 126
Godard, Vic, 249
Godfrey, Charlie, 16
Godin, Dave, 194, 201, 226
Goins, Herbie, 77
Gold Coast, London, 275
Golden Eagle, Birmingham, 301
Golden Guinea, New Brighton, 222
Golden Lion, London, 239
Golden Torch, Tunstall, 124, 178–9, 202–5, 224, 419

Goldie, 316–17, 360
Goldmine, Canvey Island, 219, 224
Gomelsky, Giorgio, 112–13, 119, 141, 417
Good, the Bad & the Queen, 393
Good Mixer, London, 412
The Good Old Days, 29
Good Vibrations, 282, 364, 420
Gopal, Sam, 173
Gordon, Aloysius 'Lucky', 145
Gordon, Dexter, 86
Gordon, Noele, 212
Gordon, Robert, 341–2
Gorilla, Manchester, 413
Gossips, London, xi, xii, xv, 267, 269, 271, 275, 405
Graham Bond Organisation, 118, 153
Granary, Bristol, 187–8, 407
Grand Hotel, Bristol, 116, 166
Grant, John, 293
Gray, David, 163
Gray, Phil, 315
Gray, Wardell, 86
Grayson, Larry, 212
Green, Jonathon, 165
Green Moose Café, Liverpool, 187
Green Note, London, 412
Greer, Germaine, 161, 184–5
Gretton, Rob, 294, 295, 302, 304, 367
Grey Topper, Jacksdale, 285
Grooverider, 345, 347, 355–6, 387
Grosvenor House Hotel, Birmingham, 212
Grundy, Bill, 236, 243, 309
guerrilla gigs, 398–9
Guetta, David, 381
Guilded Cage, Birmingham, 223
Gullivers, London, 218
Gunnell, Rik, 85, 144
Guthrie, Woody, 89
Guy, Buddy, 111, 191
Guys, Birmingham, 212

Haçienda, Manchester, viii, ix, xii, 75, 204, 222, 286, 294, 303–5 passim, 308, 317, 318, 319–21, 322–3, 327, 328, 330, 334–5, 337–40, 341, 349, 351, 359, 367–8, 370–2, 388, 419
Hagan, Joe, 275
Hague, Sam, 18, 22
Haines, Perry, 271
Haisman, Gary, 329
Haley, Bill, 78, 79

Hall, Terry, 225, 283 (see also Specials)
Hallamshire, Sheffield, 289
Hambone, London, viii, 35, 71–2
Hamilton, James, 218
Hamilton, Kate, 25–6
Hammersmith Palais, 37–8, 39, 42, 50, 62, 135, 252, 254–5, 393
Hangar 13, Ayr, 366
Hannett, Martin, 298, 299, 302
Hanton, Colin, 89
Happening 44, London, 176
Happy Jack's, London, 364
Happy Mondays, 335, 340
Hard Times, Leeds, 354–5
Hard Times, Mirfield, 354
Haring, Keith, 304
Harley, Sheffield, 288, 418
Harp Bar, Belfast, 282, 407
Harper, Roy, 183, 186
Harriott, Chester, 209
Harris, Calvin, 381, 406
Harris, Jack, 51
Harris, Rufus, 178
Harrison, George, 108 (see also Beatles)
Harry, Bill, 107
Harry, Debbie, 285 (see also Blondie)
Harvey, Eddie, 34
Haslam, Dave (author), 320, 339, 342
Haughton, Yogi, 406
Havinoo, London, 54 (see also New Avenue)
Hawkins, Screamin' Jay, 138
Hawkwind, 186
Hawley, Dave, 152–3
Hawley, Richard, 153
Haydock, Eric, 276 (see also Hollies)
Hayes, Tubby, 119
Haylor, Phyllis, 50
Haynes, Jim, 164
Haysi Fantayzee, 268, 315
Hayward, Philip, 172
Hazel, Winston, 321, 341
Healy, Jeremy, 268, 315
Heartbreakers, 247, 248
Heatwave, 220
Heaven, London, 226, 325, 326, 329, 332, 355, 362
Heavenly Social, 364–5, 372, 405
Hedonism, London, 329
Heidi, 315
Heimann, C.L., 51–2
Hell, London, 272
Hellfire, Wakefield, 274

Helpyourself Manchester, 398, 399
Hemment, Drew, 332, 336
Henderson, Tony, 118
Hendrix, Jimi, 84, 123–4, 158, 160, 163, 164, 171, 172, 178, 190, 228, 278–80, 283, 419 (see also Jimi Hendrix Experience)
Henry's Blues House, Birmingham, 184
Herbal Tea Party, Manchester, 364
Herbert, Lesley, 277
Hero's, Manchester, 226, 352, 353
Hey!, Manchester, 397, 400
High Numbers, 144, 147 (see also Who)
High on Hope, London, 329, 354
High Society, Chester, 357
High Society, Manchester, 352
Highland Room, Blackpool, 201, 202, 204, 215, 220
Hill, Chris, 215, 219, 329
Hill, Dave, 98, 99, 102
Hillier, John-Joseph, 23
Hilton, Paris, 381
Hippodrome, Middleton, 351
Hit Squad, 331
Hobbs, Mary Anne, 379
Hoellering, George, 87
Hogan, Anni, 273
Hoggart, Richard, 82
Hoggetts, Brian, 116
Holder, Noddy, 98–9, 100, 102–3, 116, 122, 124 (see also Slade)
Holiday, Billie, 85
Holland, Dave, 102
Holland, Tom, 219
Hollies, 115, 138, 140, 275–6
Hollingshead, Michael, 167
Holloway, Nicky, 324, 329, 335
Holmes, David, 364
Home, London, 374, 376, 383
HomoElectric, Manchester, 389, 390–1, 408–9
Hooker, John Lee, 111, 118, 119, 123, 138, 141, 152, 179
Hooley, Terri, 173, 213, 282, 364
Hooper, Nellee, 311, 313–14, 342–3
Hope & Anchor, London, 230
Hopkins, John 'Hoppy', 168, 169–70, 173
Hopper, Dennis, 85
Horkan, Chris, 400
Horn, Adrian, 80–1
Horne, Charlotte, 357, 361
Horovitz, Michael, 164, 174
Horseshoe, London, 219

Horton, Jeff, 65, 66, 67–8, 69, 70
Horton, Roger, 66, 67, 68, 71
Hosteria, Birmingham, 237, 258
Hot Bananas, 393
Hot, at the Haçienda, Manchester, 330 (see also Haçienda)
Hot Space, Manchester, 415
Houldsworth Hall, 180, 185–6
Howard, Vince, 267
Howlett, Steve 'Froggy', 218, 219
Howlin' Wolf, 141, 152
Hoxton Hall, London, 3
Hoy at Anchor, Southend, 90
Hucknall, Mick, 200, 243
Hughes, Darren, 52, 357–9, 366, 367, 374, 376
Hulley, Harold, 197
Hulme Hall, Port Sunlight, 108
Human League, 262, 284, 290–2, 297, 302
Humble Pie, 144
Humphries, Tony, 329, 345, 354
Hunter, Terry, 329
Huntsman, London, 209
Hussey, Wayne, 274
Hylton, Jack, 56, 60
Hynde, Chrissie, 241
Hypnosis, Manchester, 337
Hyslop, Alf, 285

I-Roy, 215
Ian Campbell Folk Group, 90, 184
Iggy Pop, 250
Ilford Palais, 36, 37, 130, 131–2
I'm So Hollow, 299
Impressions, 142
Incredible String Band, 90, 176
Indica, London, 167–8
Indigo, London, 412
Inner Mind, 288
Inspiral Carpets, 359
Iommi, Tony, 109, 184 (see also Black Sabbath)
Isabella's, Sheffield, 305
Islington Assembly Hall, 412
Islington Mill, 414
Ivanhoe's, Huddersfield, 252, 253

Jacaranda, Liverpool, 83–4, 105–6
Jacko Ogg & the Head People, 179, 180
Jackson, Chad, 319
Jackson, Paul, 395
Jackson, Steve, 319

Jagger, Mick, 66, 103, 112, 114, 116, 163, 169, 210 (*see also* Rolling Stones)
Jam, 286
Jam MCs, 335, 337
James, 307, 359
James, Daniel, 272
James, Greg, 218
Jansch, Bert, 90, 156
Jay, Norman, 224, 314, 316, 329
Jazz Defektors, 317
Jazz Room, London, 316
Jazzie B, 316
Jean Machine, 215
Jebb, Tony, 201, 203
Jeff Beck Group, 177
Jefferson Airplane, 189, 190, 191
Jeffery, Mike, 82, 84, 117, 124, 280
Jenner, Peter, 157, 169, 174–5
Jester, Birmingham, 212
Jesters, Southampton, 415
Jethro Tull, 158, 180
Jett, Joan, 396
Jig's, London, 56
Jilted John, 295, 296
Jimi Hendrix Experience, 123, 280
Jive-A-Tones, 128
Jive Turkey, Sheffield, 307, 308, 318, 321, 322, 341, 417
John Willie Lees, Manchester, 390–1
Johnny Thunders and the Heartbreakers, 191
Johnson, Dean, 320
Johnson, Holly, 242, 251, 295
Johnson, Kevan, 284
Johnson, Miles, *see* Milo
Johnson, 'White Tony', 340
Joiners, Southampton, 415
Jones, Al, 156
Jones, Alan, 208, 211, 232, 239
Jones, Allen, 272
Jones, Brian, 112, 113, 114, 116, 144, 416 (*see also* Rolling Stones)
Jones, Mick, 228, 235 (*see also* Clash)
Jordan (at SEX), 211, 234
Joseph, Harry, 28, 93
Joy Division (later New Order, *q.v.*), 250, 254, 255, 283, 285, 293–4, 295, 296, 297, 298–9, 301, 302, 389
Joy, Rochdale, 335, 346
Joy, Ruth, 331
Judge Jules, 314, 316, 334, 375
Jug o'Punch, Digbeth, 90

Junco Partners, 117, 118
Jungfrau, Manchester, 138

K-Klass, 357
Kalima, 317
Kamins, Mark, 303–4
Kandy Lounge, London, 208
Kane, Eden, 81
Kansas City Five, 89
Kaos, Leeds, 349
Kapoor, Sweety, 377–8
Kardashian, Kim, 381
Kazimier, Liverpool, 412
Keeler, Christine, 145
Keenan, John, 175, 255–7, 284, 286, 297, 300, 308, 416
Keita, Salif, 314
Kelly, Bair, 106
Kelly, John, 333, 335
Kelly, Martin, 365
Kemistry, 356, 360, 361
Kemp, Fiona, 266
Kendrick, Dave, 371
Kennedy, John, 317
Kent, Nick, 240
Kerr, Andrew, 189
Kerr, Jim, 283
Kershaw, Nik, 200
Kid Unknown, 352
Killing Joke, 301
Killjoys, 257
Killon, Norman, 250
King, Andrew, 169
King, Ben E., 124
King Crimson, 158
King, Jonathan, 126
King, Pete, 87
King & Queen, London, 90
King, Rob, 325, 417
King Tut's Wah Wah Hut, Glasgow, 395
Kingdon, H.S., 91–2
King's Hall, Stoke, 202
King's Place, London, 412
Kinks, 62, 65, 112, 152
Kirk, Richard, 287–9, 293, 308, 342
Kit Cat Club, London, 40
Klein, John, 273
Klooks Kleek, London, 144, 220
Knowler, Mike, 323, 347
Knuckles, Frankie, 325, 347, 354
Konspiracy, Manchester, 337, 338, 352
Kontors, 89

Korner, Alexis, 79, 94, 96, 111, 117, 136, 141
Kosmo Club, Edinburgh, 49–50, 62
Kraak Gallery, Manchester, 414–15
Kraftwerk, 262–3, 283
Kramer, Billy J., 151, 202
Kray twins, 260–2
Krevine, John, 235
Kruger, Jeff, 85
Krush, 331
Krust, 342

La Belle Angele, 413
La Chasse, London, 159
La Discotheque, London, 135, 146
La Phonographique, Leeds, 256, 274–5, 408
La Rocca, Nick, 38
Lacy Lady, London, 215, 219, 224
Lafayette, Wolverhampton, 124, 252
Laine, Denny, 121 (see also Denny Laine & the Diplomats; Moody Blues)
Lambert, Kit, 147, 149
Lambeth Town Hall, London, 92
Lammar, Frank 'Foo Foo', 237, 300
Lamp, Hull, 395
Land of Oz, London, 332
Lane, Sam, 5
Langer, Clive, 250
Laserdome, Longton, 344, 347
Lashes, Lisa, 361
Laurel Tree, London, 412
Laurie, Cy, viii, 74–5, 76, 139, 416
Le Beat Route, London, 273, 315
Le Bon, Simon, 266 (see also Duran Duran)
Le Duce, London, 209, 210
le Sage, Bill, 73
Lea, Jim, 98
Leadmill, Sheffield, vii, 301–2, 305, 306, 307, 394
Lear, Amanda, 226
Leary, Timothy, 167
Led Zeppelin, 81, 100, 163, 182, 188, 212–13, 284
Lee, Brenda, 121
Lee, CP, 179, 182, 300
Lee, Jeannette, 235, 254
Leeds Poly, 256, 349
Left Wing, Manchester, 95, 137 (see also Twisted Wheel, Manchester)
Leftfield, 350
Legend, Manchester (Princess St), 222, 317

Legends, Manchester (Whitworth St), 222, 389, 408–10, 414
Legends, Sheffield, 302
Legends, Warrington, 351
Leighton, Clare, 335
Lennaine, Terry, 221
Lennon, John, 83, 89, 104, 106, 116, 122, 167, 174 (see also Beatles)
Lennox, Annie, 276
Lennox, Tim, 352, 371
Leno, Dan, 18, 19, 317
Leno family, 18–19
Leofric, Coventry, 132, 191–2, 393–4
Lesser Free Trade Hall, Manchester, 83, 229, 234, 245, 404
Letts, Don, 215–16, 235, 246–7, 251–2, 253
Levan, Larry, 303–4, 354
Levene, Keith, 239, 241, 253 (see also Clash)
Levine, Ian, 215, 225–6
Lewis, Jerry Lee, 79, 89, 141
Lewis, Linda, 189–90
Lewis, Steve, 315
Lexington, London, 412
Leybourne, George, 17
Libertines, 398, 399, 400, 411
Life, Manchester, 352
Lilley, Patrick, 237, 258–9, 267, 277, 315, 329, 392, 417
Limit, Sheffield, vii, 281, 283–4, 285–6, 290, 291–2, 299, 394
Limpopo, 314
Listen, 121, 122
Litherland Town Hall, 106
Little Joe & the Thrillers, 128
Little Richard, 121
Littlewood, Joan, 80, 84
Live the Dream, Blackburn, 335–6
Liverpool Scene, 185, 188
LL Cool J, 325
Locarno, Bristol, 154–5, 206, 393–4
Locarno, Coventry, 132–3, 134–5, 154, 200, 206, 214, 225, 350
Locarno, Glasgow, 52, 62
Locarno, Leeds, 131
Locarno, Streatham, 34, 42, 50, 52, 63, 91–2, 379–80, 389
Locke, John, 357
Loco Dice, 315
London Blues and Barrelhouse Club, 94
London, Brian, 261
London, Gary, 217

Lord Woodbine, 84, 96
Lottie, *see* Horne, Charlotte
Loud, Lisa, 326, 328, 361
Louise's, London, 210, 226, 237
Love, 176, 186, 191
Love, Courtney, x
Love Decade, Gildersome, 336
Love Ranch, London, 341
Lucas, Chris, 211, 217
Ludus, 301
Luminaire, London, 412
Lunch, Lydia, 273, 306
Lunt, Max, 175
Lyceum, London, 31, 92, 145, 215, 216, 300
Lydon, John, *see* Rotten, Johnny
Lyons, Betty, 50
Lyttleton, Humphrey, 61, 66, 67, 71

Maal, Baaba, 314
MC5, 246
McAleer, Dave, 140, 141, 143, 148
McCartney, James, 103
McCartney, Paul, 70, 83, 89, 103, 104, 108, 114, 116, 122, 167, 169 (*see also* Beatles)
McClanahan, Mary, 59
MacColl, Ewan, 90
McCready, John, 333
McCulloch, Ian, 251
McCulloch, Ron, 374
McDermott, Kath, 371
Macdonald, Country Joe, 190–1
MacDonald, Hamish, 273
MacDonald, Mark 'Mack', 305–6
McEwen, Sam, 414, 415
McFall, Ray, 106
McFly, 163
McGeoch, John, 270
McGinnis, Richard, 315
MacGowan, Shane, 241, 254
McGregor, Billy, 51
McGriff, Jimmy, 141, 146
MacInnes, Colin, 82
McIver, Margaret, 51
Mackintosh, C.J., 314
McLagan, Ian, 86
McLaren, Malcolm, 208, 211, 232, 233, 235, 237, 239, 240, 241 (*see also* Sex Pistols)
McLusky, Sean, 341
McMillan, Len, 358
McNair, Harold, 87

McNeish, Peter, 404
McQueen, Alexander, 346
McRae, George, 214
McTell, Ralph, 186
Mad Stuntman, 354–5
Madame Jojo's, London, 410
'Madchester', 320, 359, 372
Madonna, 304, 343
Magazine, 270, 297
Magic Otters, 393
Magic Village, Manchester, viii, 160, 180–2, 186, 191, 193
Mahogany Hall, Newcastle, 76
Major Lance, 203
Malice, Laurence, 361
Mall, Stockton-on-Tees, 350
Mallinder, Stephen, 288, 293
Malvern Winter Gardens, 186
Mambo, London, 209
Manchester Cavern, 180
Manchester, England (Haslam), 41
Manchester Odeon, 79
Mandrake, London, xiv–xv, 268
Mandy's, London, 272
Manhattan Sound, Manchester, 352
Manic Street Preachers, 63, 308
Manicured Noise, 295, 296
Mansfield, John, 172
Manumission, 345
Marc and the Mambas, 273
March Violets, 274
Margox & the Zinc, 295, 296
Marilyn, 267, 268
Marimba, Newcastle, 82, 84
Maritime Hotel, Belfast, viii, 120–1, 173, 407
Marley, Bob, 188, 215, 216, 224, 235
Marquee, London, 87–8, 96, 112, 119, 137, 148–9, 157–9, 167, 228, 237–8
Marr, Johnny, 340
Marriott, Steve, 144 (*see also* Humble Pie; Small Faces)
Mars Bar, Glasgow, 283
Mars Bar, London, 360
Marsden, Gerry, 103
Marsh, Helena, 327, 340
Marsh, Ian Craig, 290, 302 (*see also* Human League)
Marsh, Jon, 340
Marshall, Grant, *see* Daddy G
Martin, George, 20
Martyn, John, 186
Marvin, Hank, 81

Mash House, Edinburgh, 413
Mason, Paul, 225, 319–20, 337, 414
Masquerade, London, 211
Mass, London, 378
Massey, Graham, 331
Massive Attack, 154, 251, 310, 311, 314, 342
Master Juba, 19
Maximes, Wigan, 351
Maximum Joy, 311
Maximus, London, 315, 341
May Fair Hotel, London, 51
May, Jack (a.k.a. Gerald Walter), 40, 41, 45
Mayall, Gaz, 275
Mayall, John, 77, 111, 129, 180, 188
Mayhem Studios, London, 314
Mayhew, Henry, 24–5, 26, 43
Meaden, Pete, 86, 144, 147
Mecca dance halls, ix, 35, 51–2, 63, 130, 131–2, 134–6, 154, 155, 196–7, 201
Mecca Empire, London, 135
Media, Nottingham, 375
Megadog, 362, 363, 373
Megatripolis, London, 362
Mekons, 284, 297
Melloy, Peter, 32–3
Melly, George, 74, 75, 96–7, 111, 161
Memphis Cutouts, 102, 107, 124
Memphis Slim, 94
Merridy, T.H., 20
Metalheadz, 360, 405
Metallica, 406
Meteors, 274
Metropolitan Music Hall, London, 7
Meyrick, Kate, 40–1, 54
Middle Earth, London, 160, 177–8
Middlesbrough Rock Garden, 249, 252
Middlesbrough Town Hall, 239
Midnight City, Digbeth, 183
Midnight Express, Bournemouth, 304
Mighty Joe Young Jazzmen, 77
Mighty, Ray, 313, 314
Miles, Barry, 164, 167, 177
Milk & Honey, London, 226
Miller, Alec, 50
Miller, John, 253
Millionaire Club, Manchester, 225
Millstone Concert Hall, Bolton, 20
Milo, 311, 312, 314
Milton, Rob, 315
Mineshaft, Manchester, 352, 389, 409
Ministry of Sound, London, 345, 354, 355, 359, 364, 380, 403, 416–17

Minogue, Kylie, 350
Minshull, Keith, 203
Miracles, 142
Miss Moneypenny's, Birmingham, 357
Mission, 274
Mr C, 327, 331
Mr Scruff, 377
Mr Smiths, Manchester, 276
Mitchell, Adrian, 164
Mitchell, Bruce, 179
Mitchell, Joni, 83, 190
Mitchell, Rob, 341–2, 417
MK, 315
MMU, Manchester, 185
Moby, 350, 351
mods, 86, 119, 140, 142–4, 145–50 passim, 156, 178
Mojo, 31
Mojo, Sheffield, 137, 153, 178, 287
Moles, Bath, 304, 394, 397, 416
molly houses, 13–14
Mona Lisa's, Sheffield, 307, 308
Money, Zoot, 177
Monkees, 172
Moody Blues, 100, 121, 151
Moon, Keith, 158, 171, 185 (see also Who)
Moore, Jack Henry, 170
Moore, Mark, 319, 326, 330, 331
Moran, Simon, xii
Morgan, Laurie, 61, 72
Morgan, Marino, 337, 338
Morillo, Erick, 354–5
Morley, Eric, 63
Morley, Paul, 229, 234, 287, 297, 305
Morris, Harry, 72
Morris, William, 195
Morrison, Van, 83, 120
Morrissey, Steven, 229, 296, 301, 304, 306, 389 (see also Smiths)
Mort, Alan, 134
Morton, Jelly Roll, 61, 67
Morton, Samantha, 357, 417
Moss, Edward, 27–8
Moss Empires, 28
Moss, Jon, 254
Moss, Phil, 134
Most Excellent, Manchester, 364
Mother Clap's, London, 13
Mothers, Birmingham, viii, 160–1, 162, 182–5, 186, 191, 407
Mothers of Invention, 185
Mott the Hoople, 178

Moulin Rouge, Ainsdale, 175, 255
Move, 100, 174
Mud, 198
Mud Club, London, 316
Mulligan, Gerry, 142
Mulligan, John, 267
Mulligan, Mick, 74, 75
Mullin, Geoff, 138
Murkage, Manchester, 378, 405
Murphy, Paul, 65, 69, 219, 316, 317
Murray, Charles Shaar, 291
Murray's, London, 39, 44, 45
Mushroom, 311, 314
Music Box, Manchester, 377, 389
Music Factory, Leeds, 341, 354
Music Machine, London, 291
Myatt, Phil, 186
Myster E, 331

'N Betweens, 102, 121, 122
N-Joi, 347
Nag's Head, High Wycombe, 68, 233
Nail, Jimmy, 278, 279
Naked Under Leather, 365, 389
Napoleon's, Manchester, 352
Nash, Graham, 275–6 (see also Hollies)
Nashville, London, 230–1, 239
Nashville Men, 138
Nasty, Billy, 364
Nation, Liverpool, 412
Needs, Kris, 227, 249
Nell Gwyn's, London, 268
Nelson, Chris, 337, 338
Nelson, Shara, 313
Nelson, Trevor 'Madhatter', 224, 314
Nervo, 381
Neutron Records, 299
Neville, Richard, 190
New Ardri, Manchester, 363–4
New Avenue, London, 54
New Cabaret, Liverpool, 96
New Cellar, South Shields, 278
New Hormones, 289, 297, 300
New Order (formerly Joy Division, q.v.), 37, 281, 301, 302–3, 319
New Orleans Jazz Club, Newcastle, 76–7, 89, 94, 117, 123
New Osborne, Manchester, 298, 336
New York Dolls, 231, 232
Newman, John, 361
Newsom, Ed, 188
Night & Day, Manchester, 403
Nightingale, Birmingham, 211–12

Nightlife, Ibiza, 324
Nights Alive, Liverpool, 333
Nile, Manchester, 222, 317, 318
999, 255
Nipper, 352
Nipple Erectors, 254
Nirvana, 63, 308
Nite Club, Edinburgh, 281
Nite Spot, Bedford, 196
Noise, Nancy, 326
Noon, Jeff, 296
Norman, Jeremy, 217, 226
Norrie Paramor & His Orchestra, 113
North Westward Ho, Manchester, 199
Northallerton Sayers, 239
Northern Soul, 193–4, 201–6, 218, 220, 224–5, 419
Northwich Memorial Hall, 131
Norwich Boogie House, 282
Not Abba (Haslam), 239–40
Nottingham Palais, 36, 63, 249
Now Wave, Manchester, 397–8, 416
Nude, at the Haçienda, Manchester, 318, 321, 322, 334, 339 (see also Haçienda)
No. 1, Manchester, 352, 353
Nuttall, Jeff, 164

Oakenfold, Paul, 324, 325, 326, 329, 332, 335, 340, 345, 374, 381, 391
Oakes, Geoff, 375
Oakey, Phil, 290, 292, 302 (see also Human League)
Oasis, 65, 69, 308
Oasis, Manchester, 138
Oceana, Nottingham, 36
October, Gene, 246
O'Donnell, Ollie, 268, 316
O'Dowd, George, see Boy George
051, Liverpool, 348, 357
Oh, Hyeonje, 310, 342–3
Ohio Players, 215, 220
O'Hooligan, Shane, see MacGowan, Shane
O'Jays, 214
Oldham, Andrew Loog, 86–7, 114–15, 116, 128–9, 143, 144
Oliver, Andrea, 316
Oliver, King, 61, 67
Oliver, Sean, 315
On The Eighth Day, Manchester, 186, 191
100 Club, London, 60–1, 65–71, 96,

137, 215, 219, 233, 240–1, 396, 405
101ers, 230–1, 232, 239
One Kew Road, 158
Ono, Yoko, 170, 174, 177
Oozits, Manchester, 300
Opposite Lock, Birmingham, 264
O'Rahilly, Ronan, 141, 146
Orbison, Roy, 121
Orbital, 341, 362–3, 364, 373
Orchestral Manoeuvres in the Dark, 127, 298, 299
Original Dixieland Jazz Band, 170
Osbourne, Ozzie, 184 (see also Black Sabbath)
O'Sullivan, Jacquie, 276
Others, 399
O2 Academy, Bristol, 394
O2, London, 412
Outlook, Doncaster, 252, 292
Outlook, Middlesbrough, 115

Pagans, 77
Page, Jimmy, 83 (see also Led Zeppelin)
Palais, Chorlton (later Princess), 46, 62
Palmer, Clive, 90, 186
Palmolive, 249, 254
Palumbo, James, 354
Paper Lace, 198
Paradise Factory, Manchester, 353
Paramounts, 129
Paras, Fabi, 358
Park, Graeme, 327, 330, 370
Park Hall, Chorley, 195
Park Hall, Wolverhampton, 124
Parker, Andrea, 361
Parker, Charlie, 60, 72
Parker, Howard, 190
Parnes, Larry, 81, 107
Parrot, 307–8, 321, 342
Parry, Crispin, 397
Parthenon Music Saloon, Liverpool, 6, 27
Partington, Darren, 336
Pastels, 306
Patten, Brian, 170
Paulette, 361
Payne, Jack, 60
Peace, David, 274
Pearce, Ben, 381
Peel, John, 94, 131, 161, 176, 178, 182–3, 184–5, 188, 254, 263, 281, 282, 291
Pendleton, Harold, 88, 148, 158
Penetration, 285, 297

Penny's Sheffield, 299, 305
Pentangle, 90, 186
Penthouse, Sheffield, 289
Penzance Winter Gardens, 252
People Show, 164
Perfect, Christine, 90
Perkins, Carl, 141
Perry, Lee 'Scratch', 378
Persian, 318
Peshay, 360
Pet Shop Boys, 207
Peterson, Gilles, 65, 69, 226, 316, 342, 379
Phantoms, 102
Phillips, Dom, 370
Photek, 360
Picador, Manchester, 300
Piccadilly Jazz Club, 112, 141
Pickering, Mike, 304–5, 318, 321, 323, 330, 334, 337, 387, 417
Pickett, Wilson, 153
Pier Pavilion, Hastings, 240
Pigbag, 311
Piller, Eddie, 406
Pink Floyd, 156–7, 160, 169, 170, 172, 173, 174–5, 176, 185, 189, 213, 228, 284
Pink Industry, 365
Pink Military, 127, 365
Pips, Manchester, 263, 293
Place, Hanley, 388
Placemate 7, Manchester, 195–6, 293, 389
Plant, Robert, 100, 121–2, 179, 184, 212–13, 417 (see also Led Zeppelin)
Plastic Dog, Bristol, 187–8
Plastic People, London, 378
Playboy, London, 198
Playpen, Manchester, 317
Plaza, Edinburgh, 133–4
Plaza, Handsworth, 99, 115, 125
Plaza, London, 197
Plaza, Manchester, 132, 134
Plaza, Old Hill, 99, 100, 102, 108–11, 115–16, 121–2, 124–5, 212–13
Pleasuredome, Bolton, 351–2
Plug, Sheffield, 417–18
Police, 256, 283
Pollen, Manchester, 364
Pollyanna's, Birmingham, 223, 260
Polsky, Ruth, 304
Pomona Palace, Manchester, 20, 199
Pop Group, 254, 285, 311

Poptastic, Manchester, 391
Portishead, 310
Powell, Don, 98, 102
Power, George, 218, 219
Preager, Lou, 50
Prendergast, Martin, 318
Presley, Elvis, 78, 89
Prestatyn Soul Weekender, 329
Pretenders, 357
Pretty Things, 174
Price, Alan, 77, 89 (see also Alan Price
    Set; Animals)
Price, Martin, 331
Priestley, J.B., 38–9, 46
Primal Scream, 340
Princess Charlotte, Leicester, 395
Princess Julia, 270, 371
Principal Edwards Magic Theatre, 185
Pritchard, Frank, 134
Probe, Liverpool, 420
Proctor, Steve, 323
Procul Harum, 129, 140
Prodigy, 350, 373, 419
Profumo, John, 145
Progress, Derby, 357, 375, 388
Project, London, 325, 326
Psychick Warriors Ov Gaia, 363
Public Enemy, 323
Public Image Limited (PiL), 215, 253,
    254, 299
Pullan, Henry, 19
Pulp, 307, 308
Pun, Liverpool, 220
Pure, Edinburgh, 357, 375

Q Club, London, 215
Quadrant Park, Bootle, 345, 347–8, 367
Quaintways, Chester, 240, 253
Quando Quango, 304, 318
Quant, Mary, 84–5, 86
Quarry Men (later Beatles, q.v.), 83, 89,
    101, 103, 104–5
Que, Birmingham, 357, 375
Queen's Hall, Leeds, 299
Queer Nation, London, 277

Radcliffe's, Manchester, 389
Radiohead, 63, 308, 361, 395
Rae, Brian, 131, 151, 153–4
Raffles, Wakefield, 274
Rafters, Manchester, 293–5, 301, 389
Rage, London, 355–6, 360
Railway Hotel, Harrow, London, 150,

158, 272, 279
Rainbow Theatre, London, 163
Raincoats, 285
Ralphy, 347
Ram Jam, London, 316
Ramones, 239
Rampling, Danny, 324, 326, 375
Rampling, Jenni, 326
Ranch, Manchester, 237
Random, Eric, 297, 300
Ranking Roger, 251
Ravensbourne College, Chislehurst, 236
raves, 332–6, 384–5
Ray's Bar, Coventry, 132
Read, Al, 188, 191
Rebecca's, Birmingham, 223, 259, 260
Rector's London, 38
Red Barn, Barnehurst, 61, 74
Red Rooster Café, Lisburn, 187
Red Snapper, 377
Redcaps, 115–16
Reed, Jimmy, 91, 123, 141, 144
Reel 2 Real, 355
Regan, Joe, 99, 110, 125
Regan, Mary 'Ma', 99–100, 108,
    109–10, 115, 125, 416
Reid, Stuart, 348–9, 350, 360, 406
Reid, Terry, 189–90
Reilly, Vini, 294
Reiner, 251
REM, 396
Rembrandt, Manchester, 352
Renaissance, 315, 345, 355, 360, 375
Renbourn, John, 156
Rendell, Ron, 72
Reno, Manchester, 222, 317–18, 331,
    393
Revillos, 283
Revolution, Liverpool, 242, 243
Revolver, 312, 420
Rezillos, 250, 255, 256, 291
Rhodes, Bernard, 235, 239
Rhodes, Nick, 262, 263–4, 266–7 (see
    also Duran Duran)
Rice, Dan, 5
Richard, Cliff, 81, 84, 136
Richards, 'Evil' Eddie, 327, 331, 334
Richards, Keith, 112, 116 (see also
    Rolling Stones)
Ricky & the Rebels, 95
Ricky Tick venues, 172–3
Ridgers, Derek, xv
Ridley, George 'Geordie', 6

RiP (Rave in Peace), 327, 331
Rip Rig & Panic, 311
Ritz, King's Heath, Birmingham, 99, 108, 125
Ritz, Manchester, 36, 52, 57, 134, 317
Ritzy, Leeds, 350
Ritzy, Streatham, 63 (see also Locarno, Streatham)
Roadhouse, Manchester, 404
Roaring Twenties, 146
Roberts, David, 332
Roberts, Paul, 357
Roberts, Pete, 409
Robertson, Joe, 118
Robertson, Justin, 320, 337, 357
Rochester, Lord, 35–6, 46
Rock Around the Clock, 78–9
Rock City, Nottingham, ix, 301, 316, 396
Rock, Mick, 207
Rocket, London, 363
Rockets, 93–4
Rockin' Chevrolets, 109
Rodgers, Nile, 328, 387
Rodigan, David, 275, 418
Rodriguez, Rico, 145
Rolling Stones, 62, 86, 96, 100, 101, 111, 112–13, 114–17, 122, 123, 139, 144, 145, 153, 163, 166, 420
Roman, Mark, 218
Romulus, Birmingham, 299
Ronnie Scott's, London, 86–7, 96, 215 (see also Scott, Ronnie)
Ronson, Mick, 207, 262
Room at the Top, Wigan, 194
Roots Rockers, London, 275
Rooty, London, 388
Rory Storm & the Hurricanes, 106
Rose, Denis, 72, 73, 416
Rose, Tim, 180
Rosies, Chester, 253
Rossi, Aldo, xi
Rotten, Johnny, 68, 232, 234, 235–6, 237, 238, 240, 251, 253 (see also Public Image Limited; Sex Pistols)
Rotters, Manchester, 322
Rough Trade, 254, 297, 298, 398, 420
Roundhouse, London, 155, 160, 162, 168–9, 173, 176, 413
Rowe, Dick, 120
Rowland, Kevin, 150, 257, 272 (see also Dexys Midnight Runners)
Rowlands, Tom, 364–5, 372, 417 (see also Chemical Brothers)

Roxy Art House, Edinburgh, 402
Roxy, London, 226, 245–8, 251, 253, 254, 255
Royal Albert Hall, 27, 55, 114, 162–6
Royal, London, 57
Rudi, 210
Rum Runner, Birmingham, xii, 139, 259–60, 264–7, 270–2 passim, 276, 393
Rumours, London, 324
Run DMC, 325
Runaways, 242–3
Running Horse, London, 55
Russell, Manchester, 222, 255, 286, 295, 298
Russell, Willy, 187
Rutherford, Paul, 242

Sabresonic, London, 364
Sachs, Leonard, 29
Saddle Room, London, 135
Sade, 317
Sager, Gareth, 311
St Albans City Hall, 249
St George's Hall, Liverpool, 26
St James's Hall, Liverpool, 2, 18
  fire at, 22
St Pancras Town Hall, London, 92
St Paul, Ian, 329
Salt 'n' Pepa, 325
Sam & Dave, 203
Sammy Houston's Jazz Club, Belfast, 121
Samwell, Ian, 145
Sanchez, Roger, 354
Sanctuary, Milton Keynes, 345
Sandpiper, Nottingham, 281, 285
Sankey's Manchester, 388
Santana, 189
Sarjeant, Sandy, 146
Sasha, 324, 337, 345, 346–7, 349, 376, 388
Savage, Anne, 361
Savage, Jon, 287, 296, 321, 322
Savile, Jimmy, 93, 130–2, 141, 200
Saville, Peter, 298
Sawhney, Nitin, 163
Scala, Wolverhampton, 92
Scanes, Richard 'Tricky Dicky', 211, 217
Scene, London, viii, 119, 136, 138–40, 141, 143–4, 146, 147, 149, 383, 405, 416
Scher, Lucy, 370
Scotch, London, 171

Scott, Doc, 347, 360
Scott, Norman, 211, 217
Scott, Ronnie, 60, 71, 72, 73, 86–7
Screen on the Green, London, 245
Scritti Politti, 254
Seaman, Dave, 347
Searling, Richard, 206
Secombe, Harry, 163
Seeger, Pete, 90
Sensateria, Birmingham, 305–6, 417
Sergeant Pepper's, Majorca, 280
SEX, London, 211, 232, 234–5
Sex Pistols, 65, 68, 83, 157, 228–30,
    232–9 passim, 240–1, 243–4, 252–3,
    262, 285, 294, 404
Seymour Hall, London, 92
Shades of Rhythm, 350
Shades, Sheffield, 288
Shades, Southend, 129
Shadows, 81
Shaft, Mike, 293, 389
Shake 'n' Fingerpop, London, 316, 329
Shamen, 341, 373
Shanes, London, 217
Shante, Roxanne, 325
Sharples, Thomas, 2, 6
Shaw, Fiona, 31
Shaw, Hank, 72
Shaw, Sandie, 121
Shearsby, Claire, 256, 274–5
Shelley, Pete, 229, 245, 296–7 (see also
    Buzzcocks)
Shelley's, Longton, 337, 344–5, 346–7,
    352, 355, 380, 387
Sherry's, Brighton, 51–2
Shim Sham Club, London, 56
Shiva's Children, 176
Shoom, London, 75, 312, 326–7, 364
Shop Assistants, 306
Shotton, Pete, 89
Shrimpton, Chrissie, 114
Sicolo, Ashley, 402
Sicolo, John, x, 402
Silver Convention, 219
Simonon, Paul, 63, 393
Simons, Ed, 364–5, 372–4, 417 (see also
    Chemical Brothers)
Simple Minds, 283
Simpson, Gerald, 331
Simpson, Jim, 184
Sims, Zoot, 87, 115
Sindrome, Longton, 346, 347
Singh, Talvin, 377–8

Singleton, Stephen, 292–3, 299
Sioux, Siouxsie, 236, 237, 241, 251, 285
Siouxsie and the Banshees, 37, 65, 236,
    248, 254, 256, 297, 299
Sisters of Mercy, 273–4, 304
69 Dean Street, London, xi–xii, xiii, 268,
    273
Size, Roni, 342
Skin Two, London, 272–3, 276–7, 315
SL2, 350
Slack Alice, Manchester, 199
Slade, 37, 98–9, 102–3, 124, 206
Slinkey, 329
Slits, 235, 249–50, 254, 255, 256, 290,
    351
Slug and Lettuce, Manchester, 390
Slugs, 255
Small Faces, 86, 140, 150
Smart, Leroy, 252
Smarties, Chester, 357
Smee, Phil, 234
Smile, Manchester, 410
Smith, Alan, 206
Smith, Bessie, 61
Smith, Bruce, 311
Smith, Jimmy, 141, 142
Smith, Mark E., 393
Smith & Mighty, 342
Smith, Patti, 231
Smith, Rob, 313, 314
Smith, Robert, xiii
Smith, Tommy, 332, 336
Smith, Viola, 59
Smiths, 304, 317, 406
Smokey Robinson and the Miracles, 243
Smokin' Joe, 361
Sneaky Pete's, Edinburgh, 413
Soft Cell, 299
Soft Machine, 160, 169, 174, 184
Soho Theatre Club, London, 341
'Sombrero' (Yours and Mine), London,
    210
Sonic Youth, 306, 319
Soul Sam, 206
Soul II Soul, London, 313–14, 316, 342,
    405
Sounds Incorporated, 151
Southern Death Cult, 274
Space, Ibiza, 372, 376
Spaine, Les, 220–1
Spandau Ballet, 270
Special Branch, London, 324
Specials, 225, 283

Specimen, 273
Spectrum, London, 329, 332
Spencer Davis Group, 145, 153, 193
Spice, Manchester, 337
Spiders, Hull, 380, 395–6
Spiral Tribe, 361–2
Spiritualized, 254
Spitalfields Tea Dances, 406
Spitfire Boys, 251
Splash One, Glasgow, 306
Spontaneous Underground, 157–8, 167, 169
Spooky Tooth, 179
Spoons, Sam, 170
Spungen, Nancy, 247
Spunker, Steve, 236
Squat, Manchester, 301
Stadium, Liverpool, 186, 241, 243, 244
Staines, Paul, 332
Stallions, London, 272, 315
Stamp, Chris, 147
Stanger, Nigel, 77
Stansfield, John, 8
Star, Bolton, 2
Star & Garter, Manchester, 410
Stardust, Alvin, 134
Starlight Room, London, 220
Starlight Rooms, Brighton, 147
Starr, Edwin, 124, 195, 203, 206
Starr, Freddie, 200
Starr, Ringo, 106, 108 (see also Beatles)
State, Liverpool, 323, 347
Steampacket, 153, 193
Steel, John, 77, 89, 119
Steele, Tommy, 78, 81, 136, 161
Stephen, John, 86
Sterling, Linder, 229, 296, 301
Steve Brett & the Mavericks, 102, 122
Stevens, Guy, 136, 139, 140, 141–2, 143–4, 152, 191, 405, 416
Stevenson, Nils, 239
Stewart, Al, 156
Stewart, Ian, 112, 115
Stewart, Mark, 311, 342
Stiff Little Fingers, 262, 281–2
Sting, 279
Stipe, Michael, 396, 408
Stock, Mike, 350
Stoll, J.G. Jr, 27
Stoll, J.G. Sr, 6, 27
Stoll, Oswald, 27
Stollman, Bernard, 157
Stone, C.J., 183, 184

Stone Roses, 308, 335, 406
Storm, 356, 360, 361
Strachan, Michaela, 350–1
Strange, Steve, xi–xii, xiii, xvi, 237, 244, 267, 269–70, 272, 314, 416
Strangeways, Manchester, 353
Stranglers, 242–3, 286
Strictly Come Dancing, 63
Strindberg, Frida, 42–3
Stringfellow, Geoff, 137, 153
Stringfellow, Peter, 109, 137, 153, 178, 198, 225, 289
Stringfellows, London, 198
Strokes, 398
Strongman, Jay, 315, 316
Strummer, Joe, 230, 232, 239, 251–2 (see also Clash)
Stuart, Freeman, 201
Studio 51, London, 113
Studio 54, New York, 171, 218, 265
Studio, Streatham, 63 (see also Locarno, Streatham)
Stuffed Olives, Manchester, 352, 353
Style, Spencer, 325
Stylistics, 203–4, 224, 420
Styrene, Poly, 240
Subloaded, Bristol, 378
Subscription Rooms, Stroud, 108
Subway, London, 273
Subway Sect, 241, 249
Suckle, Count, 146, 215
Suede, 69
Sulley, Susan Ann, 302
Sullivan, Chris, 268, 272, 314, 315, 316, 317
Summer, Donna, 217
Summers, Andy, 177
Sumner, Bernard, 340
Sun City, London, 378
Sunderland Empire, 94
Sundowner, London, 217
Sunrise, London, 332, 334
Sunset Club, London, 145–6
Surakhan, Bristol, 310, 342, 343
Surrey Music Hall, Sheffield, 2, 16, 21, 418
  fire at, 22
Sutch, Screaming Lord, 68, 134, 238
Sutcliffe, John, 272
Sutcliffe, Stuart, 104
Swan, Anna, 16
Swarbrick, Dave, 90
Sweat It Out, Manchester, 346

Sweet Exorcist, 342
Swell Maps, 250
Swift, Matt, 307, 308
Sytner, Alan, 88–9, 103

T-Coy, 321, 330
T, Lyndon, 275
Tabernacle, Stockport, 174
Taboo, London, 315
Take That, 226
Tallulah, 217
Taste, 173, 188
Tatum, Art, 51
Taylor, Dick, 112
Taylor, Jeremy, 333
Taylor, John, 260, 262, 263–4, 266, 267, 270, 275 (see also Duran Duran)
Teardrop Explodes, 127, 304
Teenage Jesus & the Jerks, 273
Television, 231, 283
Temperance Club, at the Haçienda, Manchester, 320 (see also Haçienda)
Temperance Hall, Manchester, 14
Tennant, David, 408
Tennant, Neil, 207
Tennant, Stephen, xiv, 54
Terry, Todd, 354
Testi, Ken, 126, 241–2
Thatcher, Dean, 357
Theatre Workshop, 80, 84, 420
Thekla, Bristol, 199–200
Them, 120, 173
Thimblemill Baths, Smethwick, 40, 62
Thin Lizzy, 206, 291
Thomas, Erskine, 179, 183
Thomas, Evelyn, 226
Thomas, Irma, 144, 193
Thomas, Myer, 117, 118, 123, 280
Thompson's Arms, Manchester, 352, 353
Thorn, Tracey, 306
Thornton, Charles, 8
Thornton Heath Baths, Croydon, 40
Thornton, Terry, 95, 96, 152
Three Cups, Chelmsford, 213
Three Degrees, 214
3 Stripe Posse, 312, 313
3D, 311, 312, 314
Thunderdome, Manchester, 336–7, 352
Thunders, Johnny, 247
Tiffany's, Coventry (formerly Locarno), 197
Tiffany's, Edinburgh, 197
Tiffany's, Glasgow, 62

Tiffany's, Manchester, 197
Tights, 286
Tiles, London, 151–2, 176–7
Tiller Boys, 296–7
Tilley, Vesta, 17
In-Time Disco, Leeds, 84
Timepiece, Liverpool, 220–1, 226
Tin Chicken, Castleford, 195
Tissera, Rob, 336
TJ's, Newport, ix–x, 394, 402
Tomlin, 318, 337
Tong, Pete, 345, 351
Tony's Ballroom, Birmingham, 56
Top Buzz, 387
Top Hat, Lisburn, 121, 213
Top Rank, Sheffield, 287
Top Ten Club, Liverpool, 105
Topping, Simon, 318, 321
Tottenham Royal, 52
Towndrow, Roger, 254
Townshend, Pete, 140, 144, 149, 150, 279, 416 (see also Who)
Tracy, John, 305, 307, 319, 337
Trade, Farringdon, 361, 375, 388
Trades, Hebden Bridge, 397
Traffic, 140, 179
Trafford, Howard, 229, 404
Tramp, Manchester, 405
Tramps, London, 198, 382
Trans-Global Underground, 363
Travis, 69
Travis, Dave Lee, 180
Tribe of the Sacred Mushroom, 174
Tricky, 310
Trip, 75
Trip, London, 329
Trocchi, Alex, 165, 174
Trojan, 315
Tropicana, Manchester, 317
Troubadour, Bristol, 156
Troubadour, London, 90, 186–7
Troy, Doris, 193
Trulocke, Nick, 325
Tunkin, Paul, 412
Turner, Joe, 89
Turner, Robin, 365
Turnmills, Farringdon, 361, 375, 388
Tuxedo Princess, Gateshead, 200, 225
12 Bar Club, 410–11
23 Skidoo, 307
Twice as Nice, London, 378
Twisted Wheel, Manchester, viii, 95, 119, 137–8, 139, 152, 153–4, 180, 193–4,

195, 201, 205, 295, 389, 409–10, 414
(*see also* Left Wing, Manchester)
Twitch & Brainstorm, 357
Twitch, Mickey, 179
200 Club, Newport, 403
2i's, London, 81, 88
Two Rage, 356
2-Way Club, London, 85
Tyrannosaurus Rex, 180, 182
Tyson, Nicola, 268

U Boat, 196
U-Roy, 215
UB40, 301
UFO, London, viii, 160, 169–71, 175–6, 177, 228
Ultramarine, 363
Ultravox, 262, 270
Unabomber, Luke, 390, 408
Undead, 234
Underground, Liverpool, 333, 348, 367, 405
Undertones, 282, 283
Underworld, 363
Union, Manchester, 352
Union Saloon, London, 5, 384
Unwin, Paul, 285
Up, Ari, 249, 251
Ure, Midge, 270 (*see also* Ultravox)
U2, 37, 62, 281, 283, 299–300, 343

Va Va's, Bolton, 206
Vaccines, 415
Valentine, Hilton, 119–20, 122 (*see also* Animals)
Valentino's, Edinburgh, 281
Van Dike, Plymouth, 187
van Dyk, Paul, 373, 375, 381
Van McCoy and the Soul City Symphony, 215
Vath, Sven, 315, 364
Vaughan, Sarah, 85
Velvet Underground, 186
Vendetta, Arcane, 254
Vendors, 102
Venue, Edinburgh, 402
Venue, Manchester, 320
Venus, Nottingham, 357, 388
Verve, 415
Vibrators, 256
Vice Versa (later ABC, *q.v.*), 292–3, 299
Vicious, Sid, 65, 68, 240, 241, 247, 253
(*see also* Sex Pistols)

Victim, 282
Videotech, Huddersfield, 293
View, 400
Vin, Duke, 92, 130, 145, 313
Vincent, Gene, 228
Vincent, Robbie, 218, 219, 329
Vinegar Joe, 206
Vines, 398
Vipers Skiffle Group, 81
Visage, 270
Voodoo Rooms, Edinburgh, 413
Vortex, London, 253
Vowles, Andrew, *see* Mushroom

Waddicker, John, 352
Wade, Michael, 92
Wag, London, 316, 326
Wagner, Malcolm 'Waggy', 199
Wah Heat, 127
Wainwright, tom, 370
Waits, Tom, 83
Waldorf, London, 407
Walker, Johnny, 324
Walker, Junior, 203
Walker, Kris, 408
Waller, Fats, 209
Walsh, Steve, 63, 275, 324
Walter, Gerald, *see* May, Jack
Walters, John (musician), 77, 94
Walters, John (venue owner), 212
Wangford, Hank, 307
Ware, Gina, 209
Ware, Martyn, 287, 290, 302 (*see also* Human League)
Ware, Ted, 209
Warehouse, Leeds, 218, 274, 304, 349
Warehouse Project, Manchester, 381
Warp, 342
Warsaw, 255
Washington, Geno, 150
Waterhouse, Humphrey, 354
Waterhouse, Keith, 80
Waterman, Pete, 192, 200, 214, 350–1, 393
Waters, Muddy, 65, 94, 111, 141, 148
Watson, Boris, xv
Watson, Chris, 288, 296
Watson, Maurice, 315–16, 325, 329
Watson, Noel, 315–16, 325, 329
Watts, Charlie, 112, 116 (*see also* Rolling Stones)
Watts, Ron, 68, 238, 240
Wax Doctor, 360

Way of Life, 121
Wayne Fontana and the Mindbenders, 202
Wearden, Jay, 337
Weatherall, Andy, 328, 340, 364, 381
Webb, George, 61, 67, 71, 80
Webb, Stan, 184
Webster, George, 284
Wee Reed Bar, Edinburgh, 413
Wellington, Dereham, 279
Welly, 351, 352
Welsh, Paul, 229
Wembley Studios, 332
Wesker, Arnold, 168
Weston, Gil, 257
Westwood, Tim, 275
Westwood, Vivienne, 211
Wheeler, Caron, 342
Whiskey A-Go-Go, London, 85, 316
Whiskey, Birmingham, 179
White, Mark, 293
White Stripes, 65, 69
Whitehead, Allister, 357
Who, 62, 65, 75, 140, 144, 147, 148, 149–50, 152, 153, 155, 158, 184–5, 193, 213
Whodini, 325
Whyton, Wally, 81
Wigan Casino, 75, 194, 205, 224
Wild Bunch, 311, 312, 313, 342
Wilde, Marty, 105
Wilkinson, Tony, 129
Williams, Allan, 83, 105
Williams, Claude, 311
Williams, Guy, 371
Williams, Larry, 141
Williams, Mark 'Wigan', 341
Williams, Steve, 335, 337, 348, 349
Williamson, Robin, 90
Williamson, Sonny Boy, 119, 123, 136, 138, 179
Willot, Daz, 347
Wilson, Delroy, 252
Wilson, Greg, 221–2, 223, 317, 319, 377
Wilson, Jackie, 206
Wilson, Lindsay, 300
Wilson, Tony, 229, 240, 294–5, 298, 302, 339–40, 367, 371, 389
Wilton, John, 30, 31
Wilton's, London, 3, 30–3, 413
Windmill, Birmingham, 212
Windross, Rose, 342
Windsor Old Trout, 395
Winstanley, Russ, 206
Winter Gardens, Malvern, 157, 186, 286
Wire, 283, 292, 306
Wire and Sonic Youth, 306
Wisdom, Olli, 273
Wise, Alan, 298, 336
Wobble, Birmingham, 357
Wobble, Jah, 215, 253
Wolf, Patrick, 390
Wolfe, Tom, 152
Wonder, Stevie, 124
Wood, Fred, 8
Woodliffe, Jonathan, 316, 320, 396
Wooler, Bob, 105–6, 250
Worthington, Frank, 198, 382
Worthington, Geoffrey, 209
Wright, David, 259, 265
Wylie, Pete, 126–7, 251, 306
Wyman, Bill, 112, 113, 116 (see also Rolling Stones)

X-Ray Spex, 240, 256

Yard, London, 410–11
Yardbirds, 111, 148, 152, 153, 173
Yellow, Manchester, 377
Yes, 213
York, Chris, 69
Youdan, Thomas, 16, 21–2
Young, Jeff, 219
Young Marble Giants, 301
Yours or Mine ('Sombrero'), London, 210

Zaher, Yousef, 380
Zap, Brighton, 306–7, 394
Zappa, Frank, 83, 188–9
Zebra, London, 169
Ziggy's, London, 325
Zodiac, Brighton, 147
Zukie, Tapper, 243